The People's Zion

THE PEOPLE'S ZION

SOUTHERN AFRICA, THE UNITED STATES, AND A TRANSATLANTIC FAITH-HEALING MOVEMENT

Joel Cabrita

THE BELKNAP PRESS OF
HARVARD UNIVERSITY PRESS

Cambridge, Massachusetts
London, England
2018

First printing

Library of Congress Cataloging-in-Publication Data
Names: Cabrita, Joel, 1980– author.
Title: The people's Zion : southern Africa, the United States, and a transatlantic
faith-healing movement / Joel Cabrita.
Description: Cambridge, Massachusetts : The Belknap Press of Harvard University Press,
2018. | Includes bibliographical references and index.
Identifiers: LCCN 2017042704 | ISBN 9780674737785 (alk. paper)
Subjects: LCSH: Zionist churches (Africa)—Africa, Southern. | Zionist churches (Africa)—
South Africa—Johannesburg. | Zionist churches (Africa)—Illinois—Zion—History—
20th century. | Spiritual healing—Africa, Southern. | Spiritual healing—Illinois—Zion. |
Africa, Southern—Race relations. | Africa, Southern—Church history—20th century. |
Zion (Ill.)—Church history—20th century.
Classification: LCC BR1446 .C33 2018 | DDC 276.8/082—dc23
LC record available at https://lccn.loc.gov/2017042704

To Tarik

Contents

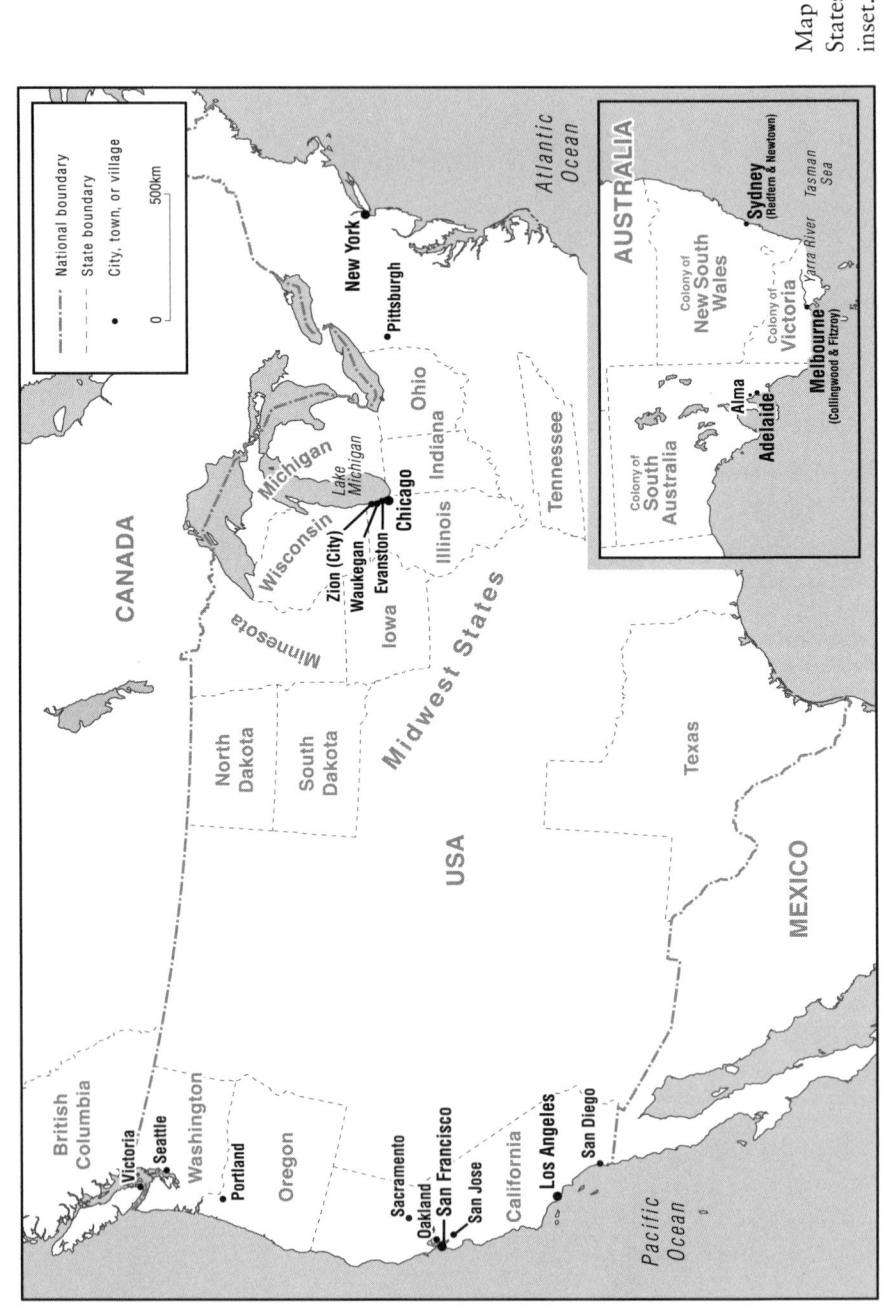

Map of the United States, with Australia inset.

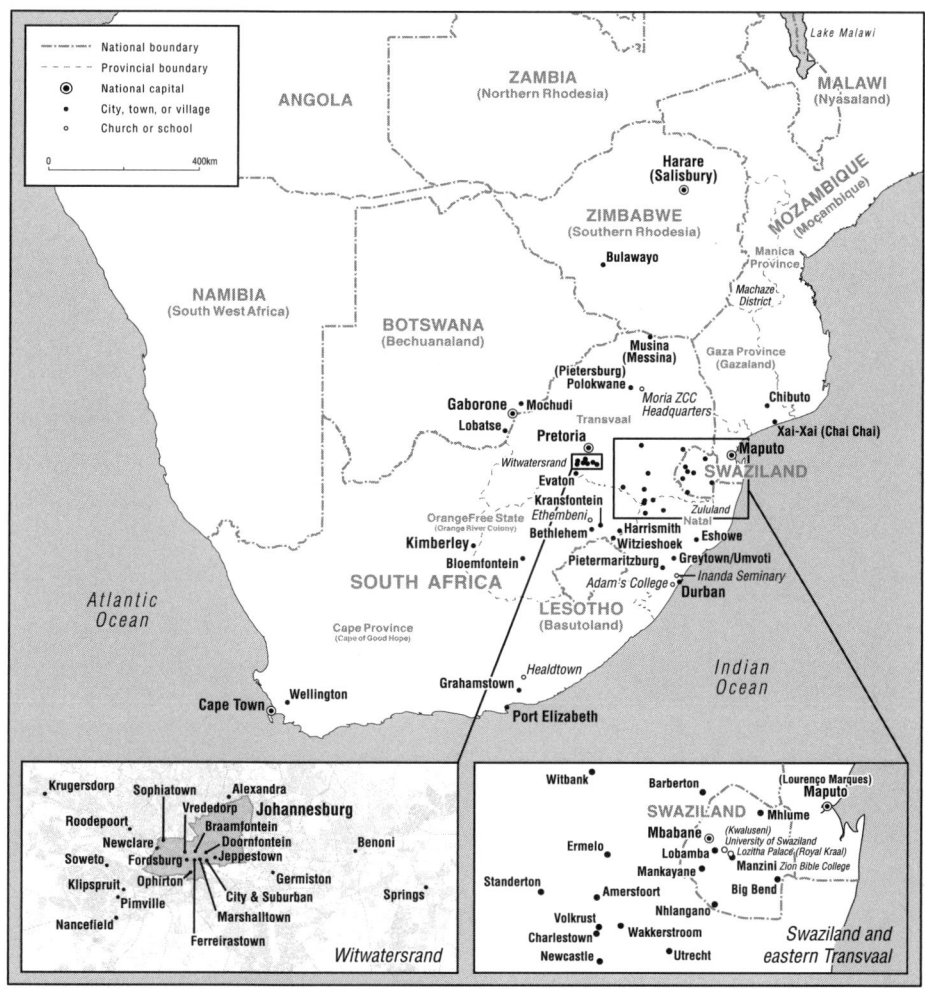

Map of Southern Africa.

The People's Zion

Louise Harrison
LMA.

Name of place

Date of complaint
n°ode

Date of entry of complaint

Date of remedy

time between
receipt, entry + remedy of complaint

① ② ③ ④ ⑤

Introduction

The People's Zion

D ANIEL NKONYANE was an early twentieth-century small-scale farmer who was born, lived, and died within a small region in the South African Highveld, a plateau of arable farmland in the middle of the country. In common with many thousands in this area, Nkonyane's horizons were much broader than the narrow world of his farm. Nkonyane's life had been dramatically impacted by a series of world events, including the discovery of precious minerals in the Witwatersrand in the 1880s and the ensuing international gold rush as the city of Johannesburg rapidly industrialized, the devastation to African farmers by the global South African War (1899– 1902), and the subsequent annexation of the region and its subjects as a possession of the British Empire. But there was one international event that perhaps defined the course of Nkonyane's life more profoundly than any other. This was the arrival in South Africa in 1904 of a Christian church known as "Zion." With roots that spanned nineteenth-century imperial Australia and the North American industrial metropolis of Chicago, Zion was a worldwide faith-healing movement that instructed its working-class followers to pray for bodily health and to renounce medical assistance. Upon joining this international Protestant movement, Zionists such as Daniel Nkonyane were immersed in a worldwide fraternity of evangelical Christians—black and white—who eschewed the elite expertise of doctors for the ministrations of the Holy Spirit. A life-long member of Zion, Nkonyane corresponded with representatives of the church outside of Chicago and eagerly received and read its faith healing tracts and periodicals. In addi- tion, he regularly sent across the Atlantic tithes from his congregation to the North American headquarters, as well as posted lengthy baptismal lists of his members in South Africa, a sign of his literal "registration" of his

regional church within the international movement. Nkonyane, as was
the case for many other Africans of this period, felt himself intimately
part of what Zion's founder, John Alexander Dowie, dubbed "one great,
universal church [in which] there are no foreign fields, no home fields . . .
everywhere Zion is one."[1]

This book tells the story of transatlantic Zion, an international evangelical Christian faith-healing church that originated in Australia, and
subsequently spread from the United States across the Atlantic Ocean to
become what is now the single largest religious movement of modern
Southern Africa.[2] *The People's Zion* argues that Zion's remarkable success
in Southern Africa demonstrates the saliency of Christian evangelicalism
for diverse societies undergoing profound social changes—industrialization,
urbanization, widespread migration, nativist and colonial racially in-
flected legislation—throughout the nineteenth and twentieth centuries. In
North America and Southern Africa, Zion flourished as the faith of choice
for working-class people attempting to navigate the stark social inequalities resulting from these transformations. Part of the international Protestant divine healing movement of the late nineteenth century, Zion's emancipatory teaching was that ordinary Christians such as Daniel Nkonyane
could access dramatic powers of healing through prayerful reliance on
God, relegating the expertise of doctors and other biomedical professionals irrelevant at best, and ungodly at worst. North American and African Zionists' criticism of medical experts was part of their larger attack
on all those—within the church and without—who claimed prestige and
status according to worldly criteria of education or wealth or social
standing. Over the past century and a half, Zionist believers of different
races on both sides of the Atlantic Ocean have joined company with count-
less working-class people who found in evangelical Protestant Christianity
a Bible-derived faith that claimed to topple the new stratum of upper-
class elites emerging from the crucible of industrialization and urbanization. In Melbourne, Chicago, and Johannesburg, for more than a century,
Zion emerged as a vast, loosely defined evangelical Christian movement
of and for the people. It has consistently spoken most powerfully to those
who found themselves on the margins of power during a century of great
fluidity and social change, and it has equipped these believers with the
conviction that it is precisely they who possess the spiritual credentials to
disrupt established authorities. In modern Southern Africa, as across the
American Midwest, transatlantic Zion has taught its members the democratic lessons of populist evangelicalism: how to resist the new medical,
religious, economic, and social elite who emerged throughout the nine-

teenth and twentieth centuries, as well as how to subvert restrictive strati-
fications of humanity by mobilizing Zion's vision of the equality of all.

Today, approximately fifteen million Southern Africans belong to Zion.[3]
Although little known outside of the African continent, these astonishing
figures make the transatlantic Zion movement one of the most significant
phenomena within modern Christianity. Zion's early numerical strength
lay in the American Midwest, where at its height in 1904, it had about
twenty thousand members, mostly drawn from first- and second-generation
Northern European immigrants and African Americans. As of 2017, however, only several hundred in the United States—almost exclusively white—
identify as heirs to the original Zion church. Christian faith healing fell
out of favor in American Protestantism just as it began to expand across
sub-Saharan Africa in the early twentieth century. Zionist demographics
thus echo the dramatic numerical shift of twentieth-century Christianity
from the northern to the southern hemisphere.[4] From a thriving North
American church sending missionaries across the world, Zion is now the
faith of millions of Africans with only a handful of believers in the northern
hemisphere. By the 1960s in South Africa, Zionists constituted the single
largest religious bloc in the country, accounting for 21 percent of all those
who were religiously active, and outnumbering both other Protestants and
Catholics.[5] Today, one in three South Africans are Zionist, while in neighboring Swaziland—the country with the highest concentration of Zionists
in the region—around one-half of the population professed allegiance to
Zion in the 1990s. Today it is estimated that between 30 and 40 percent of
all Swazis are Zionists.[6]

This book argues that a transnational lens is the best way to view the
story of Zion's remarkable success in diverse regions and societies across
the world. In addition to its staggering size, Zion's story exceeds national
and territorial boundaries. The movement had its roots in colonial Australia, came to fruition in the American Midwest and found its greatest
success in Southern Africa. Today, Zion retains its border-crossing character, spanning South Africa, Swaziland, Mozambique, Botswana, Zimbabwe, Zambia, and Malawi. Reflecting the highly interconnected nature
of Southern Africa itself, Zion is best understood as a network of exchanges
between believers across the region. Further adding to its complex border-
crossing nature, Zion is no longer a single organization, as it was in the
American Midwest of the 1890s. Instead, it constitutes a loose evangelical
federation of thousands of Zion churches displaying much diversity in theology and practice. Indeed, it is partly Zion's decentralized, diffuse nature
that has enabled the movement to travel so nimbly across territories,

cultures, and languages, predisposing Zionists to rapidly adapt to local conditions and assume protean forms. Yet alongside this diversity (itself an enduring characteristic of the Protestant tradition), most of these believers continue identifying themselves with the evangelical values of Zion—reflected in their choice of names for their disparate organizations—and some still express loyalty to the original faith-healing church of the nineteenth-century Midwest, continuing to use its devotional literature and reiterate its doctrinal credos.

Yet despite this evidence of an interconnected landscape of populist transatlantic evangelicalism, scholars have largely failed to understand African and American Zionists as two products of a single Protestant Christian tradition. Most scholars of the evangelical divine healing movement in the United States treat the Western story in almost complete isolation from its worldwide context (although Western Europe is usually factored into analyses of the development of divine healing in the United States).[7] Despite the now-widespread "transnational turn" in American Studies, including in religious history, historians of Protestantism rarely consider divine healing's role in the global spread of Christianity, still largely focusing on the Anglophone Atlantic world.[8] Seldom discussed is the fact that the divine healing movement was—as was evangelicalism more broadly—constituted by North American and European trade, military expansion, and missionary networks across the imperial world, including to South Africa, Australia, and India.[9] If mentioned, the story of Zion's explosion in Southern Africa is relegated to a brief footnote commenting on the oddity of divine healing expanding in Africa as it lost popularity in the West.[10] Belying this lack of scholarly interest in divine healing's international dimensions were the nineteenth-century advocates of the movement themselves, who consistently argued an important consequence of divine healing was increased efficacy in international missions.[11] In the words of Zion's founder, John Alexander Dowie, himself "When the Gospel of Divine Healing comes back to the church in all its glory and its power, multitudes from foreign lands will press into the temple of the church of God."[12]

In parallel fashion, Africanist scholars similarly ignore the impact of the international divine healing movement in Southern Africa.[13] Two regional literatures on evangelical Christian faith healing exist in almost entire isolation of each other, despite sharing intertwined historical trajectories and significantly overlapping themes. In the case of Southern Africa, this omission is part of a lengthy tradition of viewing Christianity in Africa in insular local terms. Zionist and other black healing churches on the continent are cited as evidence of indigenized "African" Christianity, and of the continued potency of local healing traditions. This Africa-centric mode of interpretation arose amid decolonization and independence.[14] Black churches practicing divine healing were celebrated by scholars, clerics, and politicians as evidence of the resilience of African healing traditions in the face of Western colonialism and European Christianity. These churches' emphasis on bodily healing were taken as instances, not of Protestant evangelicalism, but of the strength of African cosmologies—themselves historically preoccupied with health and healing—in transforming Western Christianity. Scholars also seized upon the fact that many healing churches had broken from American missionaries to form independent black-led denominations (not perceiving that schism was a feature of evangelicalism worldwide, not just in Africa). In the case of Southern Africa's Zion movement, a huge literature charts and classifies its "African" elements. Scholars map Zion healing rituals onto indigenous therapies as well as argue that the color schemes of Zionist church uniforms echo symbolic patterns in local cosmology; other studies maintain the Zion "prophet" is a Christianized version of the African diviner-healer specialist.[15]

There is much value in emphasizing Zion's indigenous saliency. Prior to the arrival of Christianity in the region, Southern African medical-therapeutic systems had long taught that health was more than physiology, and that underlying spiritual causes required attention. Evangelical Zion—with its spiritualized interpretation of sickness and health—undoubtedly flourished in sub-Saharan Africa due to its similarities with existing conceptions of healing. Moreover, Zion in Southern Africa developed uniquely local features including the prominent figure of the prophet from the mid-twentieth-century on, something largely absent from the North American tradition. The validity of an analytical approach stressing African agency in transforming Christianity is now self-evident, thanks to much scholarship that emphasized Christianity's inculturation in Africa, and its status as an indigenous—rather than colonial—faith.[16]

While recognizing the importance of locating Zion within a regional context, this book argues that divine healing in Southern Africa cannot be understood without reference to the broader international religious tradition from which it stemmed. Transnational evangelicalism infused important characteristics into the multiple forms that Zion assumed throughout both North America and Southern Africa over the last century. Zionists in both regions were shaped by a potent evangelical arsenal of ideas and practices surrounding the human body, spiritual and physical perfectibility, and the reality of evil in the world. By recognizing these influences, the significance of the small-scale and the local, however, is not sidelined. Rather, this book pursues a cohesive approach that holds together particularity and internationalism, local specificity with worldwide resonance. The following chapters analyze and describe how a global evangelical tradition came to make sense for specific communities of North Americans and Southern Africans pursuing well-being amid a range of local concerns. In considering the local and the global alongside each other, a transnational approach also muddies a hard and fast distinction between the two, demonstrating that the divide between Christian evangelicalism and African religiosity was not as great as commonly supposed.[17] Older scholarship portrayed indigenous healing in Africa as static knowledge, preserving a timeless local culture. In fact, African healing practitioners have a long history of experimentally importing new practices into their repertoires. Many healers incorporated biomedical practice as well as the healing therapies brought by Western Christian missionaries, investing these new techniques with novel meaning in their transplanted contexts.[18]

Moreover, this is not just a story charting the arrival and adoption of North American evangelicalism as a ready-made product in Southern Africa. Throughout the twentieth century and into the present one, millions of African Zionists were not merely the recipients of international Christianity but the active cocreators of it. The following chapters show how in mobilizing the resources of evangelical Protestantism for their own purposes, Southern Africans significantly transformed the divine healing tradition and global evangelicalism in the process. For example, the unique convergence between divine healing and regional curative therapies gave rise to the important figure of the prophet who dominated many Zion congregations with their claims to direct access to extraordinary direct revelation. Prophetic figures are far from absent from the Western evangelical tradition (look at the example of charismatic televangelists or famous healing figures such as Oral Roberts and Billy Sunday). However, the ubiquity and power of prophets is a distinctive contribution to evangelicalism from the African continent, illuminating the new forms of selfhood and religious legitimacy that African evangelicals have offered the worldwide tradition. Above all, Southern African Zionists have shaped international evangelicalism by their continued emphasis on the Holiness-rooted tradition of divine healing. Although divine healing declined in importance in North American Christianity throughout the twentieth century (with the important exception of Pentecostal and Charismatic denominations), its principles continued to inspire millions of Africans. This meant that the evangelicalism of African Zionists did not look much like Christianity as defined by North Americans; and it is for this reason, perhaps, that African Zion has often been discarded as a legitimate expression of the tradition. But religious developments on the African continent were just as constitutive of worldwide Protestantism as developments in North America, as

Protestantism's demographic shift from the northern to southern hemisphere only further underscores.

In challenging an exclusively local approach to the history of Christianity in Southern Africa, this book argues that Zion emerged from the convergence of Southern African perspectives (African, Boer, and British) with an international Protestant tradition. Furthermore, Zion was not only the product of transatlantic Christianity, but also of global repertoires of biomedical and heterodox healing, all modes of articulating the health concerns of those who lived in the modern world. The collision and ongoing transformation of these disparate elements—dynamically interacting with each other as they transformed—was enabled through interlocking dynamics of social change occurring across the world at this time. Imperialism, industrialization, unprecedented population mobility, and a technology and communications revolution, all meant the arrival of a Midwestern church in the cities and farming lands of Southern Africa could have transformative consequences across a large region.[19] In the light of Zion's eclectic international history, a hard and fast distinction between local and global, African and American, indigenous religion and Christian evangelicalism, black convert and white missionary, seems far less secure than scholars have often assumed. Detailed historical investigation, drawing on archival sources located across the globe, lays bare the intertwined stories of Christianity in imperial Australia, the industrializing Midwest, segregationist South Africa, and independence-era Swaziland, to name but a few of the regions this book delves into. Developments usually thought of as insulated from each other in fact shared long histories of exchange and borrowing. By emphasizing this, the book brings into focus the significance of a transnational repertoire of evangelical Christianity for industrializing societies across the globe, and the importance of the worldwide circulation of divine healing in an era marked by the wide-scale labor migration and the dispossession of colonized peoples.

Despite the enormous size, diversity, and complexity of this worldwide evangelical movement, three enduring features of transatlantic Zion are nonetheless discernible. First, Zionists on both sides of the Atlantic have first and foremost been egalitarians, propelled by the belief that all Christians are equal regardless of status, and committed to attacking and bringing down hierarchies of all kinds. Zionists argued that ministers, clerics, and other specialized experts occupy no privileged position in the Kingdom of God. Second, the people of Zion were reformers, committed to pursuing the purest realization of God's Kingdom on earth. Zionists were rarely satisfied with orthodox ways of being religious, continually engaging in dissenting debate about whether God's will was enacted in a sufficiently radical fashion. Their egalitarianism well equipped Zionist reformers to challenge and undermine established ways of being religious. Finally, devotees of this vast movement were—and are—cosmopolitans. They believed that all humanity belonged to a single community transcending differences not only of class, education, and wealth, but also of race, ethnicity, and language. In nineteenth- and twentieth-century societies marked by rigid efforts to categorize people into distinct boxes, evangelical Zionists have stood for the common nature of humankind. To be part of Zion was to proclaim yourself a brother and a sister to all of humanity. To be a Zionist was to point to a common parentage in the Fatherhood of God, and to assert no woman or man was better than any other.

Egalitarians

Zionists' egalitarian qualities were shaped by the broader Christian evangelical tradition from which they stemmed. Evangelicalism was the product of religious revivals known as the "Great Awakenings" in the eighteenth and nineteenth centuries in Britain and New England. Its devotees rejected what they perceived as the stultifying hierarchies of the established churches, and they instead valorized simple preaching of the Bible by ordinary people, and emotive spiritual experience over learned theological formulations.[20] In this respect, evangelicals were indebted to the earlier Protestant reformers' laity-empowering emphasis on individual conscience and the Bible against the authority of ecclesial hierarchies. Evangelicals' egalitarian message found great success worldwide, in particular in the New World. The vast territory of North America, combined with its sparse population, meant new religious ideas could travel more rapidly than in Europe, whereas the democratic leanings of the American Revolution primed Christians to value individualistic self-determination as well as complemented evangelicals' hostility to the established churches. Furthermore, the lack of an official state denomination created an open religious marketplace that allowed these disruptive new religious ideas to come to the fore.[21] The evangelical tradition was in a state of continual flux (this was itself a key feature of the movement), and by the early to mid-nineteenth-century, a new group of evangelicals in North America and Great Britain emerged identifying themselves as Holiness or Higher-Life practitioners. In this revival, too, the egalitarian qualities of evangelicalism were evident. Holiness and Higher-Life devotees stressed the necessity of a "second work of grace," a transformative spiritual experience subsequent to a believer's original conversion that resulted in complete regeneration unblemished by sin or moral failing.[22] Adherents thus placed optimistic emphasis on human agency and inherent goodness, regardless of worldly status, and affirmed the ability of all—whether clergy or laity—to attain holiness.

The Holiness and Higher-Life movement gave rise to a new interest in "divine healing" in major evangelical denominations across the world.[23] The international divine healing movement was the product of a fusion between Holiness evangelicalism, on the one hand, and European Pietist faith healing, on the other; in particular, Pietism's view of the Bible as a literally true document whose miracles could be replicated in the present. Also relevant was the growing practice of heterodox health therapies such as magnetism, hydrotherapy, and homeopathy, many prompted by anxiety regarding the unhealthy effects of life in the new industrialized cities. All these factors converged into widespread Christian interest in bodily vigor as the definitive evidence of a sanctified life.[24] Contravening Victorian piety that recommended passive resignation to ill-health, these Protestants argued that sickness was Satan's work rather than the will of a loving, all-powerful God. Furthermore, there was a radical solution to ill-health: devotees of diving healing were convinced that Christ's atonement on the Cross had effected complete spiritual and physical health.[25] Advocates advised the renunciation of medicine and doctors in favor of exclusive reliance on the deity.[26] The up-shot was that ordinary Christians found themselves empowered to retain control and management over their bodies and their experiences of sickness and of health. Rather than the learning of medical experts, the Bible and a devout prayer life were cast as the only requirements for earnest Christians in search of full health. Women were key to the early movement, finding particular relevance in a healing practice that reoriented health away from the purview of male experts and firmly into the hands of female laity.[27]

Zion—perhaps the most famous (certainly the most controversial) of the nineteenth-century divine healing organizations—exemplified evangelicals' efforts to pursue personal holiness at all costs, even if this meant subverting the authority of learned experts and religious elite. In the 1860s, the Scottish-Australian Congregationalist clergyman, John Alexander Dowie, founded an embryonic form of the Zion church in Melbourne, Australia. Early devotees—many working-class laborers in the new city's slums— embraced Dowie's brand of divine healing as a populist mode of self-improvement, despite the disapproval of the clerical elite and the medical establishment. Divine healing especially resonated with Melbourne's working-class women, who found potent resources there for anxieties related to fertility and natal health. Once transplanted by Dowie and his family to the Californian cities of the Pacific Coast, and then to boom-time

Chicago in Illinois, Zion preached a similarly egalitarian message regarding the empowerment of ordinary working people. Here it evolved into a new church—the Christian Catholic Apostolic Church in Zion—and still prescribed the renunciation of medicine and doctors in favor of exclusive reliance upon God for health.

During the church's years in turbulent industrializing Chicago, Zion's egalitarian message broadened out beyond the purview of medical matters, espousing a wider theology of human equality and the eradication of class differences. Dowie's audiences were drawn from Chicago's working-class Northern European and African American migrants during an era of great labor unrest. At a time in which new migrants to the city were attempting to carve out economic and social standing amid hostility from white native-born populations, Zion's eschewal of doctors' expertise in favor of the prayer of common-place people, and its promotion of innate human equality before God, were powerful assertions of the radical nature of the Kingdom of God. In 1900 Dowie had raised enough funds from supporters to purchase land north of Chicago where he and church members founded Zion City. The town banned doctors and pharmacists from its precincts, and styled itself as an experiment in a model working peoples' town. Dowie established industries where workers would reclaim the profits, and strove to create a community where the class distinctions fragmenting Chicago would be transcended by an egalitarian community of Christians.

From its hub on the shores of Lake Michigan, the church circulated missionaries around the world, including to Australia, New Zealand, India, China, Japan, and to the West African Gold Coast. But nowhere did Dowie's church find greater success than in the territory that would shortly become the Union of South Africa (1910) and in the surrounding regions under British and Portuguese colonial rule. Late nineteenth-century Southern Africa was not, after all, so different from the newly industrialized Midwest. Indeed, as has been more broadly noted with the rise of populist reform movements within Christianity, Islam, and Hinduism, Zion's egalitarian teachings particularly flourished in societies characterized by social change and stark inequalities.[28] Both Southern Africa and the Midwest were gripped by dramatic processes of urbanization resulting in the disruption of agrarian lifestyles and the creation of a new class of urban poor. In the case of the South African Witwatersrand—a thirty-five-mile long seam of gold running east to west—the discovery of precious minerals in the 1880s had attracted hundreds of thousands of workers from across the continent and the entire globe. It also set into motion repressive legisla-
·tion to displace Africans from rural farmlands into the mines as cheap labor. The take-up of Zion's healing techniques among newly industrial-

ized whites (for a limited initial phase) and blacks in the city and nearby farmlands was electrifying. In the early years of the new century, many thousands were baptized in the city and the surrounding countryside, committing themselves to God's triumphant power over body and soul, and to bucking the religious and biomedical establishments of the day. At a time when Africans were increasingly subject to political disenfranchisement and territorial dispossession, Zion's message of equality for all was deeply attractive. Zion not only taught its African adherents to eschew the authority of medical experts, but also to resist the stratification of humanity into the racial and economic hierarchies that were evermore structuring colonial Southern Africa.

Midwestern Zion declined (part of a demise in divine healing in the northern hemisphere), but Zion in Southern Africa mushroomed in tandem with the explosive growth of the black working-class population of the mining city of Johannesburg. During the interwar period, Zion became the religion of choice for a constituency of migrant male African laborers. Here, too, its egalitarian resources were eagerly seized upon by devotees. Being Zionist came to stand for a youthful Spirit-driven religiosity that eschewed the decorous codes of black society, subverted the hitherto unquestioned value of education, and criticized the respectable churches of the middle classes. Southern African Zion in this period represented a populist Christian insurgency, one led by those without formal education, and which subverted the presumptions of a powerful African elite who had long assumed control over "correct" Christianity and respectable black society. This dynamic shake-up of the status quo in interwar Johannesburg echoes the explosion of popular evangelical Christianity—mainly Methodism and Baptism—in the early American Republic, echoing worldwide processes through which "common people" without learning, money or social status have repeatedly commandeered interpretative and popular control of Protestantism.[29]

Wherever they went, youthful Zionists stirred dissent against decorum in the name of their commitment to a life of holiness. Whereas traditional leaders and family elders insisted on obedient youth domiciled at home, itinerant Zionists embarked on religious pilgrimages and evangelistic journeys that took them far beyond their home regions.[30] And whereas African chiefs attempted to impress on women their roles as mothers and housekeepers, Zion taught converts that the radical disciplines of personal holiness made identical demands on women and men, and called for women to forsake fathers, husbands, and brother in pursuit of Christian purity. In the context of societies already fractured by industrialization and imperialism, chiefs, elders, and other largely male African authorities perceived

Zion's egalitarian disciplines as a further threat to the communities they were attempting to preserve. On the side of these young Zionists, divine healing was a route to detaching themselves from older hierarchies constituted by patriarchal family heads and by husbands, to separating themselves from gerontocratic chiefs and from the power of traditional healers and diviners, and to liberating themselves from the stultifying mores of respectable African Christian society. As the photographer Sabelo Mlangeni's cover image for this book portrays, being part of Zion meant setting oneself on the road to a new life, a new identity, and a new vision of the Kingdom of God.

Zion's pursuit of egalitarian religious community has not been a story of unmitigated success. In common with other radical movements throughout history—religious or otherwise—Zion has been marked by discrepancies between its ideals and its actual attainments. Zionists professed themselves committed to a radically democratic vision of the Kingdom of God; but, in reality, Zion's history has been peopled by highly autocratic leaders. In 1904, Zion's founder, John Alexander Dowie, declared himself the reincarnation of the Prophet Elijah from the Old Testament, and entirely above any human criticism, much to the disgust of many followers and the ridicule of the contemporary press. Despite the promotion of men and women as equals in Christ, it is men who have lionized power within the Zion movement, in keeping with broader social mores of the time. Female members in both North America and Southern Africa were consistently excluded from high-up leadership. And within Southern Africa, the figure of the charismatic male prophet, unassailable on account of their claim to heavenly revelations, exercised near-absolute power over millions of Zionist young men and women. The tradition's failures to sustain egalitarianism, as much as its successes in doing so, are an integral component of the story of transatlantic Zion.

Moreover, many Southern African Zionists steered clear of challenging the white states that dominated the region throughout the twentieth century. During the interwar period, one of Johannesburg's leading black Zion ministers, the Malawian John George Phillips, instructed his congregation that "rebellion against higher powers, either church or state, is strictly forbidden."[31] During apartheid, frequent speeches from leaders of the Zion Christian Church—South Africa's largest Zion organization—celebrating apartheid officials as "God's servants for your [own] good" sealed many Africanist scholars' impression of Zionist leaders as cravenly acquiescent at worst, or passively disengaged at best.[32] In fact, Zionists' attitude toward political power has been more complex than simple disengagement or collusion, in keeping with the fact that evangelicals the world over—not solely in Southern Africa—have long inhabited a paradoxical relationship with secular authorities.[33] Examples abound of evangelicals who withdraw from the public sphere citing their belief that Christ's kingdom "is not of this world," yet at the same time work hard to ensure politicians committed to "biblical" values come to power. In like fashion, Zionists in both the United States and in Southern Africa have eschewed politics as ungodly (Dowie famously denounced trade union membership a perfidious sin); yet others have been active in nationalist organizations and even in labor movements. Although Phillips forbade Christians to question the authorities of the day, he was also a founding member of the new Nyasaland Native National Congress in Johannesburg, a political organization viewed with much suspicion by white authorities on account of its proto-nationalist activities.

A key theme of this book is how Zion's evangelical piety has had transformative social consequences in industrializing societies across the globe, but these have been effects that do not necessarily translate into explicit political engagement. For most Zionists—in common with other evangelical Protestants—their egalitarian ambitions were not channeled into activist resistance to repressive states. Undoubtedly, this has been an important factor in the lack of interest Southern African historians—influenced by a Marxist-orientated economic and political tradition—have shown toward Zionists. The last historical monograph on Zion appeared in the 1970s, and an authoritative survey of South African history published in 2014 makes one sole fleeting reference to Zion.[34] It is certainly the case that Zion's particular brand of egalitarianism shared little common ground with the resistance movements favored by this historical tradition. In keeping with the broader evangelical Holiness tradition, American and African Zionists' ultimate goal was to save and sanctify their own souls and save the souls of as many around them. Everything else was secondary. Political participation could be pursued when it promised to further their spiritual goals, such as when secular authorities were threatening their freedom to worship. The widespread mobilization across Southern Africa of Zionists against state-led vaccination during the interwar period is evidence of this. Normally unwilling to rock the political boat, when it came to a mandate to submit to medical care, Zionists reluctantly mobilized; many were jailed and paid hefty fines.[35] But equally, activism in the public sphere could be renounced as a worldly distraction when there seemed little discernible spiritual gain. As much as Zionists have energetically prayed to rehabilitate bodies broken by illness and sin, the premillennial evangelical theology of many Zionists—their belief that the Antichrist would overtake the world before Christ's eventual return—legitimized an apolitical attitude of resignation to societal injustice.

The Zionist egalitarians discussed in this book were a complex mixture of subversive and conservative, revolutionary and reactionary. The egalitarian promises of evangelical Christianity were mobilized by these individuals to transformative effect, yet not always in terms that made sense according to a secular political vocabulary of democratic reform. Moreover, even if judged according to their own standards, Zionists have frequently fallen short of the radical principles of Holiness Christianity, lapsing into authoritarianism and excluding women and youths from power. Yet the story of the People's Zion does not end there. This tendency to lapse from egalitarianism leads us directly to the second feature of Zionists worldwide. This is their endless propensity for dissent, criticism, and rebellion against established ways of being religious, a tendency broadly labeled here as "reformist." Zionists in both North America and Southern Africa may have been quick to lose sight of their egalitarian ideals, but others in their ranks were even quicker to criticize them for doing so, and to institute reformed churches they believed better exemplified the Kingdom of God on earth.

Reformers

Zionists' identity as reformers springs from the heartfelt zeal that characterized their faith. This is a feature Zionists shared with Protestants more broadly; as one historian recently commented, "from the beginning, a love affair with God has been at the heart of [Protestants'] faith."[36] Certainly, one of the most important characteristics of the Great Awakenings—influenced by European Pietists' quest for a deeper spiritual experience—was the emphasis adherents placed on unqualified devotion to God, and the contrasts they drew between their own emotive quest for God, and the stultified formalism of more established churches. This lengthy Protestant tradition of valorizing an ardent life of faith is evident in the history of Zion. Early Zionists spoke of their miraculous experiences of healing as evidence not only of the power of God over sickness and Satan, but as signs of "the wonderful love of Jesus for them." They phrased their quest for bodily healing not only as a desire for wellness, but also as an overpowering "hunger for God," characterized by a "melting heart."[37] Embracing divine healing and renouncing medicine was cast as devotion toward a lover, a leap of faith into the embracing arms of God. As one early Zion convert put it: "Father,

You are the Healer, I will never take medicine as long as I live. If I die I'll die in Your hands and You shall be responsible for me."[38]

Zionists' experience of the religious life as an ardent love affair gave rise to their restless reformist instinct. Devotees were propelled forwards in passionate commitment to deepening their spiritual experience by breaking away from established modes of religious life. Early twentieth-century Johannesburg Zionist Arie van Woerkom left the Methodist church because he found in Zion a compelling Christianity of the "heart": "I do not regret that I left the skeleton of Methodism. This was worth it . . . instead God led me to the heart of Jesus, to the real living Zion."[39] For Zionists such as van Woerkom, it was their suspicion of ecclesial hierarchies that freed them to pursue ever-greater intimacy with the divine. Invested in commitment to the Bible rather than to denominational orthodoxies, Zionists valued individual conscience rather than clerical authority and preached religious liberty rather than dogmatic obedience. Lacking a strong institutional center, individual Zionists were confident in their ability—grounded on direct revelation from God and the Bible—to improve upon the religious establishments of the day (including even their own Zion tradition, which could also be lambasted by internal reformers as "dead" status quo religion). Many Zionists invoked the direct promptings of God straight to their "hearts" to dissent from Dowie's grandiose insistence he was the reincarnation of the prophet Elijah. Zion City's top lawyer dramatically left the church after a personal revelation from God outweighed the ecclesial leadership who affirmed Dowie's declaration; this reformist figure aspired for nothing more than to "keep my heart open to the reception of God's truth, as He may show it to me."[40]

Zionists' reformist attitudes—a potent combination of religious ardor and antiestablishment logic—inevitably led to schism within the movement.[41] The existence of competing, contradictory voices is one of the most enduring features of the divided Protestant tradition the world over, and these same restless dynamics were discernible from an early date in Dowie's church. Many critics of Dowie's "Elijah Declaration" proclaimed themselves mandated by the authority of Scripture, direct revelation, and their own consciences to form new congregations correcting the grievous errors they believed the church had fallen into. A spate of breakaways by high-minded dissenters meant the church rapidly splintered into disparate rival Zions all claiming loyalty to a supposedly more authentic version of the faith. In the 1920s, one resident of Zion City estimated there were at least twenty different versions of the Christian Catholic Apostolic Church in Zion in the town, all almost identically named, and all claiming to be the purest and most biblically faithful version of Dowie's original organization.

One of the most contentious debates within the increasingly fractious Zionist community was over the new teachings of Pentecostal Christianity—an early twentieth-century sub-group within evangelicalism that stressed the importance of "speaking in tongues" (believed to be a miraculous language inspired by the Holy Spirit)—as the definitive marker of holiness. Many of the reformist churches emerging from within North American Zion throughout the twentieth century were products of arguments over whether Pentecostalism was the culmination of divine healing, as supporters argued, or the repudiation of the tradition, as detractors maintained.

Zion's reformist qualities manifested in Southern Africa around the same time as in the United States. But the much greater numbers of Zionists involved in the Southern African movement meant denominationalism exploded on a scale unprecedented in the North American context. As in the Midwest, African reformers appealed to their direct experience of divine guidance that trumped the pronouncements of their church seniors. One schismatic church founder from Johannesburg told of the "wonderful appearance of the Heavenly Choir to him," in which he "received Baptism by Fire, and God's power as . . . in the days of the Apostles."[42] Another African Zionist of this period maintained he broke away from his minister due to "two visions which revealed to me the name of the church, and called upon me to found my own church."[43] As was the case in North America, the religious multiplicity characterizing Zionist churches in Southern Africa was a barometer of the lively debates over adherents' quest for spiritual purity as well as a sign of the absence of an authoritative, universally recognized center.

By the end of the 1930s, approximately 300 rival Zionist organizations existed across South Africa, each led by individuals professing themselves directly led by the Holy Spirit and the Bible.[44] In the 1940s, this number had jumped to 800 "Zions" in South Africa alone, with doubtless many hundreds in neighboring countries such as Swaziland.[45] By the 1960s, a continent-wide survey of black Holiness churches in Africa concluded there were 6,000 separate organizations active on the continent, many in Southern Africa bearing the name of "Zion" or "Apostolic" (a related Pentecostal movement we shall hear more about).[46] Doubtless, the hostility of white governments to large African-led churches, and the greater ease with which a small denomination could survive under the official radar, also facilitated the rapidity with which Zionist reformers broke away from established bodies to form new churches. An important consequence of these anti-institutional dynamics was that North American missionary oversight of the Zionist movement in Southern Africa receded to the point where

Zion was widely perceived as a vast and decentralized collection of indigenous African churches with no common origins within a Midwestern evangelical church. Zion's highly fissured character obscured from sight its historical roots within the North American Christian Catholic Apostolic Church in Zion, and its ongoing indebtedness to the international divine healing movement. Yet, paradoxically, it is precisely Southern African Zion's schismatic character that identifies it as a faithful heir of the North American church in Illinois.

Telling the history of this contrary group of transatlantic evangelical reformers presents challenges. Histories of Africa have long focused on stories of collective action and of group consensus, tending to tell narratives of large groups of people mobilized in unity to ethno-nationalist projects, labor movements, and social causes, and characterized by their invocation of a shared past and common history.[47] By contrast, the history of evangelical nonconformity in Africa, as elsewhere in the world, is not one of consensus, but one of fragmentation. On the African continent, in particular, Zionists' history is one of a divided factional movement, marked by great difficulty in achieving any form of unity or stability. The story that follows charts the main contours of the key reformist groups to emerge within both the United States and South Africa, while attempting to steer clear of an overwhelming welter of confusing denominational detail. Yet attending to the contentious divided state of Zion in both regions should not merely be dismissed as a narrative challenge to a coherent story. Tracing these fissures offers invaluable insight into the independent-minded, passion-driven values that have animated the African and American Zionist women and men described throughout this book. The idiosyncratic, fissured story of Zion offers an important counterpoint to the more usual narratives of consensus and mass mobilization that characterize the annals of African history, underscoring the importance of disagreement and debate in the history of the continent.

Yet Zionists' diversity is, once again, far from the whole story. Echoing broader patterns in Protestantism, a dialectic between difference and uniformity, between individual diversity and institutional unity, lies at the heart of this evangelical movement. As much as Zionists have fragmented and splintered over the last century, they have also sought out unity, federation, and collective action. There is, after all, something discernibly "Zion" in the fissiparous expressions of this faith-healing movement. One of the most significant ways in which Zionists have sought to unify—amid all the divisions that fragment them—is in their pursuit of cosmopolitanism.

Cosmopolitans

Zionists in both the United States and Southern Africa were cosmopolitans who rejected the notion that humanity could be divided up according to race, nationality, or language. In doing so, Zionists were drawing on a long tradition in Christian thought—for example, the New Testament's advocacy of Christians as "citizens of the world," eradicating former differences between "Jew and Gentile"—that presented the church as a template for a redeemed society unified under God and across biological and social differences. In an age when great population mobility was twinned with burgeoning pseudoscientific racism, these expansive beliefs had profound meaning for many across the world. In 1901, preaching a sermon to his Chicago following, Dowie proclaimed "the man who hates another man because of his race or color or his creed is not a true Christian . . . and he cannot stay in the Christian Catholic Church in Zion."[48] This inclusive sentiment was widespread among Dowie's early following of first and second-generation immigrant American Scandinavians, German, Britons, Italians, Dutch, and African Americans. Indeed, this eclectic group of Midwestern Zionists fast put their conviction that the Kingdom of God transcended earthly differences into practice by founding Zion City as a cosmopolitan home for all nationalities and races, explicitly pitting it against the tensions that characterized Gilded-Era United States. As Dowie celebrated in 1902, "almost every race and nation under heaven has its representatives setting their faces towards Zion, seeking for help and guidance . . . there are over 60 nationalities represented in this City of Zion."[49] Residents of the new city sought to build an alternative society characterized by the harmonious and equal fraternizing of all. The rights of the small community of blacks within the church were frequently at the fore of sermons and articles published in Zion City's new press. The frequent lynchings taking place in the southern states at the turn of the century, for example, were meticulously documented, and much time was devoted to celebrating the successes of black Americans in enterprise.[50]

Dowie's message of racial cosmopolitanism especially resonated with believers throughout Southern Africa, a region evermore marked by harsh discrimination toward African people. Early twentieth-century British victory in the region had resulted in a strategic alliance between imperial interests and a local white settler community, a union which increasingly compromised the rights and standing of the region's black African population. Black divine healing adherents seized upon Zion as an alternative model for human society. South African Zionist, Elijah Lutango, for example, celebrated that in Zion's arrival in South Africa he had at last found "the True Love which does not separate brethren because of differences in the colours of their skins."[51] Throughout the region, in a manner profoundly countercultural for Christian and other organizations of the period, black and white Zionists were baptized together, sat next to each other in church services, and met in their houses at night to pray and sing together. Perhaps most important, they laid hands on believers of different races in joint supplication for divine healing. Both African and American Zionists deeply valued their relationships with counterparts on opposite sides of the Ocean, perceiving themselves as members within a multiracial, worldwide fraternity. In 1902, Zion City's periodical, *Leaves of Healing,* celebrated that the great advantage to the telephone was that it enabled Zion City residents to receive from "distant cities" in South Africa their "cries for prayer on behalf of the sick and dying . . . when we utter over the wire the words of prayer it is touching to hear the grateful 'Amen.' "[52] Most studies of religious exchanges between Africans and Americans rely on the notion of the "black Atlantic," a solidarity predicated on shared race. By contrast, the example of transatlantic Zionism was a self-consciously interracial collaboration, at least in ambition if not always reality.[53]

Despite its saliency for millions of black and white American and African Zionists, cosmopolitanism is a surprisingly absent theme in much literature on evangelicalism in the United States and Southern Africa. Ignoring the extensive collaborations between black and white evangelicals at various moments—not least within the abolitionist movement—a recent history of evangelicalism in the United States paid virtually no attention to blacks on the grounds that white and black evangelicals were simply too different to consider alongside each other.[54] The stories of black and white Christianity more frequently tend to be told in parallel fashion—running alongside each other, but seldom intersecting. In like fashion, the cosmopolitan aspirations of Christians of all races is invisible in many studies of Christianity in Southern Africa.[55] A large and lively literature on Christian missions in Southern Africa has mainly focused on the mutual incomprehension and even hostility that existed between white missionaries and black converts, as well as on the efforts of black Christians in Southern Africa to build links across the continent and internationally with other Christians of color, eschewing relations with white Christians.[56] The deliberate ways in which Christians of all races sought to mitigate and overcome—rather than work with—the racial classifications of their period is still a largely untold story.

Outside of the realm of scholarship, racial cosmopolitanism seems an increasingly detached concern from the present-day world. South Africa may have overthrown institutional racism in the form of the apartheid state in the 1990s, but it is today a nation divided by racial tensions and spates of deadly xenophobic violence against migrants. In 2017, Johannesburg's mayor announced that the city would not provide housing for foreign nationals (the large Nigerian community in the city was his target). The political developments subsequent to the 2016 presidential election in the United States can also be interpreted as part of a broader worldwide shift toward an insular nativism on the part of ideologues and elected officials. With its evidence of believers' radical commitment to Christian cosmopolitanism, the story of Zionists in Southern Africa and the United States offers an important counterpoint to the more frequently told histories of racial segregation in the United States, the apartheid state's manufacture of ethnic and racial identities, and the current wave of anti-immigrant nativism sweeping the world.

American and Southern African Zionists, nonetheless, were enacting their cosmopolitan experiments in the context of highly stratified societies. The nineteenth and twentieth centuries were the age of colonial rule and apartheid in Southern Africa—both systems predicated on hierarchies of race and ethnicity—while the United States was characterized throughout much of the twentieth century by the "Jim Crow" laws of segregation and disenfranchisement of nonwhites. The conditions of these wider societies produced a profound tension within Zion between cosmopolitanism and racialized thinking. Belying the original cosmopolitan aims of the movement, ethnic divisions soon permeated most branches of the worldwide church. Since the 1920s, Zion has been organized along racial lines: Zion in Africa is entirely black, and Zion in North America almost exclusively white. In Southern Africa, it simply proved too difficult to maintain a racially unified church in the face of legislation prohibiting and discouraging interaction between races. The chapters that follow provide numerous examples of lapses from the cosmopolitan ideal, even in the early more idealistic days of the transatlantic church. Although all this might rightly be read as the failure of cosmopolitanism within the Zion movement, scholars nonetheless remind us that cosmopolitanism has rarely existed in complete opposition to localism or to nativism. The term "vernacular cosmopolitanism" conveys the sense in which the local and the particular (including individuals' commitment to ethnic and racial identities) continually pull cosmopolitans in contradictory directions.[57]

Zion cosmopolitans did seek other outlets for their connective aspirations, even when their vision of interaction between whites and blacks faltered. Johannesburg's migrant labor networks ensured that believers of very many different language groups and ethnicities were extensively linked to each other. Individuals traveling between Johannesburg and regions as far away as Nyasaland (present-day Malawi) created a dense transfer and exchange of religious beliefs and practices across the African subcontinent.

Mobile Zionists were constituting themselves as a new people—affiliated not to kith and to kin, but to the Kingdom of God that knew no borders, and to the people of God who held aloof from classifications of race, ethnicity, or geography. While white government officials across the continent were trying to pinion Africans into fixed racial identities, casting different ethnicities as locked into pre-ordained slots on a civilizational "ladder," Zionists were making their contradictory claim that believers were characterized by fundamental sameness. Zionists were not alone in their efforts to combat the segregated logic of the day. This was an era when many across Southern Africa were experimenting with expansive ideologies of nationalism, socialism, and pan-Africanism, all seeking to erase local differences and to transcend racial or ethnic divisions. But Zion was one of the first movements to successfully put into action its cross-cutting solidarities. While the nationalist African National Congress struggled to mobilize popular support for much of the twentieth century, hundreds of thousands of Zionists from across Southern Africa regularly streamed to their holy hubs for annual sacred festivals, eclectic, cosmopolitan crowds all unifying under the expansive mantle of Zion.

Moreover, while by the interwar years Zionists in Southern Africa had largely broken away from North American Zionists, by the end of the twentieth century there was a new interest in reestablishing the multiracial transatlantic foundations of Zion. In the 1980s, American Zionists—long detached from African Zion—renewed their efforts to engage with their African brethren, largely through the provision of subsidized biblical education rather than the overt proselytization of a previous era. This development owed much to a desire among Western evangelicals to position themselves as relevant actors in a postcolonial age of Christianity. African Zionists responded with alacrity to renewed relations, not least because the Bible training on offer from North Americans was mobilized by youthful Zionists to contest the older church elite who claimed exclusive ownership over scriptural texts. African Zionists, in common with black Christians throughout the continent, have strategically leveraged interracial relations with white North American churches to gain access to much-needed resources. As Anthony Kwame Appiah reminds us, cosmopolitans are rarely divorced from mundane local struggles for survival.[58]

Sources and Chapter Summaries

The method of writing this book reflects its transnational themes. It uses archival material and newspapers in Johannesburg, Pretoria, Bloemfontein, Lobamba (Swaziland), Gaborone, Uppsala, London, Chicago and Zion,

Illinois. The book also relies on my interviews conducted with Zionists in Southern Africa and the United States. Many of the aforementioned documents are the official records of the South African government as well as of various colonial administrations. Reflecting the fact that colonial governments and the apartheid state took a great interest in these itinerant subversives, regional administrations meticulously detailed the affairs of Zionist churches, including filing their applications for official recognition of their organizations as well as their applications to erect buildings and secure permits for sacramental wine and railway travel. The South African National Archives Repository contains nearly 4,000 files on the topic of "Zion."

This book also draws on the documentary material generated by Zionists themselves, ranging from the periodicals, tracts, and pamphlets housed in church archives in Zion and Chicago, to the correspondence exchanged between Zionist ministers in Southern Africa and the United States, to the internal church histories and constitutions produced by Zion churches in both regions. I have accessed some of this material through the generosity of Zionists who have shared their private, family, and church papers; these individuals are listed in my acknowledgements. Similar material is in the archives of the University of Uppsala, part of a rich collection on Zion churches gathered by Bengt Sundkler throughout his seventy-year career in sub-Saharan Africa. A major blow to historians' understanding of the movement was dealt by the two fires that burned down Dowie's church in Zion in the 1930s and 1950s, destroying many personal papers such as letters and diaries.

Taken as a whole this material supplies a view of church life from the perspective of North Americans and Southern Africans, but many documents are largely weighted toward the perspective of clergy on both continents, rather than expressing the ideas of laity. One of the implications of this rather skewed representation is that female voices are relatively absent from the historical record. Very few women were or are formally ordained—at least to high levels—in transatlantic Zion. This means that documentary evidence is largely populated by the stories of male church founders, ministers, evangelists, prophets, and reformers. Where possible, this book has read these male-dominated sources "against the grain" and has used supplementary evidence, including from newspapers, to understand the female religious activity that formed Zion's backbone on both continents. Also, where possible interviews have been used to flesh out the paucity of the documentary record. This book is far from a complete history of female experience within Zion, which remains a lacuna in our understanding of the implications of this movement for all strata of Southern African society.

The book begins in the Australian cities of Adelaide, Sydney, and Melbourne in the second half of the nineteenth century. Demonstrating that evangelical Protestantism was forged just as much as in the wider imperial world as in the West, Chapter 1 shows how Dowie's inspiration for a populist working-people's church crystallized amid the Protestant temperance drives of the period. Influenced by the newly formed Salvation Army, temperance and divine healing both sought to forge a new language of redemptive holiness for working-class people.

Chapter 2 charts Dowie and his family's move to the American Midwest, via a several-year sojourn in California. In Chicago, Dowie first encountered the dizzying heterogeneity of one of the world's great immigrant cities. This prompted him to incorporate notions of cosmopolitanism within his new church—the Christian Catholic Apostolic Church in Zion—arguing that the Kingdom of God not only disregarded distinction in financial and social standing, but also differences of nationality, race, language, and geography.

Chapter 3 narrates the enthusiastic reception of Dowie's teachings in the goldfields of the South African Transvaal. There, another recently industrialized population used divine healing as a route to flourishing in the aftermath of a recent imperial conflict between Afrikaners and Britons. Although its success was limited, South African members of Dowie's church drew upon Zion's cosmopolitan teachings to argue for a new postwar white South Africanism, one that intermingled formerly estranged white "races."

Chapter 4 examines the transfer of Zion teachings to African Christian farmers on the rural South African Highveld. Disheartened by the hardening racism toward Africans that accompanied white South Africanism, this aspirational class found in Zion an affirmation of much-threatened values of progress, equality, and uplift for all. Divine healing's egalitarian values helped black Zionists assert their distance from the "heathen" healing techniques of their forefathers, and to proclaim their membership of a global community of civilized Christian moderns.

Zion's character in Southern Africa soon took a more populist twist. Chapter 5 shows how the explosive growth of Johannesburg as an immigrant mining hub transformed Zion from a relatively small movement of an elite African farming community to the faith of choice for many thousands of youthful African immigrants to the city. In capitalizing on Zion's affirmation of equality for all, these new devotees seized a chance to topple the orthodoxies characterizing black society of the day.

Chapter 6 returns to the twinned themes of transnationalism and cosmopolitanism. Throughout the twentieth century, Zion rapidly extended across Southern Africa, a phenomenon precipitated by the labor migrant networks that connected the region's population to Johannesburg. Disseminated by young urban evangelists, Zion urged continent-wide converts to renounce fidelity to chiefs, to ethnic homelands, and to biological families in favor of the expansive community of the Kingdom of God.

The book ends by bringing full circle the intertwined stories of American and African Zion. In recent years, North American evangelical missionaries funded by Dowie's original church in the Midwest offered "bible school" teaching to black Zionists. African Zionists mobilized these resources to embark upon one of Zion's typical cycles of reform. In Swaziland, youthful Zionist bible students contested the authority of older Zion elite by invoking their superior knowledge of the Scriptures. This final chapter demonstrates, once again, the seemingly inexhaustible capacity of the transatlantic People's Zion to generate fresh critiques of religious, political, and social authorities, and to propose novel visions of the democratic Kingdom of God.

CHAPTER ONE

Temperance, Divine Healing, and Urban Reform in Nineteenth-Century Australia

I N N O V E M B E R 1884, the *Melbourne Punch,* an illustrated magazine modeled closely on the British *Punch,* published a scathingly satirical poem on John Alexander Dowie, the controversial and outspoken divine healing practitioner who ministered to Melbourne's working-class suburbs of Collingwood and Fitzroy. The *Punch* poem lambasted Dowie for his pretensions to greatness, dubbing him "Alexander the Great: The Modern Miracle Monger," and mocking his claims to heal the sick as "the balderdash you talk." Portraying Dowie as a deluded religious crank, the poem went on to jab fun at Dowie's propensity to rail against the religious, political and medical establishment of the city, reminding him to "mind your Ps and Qs, or you'll be sat upon":

> Don't abuse the Bishop—really tis a shame
> Thus to flout his Lordship—much you are to blame
> Why such bitter railing at the Upper Ten?[1]
> Do you think reviling will make them better men?[2]

This poem was one of many critical commentaries on Dowie's frequent and well-publicized attacks on the middle-class Protestant establishment as self-interested and ineffectual. Amid public anxiety around the "problem" of the urban poor (a concern shared by many nineteenth-century metropolitan elite of Britain and the Britannic world), the reform-minded Protestant establishment of Melbourne proposed paternalistic solutions to urban poverty that lent upon the notion of the working classes as inherently degenerate. Dowie, by contrast, cast himself as a religious outsider, an outspoken advocate of the city's working people, and as deeply skeptical about the corruption and insincerity of the Protestant reforming classes. Part of a broader milieu of competition in Australia between traditional Protestant denominations and a new swathe of independent churches, Dowie and his hundreds of urban followers advocated a return to what they cast as a heartfelt Christianity that reclaimed the faith of the Apostolic age, including the practice of miracles. By promoting divine healing (the results of which were exuberantly proclaimed in public testimonies) as the essence of true Christian faith, Dowie negated not only the decorous codes of middle-class Australian Protestantism, but also the necessity of expensive physicians and surgeons. Dowie's egalitarian, antimedical message proved particularly attractive to a group of working-class women disillusioned with male surgeons' propensity for experimenting with scalpels and saws on female reproductive organs. For these women, as well as many men, Dowie proclaimed that total holiness and revolutionary improvement of both mind and body was within the grasp of the most humble resident of working-class areas such as Collingwood or Fitzroy. And against the backdrop of the Protestant establishment's rhetoric of "poor-shaming," Dowie's followers argued that divine healing empowered themselves as working women and men to radically transform their lives for the better—rendering the social reform campaigns of the city's churches superfluous. Dowie's new Holiness church instructed working-class attendees not only to regain control over their bodily health—reclaiming power from the intrusive, even dangerous, interventions of medical elite—but also to assert new autonomy over their personal narratives of faith, recounting in their testimonies how they had attained full spiritual perfection.

The story of the People's Zion thus begins far from either the United States or Southern Africa. It opens in colonial-era Australia, following Dowie's early career as a young Congregationalist cleric in Australia's new cities. In doing so, this chapter places the evangelical divine healing movement amid a much broader wave of religious urban reform programs of the late nineteenth century, emphasizing the saliency of the practice for new configurations of sociability and urbanity arising in this period. Recent studies of divine healing stress its influence on private devotional practices and the importance of the tradition's sanctuary-like residential healing homes; others examine how individuals accessed startling new bodily experiences (the physical body as a crucible for the divine, for example) through their practice of divine healing.[3] This chapter expands its gaze beyond the formation of selfhood to examine the rather more public dimensions of divine healing in the context of the explosively large cities of the imperial Anglo world. As Heather D. Curtis shows, divine healing's new devotional practices enabled a shift from a spirituality that was passive and acquiescent in the face of suffering to one that optimistically believed in the ability of Christ to remedy all the ills—spiritual, bodily, moral, and social—of the world.[4] Highlighting these public-minded reformist qualities, this chapter discusses the role of divine healing practitioners such as Dowie in a contested and lively milieu of social commentary regarding the industrialized poor of the Victorian era. It underscores the crucial link between divine healing and temperance: both were methods of cherishing the body as a "temple," and both offered redemptive interpretations of urban spaces depicted as full of moral and bodily danger. Moreover, while divine healing leaders in North America and Britain tended to represent an upper-class Protestant elite, in the newer cities of Australia, divine healing was far less favorably regarded by the Christian establishment.[5] As was the case with the new and controversial Salvation Army, divine healing was perceived as dangerously pandering to working-class sensibilities. In the context of nineteenth-century Melbourne, then, divine healing was a revolutionary program for working-class self-improvement that sat at odds with the interventions of the middle-class Christian and medical elite.

John Alexander Dowie's Australian years (1860–1888) are little explored. Most biographies treat Dowie's years in Australia as merely the backdrop to his arrival in the United States in 1888, offering only scanty detail on the antipodean origins of his religious career.[6] Although Dowie founded the Christian Catholic Apostolic Church in Zion in the United States, the importance of his Australian years should nonetheless not be passed over. Dowie's discovery of divine healing in urban Australia, alongside his promotion of temperance, are important for understanding both his later career in the United States as well as the success of divine healing in Southern Africa. It was during this lengthy period that Dowie's interest in portraying himself as an emissary to society's marginalized crystallized, and that his promotion of his religious organization as a self-consciously antiestablishment force came to the fore—two concerns that would resonate in both the industrialized Midwest and colonial Southern Africa. Dowie's egalitarian message that distinctions between classes were irrelevant to the possession of true holiness (an ideology forged in the streets of Melbourne inner-city slums) would be of key importance for Zionism's reception in Southern Africa among working-class whites and blacks. Moreover, Dowie's period in Australia also confirmed his opinion of the deleterious consequences of city living and industrialization, fueling his interest in creating Christian alternatives to an urbanization process cast by him as deeply degenerate.

Debates over Urban Health

Nineteenth-century Australia, a collection of British settler colonies, became a highly urbanized society with breathtaking rapidity. Melbourne, for example, grew to the size of half a million inhabitants in the space of fifty-five years, far outstripping older cities in the southern hemisphere such as Sydney, Los Angeles, Buenos Aires, and São Paulo.[7] This explosive growth— replicated in other cities across the country—was largely on account of the dominance of the manufacturing, building, and services sector, which naturally concentrated in Australia's large cities.[8] By 1850, 40 percent of the Australian population lived in medium and large-sized towns (compared to only 14 percent in the United States in the same period), and by the end of the nineteenth century, the urbanized proportion of the population sat at 70 percent.[9] Australians—both colonials and native-born—were proud of their urban civilization, viewing large and prosperous cities such as Melbourne, Sydney, and Adelaide as evidence of the new and superior (to the Old World) society being crafted by the new breed of men and women. In the 1880s—at the end of three decades of extraordinary financial prosperity—Australians found it easy to imagine themselves as the builders of a better and class-free world, where in the cities social mobility was open to all, and urban life was free of the royalty, nobility, class, corruption, and grinding poverty of Victorian England.[10] Cities such as Sydney and "Marvelous Melbourne" were lauded in booster accounts as refinements upon London, Paris, and New York, preserving their best aspects and extinguishing their worst social evils. Melbourne was admired as a "great emporium of British wealth and commerce,"[11] "London reproduced" and improved on as a "progressive, triumphal settler colonial city,"[12] whereas Sydney was the site of urban respectability and self-esteem, "drunkenness claimed to be seldom seen and riots and general disorder never."[13] The 1880 Melbourne International Exhibition—the first World's Fair in the southern hemisphere— confirmed Melburnians' opinion of the advanced state of their commerce, industry, sciences, and arts.[14]

Yet at the same time as these glowing commentaries on urban civilization were being produced, a much more skeptical rhetoric regarding the dangers of city living was emerging. For all the prosperity of the 1880s, the spoils of Australia's wealth were by no means equally shared by residents of its cities. The rapid industrialization of the second half of the century led to a deskilling of cities' work forces, supplanting older craftsmen with "an army of factory operatives performing menial tasks," and technological changes led to the creation of insecure, poorly paid occupations as telegraph clerks and tram operators with little opportunity for professional advancement.[15] Contrary to the optimistic accounts produced at the time (as well as much subsequent scholarship that echoed their views), cities such as late nineteenth-century Sydney and Melbourne were marked by a trend of downward social mobility among the working classes, and the persistence of pockets of extreme urban poverty even amid the prosperity lauded in contemporary accounts.[16] As early as the 1870s, elements among middle-class Australian city dwellers began to wake up to the presence of urban slums in their midst, uncomfortably echoing the problems of Old World cities they had hoped to eclipse.[17] This was the decade when a large group of sanitation and health reformers who included among their ranks politicians, journalists, doctors, health officials, and clergymen undertook investigation into the poorer areas of Melbourne and Sydney. Through their findings, reported in newspapers and presented before government commissions, this early generation of sanitary reformers popularized the notion that Australian cities had a "slum" problem. These were defined by them as urban spaces occupied by largely working-class residents, living in cramped, unsanitary, and unhealthy conditions, often in proximity to noxious and noisy industries.[18] Extensive measures aimed at addressing these problems—slum clearance, sewerage installation, legislation on industrial pollution, health provision—were rolled out during these years, with varying degrees of success.[19]

These reforming efforts were bound up with Australia's perception of itself as a region where the so-called Anglo-Saxon race was destined to find physical rejuvenation and repair. It is within this wider context of anxiety regarding the racial health of white Australia that nineteenth-century Australians' pursuit of health, hygiene, and cleanliness needs to be understood. Heavily industrialized European and North American cities had been long identified by contemporaries as a source of the physical and social ills supposedly plaguing Britons and Anglos the world over. A range of new occupational diseases proliferated from new factory working conditions, while the increased pace of urban life was thought to bring about a range of "nervous" complaints, making men weak and effeminate, and increasing supposedly "female" disorders among women.[20] The Australian Colonies, with their sunny climate and open spaces, were meant to have been the place where Anglo immigrants enfeebled by modern industrial civilization would be replenished.[21] But with the increased visibility of unwholesome, unsanitary slums in the midst of their cities, Australian activists of this period became acutely aware that local urban conditions, instead of replenishing the race, were further endangering it by having an enfeebling effect on racial health.[22] Compounding this anxiety about racial degeneration were worries about a declining birth rate[23] and public hysteria about newly arrived Chinese immigrants who, it was feared, threatened to drown out the Anglo-Saxon race.[24]

In attempting to address these threats to Anglo supremacy, urban sanitation reformers were also deeply infused with the values of evangelical Christianity. This was reflected in the fact that clergymen and missionaries to the inner city were a key subgroup within those who undertook pragmatic social reform.[25] From the second half of the century on, Christianity in the Australian colonies—already heavily non-Conformist—became marked with an increasingly evangelical character, influenced by the global Holiness revival brought to Australia via evangelical periodicals, visiting revivalists and the popular Holiness-style hymns and music of Moody and Sankey.[26] The Holiness tradition as it developed in Britain and North America—marked by the fervent committal of one's life to Christ and the renunciation of the past—had made its impact on social reform projects in cities around the world. In part, what became known as the "Social Gospel" was the product of the premillennial sentiment of the period: Christians believed they could usher in the second coming of Christ for his thousand-year reign by improving society as much as possible in the interim.[27] But evangelicals' interest in improving urban conditions was also the natural result of their highly optimistic theology: all aspects of human life were thought to be redeemable in the light of Christ's atonement on the Cross, and there was no imperfection either in the soul or in society too great to be redeemed and sanctified. Moreover, the evangelical emphasis on the self-disciplined and perfected human will combined with the above to form a deeply moralized understanding of poverty, whereby vice and sin were understood as both the symptom and the cause of poverty. Moral "sins" such as prostitution, gambling, horse racing, and dog and cockfighting were all considered factors leading to and cementing the poverty-stricken state of urban working classes. This moralized reading of poverty was especially applied to alcohol; Christian temperance activists in Australia, as elsewhere in this era, believed that hardship among the working classes was largely due to their excessive drinking habits.[28]

Inspired by these interlaced ideas surrounding urban poverty, racial health, and moral failings, a network of upper middle-class Christian reformers sprung up in Australia's main cities.[29] Most churches were heavily identified with values of middle-class respectability and their leading members tended to be the most active in social work among the urban poor. One author has dubbed this the "upper middle-class charity network" to refer to those—both formally within the church and those indirectly inspired by its evangelical values—who led a variety of campaigns for urban replenishment.[30] Eager to uplift the urban poor, and mindful of the fact that churches had experienced diminishing working-class attendance over the last few decades,[31] Australian cities' respectable church-going middle classes engaged in a plethora of do-gooding. Following the example of church members in British cities such as London and Manchester, Australian denominations united to form ecumenical "city missions" that sent clergymen out to live in the worst parts of the slums, ready to uplift the poor in intertwined practical and moral ways.[32] Temperance organizations that distributed tracts, campaigned for legislation change, and organized public lectures were formed, some part of transnational evangelical networks such as the Women's Christian Temperance Union, which reached Australia in the mid-1880s.[33] Sexual restraint and urban uplift were thought particularly interconnected by evangelical reformers. The moral being of young women newly arrived in cities was a point of particular concern as they were thought to be vulnerable to falling into prostitution. The Baptist medical doctor, John Singleton, launched "anti-vice crusades" for recent female emigrants, while the charismatic Henry Varley became a famous purity preacher in both England and Melbourne, railing that the sexual licentiousness thought to characterize working-class urbanites was "cursing the city."[34] In cities like Sydney, members of the international Young Men's Christian Association—a movement especially aimed at uplifting urban working-class young men set adrift from wholesome influences in the city—patrolled the streets, inviting wandering men to large meetings in the Sydney Opera House where short, simple, evangelical sermons about sexual purity and temperance were preached.[35]

The urban working classes expressed considerable ambivalence about this efflorescence of evangelical interventions. On the one hand, churches were often the only organizations offering practical assistance and aid in working-class inner-city areas such as Collingwood in Melbourne and Redfern and Newtown in Sydney. On the other hand, there was a high price to be paid for such assistance. Middle-class evangelicals typically divided the recipients of their charity into categories of "undeserving" and "deserving," maintaining that those who persisted in sinful behavior were the authors of their own misfortune and were thus ineligible for assistance.[36] Churches' intractable stance on drinking alcohol was one of the factors that drove a wedge between moral reformers and the working classes of areas such as Collingwood, where the local drinking hotel was a hub of community life, viewed by its patrons as far less elitist than middle-class churches that charged pew rents and required fancy clothes for Sunday services.[37] Reformers' negative portrayals of the urban poor as lazy, indolent, deeply immoral—some accounts cast them as a barely human subspecies[38]—sat ill with the working-classes, who valued Victorian ideals of cleanliness, sobriety, self-discipline, and thrift as much as the middle classes, and whose predicaments stemmed from structural inequalities rather than moral lassitude.[39] A visit from an inner-city missionary to a home in a poorer area "carried [with it] a degree of odium, implying fecklessness or degradation."[40] Furthermore, over the course of the nineteenth-century, evangelical and popular rhetoric surrounding working-class poverty in Australia as well as in British cities such as London became increasingly antagonistic and pessimistic.[41] Rather than being a temporary state that could be remedied given correct interventions, urban poverty began to be seen as a permanent fixture of cities, and the urban poor an inherently pauperized class who were incapable of uplift, and who posed a potent danger for racial degeneration.[42] Finally, as well as refusing to see themselves through the categories of degeneracy and infirmity popularized by middle-class reformers, the aspirational working classes of Sydney and Melbourne objected to reformers lowering the tone of their neighborhoods through the introduction of charitable institutions for the destitute and down-and-out. A municipal councilor in Melbourne complained that "what with lunatic asylums, drunkards' hospitals, reformatories for juvenile criminals, and fallen women . . . the place would soon become the Lazar House of the colony."[43]

Middle-class reformers were not the only ones offering commentary on what virtuous urban life should look like; working-class city dwellers also developed their own unique responses to the social pressures of the city. The second half of the nineteenth century thus saw the growth in a more militant working-class solidarity characterized by labor unrest, strikes, and agitation for an eight-hour working day.[44] This was also the period when new forms of working-class leisured sociability emerged. The figure of the "larrikin" first emerged as a pejorative term in popular middle-class discourse of the 1870s. It referred to gangs of working-class youth infamous for attacks against women and Chinese immigrants (the perception was that both groups were stealing jobs from them), as well as for engaging in street warfare with police and rival gangs.[45] With their flamboyant "street style," larrikins both participated in the culture of display and ornamentation that marked the prosperity of Australian urban living in these well-off decades (for example, larrikins were renowned for their eclectic fashions and haircuts) but were simultaneously excluded from full participation in the spoils of wealth enjoyed by the middle-classes of the city.[46] Indeed, larrikins were largely from those areas such as Collingwood in Melbourne where skilled trades such as boot making that had historically characterized the area were increasingly displaced by insecure, cash-rich jobs with little opportunities for advancement.[47] Larrikins were thus typically unskilled laborers, messenger boys, carters, and hawkers on the streets.[48] In their noisy, disruptive street ethos, larrikins—much bemoaned and criticized in the press of the period—challenged the dominant middle-class consensus about a well-behaved and respectful urban working class.

Middle-class commentaries on urban poverty were also challenged from within the ranks of the church. The arrival of the Salvation Army in the Colony of Victoria in 1881 marked one of the most sustained challenges to established Christian notions of how best to reform the urban poor. In many ways, the Salvation Army espoused near identical values and perspectives to those of the Christian establishment of Melbourne and Sydney. Started in the East End of London, William and Catherine Booth's evangelical organization drew its members overwhelmingly from the ranks of the working classes, and specialized in a focus on the urban poor that combined spiritual uplift with practical solutions. Booth, as were other Christian commentators of the period, was deeply concerned at the plight of London's working classes, likened to the "cannibals and pygmies of Darkest Africa,"[49] and similarly identified the city as a demoralizing environment on residents' spiritual and physical health. Indeed, in 1890 Booth proposed to establish "City, Farm and Overseas Colonies" where the enervated urban worker could recover from the demoralizing effects of the modern city.[50] Expansion of the Army into British colonies across the world was a key component both of Booth's thought, reflecting the wider societal perception that racial rejuvenation of the diminished Anglo race lay in outward expansion. In 1881, Major James Barker—commissioned by Booth to found the organization in Australasia, and to liaise with existing local Salvationists— landed in Melbourne with his wife, Alice, and within a few weeks was reporting to headquarters in Britain that its services attracted crowds of 600 in the working-class suburb of North Melbourne alone.[51] Soon, the Army had branches in Sydney as well as Adelaide in South Australia. By 1891 it claimed 1 percent of the Australian population in its membership.[52]

Yet for all its overlap with the reformist mood of the period, the Salvation Army's approach to urban poverty was radically different to that of the traditional denominations. The Army became notorious in Australian cities—as it had been in Britain—for its forthright appropriation of working-class culture and idioms. This included its use of populist methods of advertising its meetings (drawing on the popular broadsheet culture of the day, for example) and appropriating venues for its services usually shunned by the respectable classes, such as brothels, saloons, and dance halls.[53] Newly arrived in Melbourne, this sensationalist engagement with the nitty-gritty of urban life undoubtedly contributed to the organization's popularity, as did

its huge outdoor processions of bands of music-playing and singing Salvationists through the streets of the inner city, calling people to repentance.[54]
Its meetings featured riveting lineups of hardened former criminals detailing
their reprobate pasts and relating their dramatic conversion experiences;
such individuals were known as the Army's "trophies," which indicated their
interest in reclaiming and sanctifying members of the urban underclasses.[55]
The large membership of the Army undoubtedly reflected its success in
capturing the moral imagination of the urban working classes in ways that
the older and more established Protestant denominations largely failed to
do. In Australia, as in Britain, it drew its members—which included many
women—from "the most precarious stratum of working class single women,
tailoresses, washerwomen and labourers."[56]

In a climate in which traditional denominations were struggling with
declining church attendance and the proliferation of independent evangelical churches and para-church movements, it is perhaps not surprising that
the Christian establishment of Australia's cities were united in their condemnation of the Army.[57] In appealing to the working classes of the city,
the Army was thought to lower itself—and by extension, the entire "tone"
of Christianity—in a most undignified manner. In 1884 Dr. James Moorhouse, the Anglican Bishop of Melbourne, announced that he "griev[ed] to
see noble men and women descending to unworthy vulgarities for any cause
whatsoever . . . I fear that instead of lifting the mob up to Jesus Christ's
level, they will in time let the mob pull them down to its own."[58] City officials objected to the Army's considerable noise and the disruption this oc-
casioned, particularly during the famous street processions, where thousands could follow the marching, singing, preaching Salvationists—in the
words of one Collingwood councilor—"gyrating through the streets like a
lot of fools."[59] The city of Melbourne soon passed a bylaw banning street
processions other than funerals (legislation directly targeting the Salvationists), but to no avail as Army members—confident that they were following Christ's command to preach among ordinary people—broke the
new law, steadfastly refused to pay the fines and were imprisoned.[60] The
middle-class representatives of the establishment were not the only critics
of the Army; it also drew hostility from larrikin gangs in the cities, who
raided its meetings, behaved in disorderly fashion, and even took pot shots
at Salvationists. In 1886, at the North Fitzroy Army barracks, one "Dunkley,"
a "labourer of nineteen years of age and a member of the larrikin class
pulled a pistol from his pocket and pointed it at the temple of Quartermaster Rain." The reason was the quartermaster's frequent "putting out"
of meetings of Dunkley and other disruptive youths, meaning that the
Salvationist "had incurred the dislike of larrikins in and around North

Fitzroy."[61] Larrikins especially disliked the Salvationists because they were two highly popular groups competing for the loyalty of the same urban constituency. Their mutual antipathy thus represented tension between closely related social strata, the "respectable and rough elements in working class life."[62] In fact, middle-class commentators, including clerics and city officials, often confused the activities of the two groups, concluding that the Salvation Army was itself a form of "religious larrikinism." Collingwood's mayor stated: "two of the most noted and foul-mouthed larrikins of Collingwood were no more obstructive than the leaders of the Salvation Army,"[63] a "body that caused a very great deal of discord" in the area.[64] It was this same tension between elite and popular forms of Christian urban reform that characterized the early divine healing ministry of the young South Australian Congregationalist minister, John Alexander Dowie.

John Alexander Dowie: An Elite to a Populist Reformer

John Alexander Dowie was born in Edinburgh, in 1847, the son of John Dowie, a tailor and part-time Congregationalist preacher. Dowie's childhood in Edinburgh was shaped by the effects of the first Great Awakening. By the middle of the nineteenth century, the official Church of Scotland was competing with a large number of nonconformist churches—including the Congregationalists—that advocated for the necessity of a simple, practical, missionary-inspired Christianity.[65] In later life describing his childhood as sickly, Dowie remembered it was "only my intense love for God that gave me any joy."[66] The young Dowie frequently accompanied his father on his preaching journeys around the town and its surroundings, and recalled also hearing the street preaching of Henry Wight who, throughout the 1840s and 1850s, was famed in the north of England and in Scotland for powerful revivalist-type sermons.[67] A contemporary report recounted that Wight would typically issue "an invitation to all to hear plain and simple exhibitions of the way of salvation, illustrated by anecdotes."[68] Perhaps influenced by Wight or another nonconformist preacher of the day, the whole Dowie family were ardent teetotalers (a typical stance for British evangelicals of the mid-century), and Dowie remembered that he signed the temperance pledge when he was only six.[69] Dowie recounted in later life that the family was "poor," as were many mid-century Scots caught up in a period of rapid industrialization and famine.[70] Doubtless this prompted their decision to emigrate in 1860 to Adelaide in the colony of South Australia, where the rumored level of living standards continued to attract immigrants from Scotland.[71] Dowie Senior's brother—Alexander—had already immigrated here, and was making a good living in boot manufacturing.[72] It was common for Scottish immigrants of this period to settle in Australian towns where they had a family member who could host and orientate them.[73] Following this pattern, the family arrived in Adelaide where John Dowie continued his trade as a tailor, and the thirteen-year old Dowie was apprenticed as a clerk in a wholesale grocery firm, G. and R. Wills.[74]

A Colony of free settlement, based on principles of "scientific colonization"—designed to open up new agricultural land, accommodate surplus British farmers displaced by industrialization, and to provide food for Britain—South Australians considered themselves superior immigrants to those found in many of the other Australasian colonies.[75] These self-perceptions of middle-class respectability were particularly pronounced in its capital, Adelaide, which also prided itself on its Christian evangelical zeal. From its inception, South Australia had refused support for an established church, and so nonconformist denominations such as Methodists, Baptists, and Congregationalists flourished.[76] In addition to this, the Colony was also the site of an extraordinarily successful revival within the Methodist church in the 1870s which "shook the foundations of society" with intense anxiety about personal sin and a heartfelt desire to cultivate holiness.[77] The Dowies worshipped at the Hindmarsh Square Congregational Church, under the Rev. Francis William Cox, where John Dowie Senior became a "respected deacon and lay preacher."[78] Of all the denominations in South Australia, Congregationalism was perhaps the most allied with the bourgeois metropolitan classes—an influential, elite, and politically active minority in the cities, but which had even by this date already lost ground to revivalist Methodists in the rural areas.[79] Of a pious bent, the young Dowie studied for the Congregationalist ministry in Adelaide for thirteen months, and then in 1868 returned to Edinburgh for three years "to take voluntary courses in the Free Church School."[80] By 1872—partly at the urging of his family—Dowie returned to South Australia, where he was ordained a minister of the Congregational Church, and took up his first position as pastor of the tiny rural settlement of Alma, fifty miles north of Adelaide.[81]

From the start of Dowie's ordained ministry, the issue of temperance—principled abstinence from alcohol on religious grounds—was of central importance for him, and for his understanding and practice both of his personal faith, and of the role of the church in society. The late nineteenth-century Australian colonies had high levels of alcohol consumption; until the 1860s, Australians drank considerably more than the British, perhaps attributable to the high proportion of single men.[82] However, the colonies were also places where anti-alcohol activism in the form of temperance societies flourished. Organizations such as the Sons of Temperance and the

Order of Good Templars first arrived in the 1870s, and had 63,000 Australian members by 1890.[83] The colonies' Protestant churches were particularly active in the fight against alcohol, and the "liquor trade." For evangelical Christians of this period, in Australia as in Britain and elsewhere, abstinence was understood to be integral to the cultivation of personal holiness. The issue of alcohol consumption also became a key feature of the churches' commentary on the evils of urban existence and the problems besetting working-class existence. It was true that drinking lay at the heart of many late nineteenth-century working-class areas in Australian cities. "Hotel keeping" was in this period a source of economic survival for many men and women, and urban pubs became centers of sociability and recreation.[84] Working-class areas like Melbourne's Collingwood had sixty licensed liquor houses in the 1860s, and their social function far exceeded drinking with early labor movement meetings held in them—working men's clubs and sporting bodies.[85] But in keeping with their tendency to locate the causes of poverty among personal habits—rather than amid structural factors—evangelical Christian temperance advocates saw hotels and licensed liquor as the major, unnecessary cause of poverty among the working classes, whom they stereotyped as fecklessly drinking away their salaries at the expense of their health and their family lives. The temperance evangelist, William Noble, told his Sydney audience in 1886 that "we should hear very little of poverty or the unemployment question if a stop were put to the drinking habits of our land."[86]

As a pious Congregationalist churchman, it was a natural step for the young Dowie to become intensely involved in temperance reform and activism; many of his Congregationalist colleagues in Adelaide, such as the well-known Joseph Coles Kirby, were tireless pamphleteers and lecturers on the topic.[87] Indeed, Dowie's devotion to the temperance cause was part of his dissatisfaction with his first pastorate in the small town of Alma. Being the only minister in a largely rural area meant traveling gruelingly long distances every week to minister to far-flung parishes. In combination with this, Dowie lamented "the perfect mine of evils sprung in the midst of the nominal church here." The fact that many of his fellow Congregationalist ministers continued to indulge in alcohol was "a painful discouragement" to him.[88] In Dowie's opinion, drink was not just a personal, individual sin but at the root of social, national, and racial woes of the British people, both at home and in their overseas colonies. In a letter to the editor of the *South Australian Register* in 1873, while still at Alma, he lamented "that there is no single habit in this country which so much deteriorates the qualities of the race, and disqualifies it for endurance in the struggle for the prize of superiority."[89] In the same year, after just several months in this post, Dowie resigned from Alma, and soon took up a new position as pastor of the Manly Beach Congregational Church in Sydney.[90] Here, in the middle of the second largest metropolis of Australia, Dowie found plenty of further evidence of the ruin wrought by drink. All around him, as he wrote to his parents in his regular letters home to Adelaide, he saw "the most heart-rending sights of men and women being dragged down into awful depths through this curse."[91] He could only conclude that "Christ's work in this city is a sad state."[92] Immediately upon arriving at the Manley congregation, Dowie began an energetic program of temperance work, reporting with triumph that about fourteen in his congregation had become avowed abstainers in the space of several weeks, signing the temperance pledge book.[93] Like many others, Dowie was certain that temperance was the key to correcting the excesses of city living and to resolving the predicament of the urban poor. In a letter to his parents in 1873, Dowie proclaimed that "when I think of the mighty moral force which the destruction of that fearful trade would liberate for the destruction of ignorance, crime, disease, insanity, destitution . . . drunkards clothed and in their right minds, homes made happy, children cared for, fed."[94]

Like many other Christian reformers of the period, Dowie focused not merely on personal perfection within the individual, but on affecting society at the highest levels possible via legislation reform. As early as 1872 when he was still in Adelaide, Dowie was addressing Congregational Union meetings and gatherings, "calling upon all members to endeavor by every private and public effort to diminish so man-destroying and God-dishonouring a trade."[95] And in Sydney's Congregationalist circles, Dowie found more prominent and influential platforms from which to advocate for legislation change. He became a frequent speaker at the New South Wales Association for the Promotion of Morality—in company with other clerical luminaries of the city such as the Anglican Dean of Sydney—drawing up proposed amendments to the laws regulating the sale of alcohol, and making plans to present a petition to Parliament.[96] By 1876, Dowie was part of a committee representing forty Sydney clergymen of various denominations charged with the task of drawing up the amendments. These included, among other points, the removal of the power to licenses for drinking establishments from magistrates (supposedly corrupt, and in the pocket of local "liquorocracies") to the people, constituted in democratically elected Boards of License.[97] The next year, Dowie was one of the founding members behind Sydney's Liquor License Amendment Association.[98] He was charged not only with attending upon the Premier of the Colony with its aims, but also encouraging the establishment of branches in towns across the colony and issuing circulars about its legislative reform aims to the political and administrative elite of the colony.[99]

Over the next few years Dowie's relationship with this stratum of middle-class Christian reformers would become increasingly strained. For one, Dowie's stance on liquor reform was viewed as far more extreme than that of the majority of his clerical colleagues. Most Temperance Societies in Sydney were by 1880 ready to accept a proposed amendment that would give inhabitants of an area the right to petition against the opening of a public house. But Dowie could see this only as a "lowering of standards" as the Bill did not embrace Sunday closing for public houses, nor his hoped-for two-year suspension of all new licenses for public houses.[100] His temperance colleagues in the Liquor Licensing Amendment Association were increasingly wondering whether "Mr Dowie was a very enthusiastic worker but not a very practical one."[101] Compounding Dowie's temperance zeal was the fact that he was undoubtedly a character given to personal conflict and friction with everyone around him. As early as 1877, he lamented in a letter to his new wife, Jane, or Jeannie, (a first cousin from Adelaide, whom he had married in 1876) about why "I never seem to get along with some classes of minds—and these not a few in the Christian Church—to whom my words seem to act like a red flag."[102] Dowie increasingly lambasted those respectables within the Congregationalist church for "narrow denominationalism ... and cliqueism ... rather than the claims of perishing multitudes who want bread and not theological stones."[103] In particular, he was deeply frustrated by the moderate stance Congregationalists were taking on the temperance issue, bemoaning "the languid state in our churches."[104] In fact, Dowie was becoming increasingly irate and outspoken on a number of issues. These included not just temperance but also Roman Catholicism, spiritualism, and horse racing. Dowie's views were aired in such a polemical and provocative manner in both public lectures and printed tracts that he outraged the news organs of the respectable middle classes, precipitating what would be an enduring antagonism between him and the press in Australia, and later in the United States. One newspaper considered that Dowie's public lectures directed toward Sydney's Catholic Archbishop were "needlessly offensive ... its uncompromising hostility to a cause is not incompatible with charity and gentlemanness."[105] In 1878, Dowie finally broke the ties between himself and the Congregationalist church, resigning after a dramatic sermon in Sydney, where he mounted his pulpit in "full canonicals carrying a glass of wine ... [he] held the intoxicating glass before the astonished congregation, dramatically exclaiming, 'these be thy gods, O Israel!!' "[106]

From this year on, Dowie positioned himself as an independent minister, on a "Free Christian Platform," unconstrained by "narrow denominationalism" nor by the class interests and notions of respectability that he believed impeded Sydney's churches from acting effectively in the world.[107] Without a building for his ministry, he began holding services in a variety of public venues. This was done partly out of pragmatism, but also inspired by his vision that Christianity should exist among the people rather than being constrained by the elite interests of the "snobocracy of Sydney who are such a curse to the people generally . . . and promote vice under high patronage."[108] Thus he proclaimed several years later: "I have felt it my duty to reach more directly perishing multitudes around me, preaching in the theatres and public halls of Sydney."[109] After denouncing the sinfulness of theatergoing, he affirmed his strategy of discarding norms of respectable behavior by meeting the working classes of the city where they were, declaring that "the theatre is the best place to speak in the city . . . In the name of God, I would consecrate every stage for his service, and take possession of them for the Lord God."[110] When the rent on theaters became too high, he transferred his ministry to a "stuffy room up one pair of stairs in Pitt Street," grandly named by him "International Hall."[111] His vehement Holiness message—still focused at this point on the issue of temperance and denouncing the evils of the city's "liquorocracy"—seem to have found some success with a working-class audience. A reporter visiting International Hall remarked on the "fifty or sixty people present," commenting snidely they were "without exception of the lower orders, such a collection of pinched bonnets, turned gowns, patched boots and five and ninepenny costumes I never saw collected together."[112] These were years of difficult financial struggle for Dowie and his family, and he relied on the financial support of several more prosperous evangelical sympathizers to keep afloat.[113]

Dowie's final break with the Australian Christian establishment occurred at the end of 1879 when he unsuccessfully campaigned to represent the constituency of East Sydney. From an early date, Dowie had perceived that "the only real battle field of drink was at the ballot box . . . only there that they would bring influence to bear on the legislature of the land."[114] In 1879 Dowie proclaimed that a life in politics, where he could influence temperance reform, was the fulfillment of his ministerial vocation: "I believe my ministry in the city must carry me into the legislature ere I can fulfill it, to promote righteousness in our Government and its laws, our young men are decaying fast."[115] Bolstered by the support of a small group of temperance backers, Dowie campaigned against another Christian temperance candidate, Dr. Arthur Renwick. However, Sydney's temperance associations were by now deeply wary of Dowie, who was increasingly lambasted by the city's newspapers as "a ridiculous and comical personage of a semi-public position,"[116] and whom they viewed as a distinct liability. The Protestant temperance establishment thus gave their support to the more moderate Renwick, leading to the temperance vote being divided, and the victory of another candidate.[117] It was this Christian political elite whom Dowie came to cast in later years as "the betrayers of the Temperance cause," accusing them being "dupes of men who are either office seekers or who made the temperance platform a political and social stalking horse."[118] In his view, Renwick had been supported because while publicly taking a temperance line, in private he was a paid man of the "liquorocracy"—something that suited the financial interests of the Christian establishment. In a bitter letter to his parents, Dowie maintained that "everyone in Sydney who knows anything about this election knows that I was not defeated, I was sacrificed, in a panic . . . this shows us more clearly than ever that money and alcohol are the tyrants of men who are destroyers of the people and dishonorers of God."[119]

In Dowie's progressive shift away from the values of the urban Christian elite—from whom he now felt alienated—the events of 1881 would be decisive. It was in this year that Dowie first made contact with the newly arrived Salvation Army in Adelaide. The financially struggling Dowie had been promised a huge donation by a young follower called William Holding. The sum was meant for the construction of a new church for Dowie's ministry in Sydney, and it would supposedly come out of Holding's inheritance. Holding borrowed £300 from Dowie to return to England to collect the inheritance; the plan being that he would meet Dowie in Adelaide upon his return. The whole affair turned out to be a painful and much publicized fraud. Once in England, Holding faked news of his death to be sent to Dowie in Adelaide and made off with the money, which considerably added to the financial strain Dowie experienced during these years.[120] During his months of fruitlessly waiting for Holding in Adelaide, Dowie started attending meetings of the Salvation Army corps in the city, also delivering lectures to Salvationists in their barracks on topics such as "General Booth and the Salvation Army: Its Origin, Victories, Methods and Prophecies."[121] From the content of sermons such as these, it is evident that Dowie found much to admire in the Army's bold methods in forthrightly penetrating working-class areas. In Dowie's opinion, "this movement was second only to the Reformation," and the opposition of Adelaide's Christian establishment to its work, was akin to the attitude of the "church of Thessalonica at the time of the advent of the Apostles Paul and Silas, when it was said, 'Those that have turned the world upside down have come hither also.' "[122]

Dowie emerged as a prominent defender of the Salvation Army's right to "claim the streets for Jesus," asserting that the Army was performing a vital service in redeeming the urban poor by street processions. In his view, rather than being a public nuisance, as the Christian establishment of Adelaide were claiming, the Army only sought "the moral elevation of the people and to save them from drunkenness and crime."[123] And while Dowie claimed that he was only a "friend of the Army, not an Associate," contemporary newspapers make it clear that Dowie played a pivotal role in a power struggle between two factions of the Army in Adelaide—one loyal to Booth's appointed deputy, Captain Thomas Sutherland, and the other to Dowie himself.[124] It was certainly the perception of Adelaide's newspapers that "the so-called Salvation Army, an assemblage of rough, consisting of all the tag rag and bob tail of the back slums of Adelaide are headed by a clergyman, the Rev. Mr. Dowie and parade the streets on the Sabbath evening singing hymns that border on the ludicrous to the disgust and annoyance of all right-thinking people."[125] As it happened, Dowie's attempt to wrest power away from Sutherland was unsuccessful. The hierarchies of the Army were absolute, and his moral legitimacy was quashed in the face of a leader appointed by General Booth himself.[126] By October 1881, Dowie had left Adelaide and set out for what he called "the moral wastes" of the city of Melbourne to once again start a new phase in his ministry.[127]

In his subsequent seven years in Melbourne, Dowie would put the lessons he had learned from the Salvation Army to good use. Settled by early European colonials on the banks of the Yarra River, by the 1850s, the gold rush had caused the city of Melbourne to rapidly expand in population, buildings, and infrastructure. Unsanitary and disease-ridden residential areas now clustered around the low-lying, damp banks of the highly polluted river, and streets dense with saloons and opium dens proliferated in areas like Little Bourke Street. For Dowie, viewing the city for the first time in 1881, his evangelical zeal was "deeply stirred by the moral wastes of the city." He found "that infidelity and spiritualism were slaying their thousands, that the liquor traffic was slaying its tens of thousands, and that a formal and cold travesty of Christianity was responsible for the awful condition of hundreds of thousands."[128] And at the same time, Dowie discerned the manifold advantages of starting a new urban ministry in a city that seemed "the powerful centre of Australian life, the real capital of Oceania . . . where good work done for Christ must permeate throughout this New World in the south."[129] Dowie briefly took over the pastorship of a Baptist church on Sackville Street in the working-class area of Collingwood, while the minister was on sick leave in Europe. He particularly appreciated the location of the "large weatherboard Tabernacle," "within easy reach of thousands of working people . . . those whom Jesus loved so well, "the common people" who "heard Him gladly."[130] But soon the minister returned, and despite an unsuccessful attempt to wrest power from him, the contentious Dowie was ejected in early 1883.[131]

Dowie took with him a number of supporters from the Sackville Tabernacle, and by February 1883, he had founded his own Free Christian Church, constituted with "99 brethren and sisters" from Collingwood.[132] The church's newly written "Declaration of Fellowship" explicitly distanced itself from the "formalism" of the city's Christian establishment, announcing that "we declare ourselves FREE from all allegiance to human definitions of doctrines and church systems."[133] Initially without a building (they would erect a Tabernacle the following year that could seat 3,000[134]), the members met in the Fitzroy Town Hall, a working-class area adjacent to Collingwood.[135] Dowie's vision was to preach salvation among the urban poor in a manner he hoped would be far more efficacious than that of the reformist elite he had now entirely broken with: "this church exists for practical work, and aims at the conversion of sinners and the sanctification of believers."[136] In particular, his new Free Christian Church would be characterized by a teaching that middle-class Christians would find particularly objectionable. The final clause of the new church's "Declaration" listed that "sin, disease and death are three links in one chain of evil, every one of which Christ has broken."[137] The refusal of the inevitability of disease, the eschewal of medicine, and the exclusive reliance on Christ for healing would distinguish Dowie's radical urban ministry from this time forward.

Divine Healing and Melbourne's Working Classes

There was a natural affinity between the international divine healing movement and the urban social reform projects so beloved of the Christian middle classes of the period. Leading Canadian divine healing figure, A. B. Simpson, resigned from his genteel Presbyterian church to become an urban minister in New York City, convinced that the alienated working classes ought to be more directly engaged. For Simpson as for other divine healing advocates, clear parallels existed between the "energetic resistance" offered by divine healing practitioners to personal infirmity, on the one hand, and the "aggressive work" needed to counter the social and spiritual maladies of contemporary cities, on the other.[138] Simpson and other divine healing practitioners in cities such as New York and Boston formed committees on charitable aid, sought to create jobs for the poor, and took care of the sick and dying, regularly seeking out the urban poor in their own spaces. Simpson reported that "many of the ladies visit regularly the tenements, distributing cards of invitation and tracts."[139] Other divine healing figures pushed for legislative and structural reform. After her own dramatic experience of bodily healing, Emma Whittemore, a prominent member of New York's social elite, opened a home for "fallen girls," and agitated for regulation of female wages and protection in their workplaces.[140] Many other women and men of this era echoed this pattern, celebrating that they were now physically and practically able to undertake good works for the poor; no longer sick and enfeebled, they were empowered to participate in urban ministries and temperance movements.[141]

An interest in divine healing, then, was not so far a stretch for the intensely reform-minded Dowie. In later life, he claimed he had begun practicing divine healing as early as 1874, the date of an outbreak of plague in Sydney, during his time at the Manly congregation. Confronted with the death of many parishioners, he realized that sickness "is the devil's work and it is time we called on Him Who came to 'destroy the work of the devil', to slay that deadly foul destroyer."[142] Yet it would not be until 1882, during his time at the Collingwood Baptist Tabernacle, that divine healing first became a prominent part of Dowie's preaching and writing, suggesting that Dowie was more influenced by the increased prominence of divine healing in Christian circles around him than his earlier 1874 date would suggest.[143] The 1880s were the decade when international divine healing teachings first began to circulate within the mainstream of Australian Protestantism, finding support from individuals within established as well as newer denominations.[144] Anglican clergymen offered support to independent divine healing practitioners such as James William Wood in Adelaide, who had worked with the Salvation Army in the "back slums" for many years, and claimed to have healed between 2,000 and 3,000 through Christ's power.[145] Baptists and Methodists, along with Anglicans, also lent meeting places to divine healer Isabel Penny's ministry in North Brighton, Victoria.[146] Both Wood and Penny attended William Boardman's influential International Divine Healing Conference in London in 1885, indicating the participation of Australian evangelicals within an international landscape (Dowie, unable to attend, instead sent a lengthy letter describing his healing ministry in Melbourne).[147] Books and periodicals airing the views of leading international divine healing figures such as Andrew Murray, A. B. Simpson, and Carrie Judd were widely read in Australian Protestant circles in these years, perhaps another channel through which Dowie accessed the movement's teachings.[148] For Dowie, the link between temperance activism and divine healing would have been an obvious one: both emphasized the intertwined health of the individual and the social body, and both portrayed the body as a temple of the divine.[149] Dowie was prone to denounce both alcohol and pharmaceuticals as having a similarly corrupting effect, lamenting the "unclean souls and bodies" that were "temples of disease . . . temples of patent medicine, temples of vegetable and mineral poisons—perhaps alcohol—bodies saturated with nicotine and other kinds of poison."[150] Moreover, the ever-polemical Dowie seems to have perceived divine healing as a decisive return to the values of a nonelitist Christianity, a repudiation of the "social" Christianity of the city's establishment. His letter to Boardman's 1885 Conference rejoiced in the "signs that the 'old time religion' is returning to its primitive lines of spiritual power and despite the forces of an organized and widespread formalism, true Christians are realizing 'The Spirit gives life,' amongst these signs the revival of faith in Jesus as the Healer."[151]

By 1883, Dowie had incorporated divine healing as a regular part of the activities of his new Free Christian Church. This typically involved prayer while laying hands on supplicants, usually in their own homes, or in the back room of his Tabernacle. On these occasions, his wife, Jeannie Dowie, was usually in attendance to forestall accusations of impropriety in the case of female congregants, who by all accounts, made up the majority of his followers.[152] Dowie would also silently pray for sufferers from afar, something that was especially done in his early healing career to counter the frequently made claim that he was a mesmerist or spiritualist, and worked by transmitting electrical currents to supplicants' bodies through his hands.[153] Many for whom he prayed told of experiencing a bodily jolt during the experience of the laying-on of hands: a "shock . . . [as] the Holy Spirit's power" pass through them.[154] Some claimed that they experienced healing instantaneously. Mrs. Parker of Napier Street in Fitzroy, who was a tailoress and so relied on her sight for earning a living, recalled Dowie prayed for a "running cancer" in her eye, and that upon his touch it burst and "poured" out.[155] For others, healing took a little more time to set in. For a Mr. Spinks, who received prayer for an internal tumor "so large in front of me I was ashamed," it was three days, and then "every particle of the tumour was gone altogether."[156] As were other divine healers, Dowie was always eager to claim that healing did not come from him, but from Christ, "the great physician." In keeping with the conventions of the broader movement, Dowie stressed to his followers that healing only followed from faith, and was bound up with a holistic dedication of one's life to Christ. An example of this interpretation of divine healing is found in the testimony of Mrs. Trickett of Geelong near Melbourne, who had experienced a life of infirmities, including "scarlet fever, brain fever, hydatide and enlargement of the liver." A relative wheeled her in an "invalid chair" to the Mechanics' Institute Hall in Melbourne—a popular working-class meeting venue—where the Dowies were holding their "faith missions." Approaching Dowie for prayer for her conditions after the service, Mrs. Trickett was quizzed on whether she "believed the Lord was willing to heal [her] there and then?" She remembered that "I burst into tears and had to answer 'No.'" But by the time she came again to the meeting, next week, "my unbelief was swept away." She remembered that "I had no fear, calmly waited . . . Mr Dowie prayed and laid hands upon me, and my back—I suffered from muscular paralysis of the spine—I was healed instantaneously."[157]

Although the experience of the laying-on of hands was evidently a powerful part of this ritual, divine healing was above all a profoundly verbal process. The act of publicly offering a testimony was an integral component of the healing ritual. Regular testimonial meetings were scheduled, initially held in the Fitzroy Town Hall, in which members of the congregation would come forward, take the stand, and testify to their miraculous healings received through the prayerful intercession of Dowie.[158] Individuals' testimonies occupied as prominent a place—if not more so—than their actual experiences of receiving healing prayer, which usually occurred in private spaces. A journalist who attended a service at Dowie's Free Christian Tabernacle in Fitzroy confessed himself surprised and "disappointed when I found I was only going to hear about the things that had been done instead of witnessing them for myself . . . it was mainly young women standing up [to talk]."[159] Dowie himself seems to have viewed the testimonial meetings as a quasi-evidentiary process, requesting those who had experienced divine healing to offer their own "proof" of these miracles in the interests of silencing his many critics and skeptics.[160] Those giving testimonies on a platform before the whole meeting were frequently cross-examined by Dowie, who asked probing questions about the length of their illness, how many doctors they had consulted, how often they had attended hospital, the length of time that had elapsed since their healing, and the current state of their health.[161] Particularly noteworthy healings—whether because of the severity of the illness or the dramatic instantaneousness of relief—were returned to by Dowie time and time again in these testimony meetings. He referred to them as "cases which are beyond all question," including Mrs. Parker of Fitzroy's healing of an eye cancer, who had "regularly testified before more than a thousand persons in the Tabernacle and never once been challenged."[162] This evidentiary strategy was not dissimilar to the techniques employed by spiritualists of the period, a class of practitioners similarly intent upon producing "scientific" proof of the miraculous.

Dowie was particularly interested in the strategic use of print to create authoritative records of miraculous healings. He printed and circulated thousands of tracts that reproduced the most impressive and dramatic testimonies he could muster from among his followers.[163] Although his detractors denigrated his "ill-printed, ill-written, ill-looking hand bills as scurrilous phillipics,"[164] Dowie was convinced that documents such as these supplied "the most convincing documentary printed evidence of divine healing's efficacy"—something that was useful both to silence critics as well as to persuade unbelievers.[165] It was for this reason that in 1888 he published his *Record of the Fifth Annual Commemoration of [Dowie's] Ministry of Healing through Faith in Jesus,* a small booklet that contained "hundreds of written testimonies from persons healed . . . it will reach tens of thousands of suffering homes where [Dowie's] voice can never be heard and [Dowie's] bodily presence never come."[166] This was also the year the regular periodical *Leaves of Healing* was launched as a further platform for the testimonies of those who had been healed. *Leaves of Healing* imitated the popular broadsheets of the period through its use of large, eye-grabbing headlines as well as dramatic "before" and "after" photographs of divine healing supplicants. With publications such as these, Dowie was also attempting to correct a popular impression that his healing techniques overlapped with the strategies used by the heterodox healers of the city such as spiritualists and mesmerists. To reiterate, in public opinion the dividing line between a self-pronounced Christian healer, like Dowie, and the city's mesmerists and spiritualists was a blurred one. A skeptical public lecturer on "Popular Delusions," held at the city's Mechanic's Institute in 1884, classed Dowie and the renowned spiritualist Stephen Milner-Stephens as part of the same fraudulent phenomena: "the cures effected by Messrs Milner-Stephen, Dowie and Co. . . . generally turned out to be unworthy of notice."[167] Another journalist, in 1887, located the Dowies as members of the "quack fraternity,"[168] while another reporter who visited a meeting at the Free Christian Church Tabernacle in Fitzroy concluded that "the faith healing of Dowie and the mental healing of the Theosophists and Christian Scientists are one and the same thing under different forms."[169] The printed testimonies of those whom Dowie had healed were thus presented as polemical documents designed to highlight the difference between divine healing and false forms of "heathen magic."[170] In his tracts he vigorously denounced spiritualists as "agents of Satan" for claiming to mediate deceased spirits to the living (a common Christian criticism of spiritualists during this time),[171] and lambasted other "diabolical counterfeits that confounded the permanent gifts of healing in the one Spirit" such as "magnetic, mesmeric and psychopathic mockeries of ancient and modern heathenism."[172]

Dowie viewed both oral and printed testimonies as indisputable evidence for the persuasion of unbelievers, drawing on a legal-scientific rhetoric to craft and present them. But those individuals who spoke publicly and at great length about their healing were engaged in a very different task. In attending divine healing testimony meetings in the Fitzroy Town Hall, and later on in the new Tabernacle, Melbourne's urban residents were forging a new language for making sense of their experiences of illness and downfall. In this respect, the practice of testimony-giving came to form a powerful counterpoint to the dominant poor-shaming rhetoric of the middle-class Christian reformers. Through their frequent attendance at the meetings of the Free Christian Church, the working classes of Fitzroy and Collingwood found new opportunities to articulate their experience in idioms that emphasized their triumphant victory over hardship. The many individuals who had experienced divine healing spoke of being charged with power and of being filled with fresh resources with which to overcome obstacles. One woman attending a meeting at the Fitzroy Town Hall recounted that she had been "'ill from head to foot' for several years, under the treatment of several medical men, been an inmate of the Lying-In Hospital, she only got worse . . . at last, she went to Mr Dowie, who asked her whether she believed Jesus could heal. She said she did, and he laid hands on her and prayed for her, and she was perfectly healed." The woman finished her testimony by remarking she "felt it to be her duty to publicly testify to the great goodness of Christ, of whom she would never be ashamed."[173] Others described in thrilling detail their entry into a world of spiritual power in terms that invoked biblical narratives of the Gospels, implying their own affinity to the "old time religion" of the Apostolic age.[174] Echoing the Gospel of Matthew, Mrs. Williams of 196 Johnstone Street, Fitzroy, testified that since her own healing of an ulcerated foot, "I have seen the blind receive sight, the deaf hearing, the lame lay aside their crutches and walk, I don't know what I have not seen done in this place by the power of the Lord."[175] Testimony after testimony recounted great personal suffering followed by joyful triumph. Mr. Dummett of North Fitzroy testified that his daughter was "healed instantaneously" after she had renounced doctors, and turned to Dowie. "I had lost two children under Dr. Wilson of East Melbourne, and you parents know what it is to lose your little ones . . . I didn't want to lose this one."[176]

Working-class Melburnians discovered in divine healing newly optimistic forms of self-description; they also found in it resources with which to denounce the medical establishment of the city. In this respect, Dowie's divine healing ministry tapped into an antimedical sentiment widely felt by working people throughout Melbourne, and especially by women. Urban reformers of the period recognized that the urban working classes ran higher risk of various illnesses, including an increased infant mortality rate and diseases such as typhoid and consumption.[177] But at the same time, the city's poor were far less likely than the wealthier residents of outlying suburbs (where doctors tended to congregate in pursuit of a roster of prosperous clients) to access the medical care they needed. In Melbourne's wealthy suburb of St. Kilda, the ratio of doctor to patients was 1:660; in Collingwood, it was 1:7,000.[178] It was true that the working classes had recourse to a range of charity institutions in their areas—for example, the Melbourne Women's Hospital catered for "homeless and friendless" women[179]—but the demand for those organizations far outstripped the supply. Even those people who accessed therapeutic care often expressed deep ambivalence about medical professionals' skills. Medicine in late nineteenth-century Victoria, as around the world, was in a state of flux, still not fully incorporating the new germ theory of how diseases were spread. As a result, hygiene in many hospitals was poor. On more than one occasion, the charitable Women's Hospital was closed due to the number of patients dying of septic diseases. Of the 600 women admitted to the hospital in 1884, 40 died, a death rate of 1 in 15.[180] Furthermore, inmates had to contend with an elite class of surgeons eager to practice their skills and improve their small scientific knowledge on their patients' bodies; in the 1880s, Australian surgeons were especially notorious for their overzealous removal of women's ovaries.[181] Working-class women were viewed as material readily available for male experimentation. James Beaney, one of Melbourne's leading surgeons (who operated with diamond encrusted fingers and had claret for breakfast) was unsuccessfully prosecuted for the "surgical homicide" of a barmaid.[182] Given all of this, it was no wonder that the historian of medicine in Melbourne, T. S. Pensabene has concluded that "the whole tenor of medical debates up to 1900 was pervaded by a feeling of mistrust for doctors."[183]

The women and men of the city who came to Dowie's services found an alternative avenue of healing, one that for many seemed superior to the expensive services of the medical-scientific profession and that reinvested command over their health in their own hands. Many who experienced healing through Dowie's prayer had both consulted multiple doctors and tried various alternative therapies over the years, usually at great financial and personal cost. In 1887, a journalist estimated that there were about "one hundred irregular medical practitioners in the metropolis, some making fortunes."[184] Hydropathic establishments, mesmerizers, homeopaths, spiritualists, and suppliers of patent medicine all flourished in Melbourne in the late nineteenth century, as they did in a range of imperial cities throughout these decades.[185] Divine healing devotees cast Christian healing as superior to all these alternatives. A recurrent trope of individuals' testimonies was to bemoan the inefficacy of medical doctors. One woman attending a divine healing service in the Fitzroy Town Hall in 1883 recounted that her left-eye sight caused her great problems, and that "although under the treatment of three doctors, she got no relief whatsoever."[186] Those who accessed Christ's healing were similarly denunciatory of the misguided cures of alternative healers, recounting at length their unsuccessful treatments. Mr. John Taylor was a metalworker whose "blood became poisoned from breathing fumes." Before discovering divine healing, he recalled that he unsuccessfully consulted "one physician, then another, one system, then another, the last idea what galvanism, I was clothed with magnetic appliances . . . What will a man not spend to get his health? I spent my all."[187] By contrast, Dowie's message of divine healing preached that there was no need of these expensive so-called "experts." In one service, he proclaimed that ordinary churchgoers had all the necessary skills to heal themselves through reliance on prayer: "Oh yes, we are all doctors— doctors of divinity!"[188] Although Dowie's prayers were considered particularly efficacious, divine healing in fact taught a more democratic message— that any faithful Christian could pray for his or her own or another's healing. It was thus that Dowie referred to "the work of Divine Healing rapidly spreading by the agency of many highly gifted fellow-labourers, holy men and women."[189] Citing their experience with hit-and-miss bio-medical and heterodox cures of the day, individuals used the practice of testimony-giving to laud divine healing's superior efficacy. Mrs. Spinks of Moreland "suffered from an internal tumour." Signaling the propensity of contemporary surgeons to operate on female reproductive organs, she related how "Drs. Danne and Singleton said it was no use me thinking of getting better without an operation." Yet in Dowie's hands, her pain soon went away.[190]

In the outspoken Dowie, the working people of the city found an advocate who was willing to public lambast the medical profession as self-enriching charlatans and to deride heterodox healers as exploitative dupes. Doctors, in particular, were cast by him as unscrupulous elite who preyed on the desperation of working people. In a sermon preached in 1887 in Fitzroy at the Tabernacle, Dowie inquired "that if he healed the sick, what would happen to the doctors? They might dig gum. Better to dig gum than dig into peoples' pockets . . . the medical profession is one of the most miserable professions a man could be in!"[191] Dowie was also outspoken in his condemnation of the lack of regard doctors showed for working-class lives—

especially female ones. Dr Beaney, the notorious medic who was charged with the homicide of a barmaid through irresponsible surgery, was so outraged that he took libel action "in consequence of a sermon preached by Mr Dowie reflecting on [his] character."[192] Dowie also vigorously denounced other types of healers. Middle-class spiritualists were a favorite target of his, and he identified them as "agents of Satan" due to their claims to mediate deceased spirits to the living (a common Christian criticism of spiritualists):[193] these healers were nothing less than "diabolical counterfeits that confounded the permanent gifts of healing in the one Spirit."[194]

Throughout the 1880s, Dowie became increasingly outspoken in his denunciation of all aspects of Melbourne's establishment, not only the medical profession, and ever-more situating himself as a spokesperson for the poorer residents of the city. As early as 1881, Dowie had publicly come out in support of the eight-hour working day. This prompted at least one working man to write to the news press to show his appreciation of the unusual clergyman who showed "sympathy" with the laboring classes, and contrast Dowie against the bulk of his clerical colleagues who "complain of the smallness of their congregations, and now the cause is put before them."[195] His much-publicized sermons were the major platform through which Dowie voiced criticisms of what he saw as the excesses of the political elite. The premier of Victoria was labeled by him as an "open adulterator," the councilors of the city supposedly came to "meetings blind drunk," and the mayor of Fitzroy was "a poor, ignorant fool." Fitzroy's head of police called Dowie's sermon on the political luminaries of the suburb "the most disgraceful and slanderous discourse he had ever heard."[196] No figure was too high to remain untouched by Dowie. The imperial elite of the day—the intercolonial British governors who visited Melbourne in 1886—were described by him in a Sunday night sermon as "snobs and genteel loafers who live upon the public purse and spend money which is not their own."[197] The Christian elite of the city was also attacked, and they responded in kind, coming out in force in their Sunday sermons to denounce Dowie. Although individuals within established denominations had supported various divine healing ministries, by the middle of the 1880s the tide of Christian opinion was turning against divine healing, in Australia as well as worldwide.[198] Melbourne's Welseyan minister maintained that any man "stood on slippery ground when he claimed the gift of healing to a degree equaled only by one man since the time of the Apostles."[199] The city's Catholic bishop announced that "any Catholic who visited this man for the purpose of being healed would be deprived of the sacraments of the Church."[200] It was thus that Dowie admitted in 1888 that "I am sorry to say our most formidable opponents are to be found in the Church."[201]

But the city's Christian establishment also objected to Dowie's flamboyant appropriation of urban space—doubtless a lesson he had learned from the Salvation Army during his days in Adelaide. Very much like Salvationists, Dowie was determined to reclaim the secular spaces of the city for the cause of Christ, holding meetings in disused theaters as well as occupying the streets of Melbourne, and evangelizing in bars. Dowie was by now regularly in trouble with officials of Melbourne for his flouting of the law of "street preaching." Mimicking Salvation Army methods, members of his Free Christian Tabernacle would process en masse along the streets, "stop[ping] outside public houses, where a hymn was sung and the hotel-keeper called out by name, and told he would go to hell for keeping such a house."[202] Often these confrontational methods resulted in street brawls with crowds of larrikins who gathered to watch and jeer. In 1885 Dowie was fined £20 for breaking the law against street processions, which he refused to pay on principle, and was consequently sent to jail for one month—an incident that did no disservice to his growing notoriety in the city.[203] Commentators and public opinion rightly noticed—as with the Salvation Army—that there was a fine line between reclaiming the streets for religious purposes and the larrikins' rowdy ownership of the streets. Newspapers of the day were unified in their condemnation of what they called Dowie's "religious larrikinism."[204] One resident of Fitzroy observed that "in this country where larrikinism is so strong, any undue excitement in the streets needs to be checked and not encouraged."[205] The middle-class establishment of the city was outraged at these "antics," seeing them as a violation of Christian respectability. The *Melbourne Advocate* ran an editorial denouncing the "eccentric Mr. Dowie," on the grounds that "when the compassionate founder of Christianity ordered his disciples to seek out the erring and the fallen, he did not mean they should parade the streets with discordant noises, inferior singing and blare of trumpets . . . street processions are a public nuisance, inconsistent with good order of everyday life."[206] Indeed, the tactics of "the Dowie crowd" (as the local Fitzroy newspaper dubbed them) were at times indistinguishable from the violent displays of the larrikins. One hotel owner received visits from Dowie's "male henchmen . . . [who were] trying to make the drink traffic as obnoxious as possible," and were left with a "smashed highly ornamental and expensive pane of glass . . . with genuine Dowie philosophy they refused to pay for the damages."[207]

But it would be an error to assume from all of this that the working classes of Melbourne were united in warming to Dowie's populist stance. Hotel keepers and bar owners objected to his outspoken denunciation of alcohol, and on at least one occasion Jane Dowie and a delegation of church women were ejected forcibly from a hotel bar in Collingwood after trying to pray in the bar with customers.[208] And others in Collingwood and Fitzroy—who although poor nonetheless prided themselves on their respectability—objected to having their "ears polluted and property depreciated" by refuges for homeless women and night shelters for the homeless. One Collingwood local resident wrote in to the local paper to announce that "the free and enlightened citizens of Collingwood object to have a lot of howling criminals gathered into a nest of vice from which pollution issues to taint the neighbourhood."[209] This resident perhaps spoke for many others when he objected to the area merely being the backdrop for Christian do-gooders: "Collingwood has a soul, it aspires! No longer must the Rev. Dowie, the Salvation Army and other "faddists" make it the scene of their philanthropic experiments!"[210] Despite Dowie's self-professed ambition to reach the "common people," he could still draw a similar link between social standing and Christian virtue that echoed the arguments made by the elite reformers of the day. Dowie could also lament that the "absence of intelligent and cultivated Christians in Collingwood was a serious hindrance to progress, inducing a low standard of piety and a contentment to abide in poverty."[211]

By the close of the 1880s, Dowie's time in Australia had come to an end. The fierce opposition he received from the Christian establishment of Melbourne was perhaps one factor in nudging him toward leaving the city. But more important, Dowie had for several years been nurturing a sense of vocation to broaden his scope beyond Australia, and to found divine healing missions across the world. Throughout the nineteenth century, concern for spreading the Gospel in foreign lands was a key component of the Holiness evangelical revival, and many practitioners of divine healing came to see an integral link between the "faith cure" and proselytizing the world. In 1883, A. B. Simpson founded the New York Missionary Training College, and the cause of foreign missions were a major focus of Boardman's 1885 Divine Healing conference in London.[212] These figures cast divine healing as a key aid to missionary work, invaluable in convincing "pagan nations" of the truths of Christianity.[213] In 1886, Dowie founded the International Divine Healing Association, branches of which were soon opened in New Zealand cities such as Auckland and Christchurch, which the Dowies visited and where they reported "great interest awakened, many saved, healed and blessed, tens of thousands attended meeting."[214] By the following year Dowie was regularly speaking of the "Macedonian cry, 'Come over and help us', that is ringing in our ears and burdening our hearts, rising into a worldwide cry of anguish from millions who are sick and sad."[215] In February 1888 Dowie resigned from the pastorate of the

Free Christian Church and announced his intention to begin, with his wife and two children, a worldwide divine healing missionary tour, first starting throughout New Zealand, the Pacific Islands, and then arriving at the West Coast of the United States.[216] Their intention was to work across North America, cross the Atlantic to Britain and then to Europe, and eventually return to Australia. The goal of this "long and uncertain period of missionary journeying" was to "preach Christ as the Savior and Sanctifier of spirit, soul and body, and to be used and blessed to a far greater extent."[217] Waved off by "hundreds of our friends," the Dowie family sailed from Melbourne in early March; by June they had docked in San Francisco and the North American phase of Dowie's career had begun.

CHAPTER TWO

Christian Cosmopolitanism and Zion City in the American Midwest

THE NEW FOLLOWERS whom Dowie encountered in the North American industrial metropolis of Chicago would profoundly transform his divine healing ministry. Although the industrial workers of Melbourne of the 1880s were relatively unorganized, in Chicago of the 1890s Dowie encountered an immigrant labor force that vigorously refused the contractual terms of capitalism offered to them by wealthy industrialists. The city was awash with socialist-inspired ideas regarding the fundamental equality of humans. Radical demands that the gulf between rich and poor be erased were made by anarchists, socialists, and trade unionists in the form of strikes and riots. Amid this ferment many immigrant workers turned for inspiration to Christianity's teachings regarding the solidarity of the human family and its promise to radically level social difference. In this turbulent context, Dowie's promotion of divine healing as a platform for working-class improvement took on new dimensions. The thousands of European and African American immigrants and industrial workers who joined his movement in this decade transformed the organization into a radical Christian experiment in communal living in which members attempted to transcend differences of class, nationality, and race by invoking ideals of solidarity, fraternity, and unity. The culmination of this egalitarian project was the formation of Zion City, a small town on the banks of Lake Michigan, in 1900. Zion City created an environment free of doctors, medicine and sought to replace the inequalities of Chicago with an empowering, worker-owned industry. This chapter charts the foundation of Zion City in the American Midwest as a crucible for Christian cosmopolitanism and egalitarianism; a site for the formation of a new and holy people of "Zion" unmarked by hierarchy, rank, or social stratification.

This chapter continues to chart evangelicalism's saliency within the newly industrialized cities of the international Anglo world, illuminating the intersections between Zion believers in the American Midwest, and a working-class tradition of organized labor. Studies have frequently bifurcated North American Protestantism into middle-class Christian progressives who saw the ultimate goal of their faith as repairing broken human society, on the one hand, and radical evangelicals, on the other hand, who espoused an individualistic Christianity more concerned with saving souls. Scholars consider the former strand of Christianity to have found its fullest expression in the early twentieth-century Social Gospel movement, exemplified in the writings of the liberal theologian Walter Rauschenbusch and propagated in universities, seminaries, and from the pulpits of leading establishment churches. By contrast, the heirs of the latter evangelical tradition—supposedly disinterested in social reform—are typically identified as the right-wing fundamentalists of the early twentieth-century, a largely working-class constituency who nonetheless rejected efforts at social amelioration in favor of spiritual revival.[1] A spate of recent books has modified this dichotomized analysis of North American Christianity, showing that Holiness Christians and liberal progressives alike were both invested in uplifting human society, particularly in the context of urbanization and industrialization, although employing different rhetoric and using divergent means to do so.[2] Social reform was never entirely the preserve of middle-class Christian elite—a fact that holds true for Chicago in the 1890s, as much as it did for Melbourne in the 1880s. Instead, Protestants of all persuasions and backgrounds formed part of a complex force for labor and social reform throughout the last decades of the nineteenth century, one that infused the nascent labor movement with the egalitarian resources of Holiness spirituality.

In particular, the activities of Dowie and his followers in the 1890s—a decade associated with the growing gulf between salvation-focused conservatives and middle-class proponents of the Social Gospel—showed that his radical Holiness salvation-focused movement was intensely interested in saving souls and healing bodies, as well as in questions of social reform, in workers' rights, in mitigating the gulf between the classes, and in advocating for a cessation of racial discrimination. In company with leaders within the Salvation Army as well as other revivalist figures populating the city in this decade such as the popular preachers Billy Sunday and Dwight L. Moody, the naturally radical, antiestablishment Dowie was a social reformer, although in a manner that denounced the insights of Social Gospel Protestants as a watered-down aberration of the true Gospel. Studies of Dowie's church largely ignore the influence of organized labor on the evolution of his divine healing ministry. However, this chapter argues that it was the radicalism of the ethnically diverse Chicago labor movement in the 1890s that spurred Dowie and his followers into launching their experiment with the urban utopian community of Zion City—an experiment that would have far-reaching consequences not only in the American Midwest but in the rapidly industrializing milieu of early twentieth-century Southern Africa.[3]

Industrial Unrest and Workers' Solidarity in the American Midwest

On June 9, 1888, Dowie and his wife, Jane, and their two children arrived in San Francisco. They were without personal contacts in California, but carried with them a letter of introduction from the New Zealand-based parents of Hugh Craig, a self-made businessman and divine healing sympathizer in San Francisco.[4] Capitalizing on introductions made on their behalf to local Protestant churches by Craig, the Dowies launched a series of divine healing missions in San Francisco and other Californian cities such as Oakland, Los Angeles, and San Diego. The next two years saw the Dowies move further up the west coast to the cities of Portland, Seattle, Oregon, and Victoria in British Columbia.[5] One of Dowie's immediate goals in this period was the formation of the American Divine Healing Association, the new continental subsidiary of his Australasian-based society. In November 1888, during his second mission in San Francisco, Dowie was elected as its President, and the Association soon grew to 700 members in cities up and down the Pacific Coast.[6] The intention of the Association was not to rival the Protestant churches of these cities, but rather to work alongside them as an ecumenical body devoted entirely to "promot[ing] the doctrine of healing through faith in Jesus . . . not primarily to promote the work of Salvation, important though it is, for it would then come into collision with the churches."[7] As had been the case in Australia, Dowie's followers were largely drawn from the ranks of Protestants with an evangelical leaning; a San Diego reporter commented that "Dowie's audience were Perfectionists, Adventists, Nonconformists and other more or less irregular Christians."[8]

Despite Dowie's intention to avoid "collision," the response of California's Protestant establishment to his Association and its healing ministry was as vehemently negative as it had been in Melbourne. Although a few churches did support their work—for example, Dowie's meetings in San Diego were hosted by a prominent German Methodist minister[9]—Presbyterian,

Congregationalist, and Methodist Episcopal ministers closed ranks against him. The more widespread acceptance divine healing had enjoyed during the past twenty years, especially in the United States, was now on the wane. By the 1890s, many practitioners were doubting the centrality of divine healing to God's plan of salvation, seeing it as "incidental rather than integral." Doubtless, the advances being made in the area of biomedicine during these years also contributed to the growing skepticism that the faith cure alone could suffice.[10] In this changing climate, Dowie's continued emphatic insistence on the non-negotiable nature of divine healing, his identification of sin as the cause of disease, and his vehement denunciation of doctors and medicine, all seemed aggressively radical to the Protestant establishment.[11] By the middle of 1889, a Los Angeles newspaper reported that "the religious people of this city are very far from being of one mind on the teachings of Mr. Dowie . . . many protest the doctrine of faith healing applied thus is not in accordance with the canons of church and is contradictory to scientific evidence."[12] Whether official hostility or not was the cause, the Association's work did not take off on the West Coast. Furthermore, it had been clear since their arrival in San Francisco that Dowie's ambitions were greater than merely California; as he announced in 1889, "I am just on my way through your great continent, I hope to pass through Canada and England."[13] By 1890, the Dowies had relocated eastward to the small Illinois town of Evanston. Within commuting distance to the great metropolis of Chicago, Evanston would become their base for the next three years before a relocation to Chicago in 1893.[14]

Throughout the early 1890s, Dowie had been on the lookout for a city of significant stature to operate his Divine Healing Association from before making his way farther eastward, to Europe and ultimately back to Australia. For a time, the steel-manufacturing city of Pittsburgh had seemed a possibility; the Dowies held a series of divine healing missions there throughout 1891, some attended by as many as one thousand individuals.[15] But Pittsburgh proved problematic in that it already had a well-entrenched divine healing tradition in the form of Bethany Home, a residential divine healing establishment founded in the previous decade, and run by the Rev. John Morrow and Miss Moorhouse.[16] Believing itself "set apart for whatever service the Lord may need for his suffering children," Bethany believed in "gradual healings" for its residents and visitors, strongly disagreeing with Dowie's insistence on God's ability to work instantaneous cures.[17] Dowie, for his part, issued typically polemical statements accusing his rival Morrow of fabricating healing testimonies.[18] Despite Dowie's best efforts, he made little inroads in Pittsburgh's evangelical circles, announcing at his final meeting that "his great difficulty in Pittsburg was the tough old church members . . . they had too much theology to get rid of for him to do anything with them." This comment reflected the juxtaposition Dowie would repeatedly make in America, as he had done in Australia, between the learned elite of the official church establishment and the popular everyday Christianity of the working classes.[19] Disillusioned with Pittsburgh's Christians, Dowie turned his gaze to the Midwestern metropolis of Chicago, conveniently close to his base in Evanston. By 1890, Chicago had already emerged as the United States' "second city," subordinate only to New York in economic power and size.[20] Chicago's unique position was as a "broker between Eastern cities and the natural resource rich Midwest," a standing enabled by its monopoly over the railroads linking the East Coast to the West.[21] Its meatpacking factories, lumber factories, and steel mills positioned it as a successful and vital city, spectacularly rebuilt after the devastating fire of 1871. In merely two decades, the city achieved a growth rate of 268 percent; in 1870 its population was 300,000, by 1890 there were 1.1 million Chicagoans.[22]

Chicago's growth as a massive industrial center occurred through large-scale immigration. By 1890, 80 percent of the city's population was of foreign, mainly European, parentage, with many more immigrants pouring in every year.[23] Germans made up the largest immigrant group in the 1890s, with industrialization and commercialized agriculture in Germany leading to a decline in the number of landholdings that could support families, and consequent mass immigration to the New World.[24] Between 1850 and 1900, German-born and their children accounted for 25–30 percent of Chicago's population, with over two-thirds of this community living in working-class households, engaged in traditional German crafts such as furniture making as well as absorbed by the city's new industrial factories.[25] Swedes were the next large immigrant group, making up 10 percent of Chicago's foreign-born population in 1890.[26] Prompted to migrate by famine in Sweden,[27] and by the allure of Chicago's economic promise described in letters home from those already emigrated as well as emigration agents,[28] many thousands of Swedes—mostly single men and women—came to Chicago and to the entire Midwest region. Their occupational profile was typically less skilled than German immigrants; Swedish women, for example, were Chicago's leading supplier of domestic servants, and the metal and mechanical industries employed many Swedes, as did the building industries.[29] By the 1890s, a newer wave of eastern and southern European immigrants was beginning to make its presence felt in the city: these were Bohemians, or Czechs, Poles, Italians, Lithuanians, and Slovaks. These immigrants tended to enter the labor pool at the lowest level, whereas many Germans and Swedes by the end of the nineteenth-century were working their way toward white-collar positions.[30]

Chicago's rising fortunes meant it had warded off intense competition from both New York and the port city of St. Louis to be selected as the site for the 1893 World's Fair, a celebration of Columbus's arrival in the Americas four hundred years ago, but more pertinently, a commentary on the perceived benefits of American technological and industrial progress. Chicago's World's Fair was held on what had formerly been the undeveloped mud flat of Jackson Park to the south of the city, transformed now into a magical, Beaux-Arts "White City" (as the Fair was dubbed) that displayed the advances of nineteenth-century America, and communicated a sense of contemporary optimism about what an ideal city might look like.[31] In fact, the Fair was attempting to present a rose-tinted vision of modern progress amid significant labor conflict in Chicago and other major cities of the 1890s, events that were the product of several decades of accelerating industrialization and corresponding social change.[32] Although a large number of wealthy industrialists emerged, there was also a growth in the urban poor as many immigrants with little capital and few skills flooded into the city, receiving low wages, working long hours, and often living in abysmal conditions that produced disease and medical problems. It was estimated that half of Chicago children died before age five due to poor sanitation and overcrowding.[33] In 1882, Chicago's Health Conditions Committee described how "the building of tenements on speculation was now a profitable means of investing capital . . . in one room alone, I found several immigrant families living huddled together with more curtains for partitions."[34] Many critics came to feel that property value was placed over the value of human tenants; more broadly, the industrial revolution was perceived as prioritizing capital before workers' welfare.[35] The depression of 1893, which lasted for five years, produced an army of unemployed and homeless men in Chicago, many immigrant construction workers newly out of work after the completion of the World's Fair.[36]

Motivated by this pressing evidence of social inequality, Chicago became a "global center of working-class organization," a hub within which radical new ideas arguing for the fundamental equality of industrialist and worker were hammered out.[37] Working class-based socialism circulated widely in the 1890s, largely propagated by German-speaking immigrants loyal to the teachings of Karl Marx, and for which trade unions were thought to serve as the platform for the overthrow of the class rule of capitalist industrialists.[38] This powerful rhetoric of workers' unity and solidarity was also widely disseminated through less explicitly revolutionary but nonetheless popular books such as Edward Bellamy's *Looking Backward*, which laid out a utopian vision of society organized around the common possession of property, including industry, and radically reduced working days for industrial laborers.[39] Inspired by ideas such as these, social and political unrest significantly increased throughout the decade as the largely immigrant-led labor movement gained traction in Chicago.[40] The massive 1894 strike of Pullman car-shop employees just outside Chicago, and spreading nation-wide, was a central event, and had been preceded by dozens of strikes earlier in the same year, leading bricklayers, carpenters, plumbers, painters and others in the building trades to down their tools in protest over working conditions.[41] These explosive events were evidence of the power of disgruntled "foreign"—non-American born—labor, and the growing influence of the unions amidst anger with big capital.[42]

Cementing the solidarity of working people meant transcending other divisions within Chicago's workforce. An important part of the rhetoric of working-class fraternity was a self-conscious effort among organizers for Chicago's workers' ethnic and national identities—dizzying in their variety and potentially divisive—to be trumped by a common class solidarity. Trade unions were important venues for early experiments in ethnic cosmopolitanism. One Lithuanian packinghouse worker commented in 1904 that joining the union "is giving me [a chance]to enjoy life like an American . . . it is combining all the nationalities, the night I joined the Cattle Butchers' Union, I was led into the room by a Negro member, with me were Bohemians, Germans, Poles, and the President is an Irishman who spoke to us in English, and three interpreters told us what he'd said."[43] But there were discernable limits to these universalistic projects. As much as some union leaders and members deliberately pursued ethnic cosmopolitanism, national, linguistic, and racial differences and divides continued to characterized Chicago's labor movement at the turn of the century. Polish-descended Chicagoans, for example, forged a fairly insular working-class solidarity by emphasizing their rural peasant traditions from Europe.[44] Furthermore, important splits existed between the Anglo-American elite craft unions, on the one hand, who espoused a moderate reform-minded program, and the revolutionary German socialist and anarchist organizations, on the other.[45]

Secular labor movements were not the only forces propagating notions of human fraternity. Elements within Chicago's Christian circles also began to draw on similar ideas of solidarity and workers' unity to mount a critique of industrial capital. It is undeniable that the majority of the city's churches were conservative in their alliances with wealthy industrialists; well-paid Protestant ministers connected to the economic elite had, for example, vehemently opposed the general strike of the 1860s for the eight-hour day, their criticism tinged with nativist prejudice against immigrant radicals. As in Melbourne, poverty continued to be cast not as a result of structural inequality but rather of the individual moral failings of the working classes.[46] For the most part, the elite-led Social Gospel movement of this period feared the hostility to organized religion on the part of socialist labor activists who denounced Christianity as antagonistic to working-class rights.[47] But while a majority of leading Protestant and Catholic ministers clung to this stance, the decade of the 1890s saw small numbers of younger ministers—both from liberal and conservative evangelical strands of Protestantism—increasingly turn toward a more radical interpretation of industrial unrest and economic woes. Many worked among immigrant communities outside of the center of the city. Their stance reflected a widespread concern about the social conditions of American workers, the growing materialism of American culture and the marginalization of Christianity as a normative code for values and behavior reflected in declining church attendance, particularly among the working classes.[48] Figures such as the Danish Lutheran pastor Thorvald Helveg and the young Baptist John. M. Lockhart sought to demonstrate the relevance of Christianity to this imperiled situation.[49] They emphasized Jesus Christ as an exemplar and reformer, an advocate for the rights of labor, and a critic of the unbridled concentration of wealth at the upper end of the economic spectrum.[50] The Kingdom of God, they proposed, would usher in all, regardless of class or economic standing.[51] Ministers from this group argued that the church should affirm its solidarity with the laboring classes, correcting the more usual perception of ecclesial institutions as bastions for Chicago's wealthy.[52] In the aftermath of the Pullman Strike, for which he had given vocal support, the radical Methodist minister William Carwardine wrote that all should seek "the gospel of applied Christianity . . . of mutual recognition, of cooperation, of the 'brotherhood of humanity.' "[53]

Significant overlaps existed, then, between organized labor's demands for workers' solidarity and a Christian rhetoric of equality. The Haymarket Riot of 1886, during which police and civilians were killed in the aftermath of a peaceful labor demonstration, displayed evidence of Chicago participants' use of intertwined idioms drawn both from Christianity and from socialism. For example, German immigrant anarchist August Spies, after being sentenced to death, linked his belief to radical German reformation preacher Thomas Muntzer who—recalled Spies—"said the Gospel did not merely promise blessings in heaven but it commanded equality and brotherhood among men on earth."[54] Christianity could also aid in workers' efforts to transcend racial division. United Mine Worker leader, Richard L. Davis, argued against racial factionalism in the union in 1892. He insisted to his fellow African Americans that far from being a "white man's organization," the union was for all, regardless of color, "because I believe in the principle of the Fatherhood of God and the brotherhood of all mankind regardless of what colour his skin may be."[55] United in their desire to reform the elite Protestantism of the city, several experiments in working-class orientated Christianity sprung up in these years. The short-lived "Modern Church" was funded and led by figures from the Trade and Labor Assembly (TLA) and its opening sermon was loudly cheered when the speaker lauded the goal of "building a church where the millionaire and tramp may worship together."[56] However, the TLA represented a minority Anglo-American workers' base, and so the goals of the Modern Church failed to appeal to the more international elements within the city's workforce. Yet there were other radical religious experiments occurring in Chicago during this turbulent decade of the 1890s that spoke more directly to the specificity of immigrant working-class discontent. It was to precisely this international constituency that Dowie's divine healing ministry would resonate the most profoundly with.

"You Are All Brethren for One Is Your Master"

For Dowie, as for so many other new arrivals to Chicago in the 1890s, the World's Fair was the magnet that drew him to the city. As did other evangelical Protestant ministers of the period, Dowie viewed the Fair as an event of critical importance for the cause of Christianity worldwide. Many religious figures vigorously criticized the "immorality" engendered by the sensual pleasures and entertainments of the Fair, including the growth in brewing companies in Chicago catalyzed by the city's vast amounts of visitors, as well as a boom in prostitution.[57] Clerics nonetheless viewed the Fair—with its millions of visitors from across the United States and the entire world—as a unique opportunity for evangelism. Much of the city's Protestant establishment rallied to this opportunity. Temperance activists and revivalist preachers, such as the popular Protestant evangelist Dwight L. Moody, all hoped to capitalize on the event as a missionary opportunity to reach international visitors who would hopefully then carry the Gospel back to their home countries, preaching in diverse languages around the Fair to further this goal.[58] Dowie shared in this general missionary fervor. As early as 1891, he announced he was trying to decide whether "he would go to Washington to pray for Congress, or go to Chicago and pray for the World's Fair."[59] Deciding on the Fair as the more important of the two, and echoing the missionary aspirations that had first led him to the West Coast,

Dowie stated his hope "that this proposed 'Vanity Fair' will afford us an opportunity of sending the truth out to the rest of the world."[60] In Dowie and others' perception of the Fair as an opportunity to convert the world's "pagan" nations, a key fault-line was revealed between the city's Christians. On the one hand, there were the evangelicals (represented by figures such as Dowie and the well-known Moody) who denounced the sinfulness of non-Christian religions and seized upon the Fair as a proselytization opportunity. On the one hand, there was the official ecumenical rhetoric of the Fair's famous "Parliament of World Religions," an event that featured seminary-trained emissaries from liberal Christianity in conversation with equally elite, well-educated representatives of Islam, Hinduism, and other world faiths. Rather than attempting to convert nonbelievers to the truths of the Gospel, these Christian figures viewed believers of other faiths as equal partners in the universal task of uplifting humanity. Indeed, liberal ecumenism would be a key tenet of what would crystallize into the Social Gospel of the early twentieth century (Christianity could be distilled to general ethical precepts, similar variations of which could be found in other world religions).[61]

Dowie established a small wooden "Zion Tabernacle"—"a plain board structure"[62]—on the perimeter of the Fair's grounds, adjacent to the Midway Plaisance, an area of amusements including the Ferris Wheel and spectacle-like ethnological exhibits, including a belly dancer, that drew the highest number of visitors of any area in the Fair.[63] Well-attended divine healing services were held at Zion Tabernacle on Monday, Tuesday, and Friday afternoons, with three services on Sundays.[64] This was one of the first occasions on which Dowie gave prominence to the term "Zion" in his divine healing ministry. Here, Zion stood for the holy place, a new Jerusalem pitted against the evils of the city of Chicago, and of the carnal pleasures of the Fair itself. Dowie's rhetoric from this period explicitly contrasted Zion Tabernacle against the Fair's degeneracy: "The Carnival of the World, the Flesh and the Devil, properly enough called the World's Fair . . . was alive with thieves, harlots, fools, cheats, patent medicine vendors, gamblers . . . Midway Plaisance was breeding a moral pestilence deadly enough to destroy a nation but Zion Tabernacle floated its flag 'Christ is All.' "[65] Much contemporary opinion celebrated the Fair as exemplary of the bright future of American civilization, epitomizing the best of its urban and industrial culture. But, in Dowie's pithy Holiness polemic, it was only within "Zion"—human society organized according to the laws of God and in obedience to divine healing—that any hope for the future lay.

Zion Tabernacle. *Source: Leaves of Healing* 1, 31 August 1894, 1. Flower Pentecostal Heritage Centre, Springfield, Missouri.

Many who flocked to Zion Tabernacle were the immigrant workers who constituted the bulk of Chicago's labor force in this period. The unique features of Chicago's international population meant that Dowie now encountered a dizzying ethnic and linguistic diversity unlike anything he had experienced in either Australia or Scotland. Dowie's marvel at Chicago's national and racial diversity—"its strangely mixed population"[66]—was frequently voiced in his periodical *Leaves of Healing,* which he had relaunched in California as a second series: "we are living in a city where all the nations of the earth, especially of the western part, are assembled . . . it is said that there are not more than 300 000 persons in Chicago were born upon American soil, so then one million and a quarter have been born on foreign soil."[67] Indeed, Dowie had remarked on this heterogeneity since his arrival in San Francisco, commenting on the African Americans, Native Americans, Swedes, Germans, and Russian immigrants who frequented his California meetings.[68] In Pittsburgh, too, Dowie found his divine healing mission meetings heavily attended by recent immigrants to the city,

including many Italians.[69] Many of the first Chicago converts to divine
healing hailed from the Northern European nations that dominated the
city's immigrant landscape in this period. Fred Trampsich was one of them,
a German-born arrival to the United States, a self-professed "low man, a
drinker, a smoker, a chewer, a filthy man" who heard of this "wunder
doctor at the World Fair." He visited Zion Tabernacle, and "Dr Dowie laid
hands of me, my disease passed away . . . today I can say I'm a healthy
man."[70] Many who came across Dowie's Tabernacle were those who had
flocked to Chicago in the months before the Fair for employment in the
booming construction industry. George Wiedeman was a second-generation
German immigrant who worked his way to Chicago from New York to
work as a painter in the construction of the Fair's buildings. While at the
Fair, he heard Dowie preach and was so impressed that he boarded with a
family near the Tabernacle so he could regularly attend its divine healing
services.[71] Another was John Nicholson, a British emigrant, who worked
as an engineer at the Fair and also attended services at "the Little Wooden
Hut"—as Zion Tabernacle came to be known by its devotees—and there
became a convert to divine healing.[72] Then there was Karin Lindquist, a
Swedish-born domestic servant in Chicago, who read about Zion Tabernacle in Chicago's daily newspaper *Inter-Ocean*. She was a sufferer from
lumbago, but found an answer to her problems under the ministrations of
Dowie: "what a relief to hear that God could heal us . . . the first time you
[Dowie] laid hands on me, the pain ceased."[73] Although contemporary
testimonies indicate that most early converts were Northern European in
origins, Dowie's first American followers also represented the other nationalities found in Chicago at that time. One was the first-generation Si-
cilian immigrant Ross Aiuppa, a carpenter by trade, whose granddaughter
remembers how "he was saved by Dr Dowie at the Little Wooden Hut in
the city of Chicago."[74] Soon, Zion Tabernacle's packed services featured a
wall displaying believers' "trophies captured from the enemy"; crutches,
metal body braces, orthopedic shoes to correct misalignments, even wheel-
chairs were triumphantly pinned to the wall as evidence of the power of
divine healing to work where biomedicine had failed.

Dowie's immigrant audiences at the World's Fair were drawn from
around the entire Midwest. In addition to Chicago residents, these were
also the many "farmers of the wheat belt who had come flocking at reduced fares to the 1893 Fair . . . emigrant Europeans already saturated
with rural evangelism."[75] Often it was the remarkable sights of the Fair
that were the initial draw. One couple from the Dakota Plains found the
"White City" of the Fair "moved [them] to tears of joy almost as poignant
as pain."[76] And once at the Fair, many discovered Zion Tabernacle and the

Scene in Zion Tabernacle: Christ Is All. *Source: Leaves of Healing* 1, no. 17,
11 January 1895, 272. Flower Pentecostal Heritage Centre, Springfield, Missouri.

divine healing practiced within its wooden walls. W. O. Dinius, a German-
born farmer from Ohio, visited the Fair, and there heard of a "Dr Dowie
having a Divine Healing Mission near the Fair grounds" (it was in this period that Dowie began to be called "Doctor" by his followers, perhaps a
mark of his own standing in their eyes as well as an ironic inversion of his
own diatribe against secular doctors). Dinius managed to get a "ticket for
the prayer rooms' where·"Dr Dowie laid hands on me and prayed."[77] Individuals such as Dinius subsequently carried news of Dowie back to their
farming communities, ensuring that further visitors streamed to the Tabernacle. Another German devotee of Dowie's was John Dietrich of Prairie
du Sac, Wisconsin, who heard from people in his rural community that
they had visited the World's Fair in Chicago and witnessed a "doctor in
Chicago who through prayer and laying on of hands wrought marvelous
cures." This news inspired Dietrich to visit the World's Fair, and to seek out
Dowie's ministrations.[78]

Many of these newly settled communities were already engaged in lively
debates over newer forms of evangelical spirituality. Far from being bastions of ethnic insularity and resistant to social and religious change as they

are sometimes cast, in fact immigrant churches in the American Midwest were deeply marked by the effects of the Great Awakenings, both in Europe and in the New World.[79] This was especially true of Swedish Lutherans who were still reverberating with the aftershocks of the evangelical awakenings of the 1850s, where "Meetingsmen" departed from the set liturgy of the National Church of Sweden to follow a regimen of individual bible study and the cultivation of personal Holiness.[80] Once transplanted to Chicago, some Swedes joined evangelical organizations such as the Salvation Army and also gravitated to evangelical preacher Dwight L. Moody's revival services.[81] Many found Dowie's divine healing teachings resonated with their existing evangelical commitments. Engry Johnson, for example, had grown up in Sweden as a Lutheran, but "praised God I was saved from this formal, dead religion where our Lutheran priest indulged freely in the filthy habit of smoking." Once in Illinois, she heard Dowie speak and was prayed for by him, cured of "heart trouble." She was ordained a deaconess in the church—an indication of the standing of female members within the new organization—and had "an intense love to work for the Lord, visiting saloons and fighting the Devil there."[82] For Johnson, divine healing tallied with her belief in temperance, the renunciation of tobacco, and the importance of a personal "nonformalistic" Christianity. German Mennonites, typically cast as supremely resistant to outside religious influences, were in fact similarly in the throes of debates over new forms of Holiness evangelicalism, leading small factions to break away and follow Dowie and divine healing. Andrew Ropp of the small farming town of Pekin, Illinois, about 170 miles from Chicago, was a leading figure in the town's close-knit German Mennonite community, where his father was a famous preacher.[83] But after Ropp had the experience of receiving healing prayer from Dowie— curing him of a "kind of jerking spell I had when I would be standing"—he led a faction of thirty-two Mennonites into membership of Dowie's organization, all of whom "earnestly [sought] a freer, deeper, more thorough Christian life." The cost of this defection was severe, splintering the community. But members of this group of German Mennonites were sure that God had led them to divine healing. Ropp reported "they have suspended us from fellowship on account of our creeds and upholding Dr. Dowie, but we uphold Dr. Dowie because God upholds him."[84]

In addition to tapping into debates over evangelical spirituality already alive in many immigrant churches, Dowie also cast divine healing as a ministry that was consciously sympathetic to the working classes of the city. Like many other Protestant clergymen of the 1890s, Dowie was highly ambivalent about the power of the unions in advancing the cause of the working-man. In this respect, then, Dowie was typical—although perhaps more forthright and polemical—in his condemnation of the unions. In 1897, he denounced the "tyranny of the unions as an idol . . . how dare men combine and say to their fellowmen, we will work for only two dollars, and if you work for a dollar and a half we will break your head?"[85] Eight years later, he insisted that "no member of Zion can retain their membership and belong to a blood stained Union."[86] Nonetheless, while denouncing the power of the unions, and their irreligious stance, Dowie was clear that his was a church precisely for the constituency targeted by unions, noting in 1902 that "many of our members were connected at one time with labor unions."[87] Many of his followers were employed in occupations that were rapidly becoming organized in Chicago. These included factory workers, male and female, such as Miss Katie Keck, a German machinist who was ill and healed by Dowie's prayer,[88] as well as those in the building and constructive trades. For example, Mr. Van Houten was a carpenter who took his sick daughter for healing prayer at the Zion Tabernacle.[89] The Guest Registration book from 1898 showed numerous carpenters, woodworkers, painters, shoemakers, and mechanics among those who patronized divine healing services.[90] Many of his church members were suffering, just as many union members did, from the financial depression. Female members frequently reported in their testimonies that their husbands had been out of work for many months, and even tithing was out-of-reach.[91]

Although Dowie repudiated the validity of the unions, divine healing nonetheless offered other resources to immigrant working men and women hungry to improve their lot amid hard conditions. Certainly, many reflected in their testimonies, delivered to listening audiences in Zion Tabernacle, how divine healing made them stronger for their work, and more able to deal with the contingencies of the industrial workplace. One G. Anderson, for example, formerly a member of the Swedish Methodist church in Chicago, fell ill with throat cancer and "took to my bed." There, he was visited by a Swedish follower of Dowie's whom he knew, and who prayed for him at his bedside. After he threw away all "swine's flesh and medicine" in his home, he recovered and "again began work at my trade, I have been at work ever since, I am an ironmonger."[92] And Ingeborg Johnson, a Swedish domestic servant in Chicago, found that after her "instant healing" in the church, she could again "do hard domestic work as well as some sewing."[93] Others, who were not in the fortunate position of having employment, believed that the prayer they received from Dowie paved the way to finding jobs. A Mr. Kelser was a factory worker who sought a position as a skilled machinist. A railroad shop initially said no, but "we kept on praying, and about a week later, I called again and was given a good position."[94] In addition to making people fit for labor, adherents of divine healing believed that its moral and bodily disciplines uplifted them in other ways. Working men were encouraged to save and put aside their earnings for future purposes because they had been released from their "drink, tobacco and secret society bills."[95] One man reported in his testimony, reprinted in *Leaves,* that "I am so much more prosperous since I have given up the filthy habit of tobacco and began paying tithes"; another said "since giving up medicine and paying tithes, I find money does not go nearly as fast."[96] Overall, Dowie's followers appear to have prided themselves on being hard working, aspirational, and determined to succeed against the odds. Commentators noted that his divine healing devotees belonged "for the most part to the better class of workingmen,"[97] while another reporter noted that "Dowieites are eminently 'respectable' . . . Dowieism means self-respect, honesty to your neighbor and the world, a high hope."[98]

Bolstered by the surge of publicity afforded by the World's Fair, Dowie's following grew rapidly among the working-class communities of Chicago and the surrounding Midwest. In early 1894 the Fair had closed down, but the numbers attending divine healing services in the Tabernacle had grown so large that services were also held in Chicago's Central Music Hall. The *Inter-Ocean* described the Hall as "packed from floor to ceiling with those drawn by necessity, sympathy or curiosity to hear the Rev. Dowie and testimonies of those who have been cured of their disease." The paper estimated as many as 4,000 were regularly attending services.[99] The same year, Dowie also began to hold divine healing meetings in Chicago's suburbs, in places like south Chicago and Englewood, and hosted by those Baptist churches whose pastors were sympathetic to the divine healing ministry.[100] When the rent of the Central Music Hall was raised, Dowie secured a new building at 60th Street and Edgerton Avenue.[101] This became known as Divine Healing Home Number 1, a few hundred feet from the 60th Street railway station, and close to Jackson Park where the Fair's Midway Plaisance had been, making it—in Dowie's estimation—"one of the most convenient and pleasant locations in the city."[102] Shortly after, the second of Dowie's residential Homes was opened two blocks away, and this too was reported as being "almost continuously filled, frequently to overflowing" with hundreds of guests in both.[103] These establishments were largely intended for out-of-town individuals who came to receive healing prayers from Dowie.[104] Much of the growth of Dowie's following in these years was because by 1894 he had raised enough money from supporters to buy a small printing press to restart the periodical from his Australian days, *Leaves of Healing.* As in its Australian incarnation, *Leaves* featured compelling personal testimonies of divine healing as well as dramatic "before" and "after"

Mr. Stuart Mutch, Before. *Source: Leaves of Healing* 4, no. 23, 21 April 1898, 437. Flower Pentecostal Heritage Centre, Springfield, Missouri.

Mr. Stuart Mutch, After. *Source: Leaves of Healing* 4, no. 23, 21 April 1898, 437. Flower Pentecostal Heritage Centre, Springfield, Missouri.

photographs of afflicted believers. Echoing the missionary aspirations he had stated when setting out from Australia, Dowie now hoped *Leaves* would be the conduit via which divine healing would spread in the United States as well as more broadly across the world. His editorial in the inaugural issue stated that "I feel that these words, feeble though they are, will be used of God to open the Beautiful Gate of Divine Healing to multitudes in many lands . . . in our daily meetings, we often count more than twenty nationalities."[105]

By 1895, the strength of Dowie's following in Chicago and the Midwest was such that he took the decision to found a new church. This meant dissolving the umbrella-like International Divine Healing Association, which had until this point acted as the organizing structure for his ministry in Chicago. While many Association members' home churches continued to show considerable antagonism toward divine healing, Dowie correctly perceived that in place of a para-church organization such as the Association, he could instead build up a new and powerful church: "we gave thousands of converts to the Churches, tens of thousands of dollars to their funds, we steadily weakened our own power financially . . . we planted and we let others reap."[106] In early 1896, Dowie formally founded the Christian Catholic Apostolic Church. The inclusion of the word "Christian" in its name suggested Dowie's longstanding and typically evangelical commitment to a faith that he cast as transcending petty denominational differences. Much in the style of his Free Christian Church in Melbourne, Christians should be loyal only to Christ as the head of the true church. In this respect Dowie was also invoking the period's interest in ecumenism, the determination exemplified by the Fair's Parliament of Religions to distill Christianity to its essence by doing away with superficial differences. Furthermore, Dowie's choice of name for his new organization reflected yet another broader societal concern of the time: that stratification by wealth and class should be done away with in favor of a society that conceived of all as equals. Dowie's explanation of the church's new name explained that it was called "Catholic or Universal, for we hold the right of every Christian to fellowship." Employing language that would have been familiar to the working-class Christian labor organizers of the city, Dowie affirmed all within the church were equal children of God: "every Christian is a citizen of Zion by birthright, God forbid that we should refuse citizenship in God's Zion on earth to a single citizen of the Heavenly Zion. Neither race, nor colour, nor education, nor position, nor wealth can be a barrier to fellowship for our Lord said 'One is your master and all ye are Brethren.'" Finally, loyal to the healing miracles reportedly practiced by the first community of Christians, the church would henceforth be known as an "Apostolic" organization.[107]

Dowie's insistence that all were welcome in the new church, regardless of wealth or ethnicity, powerfully resonated in a context where working-class immigrants often reported feeling stigmatized by the city's English-speaking Anglo Protestant establishment. Chicago's German-language newspaper *Fackel*, for example, published a satirical account of a devout working man "Zachary Godloving" who was refused entrance to the churches of the city's Anglo middle and upper classes.[108] Dowie, by contrast, proclaimed his as a church for the immigrant, booming from the pulpit of his large new Tabernacle on Michigan Avenue in downtown Chicago that "while many of us here are called 'foreigners' in this country, if you are a Christian, you are not a foreigner in the Church of God [applause]. There is one place you won't be called a stranger or a foreigner, and that will be the Christian Catholic Church . . . this is only a little prod to you, my good American friends, to let you know that we do not want to hear 'foreigner' applied to brethren or any such nonsense."[109] At the same time as celebrating the free and equal mingling of nationalities within the Christian Catholic Church—"our new Tabernacle is an international meeting place in one of the world's great Cosmopolitan centres"[110]—Dowie was cognizant of the strategic importance of specifically catering to the different ethnic groups within the church. Services were regularly translated into multiple languages, and special missions were held for different nationality groups in areas of the city where they tended to live.[111] By 1895, *Leaves of Healing* was produced in a German version, which Dowie triumphed would cater to the "half million German speaking people in Chicago alone . . . may the LEAVES be blessed in the grand old German tongue."[112] Soon editions of *Leaves* in Swedish, Norwegian, Dutch, and French were available, many translated by devout members in their own time and at no cost.[113]

Dowie's cosmopolitan rhetoric also included an effort to transcend racial divisions. By the 1890s, Chicago's work force was made up of not only of the larger European immigrant groups, but also of a community of small African American skilled and semi-skilled workers who sought a footing in the city's labor economy in the face of racial discrimination. The so-called African American "migration of the talented tenth" from southern states characterized this decade; this was largely due to deteriorating race relations and the collapse of Reconstruction in the South.[114] The World's Fair of 1893 was also a magnet for black workers, and many stayed on after the Fair had ended.[115] Yet by1896, the black population was only 22,700 out of a total of 1,600,000; these small numbers reflected the limited economic opportunities open to black workers in Chicago in this period.[116] Most of Chicago's black workers were not part of the industrial work force, which union discrimination ensured was dominated by European immigrants.[117] Black labor tended to be brought on as strike breakers, whereas only 1.4 percent of the regular workforce of Chicago's packing plants in the 1890s was made up of black workers.[118] Although there was a small black professional and business class, the vast majority of African Americans were employed as unskilled laborers, waiters, porters, and domestic servants.[119] Informal racial discriminations and exclusions operated here too; even college-educated blacks often found a job as a Pullman railway porter the only one available to them.[120] Professional segregation was echoed at a residential level. As black migration levels to the metropolis rose throughout the 1890s, a black residential enclave developed in the center of the city, along the Dearborn St. corridor.[121]

From the beginning of his time in the United States, Dowie's divine healing ministry had drawn in substantial numbers of African American adherents. Some of Dowie's black converts came from the Southern Holiness tradition, already well primed for the perfectionist message of divine healing. One such convert was Lulu Boyd of Knoxville, Tennessee, whose testimony was carried in *Leaves* in 1898. Boyd worked as a Holiness preacher at camp revival meetings, and encountered Dowie's teachings there via distributed copies of the *Leaves*. She and other like-minded Holiness adherents had an open-air meeting where they prayed for healing, "lift[ing] their hands and shout[ing] and prais[ing] the Lord."[122] Yet another convert was drawn from the prominent and socially influential African Methodist Episcopal Church, indicating divine healing's appeal across a range of denominations. Rev. Charles Augustus Portland stood up and testified in a meeting to his instantaneous healing, making him realize "since I heard Brother Dowie preach how imperfectly I am preaching and teaching the Gospel."[123] And when Dowie started his first healing homes in Chicago after the World's Fair, he reported in *Leaves* that "it delights me extremely to say that we have received into Zion lately Negro guests" (adding as a side note, perhaps to forestall critics of these mixed gatherings, that "there are none in our Home who behave themselves better than these Africans."[124] In 1896, these included individuals as diverse as Rev. Willliamson, minister of the Zion Methodist Episcopal Church in Jacksonville, Illinois, and Thomas Minor, from Springfield, Ohio, a laborer belonging to the Baptist church who came to the Healing Home for relief from his rheumatism.[125]

The Christian Catholic Church's promise of full integration into the "brotherhood of man" was as appealing to black migrants from the rural South as it was to European immigrants. In part, many African Americans joined Dowie's church because they perceived him as a progressive clergyman on issues of racial integration. In his writings and speeches, Dowie regularly criticized discrimination and violence against blacks—especially the numerous lynchings taking place in the South during the 1890s—on the grounds that this violated the sanctity of the human family.[126] He denounced Christianity in the South as a "grossly corrupted form . . . [which] decreed slavery a divine institution."[127] Many of his newly appointed elders in the Christian Catholic Apostolic Church shared his views. One Elder Brooks, after hearing the African American Holiness preacher's Lulu Boyd's testimony at Chicago's Zion Tabernacle, stood up and declared, "every time I hear one of these Ethiopians stand up, it stirs me to the deepest depths of my heart . . . although I was raised in the South, I want to stand here and say I have no sympathy for the accused, diabolical and devilish thing called slavery."[128] Furthermore, Dowie took a harsh line with those among his congregation who expressed the typical prejudices of the day against blacks. When an audience member shouted out "nigger" during a sermon he was preaching on the New Testament figure of Simeon the Ethiopian, Dowie rebuked the interrupter from his podium by booming, "in the early church many of the mightiest men were black, and the meanest thing that I know is that wretched colour line. If there is any of you who do not like to sit down with the nigger, stay outside."[129] Any church members who expressed dismay at these racially mixed services received a tongue lashing from Dowie: "never get that accursed word 'some' in there . . . I say NO! It is to ALL people, to the black man and the white man and the yellow man, to the wicked and the weary and the sin-laden."[130] African American members appear to have welcomed the church's promotion of egalitarianism. A black convert from the Midwestern state of Minnesota called Dowie "the most courageous man on earth today."[131] In 1897, the *Leaves* printed a letter from a "very intelligent coloured gentleman in Hot Springs, Virginia" who wrote to Dowie, thanking him "for your charitableness towards my people . . . in most cases the religion of ministers of your race is not enough to obliterate their prejudices, but this is not so with you for the manner in which you defend the great Christian principle, 'One is your Master, and all ye are brethren.'"[132]

For the most part, though, blacks joined Dowie's church for the same reasons other immigrant groups in late nineteenth-century Chicago did: in expectation of the promise of divine healing and in pursuit of full holiness. Many who joined the church were Chicago's poor black citizens struggling to attain lives of "respectability," and to assert themselves amidst hostility and exclusionary practices from white immigrants.[133] For these individuals, divine healing strengthened them for industriousness, health, and flourishing. Miss Carrie Coleman did "hard work every day," but landed in the

Charity Hospital due to "consumption, partial paralysis in my right limb, heart troubles and a roaring in my head." She read *Leaves,* and went to the Zion Tabernacle in Chicago for prayer. Having obtained her healing, she regained her living.[134] Another early African American convert was Mrs. Emma Parker, a domestic servant in Chicago. In 1896, she wrote to Dowie describing her healing after being "sick one year and [having] three doctors." But then she read *Leaves* and all changed: "God opened my eye ... something touched me on my head and there went through my body a strange new feeling."[135] Mr. Samuel Nelson was a waiter on the buffet car of the Wabash Railway; for about fifteen years, he had been "afflicted by strong pains in my stomach." After his wife urged him to attend Zion Tabernacle while spending a Sunday afternoon in Chicago, "I was relieved of a tape worm which I believe was in answer to prayer."[136] For a few on the margins of respectable African American society, divine healing represented redemption from societal alienation. A young woman called Hattie H. had "fallen into sin" in Chicago. But Zion's healing home looked after her during her pregnancy, and "returned her to the City, where she is now living a good life, earning her living."[137] For many African American converts, Zion's Holiness-style promise of liberation from bodily weakness and spiritual sin was understood as an emancipatory reprisal of the not-so distant experience of freedom from slavery. One "Dowiete" affirmed that the God who healed him was the same God who "put it in the power of Abraham Lincoln to liberate [me] from slavery."[138] Echoing this rhetoric was Adam Hill, "an aged colored man who was a slave for many years," and who had attended Dowie's missions in Pittsburgh, testified that "the Lord freed me from slavery and now I want to be cured of rheumatism."[139]

Dowie perceived the presence of blacks in the church as key to his project of creating a new and egalitarian community that overrode not only economic distinctions but also sought to transcend racial divides. This was the period of an expanding American economic and political empire in countries such as the Philippines, Cuba, and Hawaii, and the corresponding growth in Americans' consciousness of their perceived role in exporting Anglo-Saxon civilization throughout the world.[140] Closer to home, Chicago's World's Fair had featured "ethnological" displays—human exhibitions from Africa, Asia, and Native American communities that reflected the racist evolutionary thought that structured Western society at the close of the nineteenth century. The Fair's international exhibits—the "oriental" belly dancer on the Midway Plaisance; the Zulu, Lapp, and Eskimo communities presented in frozen "traditional" life; and the Chinese opium smokers—all projected a vision that legitimated imperial expansion abroad and confirmed white Anglo-Saxon culture's supposed supremacy amongst

Mrs. Emma Parker. *Source: Leaves of Healing* 3, no. 4, 27 November 1896, 65.
Flower Pentecostal Heritage Centre, Springfield, Missouri.

the world's peoples, both over other white "races" as well as with respect
to non-white peoples. In many respects, Dowie doubtless shared in these
contemporary notions of racial difference and hierarchy; he could, for
example, denigrate the ethnological Midway Plaisance not only for its
sensual pleasures but also for its celebration of the "filth of Cairo and the
vices of the Orient."[141]

Yet Dowie's experiences of Chicago's highly international communities
of the 1890s would, in some respects, unsettle his acceptance of the period's racist evolutionary logic. Referring specifically to the African American membership of the church, throughout the 1890s, Dowie argued for
Zion's role in reprising the original race, a single people he referred to as
the Adamic race. Many in postbellum United States argued racial variation
was innately bestowed by God at the moment of creation; this view was
usually extended to support Anglo-Saxons' superiority over other races.[142]
But Dowie was more in sympathy with the monogenists, who cited Genesis'

account of God's creation of a single human race.[143] For Dowie, then, a racial family had existed prior to the Israelites—the original human family of Adam and Eve: "there is only one race—the children of Adam and Eve."[144] Dowie's congregation seems to have supported his cosmopolitan vision. In 1903, when he declared that "all so-called races of mankind were but Families of One Great Race," his Tabernacle "rang with enthusiastic applause."[145] The church's incorporation of so-called Ethiopians into its ranks was therefore a foretaste of the reprisal of this original, unitary Adamic race: "there is victory all along the line. Prophecy is being fulfilled. Ethiopia is 'hastening to stretch out her hands unto God.' "[146] Pointing to this supposedly ancient people—an amalgamation of Anglo-Saxons and "Ethiopians"—Dowie argued that racial rejuvenation would arrive once humans recaptured their primordial unity.[147] The view that there were no races, only one Adamic race, led Dowie to controversially argue for "miscegenation," a bio-spiritual discipline that—like divine healing—rehabilitated degenerate bodies. "In Zion," he proclaimed to his followers, "black and white were blended."[148] The period's racist stereotypes underpinned his advocacy of intermarriage. In contrast to enfeebled Anglo-Saxons, and echoing contemporary assumptions about African virility, blacks were, for Dowie, the "choicest . . . embodiment of manly, healthy physique."[149] Mixed marriages would reinfuse Anglo-Saxons with potent blood. Dowie cited Moses' marriage to a Cushite woman as support for "fusing" the races into a strong "primitive" race: When you talk about different races, you talk nonsense. There is one Race and that is the Adamic race. May God grant that the time shall come speedily for the fusion of all the Races and give us back the Primitive Man, the man that was strong, the type of man that trod the soil of Eden.[150]

A Working Peoples' Town

The most ambitious aspect of Dowie's plan for reprising the true essence of humanity—the Adamic race—was the construction in 1900 of a utopian industrial town named Zion City, situated forty miles north of Chicago. The turn of the century decades in Chicago saw many utopian ideas emerge regarding the reformation of cities from degrading and anonymous environments to harmonious spaces of cooperation and community. In Chicago, as in Melbourne and Sydney, urban reform movements—many spearheaded by the Protestant middle-class establishment—were active in starting "Civic Federations" that aimed to begin a city "clean-up" campaign, including organizing garbage collection, eradicating downtown gambling saloons and organizing a municipal voters' league.[151] In the aftermath of the World's Fair, the journalist William T. Stead's condemnation of Chicago's public life *If Christ Came to Chicago* was widely read; its final chapter, however, painted a utopian picture of the future Chicago as "the ideal city of the world."[152] Moreover, Edward Bellamy's novel *Looking Backwards*—would be an important influence on the embryonic Garden City movement, which envisioned carefully planned cities with green belt areas and designated areas for industry, agriculture and commerce.[153] And the World's Fair itself—although denounced by Dowie as a "Vanity Fair"—itself took part in this idealistic impetus. The clean, white neoclassical buildings of the Fair inspired for many the image of the "White City" as a paragon of "cleanliness, beauty, visual order."[154] Perhaps the most famous city reform movement of Chicago was the model town of Pullman, founded as a factory town for car-shop workers as an experiment in urban living and social reform. The town boasted "clean, paved streets, pure air, beautiful parks and playgrounds," and was an unabashed experiment on the part of capitalist-manufacturer George Pullman in neutralizing working class radicalism by improving living conditions.[155]

Throughout the 1890s, Dowie also began to voice aspirations—and to undertake practical fundraising efforts amongst church members—that a model town would be constructed for members of the Christian Catholic Apostolic Church. In 1895, the *Leaves* made the first mention of this plan, referring to the desirability of acquiring extensive land outside the city through donations of church members. In particular, Dowie had an area of 15,000 acres in the neighboring state of Indiana in mind, to be linked to Chicago by a custom-built railway.[156] Dowie and church members' desire to vacate Chicago stemmed at least in part from the increasing legal harassment they experienced from the city's authorities from 1895 on. His healing homes began to elicit complaints from neighbors on the grounds that "the sight of the sick and afflicted flocking from buildings makes local residents nervous . . . [furthermore] the people attracted to [Dowie's] meetings are ignorant and a very undesirable class."[157] The second half of the 1890s was also the time when Chicago's medical establishment was beginning to more tightly regulate medical practice and attempting to overcome skeptical hostility from the public regarding their efficacy.[158] The controversial Dowie seemed a perfect test case against which to hone new notions of medical orthodoxy. City officials charged Dowie with keeping an unlicensed hospital; Dowie argued healing homes were not hospitals, for they did not offer medical care in any usual sense.[159] But he was found guilty and fined repeatedly throughout the 1890s.[160]

The issue of childbirth became a particularly contentious dispute between Dowie and the city's authorities. Although doctors were forbidden to attend a church member during labor, midwives were considered acceptable

as long as they did not use drugs or surgical implements. In sanctioning
female midwives, Dowie's church was in fact drawing on a rich immigrant tradition in Chicago of European midwifes who practiced within
their own ethnic communities, as well as perhaps expressing his approbation of healing therapies that abstained from more invasive treatments of
women's bodies.[161] One especially renowned figure in the church of this
period was Henrikka Bratz, described by the *Chicago Tribune* as "an elderly woman with a pronounced German method of expression . . . [and]
enthusiastic in her faith."[162] Despite her reputation among the Zion faithful,
Bratz became the target of a medical establishment attempting to clamp
down on treatments considered heterodox. After a Mrs. Flanders died
during childbirth, Bratz—who subverted the city's monopoly over medical
practitioners' licenses by claiming that "I get my license from God to admin-
ister the divine healing to the suffering women"—was fined $100 and costs
for practicing medicine without a license.[163] At the end of 1895, Dowie himself had been arrested over one hundred times, and had spent 160 days of
the year in the Courts defending himself against charges of practicing medicine without a license and of running illegitimate hospitals.[164]

Quitting Chicago meant fully implementing a practical working peoples'
Christianity freed from the social cleavages and inequalities of the outside
world. Dowie and his followers sought a community where they could fully
enact the Kingdom of God, "securing deliverance for members and their
families from the rum-soaked, tobacco-reeking streets of Chicago, since
neither saloons, tobacco shops, drugs stores, theatres, piggeries would be
allowed there."[165] At an early date it was decided that the new settlement
would be called "Zion," a term first applied to the Tabernacle at the World's
Fair. Originally denoting a synonym for the holy city of Jerusalem, for
Dowie's followers, "Zion" meant the Kingdom of God realized here and
now on earth, a perfect city that corrected the evils of worldly metropolises. As Dowie preached to the Chicago faithful in 1896, "Zion is the metropolis of the Universe."[166] Where humans created degenerate cities of
sin, marked by divisions between labor and capital, between native born
and foreigner, and between black and white, Christ's holy metropolis exemplified the solidarity of all humanity.[167] In 1900, the year that the church
relocated to the new settlement, Dowie announced that "Zion City will be
an object lesson to the people of the earth. I desire to see the doctrines of
Christianity practically worked out in a community . . . a place where people
can see a community of people acting out the principles of the Bible."[168] In
later years church members reflected that "the time had come when the
work could no longer be in the midst of the wickedness and worldliness of
Chicago, but must be transferred to the City which God had built—the city

of Zion."[169] This sense of the worldly city (Chicago) juxtaposed against the godly city (Zion City) caught the imagination of the press. A reporter from the *Albany Journal* covered the foundation of Zion City by invoking contemporary idioms of utopian communal existence: "in juxtaposition to the city of Chicago that it may stand in striking contrast to the wickedness thereof, there is to be erected a veritable Utopian City, in which the ideal of human life is to be realized, in which the Brotherhood of Man and the Fatherhood of God is to be exemplified, it will be a bright and shining example for the emulation of all the peoples' of the world."[170]

On 1 January 1900, Dowie, in company with hundreds of church members from Chicago, formally inaugurated Zion City, a town designed along biblical lines, which at its height in 1904 had probably 7000 residents.[171] Dowie had initially contemplated land in Griffith, Illinois, located south of Chicago, but poor water supply and drainage ruled it out.[172] Soon he identified an area of land forty miles north of Chicago, on the shores of Lake Michigan, in Benton County. Originally a cattle and grain farming area, farmers of the 1890s were eager to sell to Dowie because of poor climate and soil.[173] The area's proximity to Chicago, and the expanse of Lake Michigan which Dowie hoped could transport industrial products, made the area appear appealing, although local farmers in Waukegan—the neighboring town—were disappointed as they'd hoped for a large steel or automobile factory to be built there.[174] Most of the new residents of Zion—the press scathingly called them "Dowietes"—were newly urbanized lower middle-class or working-class people, for whom Dowie's condemnation of unhealthy cities resonated.[175] At least one Zion City resident relocated from the model town of Pullman.[176] Some described the shock of swopping the bustling metropolis of Chicago for life in the still unbuilt Zion City. Lucille Bidille, whose parents moved to Zion City when she was a child, remembered her astonishment at the contrast between "the large city with its advanced conveniences and diversities of urban life" and the "primitive town with its dust roads, mud, wooden sidewalks, kerosene lamps, lack of plumbing and central heating."[177] Many were from Chicago, but some relocated to Zion from surrounding rural states such as Colorado, Nebraska, and Minnesota; one journalist referred to the "prairie schooners" carrying hundreds of immigrants to Zion City from across the Midwest.[178] Rural church members—many of whom had joined Dowie's church at the time of the World's Fair—sold their farms and possessions to join the exodus to Zion. For example, John H. Schwerdt, healed by Dowie at the World's Fair of a stomach ulcer, was one of the first of the Indiana farmers who sold their farms to move to Zion in 1900.[179] A year later, a committee of Indiana farmers visited Zion City with a view to relocating there; all were impressed by the "beauty of the surroundings, the fertility of the soil and the peculiar government of the people."[180] Large numbers of Swedes from Wisconsin made their way to Zion City. Most decamped as entire families and sometimes even as extended families and whole communities.[181] Farmers also came to Zion City from much farther north in the country, as far afield as New Hampshire, most likely acquainted with the project through their reading of *Leaves of Healing*.[182] From wherever they came, all were attracted by Dowie's utopian vision of a fair working environment prizing godliness, health, and communal living.

Dowie made much of the cosmopolitan composition of Zion City's new population. By 1902, *Leaves* was celebrating that "almost every race and nation has its representative setting its face towards Zion . . . there are over 60 nationalities represented in this town of Zion."[183] Five years after the city's founding, Dowie boasted that "Zion City, ethnologically, is a miniature representation of the world . . . the citizens of our city represent over 80 nationalities."[184] For Dowie as well as regular church members, Zion City's cosmopolitanism was a sign that God's Kingdom on earth was being realized. As he told his following in a sermon in 1903, "Zion City was founded by God, and he is bringing His people into from all over the world."[185] He celebrated that a new strain of humanity was being created in Zion City, unmarked by national and race prejudices that characterized the outside world. In Zion City, "there are no less than 70 nationalities . . . yet they are so perfectly united and in such perfect harmony it would be impossible for you know to know, looking at them, they were not a people born in the same place and brought up under the same influences."[186] Zion City, in fact, did contain all the heterogeneity of a city like Chicago in microcosmic form. For the most part, as in Chicago, northern European nationalities predominated. A journalist visiting in 1901 commented that "the people already gathered at Zion are mainly . . . English, Scotch, Scandinavians and Germans principally."[187]

Zion City also had more far-flung arrivals. Reflecting Dowie's still-loyal base in Australasia, in 1904, a party of seventy church members from South Australia set out for Zion City, as Sydney's *Daily Telegraph* reported, "mostly farming people, but also artisans, shopkeepers, a couple of chemists and one bank clerk."[188] In 1905, two groups composed of thirty-three and fifty people, respectively, left New Zealand for Zion City. One individual of the group of new arrivals was Thomas McEwan, a sheep farmer, who sold his entire holdings to invest in the new city.[189] Like those who arrived from across the Midwest, these people were embarking on a new life in search of a Christian utopia. In the words of an early arrival from Australia, they were sought a place "where their money could be used for the blessing and advancement of God's Kingdom, where their children could go to Christian schools, where the air was pure and without contamination of tobacco smoke and other contaminants."[190] Dowie and *Leaves* took great pleasure in lauding the handful of Chinese- and Japanese-born converts who were soon living in Zion City, many who found their way there via the West Coast. George S. Hong had left China as a child for San Francisco with his family. There, he had converted to Holiness-style Christianity through the work of the Congregational Chinese YMCA, and later came across Dowie's teachings via *Leaves*. By the middle of 1900, he was enrolled as a student at Zion City's new college.[191] Celebrating Zion City's cosmopolitan scope, *Leaves* began to regularly feature a drawing labelled "Zion's Prayer Reminder." Intended to connect the church in Zion City with its worldwide membership at regular moments of daily prayer at 9 a.m. and 9 p.m., this was a large clock that displayed both the time in Zion City as well as the time in cities across the world, including Sydney, Calcutta, and London.

A number of African American converts also moved to Zion City. By 1906, Zion had over 200 black residents.[192] Frank and Louise Hartfield, whose grandparents had been slaves in Tennessee, were amongst the first to arrive in 1900; another was William Elliot, who served in the Union Army during the Civil War.[193] The first black child in Zion City was Naomi Williamson, who came with her parents from Chicago. The adult Williamsons had become members of the church due to attending services at the "Wooden Hut"; Naomi herself had been a seriously ill baby who recovered after Mrs. Dowie personally prayed for her.[194] In moving to Zion City, African American families such as the Williamsons found no color bar, for Dowie vehemently denounced segregated worship: "the Church of God cannot draw a color line! The Church of the Devil can and does!"[195] Overall, as reported instances of conflict between white and black Zionists were rare, white Zionists seem to have welcomed African Americans to Zion.[196] A number of black Zionists assumed prominent positions in the new town. James Brister was Zion's dentist, and the first African American graduate from the University of Pennsylvania. Brister moved to Zion with his family in 1903, was appointed Deacon and alderman, the only African American as a town official.[197] African Americans occupied key positions in Zion City's white-robed choir that preceded Dowie into the Tabernacle for services.[198] For some African American leaders, Zion City seemed a model worth emulating for their own schemes of black uplift via industrial and technical education. In 1905, the famous black educator Booker T. Washington sent a delegation of students from his Tuskegee institute to "study Dowie's industrial schemes . . . the great negro educator who has

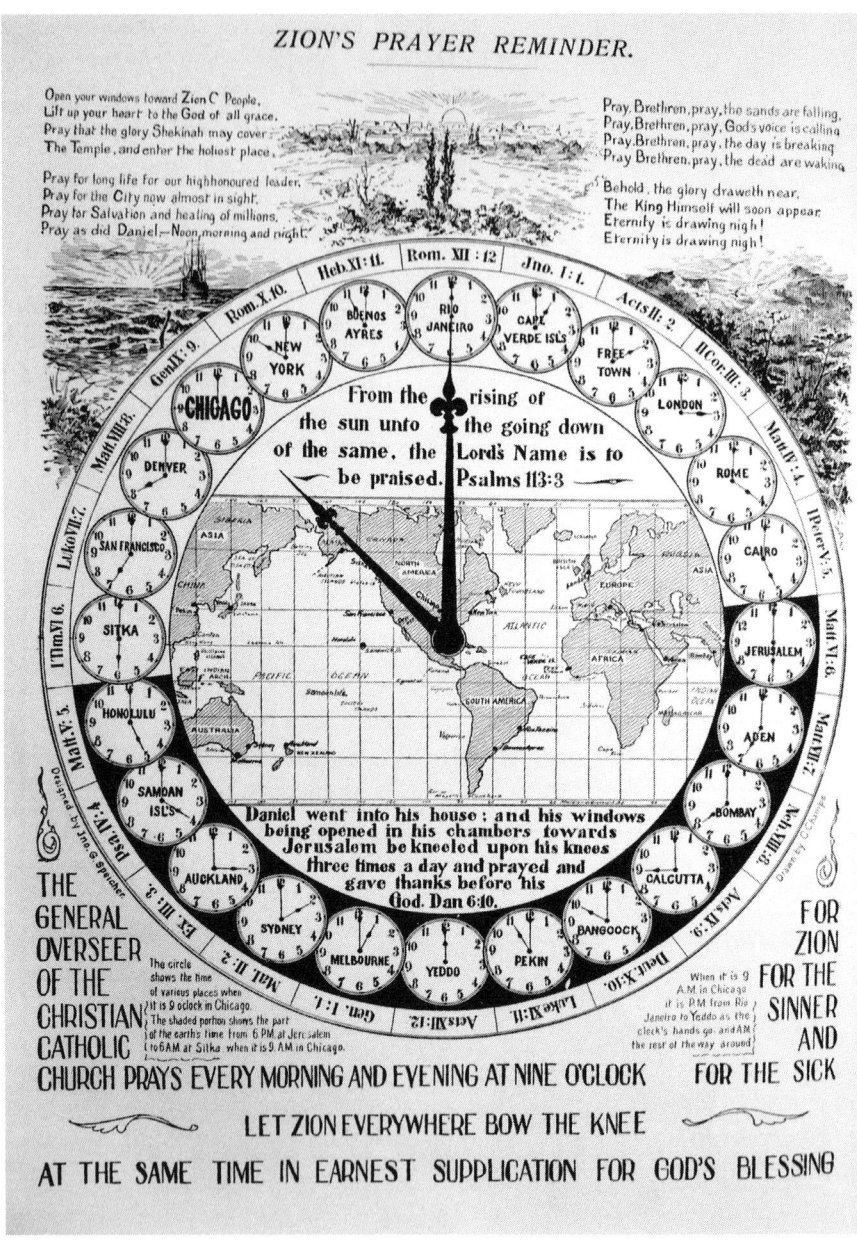

Zion Prayer Map. *Source: Leaves of Healing* 10, no. 11, 4 January 1902. Christ Community Church Archives, Zion, Illinois.

just made a visit to Zion City declares that any educator interested in an industrial community can benefit from acquaintance with Dowie's city."[199]

Outside commentators were not always sympathetic to the settlement's experiments in racial cosmopolitanism. By the early years of the century, the church had grown to include several branches in the South, especially in Texas. Ministers in the area were often unwilling to loan their facilities for services; Dowie's elders in San Antonio struggled to "hire a place in which to preach the Gospel while he allows black people to sit with white."[200] Indeed, it was particularly in the South that Dowie's advocacy of racial mingling caused grave consternation. A Baptist magazine from Birmingham, Alabama gave its opinion on Dowie's "solution for the race problem" in these terms: "he make[s] every self-respecting white shudder, and every self-respecting negro north or south turn his back on Dowie . . . we think [intermarriage] would be a manifestation of foolishness."[201] Although within Zion City the free intercourse of the races was the norm, church members venturing outside the holy city's precincts encountered obstacles. A deputation of "Zionites" were sent by Dowie to New York City in 1903 to hold a series of urban missions. At their appointed boarding houses, landladies and fellow boarders reacted in outrage when it transpired that there were black members within the Zionist group. African American boarders were compelled to find accommodation elsewhere; the irate landlady bemoaned that "the Northern boarders will return, but the Southerners entirely refuse to return."[202] In like fashion, while black ministers operated freely in Zion City, while traveling outside the city they also faced opposition. One of Dowie's black elders was Brother Wilson who—during a mission trip to the city—was refused lodging at the Christian Endeavor Hotel in New York City. For Dowie, events like this were violations of the Brotherhood of Man. Outraged, he preached a sermon on the incident the following week in Zion City, arguing that "if one God hath created us, are we not all of the race of Adam instead of being whites, blacks or peoples of other colours?"[203]

If racial prejudice was to be expunged from Zion City, Dowie and his planning committee envisioned it as an environment where workers would find uplift in a healthy environment free from divisions of class or wealth. In his efforts to design an ideal workers' town, Dowie engaged the services of Burton J. Ashley as "chief engineer of Zion City." Ashley, a member of the church after he and his daughter had been healed by prayer, was an engineer who had worked on the building of the Chicago Art Institute, and the pier at the World's Fair.[204] Ashley sought to create a model working peoples' town: his key "aims and objects were the establishment of comfortable homes, with pleasant surroundings, affording all facilities for comfortable and happy holy living."[205] While doctors, chemists, alcohol, tobacco, and gambling were all prohibited, Ashley and Dowie paid particular attention to a wide range of other factors that could uplift workers' living conditions. Ashley sent questionnaires to Boards of Public Health across the country, seeking ideal specifications on streets, alleys, lot sizes, locations of sewers, and water mains.[206] A guiding principle of Zion City's design would be that working people and the poor would have equal amenities as the wealthier in the city. As Ashley told Zion City's new magazine *The Coming City* in 1900: "every lot will have its own alley, for we determined that the best properties will have no more nor better service than the poorest lot in the city."[207] Lots for the less expensive homes were to be made approximately 40 feet in width by 140 feet in depth, larger than the average in Chicago at this time.[208] Home ownership—an elusive goal for many of Chicago's workers—was encouraged, and its attainability lauded for the working classes on the grounds that their abstemious moral disciplines led them "to save more, to buy land and have their own houses . . . out of 2000 houses in Zion City (in 1904), nineteen-twentieths belong to the working classes."[209] Sewage and waste disposal were also particular points of interest for Ashley and Dowie, while parks, shade trees, and shrubbery were considered necessary for the healthy outdoor living that Chicago denied to its workers. An article celebrating the new city rhapsodized there "will be beautifully terraced parks, beautiful gardens, velvety lawns, broad expanses for playgrounds, field sports, health producing exercises . . . God will give pure air and bright sunshine to His people."[210] In sermons given to the faithful Dowie polemically heightened the contrast between Chicago's unhealthy environment and the new community, demanding "after you have been in the Stockyards in Chicago, and in the places where they eat pig and drink liquor, after you come back from the stink, the reek, the smoke and the sin, does it not seem glorious to come back to Zion City?"[211]

But Zion City would not only reform workers' bodies; it also promised to improve their minds. Many urban reform movements placed great emphasis on educating and improving the moral and intellectual fiber of the working classes; the brotherhood of man and universal education were intrinsically intertwined concerns.[212] In the 1890s, a Scandinavian Painters and Decorators' Union in Chicago not only organized for shorter hours and higher wages but also sponsored lecture series covering topics ranging from "Consumption: Its Causes, Prevention and Cure" to briefings on public affairs.[213] Advocates of the eight-hour day in Chicago argued for reduced hours by invoking workers' need for time to improve themselves by reading and other self-study activities.[214] Dowie, too, argued that working men and women needed to improve their mental as well as moral and physical capacities. Dowie and Ashley envisioned that "schools, colleges, a university will be established in Zion City . . . night schools, popular lectures and special tutorials will be available for day workers."[215] By 1901, the *Zion Banner*—a new Zion City newspaper aimed at its residents—asked of its readers: "How do you spend your evenings?" It went on to advise that "one of the best uses of these spare hours is reading and study, for knowledge is power when used with divine wisdom. The majority of our people are not well-educated as the hard necessities of life fell upon their shoulders while young."[216] Lucille Bidille's recollection of growing up in Zion City as a young child was that learning was presented as a priority for children, and that in this matter, gender was considered entirely superfluous: "education has always been an integral part of Zion . . . little or no distinction was made between boys and girls in this matter. Each was valuable in his or her own way, at a time when the male child was still supposedly mentally superior."[217] In educating themselves, Zion City's women and men considered that they were embarking on a self-improving, upward life trajectory, an aspiration that was reflected also in the vision of the town's planners. Ashley justified Zion's equal distribution of wide alleys to all lots—wealthy and poor—on the grounds that "the labourer should become worthy of the enlightenment which he will obtain and the better he will become as a resident of Zion City . . . [this] should make him worthy of all the benefits of every service which those possessed of more expensive grounds have made."[218]

Zion City also sought to offer its residents healthy, uplifting, and self-improving employment, claiming to improve on the evils of capitalized labor represented by Chicago's many factories. While his plans for a holy city were in their infancy, Dowie had dreamed of a "rapid transit [system] so our friends could go in and out of Chicago daily or find employment in rising towns of a manufacturing region close by."[219] But by 1900 Dowie imagined a more ambitious solution to residents' need for employment. Dowie planned for a lace-producing factory as the town's main employer; the manufacturing site would located at the periphery of the new town in keeping with the Garden City model.[220] As early as 1895, *Leaves of Healing* was being read by sympathizers in the lace manufacturing town of Beeston, Nottinghamshire in England; one worker "opened [his] house for prayer meetings' in which "extracts from [Dowie's] paper were read, amid shouts of Hallelujah and Amens, together with tears of joy."[221] By 1900, Dowie had recruited about fifty skilled lace factory workers from Beeston to relocate to "Zion City to teach inhabitants of the 'sinless city' the art of lace manufacture . . . they are chiefly draughtsmen and designers and are being paid handsomely . . . they are on a three-year contract, and some are taking

Zion City Map. *Source: Leaves of Healing* 6, no. 11, 6 January 1900, 323.
Zion-Benton Public Library.

CITY.   From a Painting by Deacon Chas. W. Post.

wives and families with a view to permanently settling."[222] Immigration laws were circumvented by arguing that lace making as an industry was nonexistent in the United States, so the foreign labor would not compete with local skills.[223] Dowie also imported, at great expense, machinery piece-by-piece from Nottingham.[224] One of the first English workers to arrive in 1901 was Joseph Hazeldine of Beeston, a designer whose father had been a lace machine erector. Once arrived, Hazeldine became chief designer of Zion's lace curtains, and dress and lingerie lace trimming.[225] Hazeldine and other skilled workers trained local residents to operate the machinery. In 1902 "one operative of a large lace loom was a farmer boy of Iowa until a few months ago, yet he handled the great intricate machine like an expert."[226] Dowie ordered all "domestics, housemaids and servant girls who are members of the church to immediately quit employment in those families which use pork, rabbit, oysters, lard . . . I will give them employment in the lace factory."[227]

These industries—which also came to encompass the Zion Bakery, and the Zion Lumber and Coal Company, among others[228]—were conceived of as egalitarian undertakings, juxtaposed by Dowie and church members against the exploitative industries of the secular world. The Lace Factory (which came to employ around 500 workers) and other industries were envisioned upon a profit-sharing model, whereby workers were not only paid a "regular salary, but also a certain percent of the net profits . . . every employee must be allowed the privilege of buying an interest in the business in which he is engaged."[229] As with accommodation and with education, town planners advocated that no class divisions exist within these new industries. The first issue of *The Zion Banner* put it thus: "we have no prejudices, class hatreds or selfish interests to pursue. Beginning with the toiler in the humblest rank, and whom it has always been our privilege to serve we diligently seek opportunity to help all men and women of every rank, every colour and every creed."[230] Along these lines, Dowie's promise was also that "the capitalist class shall not be a special class in Zion, for in Zion there shall be no classes."[231] Zion City was envisioned as merely the start of a series of reformed industrial cities populated by church members. Dowie's ambitious goal was to replicate the profit-sharing model across the world. In 1903 he preached that "there is no visible end to the possibilities of this city . . . I begin to think of a city of Zion on the shores of the Atlantic Ocean, and another on the shores of the Pacific . . . I believe within twenty years we will plant ten great Zion Cities on the five great continents of the earth."[232]

Many of Zion City's residents placed a high value on what the utopian community offered them. One member estimated that "the dissatisfied ones

are but a small part of the community, perhaps less than 1/10."[233] Many
who relocated there found its unique atmosphere highly appealing. The
carpenter Rohmer had only come to Zion City to work on a construction
job, but he decided to settle there permanently: "it is really nice out here.
There is no swearing or cursing. It is easy to keep tools as no one will steal
them even if they are not locked up."[234] Others enjoyed the cosmopolitan
mixing of nationalities. One F. G. Jones—formerly of Hudson, Illinois—
wrote in a letter to a relative back home that "we have Greeks, French,
Swedes, Germans, English, Dutch from South Africa. In fact, there are not
many nationalities not represented here. But we are all living as brothers in
Christ, 'One is your Master even Christ, and all ye are brethren.' " But for
Jones the 'best thing of all in Zion City' was the regular punctuation of
working life with prayerful devotion: "every worker meets in his or her respective department at 6:45 am and prays and sings . . . it is a pleasure to
meet with them in these morning meetings where God is given the first hours
in service."[235] And for early Zion City resident Lucille Bidille, her fondest
memories related to the tight-knit fellowship of the pioneer community. In
later life she recalled, "while many creaturely comforts were missing, one
thing we did have that was precious—fellowship and understanding. Our
beliefs brought us great happiness. I often wished I could recapture some of
the 'Enthusiasm' of the time."[236]

Yet all of this is not to neglect the existence of internal tensions and
contradictions within Dowie's project. Although education for all was prioritized in Zion City, in other respects opportunities for female residents
mirrored restrictions in the outside world. The egalitarian "Brotherhood
of Man" was only partially open to women. It is true that women in the
church could progress to the respected roles of "Deaconess" and "Evangelist," and that midwives such as Bratz enjoyed high levels of prestige. Yet,
other than Dowie's wife, Jane, no female was ever ordained to the highest
level of "Overseer." And even Jane Dowie's role was designated "Overseer-
in-charge-of-women's-work," a reflection of the widespread evangelical
belief of the day that women should not be placed in positions of authority
over men.[237] Women were simultaneously viewed as equal coworkers to
men, sisters in Christ, yet were relegated to subordinate positions to male
family and church members, both within and outside of church. Dowie
declared himself opposed to female suffrage on the grounds that "you
would only add to the confusion by dragging in hundreds of thousands of
ignorant women voters."[238] Turn-of-the-century Zionists, in step with
much evangelical Christian thought of the day, viewed the ultimate destiny
of female members in terms of their reproductive and domestic utility,
imbuing these capacities with great spiritual significance. "The home,"

preached Dowie to Zion City residents, "is the most sacred thing outside of the Church of God," and it was the role of mothers to "keep it in a way pleasing to Christ." *Leaves of Healing* featured regular articles and columns aimed at its female readership on topics such as child-rearing, cooking, home sanitation, and housekeeping.[239] Echoing contemporary concerns around a declining birth rate, women were thought to carry out a particularly sacred duty in the act of childbearing, and the taking of birth control measures was denounced as one of the worst sins a female Zionist could commit.[240]

Furthermore, despite Dowie's insistence that he was a "working man's preacher,"[241] differences did arise between Dowie and residents on issues of labor and fair representation. Dowie had banned organized labor in the construction of Zion City, defiantly announcing in early 1900 that "Unions shall not control Zion City . . . they have threatened to break my head, but I told them I was not afraid."[242] But the church lacked the manpower to carry out the work itself, and by 1902 Dowie was compelled to use outside union men for building and iron work. Perhaps due to their influence, a number of Zion City workers soon began organizing. Principal among these were the carpenters, led by none other than the Rohmer who had so enjoyed not having to lock up his tools, who agitated for an eight-hour day.[243] Dowie fought back by circulating a leaflet among union members in Chicago, which painted a rosy picture of Zion City "as God's favoured city . . . there will be no favoured or privileged classes, no labor unions, no contractors' trust, no beer barons, no merchant princes . . . if it is true that the rank and file of the unions are tired of their despotic rule, let these disillusioned trade unionists become part of Zion's colony on the beautiful north shore."[244]

Yet Dowie was unable to convince the workers of the church of the iniquity of the unions. During a sermon in Zion City when he denounced unions as a "menace to society," his listening congregation shouted vociferously, 'no, no, no!' "[245] Workers seem to have ultimately won the day, for in April 1902, Rohmer, the head of the organized carpenters, was able to report to his brother in Chicago that "we now have the eight-hour day all through . . . before private contractors let the men work as much as ten hours, but now all have to obey the eight-hour rule."[246] Other disagreements arose between Dowie and his workers. All workers within Zion City—whether church members or not—were expected to abide by its laws, including abstaining from tobacco and attending daily church services. But some of the English lace factory workers refused, defiantly telling Dowie "Zion or no Zion, we smoke. If you send us away you will have to fill our places with other lace makers from England and they will be tobacco users too."[247] Others objected to the lack of choice they were able to exercise about their occupation, that "he might be made to take up a pick or a shovel at the will of Dowie." One Zion City resident, a Mr. Rodgers, "objected to this . . . I was making money as a contractor and didn't care to give up such a lucrative occupation just because someone willed it."[248]

Other discrepancies soon appeared in Zion City's promise to be an entirely egalitarian community. Dowie increasingly spoke of the need to establish a political system on earth he dubbed "theocracy." This was incompatible with all human political systems, including democracy, for "when Christ comes to reign in the glorious Millennium, His Divine Right will supersede all forms of government . . . He will not recognize hereditary rights of King, rights of popularly elected Rulers, the alleged right of the people to rule themselves."[249] While church members waited for the certain return of Christ, their responsibility in the time that remained was to establish the rule of God (or "Zion") in all spheres of life. Yet, crucially, the rule of God did not pass entirely unmediated to the brotherhood of man; despite the egalitarian rhetoric of *Leaves* and Dowie's sermons, he increasingly began to preach that it was he himself who was the bridging figure between the all-powerful Ruler and the brotherhood of man. In 1901 Dowie made the "Elijah Declaration" in the church's Chicago Auditorium, in which he identified himself as the "Elijah the Restorer" spoken of in the Old Testament of the Bible, for he alone had restored the "primitive Christian Catholic Apostolic Church."[250] Dowie's self-aggrandizing rhetoric inflated in the following years. In September 1904 he stood on the platform of Shiloh Tabernacle—the new church auditorium in Zion City—dressed for the first time in an ornate robe of white, gold, scarlet and purple and declared himself "The First Apostle of the Lord Jesus Christ," uniquely charged with mediating God's will to man.[251] His increasingly grandiose stance belied Dowie's rhetoric about the absolute equality of all humans; as he preached in 1904, "there is only one man in the world like me, and that is myself . . . there is only one man that has my commission, and that is myself."[252] Dowie's unique standing meant that absolute subordination and loyalty to himself as the "General Overseer" was a spiritual requirement; a Chicago *Daily News* reporter found on visiting the city that the autocratic "Dowie insists on complete obedience of disciples, none dare to doubt the leader."[253]

Cleavages also soon appeared in the progressive racial rhetoric of the church. Despite the rhetoric of a single Adamic race, racial distinctions continued to make themselves felt in Zion City. Much of Dowie's following in the 1890s was built up of an earlier generation of immigrants—largely Germans and Scandinavians—who were by now steadily moving into better-paid, white collar positions. Yet he, like many of this earlier generation of

Leaves of Healing, "John Alexander, First Apostle." *Source: Leaves of Healing* 15, no. 23, 24 September 1904, 796. Flower Pentecostal Heritage Centre, Springfield, Missouri.

immigrants, was scathing about the newer wave of immigrants arriving in Chicago from Southern and Eastern Europe, generally less skilled and occupying the lowest rung of the social ladder. A 1904 *Leaves* editorial commented that "while America has room for the better class of citizens, she can ill afford to permit on her shores the rabble that is pressing and crowding into larger cities."[254] Moreover, the integration of Zion City's small community of African Americans into the community was far from complete. In keeping with Chicago's exclusion of blacks from skilled industrial work, only five non-whites worked in the lace factory, out of 404 workers.[255] Overall, despite exceptions such as the talented James Brister, blacks tended to occupy the same lower-tier jobs as they did in Chicago, serving as janitors and in the hotel and restaurant industry; Richard Williamson, for example, was a long-term resident who was employed as a waiter in the dining rooms of Elijah Hospice, Zion's main healing home.[256] Although blacks and whites were buried together in the town's cemeteries, blacks' residences were clustered on Gideon, Gilead, and Gilbea Avenues.[257] The 1910 census recorded only two interracial marriages; a contemporary observer concluded that "Zion had never seemed to take [interracial marriage] seriously, and could hardly be said to believe in this."[258] In this sense, Zion's membership was composed of two working-class groups that shared much in common but also diverged significantly. White, working-class northern Europeans were by and large not racial progressives. These inherent tensions within Dowie's project, and within Zion—the impulse toward egalitarian cosmopolitanism, on the one hand, and the tug toward racial exclusivism, on the other—are the subject of the next two chapters.

CHAPTER THREE

Unity and Division in Early Twentieth-Century Johannesburg and in Transatlantic Zion

D ANIEL BRYANT, a Midwestern missionary from Zion City charged by Dowie in 1904 with establishing the Christian Catholic Apostolic Church in Zion in South Africa, described how amid the bustle of downtown Johannesburg—"buzzing street cars and whirling automobiles"—a small and devoted gathering of Zionists "clasped hands at the cross of Christ" and tirelessly worked for the ushering in of God's Kingdom on earth. A war (1899–1902) had recently ended, fought between imperial Britain and a local white settler community of Boers[1] for political and economic control of the region, and in particular, for control of the enormous wealth of the gold mines of the Witwatersrand (the long narrow rock reef of mineral resources) which by 1898 produced 2 percent% of the world's gold.[2] What made this tight-knit congregation of several hundred Zionists in their downtown Tabernacle on busy Bree Street so remarkable was their mixed ethnic composition. Commentators of the period identified Boers and Britons as different white "races," and feared that the enmity produced by Boer defeat at the hands of the British would never be overcome. However, Zion in Johannesburg brought together equal number of Britons and Boers in a concerted effort at racial reconciliation—many of those gathered in unified worship for divine healing services and who "clasped hands" would have been combatants on opposing sides of the conflict just three years earlier. For Bryant, and for Zion promoters in the United States, this remarkable state of affairs was testimony to the power of divine healing to unify humanity and to forge a single Brotherhood of Man. Using language that invoked the cosmopolitan rhetoric of Zion in Chicago in the previous decade, and emphasizing the overarching Christian loyalties that trumped national or ethnic allegiance, Bryant reflected:

From my pulpit at Johannesburg, I see that Briton and Boer have entered, and taken seats side by side. The war left them deadly enemies with open wounds fresh flowing. No power but the Love of God could make their hearts forgive. But now they had found a standard they loved more than their national colors. It was the blood-stained Banner of the Cross. Now they had found a country greater than the one they had lost and in it they had found the city that hath foundations whose Builder is God . . . Briton and Boer had clasped hands at the Cross of Christ and went forth side by side in Love's battle on earth.[3]

As in Chicago, the cosmopolitan vocabulary of Dowie's divine healing church provided a language for members in Johannesburg with which to transcend existing racial and linguistic identities. At this point Johannesburg was a city less than twenty years old, but already the new mining metropolis of Africa and composed of a heterogeneous mix of peoples from across the world eager to make their fortunes. Moreover, in the aftermath of the defeat of the Boer Republics by Britain, Johannesburg was the site of an innovative imperial experiment aimed at crafting a new, unified white "race," reflecting the contemporary redefinition of empire as an expansive amalgamation of the best of British and local white settler identities.[4] Dowie's divine healing church, in company with other Protestant evangelical organizations in the city, became an important platform for postwar Christians to articulate their aspirations toward racial unity, expressed in terms of a new white "South Africanism." Although scholars have tended to pass over Christianity's significance in Johannesburg, preferring to focus on the lively prostitution and narcotics culture that characterized this gold-rush city, in fact evangelical churches were important sites of cultural and racial experimentation.[5] In addition to encouraging new affiliations at home, Dowie's church also enabled members in Johannesburg to style themselves participants within a much larger worldwide fraternity of Christians: Zion in Johannesburg and Zion in the Midwest enjoyed a close history of exchanges and connections. At the same moment as white South Africans were imagining themselves in newly expanded terms as part of the worldwide British Empire, they were also conceiving of themselves as part of other transnational communities such as the worldwide Zion church. Johannesburg's Zion church became one of Dowie's most prized examples of his treasured program of racial cosmopolitanism, with its activities frequently lauded in *Leaves of Healing*. The unity of Boer and Briton in the Johannesburg church, as well as Johannesburg's close connections with Zion City in Illinois, seemed to perfectly exemplify Dowie's own vision of a united pan-racial Brotherhood of Man.

But this brief moment of racial unity between Boer and Briton, as well as the transatlantic unity between Johannesburg and Zion City, was short-lived.

Complex disputes and divisions typical of evangelical Protestantism soon ruptured the body of the faithful in Johannesburg and worldwide. Within three years of Bryant's landing in South Africa, the Johannesburg church had broken away from Dowie, as well as subsequently revolted against the individual who assumed leadership of the church in Zion City after Dowie's death in 1907, Wilbur Glenn Voliva. The schismatic Johannesburg church linked itself to a similarly minded rebel group within Zion City (although this alliance would itself be short-lived). A key cause for division between Johannesburg and Zion City, as well as within Zion City itself, was an argument regarding what form of religious leadership was mandated by the Bible. Voliva, representing the official heir to Dowie, declared himself divinely appointed and therefore above criticism. But the dissenting rebels in both North America and in South Africa argued that Scriptures laid out a more collaborative and democratic way of governing the Kingdom of God. A further disagreement broke out between Johannesburg and Zion City, as well as within Zion City itself, regarding the evidence by which Christian believers would know they possessed full Holiness. In the first decade of the century, a new reform movement within evangelical Christianity arose among Protestants who believed that speaking in tongues, or glossolalia, was the definitive proof of their personal sanctification. Key figures within Zion became active in what became known as the Pentecostal revival, resulting in the already divided Zion City and Johannesburg churches splintering yet further between those believers who agreed with speaking in tongues and those saw tongues as an ungodly—even demonic—manifestation.

These theological divisions—typical of this contentious tradition of evangelical Christianity—had profound consequences for the Johannesburg church's program of racial cosmopolitanism. The schismatic South African church, now loyal to the notion of collaborative leadership as well as to Pentecostal teachings, soon distanced itself from the older cosmopolitan values of Zion as they had been defined by Dowie. This shift was much influenced by the changing political climate in South Africa by the end of the century's first decade. The optimistic promotion of "White South Africanism" was replaced by a hardening Boer ethnic nationalism, deeply hostile to English-speaking Anglo identity (but even more implacably opposed to black African franchise). The postwar experiment with a unified Boer-British identity was transcended by a Boer nationalism invested in a distinct linguistic and racial identity, and which came to fruition in the 1948 ascent to power of the Afrikaans-speaking Nationalist Party. The Zion of Dowie's era now appeared to many Johannesburg believers to be an outdated experiment in universalism. The new Pentecostal-infused Christianity embraced by many Zionists had an explicitly local focus as well as renounced Dowie's former goal of racial integration, declaring the separation of the races to be in accordance with God's plan for humanity. The popularity of this church among the urban Boer poor of the city reflected these Johannesburgers' preference for a Christianity that confirmed rather than transcended racial and national identities. The brief period of unity that had characterized Dowie's early Johannesburg church had now ended, and these believers discarded their former warm relations with American brethren across the Atlantic. Highlighting the divisive qualities that lay at the heart of Dowie's church, this chapter demonstrates the protean forms Zion assumed in early twentieth-century Johannesburg—a development in no small part attributable to the primacy evangelicalism afforded to individuals' inspiration by the Holy Spirit, Scripture, and their own conscience.

The Christian Catholic Apostolic Church in Zion in Prewar Johannesburg

The doctrines of the Christian Catholic Apostolic Church in Zion rapidly fanned out far beyond Chicago and its environs, although for now this was still where its greatest numerical strength was found. By 1899, new church branches were formed throughout the state of Illinois as well as in Iowa, Ohio, Michigan, Wisconsin, Indiana, and Texas. At its height in 1904, the church had approximately 20,000 members.[6] Most of this membership was situated in the United States, particularly in the Midwestern region, with at least several thousand individuals who professed allegiance to the church living outside of the country. This was because Dowie and his leadership had successfully planted "Zion Gatherings" (as local branches came to be known) as far afield as "British Columbia, France, England, India, various parts of Africa and Australia," according to *Leaves* in 1899.[7] Immigrant church members in Chicago and later Zion City were an important conduit through which the church's teachings were funneled across the world. Zionists tended to write letters about divine healing and their experiences in the church to family members back home, as well as send used copies of *Leaves of Healing* and Dowie's tracts.[8] By the beginning of the new century, German, Swedish, Spanish, French, Italian, Danish, and Czech members had organized different editions and occasional translations of portions of *Leaves* into their native languages.[9] *Leaves* was also translated into non-European languages, again through the efforts of Zionists hailing from parts of the world outside of Western Europe or North America. A Japanese convert in Zion City named Paul Dowie Katano, for example, was the one who translated the magazine into Japanese.[10] By 1899, a new church agency, the "Zion Literature Mission," ensured that three-quarter of a million copies of *Leaves* in multiple languages were annually printed and shipped across the world, as well as two million church tracts and pamphlets, many containing reprints of Dowie's sermons.[11] It became commonplace for Dowie and church members in this period to refer to *Leaves* as the "little white dove," a mobile emissary that flew to foreign lands bearing the good news of the peaceful Kingdom. As such, *Leaves*—imagined in "bird" form—could penetrate remote areas inaccessible to Dowie and other missionaries. An 1898 issue hoped that "the Little White Dove [will] carry our stories of salvation and healing . . . around the coasts of that Great Continent of Africa, bear it up the bosom of the Nile and away across the mountains."[12] Dowie increasingly envisioned the missionary work of the church as occurring not just through *Leaves* but through physical emissaries. Australia—which already had a thriving Zion Gathering in Melbourne, due to old loyalties to Dowie—was the first country to receive Zion missionaries. In 1901, Wilburn Glenn Voliva and his wife, both members of the church since the Chicago days, were ordained as Elder and Evangelist, respectively, and sent to be Overseer of the Australian church, where they recruited around 1,300 new members over the course of five years.[13]

Some of the most important international audiences for *Leaves* were British and American Protestant missionaries stationed abroad. Many found *Leaves'* testimonies of divine healing to be stirring portends of a powerful "Full Gospel" (a favored Holiness and Higher Life phrase) that promised to successfully convert local unbelievers.[14] One female missionary "laboring in Japan," wrote to *Leaves* that "I am alone among the heathen here, but I realize the power of God in my spirit and body . . . nothing but a full Gospel will do here."[15] Missionary sympathizers also played their role in extending *Leaves'* linguistic reach. A British missionary stationed in Alexandria, Egypt translated Dowie's pamphlet *God's Way of Healing* into Arabic, intending it to circulate in "Syria, Palestine, Arabia, Egypt, Tripoli, Tunis, Algeria." Carl F. Viking was an American-Swedish missionary with the Swedish Baptist Mission in Shandong, China.[16] During a home furlough to the American Midwest, he encountered Dowie's teachings and realized the potency of divine healing for the missionary cause. He asserted that "medical missions [in China] are unscriptural, unapostolic, unscientific, pernicious." Divine healing, by contrast, was a natural complement to the work of evangelizing the world: it was "distinctly enjoined in the Great Commission . . . the first missionaries constantly exercised the Gift of Healing."[17] Upon his return to his mission field in China, Viking carried with him copies of *Leaves* as well as other church literature translated into both Japanese and Chinese characters.[18] As a result of the efforts of missionaries such as these, small communities of local converts began to spring up in countries such as China, Japan, and Egypt. Some missionaries, already in place in foreign fields, merely switched allegiance from old employers to Dowie's church after embracing divine healing. For example, the Vikings—already in China—were ordained as local Overseers for the Christian Catholic Apostolic Church once they had quit the Swedish Baptists.[19]

But the church's greatest international success during this period was in the Republic of the Transvaal, and in particular, the mining metropolis of Johannesburg. The Transvaal was an independent polity in Southern Africa governed by descendants of the early Dutch community who had settled in the Cape in the eighteenth century. Dutch-speaking settlers—who came to be known as Boers, or "farmers"—had been establishing agricultural communities in the interior of the country since the 1830s. This had been a period of mass migration of Boers from the Cape northward—also known as the Great Trek—partly in protest against their political disenfranchisement at the hands of the British government in the Cape and partly due to their objection to the British abolishment of slavery.[20] In the 1850s two independent Boer Republics were established in the interior of the country; the South African or Transvaal Republic in 1852 and the Orange Free State in 1854. Yet Boer hegemony over the region was far from secure. A series of conflicts with African polities took place over the nineteenth century, as well as brewing tension with Great Britain. In the light of the discovery of diamonds in the 1860s in the town that would become Kimberly, by this period there existed a broader Anglo imperial ambition to construct a loose federation of South African states that assured British economic and political supremacy in the region. These conflicting interests culminated in Britain's annexation of the Boer Republic of the Transvaal in 1877.[21] The Transvaal regained its independence in 1884 after several years of warfare with Britain, but the discovery of gold on the Witwatersrand in the Transvaal Republic in 1886 provoked further conflict between imperial interests in the region and the ambitions of the local white settler community. Further, the discovery of gold propelled the Transvaal Republic to massive wealth, but the Republic lacked sufficient human labor for the new mining industry. This meant that large numbers of mainly English-speaking outsiders poured in from the rest of South Africa and the entire world to work on the gold mines, further complicating the balance of power between Boer and British interests in Johannesburg. The gold mines of the Rand became a cosmopolitan crossroads of international labor, drawing into their orbit miners from across Southern Africa, Australia, North America, Britain, and the rest of Europe.

Arriving in the 1890s into this precariously balanced ethnic, racial, and linguistic milieu, Dowie's church founds its greatest initial success among the Boer residents of Johannesburg, as well as those located in the farmlands surrounding the new city. As with other areas of the world, it was *Leaves* that first promoted Zion's teachings. The residents of Johannesburg initially read the magazine in English, but by 1899 interest was so great (readers in the city were requesting 200 copies of *Leaves* every week) that Dowie decided to produce a Dutch edition of *Leaves,* estimating that readership could thus be increased to up to 1,000 weekly copies. *Bladen der Heeling* was produced by a Dutch member of the church in Chicago, Nicholas Pos, and subsidized by Chicago church members' donation of $1,000 for the purchase of a complete dress of Dutch type.[22] The interest generated by Dowie's teachings in Johannesburg was also fanned by an energetic local convert who organized a lively Zion Gathering in the city. This was a Swiss member of the Salvation Army, Johannes Buchler.[23] Influenced by the controversial Pietistic revivals of the time, Johannes' parents had left the Herisau district of Switzerland for the South African Cape as religious refugees. Once there, they became members of the Salvation Army in the small town of Grahamstown in the Eastern Cape.[24] Like many others of the period, Buchler first worked his way from the Cape to Kimberly to participate in the diamond rush, and then by the end of the 1880s, further north to the gold mines of Johannesburg.[25] Buchler became an active member of the Salvation Army in the working-class suburb of Fordsburg, and was also involved in Congregationalist meetings in the city.[26] But by 1897, having read Dowie's *Leaves,* Buchler departed from both the Army and the Congregationalists to found a "Divine Healing Home" in Jeppestown, a white working-class suburb in the center of the city. Dowie's continued emphasis on temperance doubtless would have resonated with the Army's own efforts in that direction in the city of Johannesburg, a milieu where vast levels of alcohol consumptions among a largely single male population was the norm.[27] Buchler also began selling copies of *Leaves* around the city, reporting that they "go like hotcakes."[28] In 1897, Dowie appointed Buchler as his "African Overseer," responsible for the work of organizing the Johannesburg Zion Gathering.[29]

Alongside the support of existing evangelical denominations such as the Salvation Army, the influential Dutch Reformed Church was a further conduit through which divine healing teachings circulated to the local Boer population.[30] Despite its usual portrayal as a Calvinist organization—its austere theology of predestination worlds away from the perfectionistic, optimistic Holiness theology of divine healing—in fact, laity and clergy within the Dutch Reformed Church of the late nineteenth century had been deeply influenced by the worldwide evangelical revivals.[31] In the 1820s, evangelical Church of Scotland ministers working closely with Dutch Reformed Church clergy had set the latter organization on a path that valued personal piety and spiritual fervor and proved most receptive to the Holiness movement of later in the century.[32] The Murray family—father and son—were among the leading Dutch Reformed figures in the Cape, and it was Andrew Murray junior who visited William Boardman's Bethshan Home in London for a throat ailment, and there came to believe in "Jesus our Divine Healer."[33] Murray became deeply influential in the movement, one of the most respected figures outside of North America and Western Europe, and a frequent speaker on the divine healing and Holiness conference circuit, regularly addressing meetings such as the important Keswick Convention in England.[34]

These evangelical sections of the Dutch Reformed Church—mainly located in the Cape area—energetically promoted Dowie's teachings. One of Murray's most important protégés in the Wellington district of the Cape was the young and devout Pieter Le Roux, who was sent to the small Transvaal town of Wakkerstroom (around 150 miles east of Johannesburg) in 1890 as a Dutch Reformed missionary to rural African farming communities.[35] During this decade an evangelical revival broke out in the neighboring Greytown and Umvoti districts, which Le Roux was a keen participant in, frequently visiting farms on which sympathetic farmers hosted religious meetings.[36] Le Roux also regularly corresponded with his mentor Murray in the Cape about divine healing, as well as read American and European literature on the topic, including the well-known Otto Stockmayer, a German disciple of Dorothea Trudel.[37] He felt an ever-increasing burden to practice divine healing personally and among his family, as well as to teach it to his largely Zulu congregation in Wakkerstroom, coming to view it as the culmination of the Gospel. As he reported to his Dutch Reformed Church superiors in a letter of 1898 "soon my conviction became very strong that the Lord has clearly revealed Himself in His Word as the Healer of His People."[38] One of his sons tells how inscribed on the front page of Le Roux's personal Bible were the words: "healing is the attestation of the power and genuineness of spiritual religion and ought not to have dropped out of the church."[39] Le Roux was also in regular contact with Johannes Buchler in Johannesburg (pronouncing him a "man of true and strong faith"), consulting with him on particularly difficult cases of illness, and perhaps it was even through Buchler that he first received copies of Dowie's *Leaves*.[40]

The circulation of *Leaves*, as well as the promotion of Dowie's church by key Dutch Reformed Church figures, meant that Zion in Johannesburg soon had a thriving membership of Boer believers. There was, it is true, also a handful of English-speaking members in this early period. Some among the global workforce resident in the city were deeply interested in the divine healing on offer in Dowie's church. One such individual was W. C. Clough, a Yorkshire man originally from Leeds, who had the experiences while "on one of the gold mines . . . that away in Africa, the Lord took hold of me and inspired me with assurance he was my Savior and Healer." Baptized by Buchler, Clough swore to no longer eat pork (Dowie's followers were ordered to follow the Levitical dietary laws) and repented of being a "thief and a rogue," returning the stolen twenty-five pounds to his foreman on the mine.[41] Yet for the most part, Dowie's teachings thrived among the Boers. In 1899, Buchler reported that the readers of *Leaves* were "almost entirely Boer converts in the ZAR."[42] These Boer Zionists of early Johannesburg were, according to Buchler, "mostly very poor people,"[43] drawn from the unskilled white farmers who had crowded to the city during the gold rush and since found themselves in dire straits.[44] According to Buchler, it was Boers' impoverished status that inclined them toward divine healing: Boers are "poor and scattered and often have no doctor or medicine . . . [this] predisposes them to look to the Great Physician."[45] It certainly seems to have been the case that divine healing particularly appealed to this unskilled constituency, perhaps especially given the highly unhealthy and dangerous milieu of the gold mines where many labored. White miners died from silicosis (caused by exposure to silica dust underground) at a far higher rate than black coworkers because of the longer work contracts. In 1902, underground rock drillers had average working lives of seven years, with most only surviving to the age of thirty-three. More broadly, deaths from exposure to noxious fumes underground and generally hazardous working conditions were also high.[46] Arie van Woerkom was a Methodist lay preacher and Sunday school teacher also working underground in Johannesburg's mines. His testimony describing his conversion to Dowie's church tells how "I was in a sore strait [coming] into contact on the mines with various poisons and skin irritants which got into my system, my work was in the vicinity of large quantities of mercury." Under the influence of Buchler, van Woerkom decided to "talk to God [who] did not fail me." Although ejected from the Methodist church for his allegiance to the by-then controversial divine healing, van Woerkom reported to being "permanently healed of bronchitis" and professed dramatically that he had found the true Full Gospel: "I do not regret that I left the skeleton" of Methodism."[47]

Dowie found much to admire and praise in his Boer following in the Transvaal. At this early stage at least, he deeply sympathized with the two Boer Republics' desire to assert independence against the British Empire. His stance was in keeping with much popular opinion in the United States, which had positively likened the Dutch Republican cause to their own country's independence struggle from Great Britain.[48] Along these lines, the American press tended to cast Boers as a rural, pastoral people—indeed, a different white "race"—untouched by the greedy capitalism of largely British mine "Randlords," or industrial magnates.[49] Influenced by the period's racial typology, Dowie joined in portraying Boers as members of a different race to the Anglo-Saxon family.[50] But Dowie described this separate race in glowing terms, casting his Boer converts as the antithesis of Anglo-Saxons made degenerate by an enfeebled city existence, polluted by industrial living and by toxins such as alcohol, tobacco, and medicines. To him, the Boers appeared a hardy white people, unspoiled by industrialization. Reflecting these views, Dowie featured photographs of early Boer converts in the *Leaves,* not in the urban environment of Johannesburg where they lived, but carrying out baptisms amid "lovely scenes" of rivers and hillsides. The commentary beneath one such photograph labeled Boer converts the epitome of white racial vigor: "manly men, lovely women . . . and a band of happy children."[51] A supposed propensity for healthy, simple living made Boers receptive to divine healing: "the Zion message appealed to the sturdy pioneers of that country . . . for it was a message full of vigour, virility and power."[52]

The outbreak of war between the Boer Republics and Great Britain—a conflict that lasted from October 1899 to March 1902—radically changed the position of Boers within Johannesburg, and more broadly, within the soon-to-be-formed Union of South Africa. Although the larger issue was over who would control the enormous mineral wealth of the Witwatersrand gold seam, the immediate precipitating cause was a breakdown in negotiations with Transvaal authorities over the rights of the English-speaking settle community in Johannesburg. Britain expected the war to be quickly won by Christmas. Instead, it raged on for three years, and became one of the bloodiest and most expensive conflicts in British military history. The war is often cast as a dispute between two white groups. In fact, African, Colored, and Indian South Africans were combatants and scouts on both sides, highlighting the profound impact of British and Boer expansion on formerly independent African chieftaincies in the interior of the country.[53] By 1902, at the end of three years of grueling warfare and heavy losses on both sides, Britain defeated the Boer Republics of the Transvaal and the Orange Free State and annexed them as British possessions. Yet

Zion in Africa. *Source: Leaves of Healing* 4, no. 16, 12 February 1898, 301.
Flower Pentecostal Heritage Centre, Springfield, Missouri.

at this point a surprising development occurred. Far from incorporating
the Boer territories as merely subordinate vassal states, British politicians
were increasingly envisioning ceding significant amounts of power to these
new African colonies. An innovative experiment in promoting a newly mingled Boer-British identity was underway, and great efforts were made to
mitigate the "racial" hostilities that had led to war three years previously.
The Protestant churches of the Transvaal—and especially Dowie's Christian Catholic Apostolic Church in Zion—would make an important contribution to this endeavor.

Racial Cosmopolitanism and White Unity in Postwar Johannesburg

The early years of the twentieth century witnessed a radically changed
British conception of empire as top-down rule to a more "organic"
federation-like entity. This was particularly true of areas of significant white
settlement—South Africa, Australia, New Zealand, and Canada—in which
local white communities enjoyed greater autonomy. Richard Jebb's influential 1905 *Studies in Colonial Nationalism* lent legitimacy to the notion

that local white settler nationalisms were beneficial to empire, and could form a worldwide community of the British race.[54] This shift was the result of fears regarding Anglo-Saxon racial decline in Britain. Britons lauded the supposedly innate superiority of Anglo-Saxons to rule the world,[55] but there simultaneously existed an acute sense of Anglos' vulnerability to political and economic rivals like Russia and Germany, as well as domestic unrest precipitated by industrialization. Anglo-Saxon poor health became a popular way of describing these anxieties.[56] Widespread worry existed around the detrimental effects of industrialization, thought to negatively impact Anglos' ability to rule the world.[57] Many imperialist ideologues in Britain looked to the vast expanse of the colonies to shape a new breed of rugged, outdoors "imperial colonists," loyal to the empire but also invested in local self-determination. It was thought that white Australia, New Zealand, Canada, and South Africa—incorporated into the empire as part of the single body politic—would have a reinvigorating effect on the declining race.[58] Indeed, South Africa's temperate regions had long been regarded as a healthy destination for the sick of the industrialized West, helpful in "cases of nervous breakdown . . . so common in our over-strained civilization."[59] In a speech given in 1907 in South Africa, the colonial administrator and British high commissioner Lord Alfred Milner lauded that "in South Africa men of European race thrive and multiply exceedingly . . . their splendid physique is due to the bracing air of these large expanses of lofty open air country."[60] The flourishing of Anglo-Saxons in Africa would be on the egalitarian basis whereby the national identity of "South Africanism" was promoted. As Milner famously declared in 1905: "the True Imperialist is the Best South African."[61]

Boers in the recently defeated Dutch Republics were initially unenthusiastic about their absorption into a white South Africanism. So-called race difficulties plagued the postwar reconstruction project. Many English-speakers within the Transvaal continued to view the Boers as a lesser people to Anglo-Saxons. Johannesburg's Anglophone newspaper *Rand Daily Mail* noted in 1902 that "Boers were without tradition, refinement, chivalry, the arts, literature, the Taal [early Afrikaans] was a pigeon language . . . the Briton has been the moving spirit of progress in South Africa."[62] Such attitudes gave rise to frequent friction. At a 1903 fundraiser for Dutch war orphans, attended by both Boers and Britons, the Dutch section of the audience refused to sing "God Save the King," regarding this as an instance of British insensitivity and presumptions of superiority.[63] But British-Boer animosity was not the only factor discouraging the creation of a white South Africanism. The English-speaking population in Johannesburg was also a small and a temporary one, largely made up of itinerant migrant labor, militating against the long-term flourishing of Anglophone imperial culture in South Africa. Before and immediately after the South African war, the city was overwhelmingly dominated by single men, who remitted money to their families in Britain.[64] In 1901, largely due to the astronomically high cost of housing in the mining metropolis, only 20 percent of white miners had wives and families living with them in Johannesburg.[65]

Against these odds, administrators and policy makers attempted to promote a new South African identity unifying Boer and Briton into a single white race. While the war had been marked by a jingoistic chauvinistic sense of British identity, it was clear that now crude Anglicization policies would be untenable. Boers would have to be persuaded that imperial loyalty was not incompatible with their own national identity. Milner formed a network of "Closer Union" societies in 1908, "created to spread the gospel of Dutch and British union by means of lectures, pamphlets and discussions."[66] To aid this project, his advisers produced a publication, *The State,* published in both English and Dutch, and featuring articles designed to stimulate a "common patriotism."[67] Former Boer combatants were also recruited to the notion of a united white identity in more practical ways, including financial assistance after returning to their farms.[68] Many Boer politicians, including prominent wartime generals such as Louis Botha and Jan Smuts, reconciled themselves to allying with English-speaking whites in the hopes of bolstering an independent South Africa. In 1902, Smuts wrote that his ideal was "a United South Africa . . . a compact South African nationality built up with the best elements of both parts of the colonial population."[69] The immediate postwar mood was optimistic about the prospects of incorporating a unified South Africa as a "brick" in the "arch" of empire.[70] According to the *Rand Daily Mail,* South Africa stood "on the threshold of great national life." The responsibility lay on both "Briton and Boer, brothers in one Imperial Supremacy, to make South Africa strong and true . . . a fused race with common aspirations under the mild rule of England."[71] Crucially, postwar reconciliation was forged amid intense white insecurities about African uprisings. For Smuts, regardless of historic animosities between Boer and Briton, they were nonetheless "'two white Christian peoples' surrounded by "barbarians' who had to be kept in their place."[72]

The state of white racial health became shorthand for the white South African project. Boosting the white birth rate in the postwar period was a key concern of imperial officials in South Africa and Britain, and seen as intrinsically linked to their task of creating a new unified white race. In the aftermath of the war, between 1901 and 1910, over 4,000 single women left Britain for South Africa via official women's emigrations societies, with over one-half settling in the Transvaal and most going into domestic services in white homes on the Rand.[73] Immigrant women, through their reproductive labor, would birth the new white race: "transplanted, women take deep root in South African soil and come up a graft of Imperial Africa, the new amalgamation type that is evolving every day."[74] Officials undertook other types of medical projects aimed at racial flourishing. A study into infant mortality in the city was carried out in 1904, and recommendations made for improved sanitation.[75] Transvaal newspapers carried editorials and articles on how to bolster "a nation's best asset—its childhood's health," including suggestions on home hygiene,[76] the provision of clean milk,[77] and directions on infant "gymnastics."[78] In Johannesburg, as worldwide, the patent medicine industry benefitted from a general anxiety about the therapies of regular physicians.[79] Johannesburg's newspapers advertised alternative cures, many used throughout the Anglo world, such as "California Syrup of Figs" and "Dr Williams Pink Pills."[80] Many patent medicines explicitly advertised themselves as remedies for racial health. Bolstered by "Mother Seigel's Curative Syrup," a strong "New Afrikander" would emerge: "the Dutch and British elements shall merge into one virile race . . . a grand specimen of the genus man, the great race of whites."[81] Another therapy for the new Boer-British "Afrikander" was the growing craze for "physical culture," so that "the Transvaal's learned men will not have round shoulders, narrow chests and squeaky voices."[82] And while "our beloved England is losing her place at the head of Empires, for her sons are falling away in mind as well as muscle," Mrs. Josef Conn's exercises—advertised in the pages of the *Rand Daily Mail*—"strengthen[ed] the muscles around the vital organs [for] the physical regeneration of the race."[83]

Alongside these popular and official efforts at boosting racial health, Johannesburg's Protestant evangelical churches became important sites for the promotion of white South Africanism. During the South African War of 1899–1902, several of the city's main evangelical institutions had deliberately undertaken ministry on both sides of the conflict, most famously the Salvation Army. In 1901, before the war had ended, the Salvation Army had already published its *New Territorial Song Book*, with 500 songs in both English and Dutch, as well as publishing regular articles in Dutch in its local edition of its periodical, *The War Cry*.[84] After the war, Johannesburg's evangelical community continued to work for what they viewed as Christian reconciliation of the white races. The hugely popular British evangelist Gipsy Smith held widely attended revival meetings on the Rand in 1904, preaching to audiences of several thousand Boers and Britons, proclaiming "God has used my work to bring together the two great nations of Dutch and British . . . at the Cross, those who are sundered apart are closest."[85] At the close of the popular revival meetings, he lauded the fact that "large contingent of Dutch people stood up and sang a Dutch hymn of praise."[86] Milner met personally with Gipsy Smith to convey his "sympathy with the objects of the work"—although refrained from personal attendance lest his presence should "embarrass the Dutch who were joining in cordially."[87] Other evangelical organizations prided themselves on incorporating ministers of both "races," including the regular Keswick Convention in Johannesburg, the YMCA, and the Witwatersrand Church Council.[88]

Johannesburg's churches gave their own Christian inflection to the popular preoccupation with bodily health and the flourishing of the new white imperial identity.[89] Johannesburg's YMCA, while "expressing an earnest Christian hope that men of all races may soon be found forgiving and forgetting the animosities of the last years," also instituted programs for "the physical development of men, including a physical culture class," and the provision of suitable grounds for football, cricket and tennis.[90] Its goal was to make young men of Johannesburg "decent, manlike and strong."[91] The city's evangelical churches also addressed the demographic aspect of racial health, seeking to promote a domestic culture on the Rand that was conducive to the long-term settlement of English-speaking whites in the Transvaal. Gipsy Smith expounded on the dangers of single, young men in Johannesburg, "away from restraint, away from mother, away from wife, away from children, away from old ties."[92] The YMCA led the way in solving this problem by "providing a home away from home" for young men. Echoing Milner's rhetoric of demographic engineering (indeed, Milner agreed to be the patron of Johannesburg's YMCA in February 1903[93]) for the YMCA, "the greatest asset of any country was its live men and women." It, therefore, was an institution in which to have "healthy, decent, clean social intercourse, which would [do] enormous amount for welfare of the country."[94] It was hardly surprising that an interest in divine healing was a natural step for those Protestants interested in the church's role in this project of racial rejuvenation. In 1905, the YMCA's magazine wondered whether "the Lord is the Lord of the Body as well as of the Spirit?"[95] Gipsy Smith prayed for individuals' healing from bodily illness during his 1904 Johannesburg Revival meetings, proclaiming that "someday Jesus will wipe all sin out."[96] And Christian Science in Johannesburg—which proclaimed Christ's ability to reform the body through the domination of "matter" by "spirit"—had a lively and much-debated presence in the postwar city.[97]

Dowie's church proved uniquely well suited to postwar Johannesburg's optimistic mood of racial reconciliation. Indeed, wartime networks had meant Dowie's teachings could reach combatants of both sides. Indian Ocean penal camps to which the British transported Boer prisoners proved fertile ground for divine healing. One Boer Zionist, a P. N. J. van Rensburg, voluntarily traveled to an imperial prisoner of war camp in Ceylon to minister there.[98] A camp in Diyatalawa, Ceylon, soon had thirteen Boer Zionists, part of a broader milieu of lively Christian evangelicalism.[99] Developments in Ceylon soon spread home. Van Rensburg commented that "prisoners here reside all over South Africa, consequently Zion's name will thus be more widely circulated and advertised when they return home."[100] The war also enabled Zion teachings to reach a British constituency. *Leaves* were disseminated through networks of newly arrived British soldiers to the Transvaal. James Thompson belonged to the Queen's Own Cameron Highlanders, and first read *Leaves* while stationed with his regiment in Cairo. Upon arriving in South Africa, Thompson circulated the magazine among his regiment and others.[101] *Leaves* were also distributed among convalescing British soldiers. Ernest Cox, a member of the Volunteer Lancashire Fusiliers, read about divine healing while recovering from a leg injury in a military hospital in Natal.[102] Soldierly sympathizers left *Leaves* for the men who were coming in to fill up the beds they were leaving.[103] By 1900 Dowie was receiving numerous applications for membership from the South African region, including from soldiers in a Scottish Highlander regiment in the Orange Free State.[104] A year later Dowie could celebrate that "*Leaves* has been used of God for the salvation and healing of large numbers of the British troops."[105] The wartime displacement of Johannesburg's British population also spread Zionism to English-speakers; Zionist refugees from the Transvaal planted new Gatherings in the coastal towns of Durban and Port Elizabeth.[106]

This newly mixed Boer and British readership found in Zion's teachings a compelling spiritual argument against the horrors of warfare between the two white races. For Dowie, a principled pacifist stance was a natural extension of his cosmopolitan advocacy of the universal brotherhood of man. Throughout the 1890s—a decade of burgeoning American expansion abroad under the imperial-minded Theodore Roosevelt—Dowie frequently reiterated his opposition to warfare. American intervention in the Philippines, the beginnings of the Spanish-American war, and conflict in Cuba were all denounced by him, in typically polemical fashion, as antithetical to the fraternal values of Zion—often in terms that echoed the rhetoric of contemporary organizations such as the Anti-Imperialist League,

established in 1898 to combat the American annexation of the Philippines.[107] In a stirring sermon delivered in his Chicago Tabernacle in 1896,
and reprinted in *Leaves* that week, Dowie had announced that "I can afford
to be shot and to die, but I cannot afford to kill anyone . . . I BELIEVE
WAR, IN ALL ITS FORMS, TO BE INFERNAL, and I have no intention
in becoming an American ever to fight for that flag or any flag."[108] In the
Transvaal, too, Dowie used *Leaves* as a platform for denouncing the war as
antithetical to Zion's vision of a single race. This was not a unique opinion
in turn-of-the-century South Africa. Several prewar advocates for cosmopolitan "South Africanism" had similarly criticized war for rupturing racial
unity. These included the author Olive Schreiner who wrote of the "great
blended South African people," comprised of Briton and Dutch, and lamented the impending atrocity of familial violence: "mother and daughter
up in one horrible embrace and rend[ing] each other's vitals."[109] In like
fashion, Dowie described warfare in South Africa as "fratricide," rupturing
a humanity depicted by him as a tight-knit family.[110] He instructed readers
to avoid combatant work, and to act as medical workers and chaplains:
"relieving the sufferings, both physical and spiritual, of those who fall
beneath the bayonet, the bullet and the shell."[111] True Zionists "will never
kill their fellow men . . . if drafted, they should join hospital or ambu-
lance corps."[112] Boer and British authorities objected to Dowie's pacifist
views, censoring *Leaves* in regions under their control.[113] Dowie's diag-
nosis of warfare as the ultimate sin against Christian fraternity must have
seemed deeply subversive to authorities: "We feel that *all war is wrong*. It
is sinful for Christian men to fight and destroy life. We read that the command of God is: "Thou shalt not take life."[114]

Yet although gaining the disapproval of wartime officials, Zion successfully tapped into a popular widespread spirit of disgruntlement and fatigue.
Wartime correspondence suggests that soldiers of both sides took a cynical
view of the conflict as malnutrition, high mortality rates, the scorched earth
policy of the imperial troops, and long periods of inactivity lowered mo-
rale.[115] Many British and Boer soldiers whole-heartedly agreed with Dowie
about war's depravity. One wartime convert to his church, William H.
Young, confessed that "my heart is not in this war." The reason: "it is the
very work of the Devil. I look around and see the suffering, pain and the
sorrow caused by this war."[116] Zionist John Taylor quoted a wounded ser-
geant of the Gordon Highlanders who confided how "impossible [it was]
to describe those sad sights as we brought in the poor boys, bleeding and
dying. I can only weep as I recall it all."[117] In typical Zion fashion, the care
of military doctors was described as almost worse than the shellfire and
bullets. J. Ord Armstrong's testimony to *Leaves* described "ignorant and

reckless drugging, cutting, probing and unsanitary conditions."[118] In place of violent warfare, Zionist Boer and Britons advocated that their duty was to reconcile as brethren. Converts considered it their duty to assert kinship with enemy combatants. Taylor, previously a clerk in a law firm in Pietermaritzburg, enlisted as a military chaplain for the British.[119] His motive, as he wrote in to *Leaves,* was to be "a Gospel messenger, Boer and British were all alike to me." Taylor described to *Leaves'* readers how: "[I] tended one of the enemy who was badly wounded—a Hollander."[120] Unlike Taylor, most male Zionist sympathizers almost certainly fought. But even these were keen to stress, at least rhetorically, that they avoided killing Boer brethren. One soldier reported to *Leaves* that "I had my rifle levelled at the head of a Boer, when something said to me, 'If you pull the trigger, he is a dead man' . . . I at once cocked my rifle in the air."[121] Another soldiery correspondent attributed his terrible injury to taking up arms against his Boer brother: "I [saw] that war was the Devil's work, and that God never intended me to take up arms to shoot my brother."[122] Dowie was deeply cognizant of the value of these letters as strategic evidence of Zion's catholicity, frequently reminding his readers that letters were continually received "from those who were on the firing line of both the Boer and the British side."[123]

By the end of the war, such was the success of his church among both British and Boer populations in the Transvaal that Dowie decided to send four missionaries from Zion City to Johannesburg. Although Dowie recognized the "devoted and self-sacrificing spirit of the members' who organized open-air meetings in the city as well as a regular saloon visiting to distribute temperance and divine healing tracts, Dowie felt that so far "we are only touching the fringes of this great city."[124] Most important, in the aftermath of the war, Dowie also discerned a unique opportunity to implement the church's distinctive program of racial reconciliation in this land of "terrible and bloody strife."[125] In 1904, Dowie commissioned two church members, Elder Daniel Bryant and his wife, Evangelist Emma Bryant, to travel to Johannesburg as official Zion missionaries.[126] They would be accompanied by one Nicholas Rideout and his wife, the former the "financial manager" for the church in South Africa.[127] Originally Baptists from Ohio, the Bryants had joined the church during its Chicago-based years, and had first become Dowie's emissaries in Northern Wisconsin and Michigan before being transferred to headquarters in Chicago to work on the editorial team for *Leaves.*[128] Part of Dowie's inner circle, they were among the first wave of pioneers to take residence in Zion City after its founding in 1900.

Upon arrival in postwar Johannesburg, the Bryants found a church whose British Anglophone membership of the church was much increased. This reflected the new popularity of Dowie's church with this language group, but it was also an indication of the large numbers of English-speakers pouring into the city after the war, part of the imperial government's Anglicization policies. In contrast to the impoverished Boer farmers whom Buchler had ministered to before the war, many of Zion's members were now from the city's semi-skilled English-speaking middle classes. Dowie's Transvaal followers in this postwar period numbered among them many policemen, school teachers, clerks, and solicitors. One Henry Ulyate, for example, was an electrician who played an active role in the Johannesburg Gathering and who rejoiced to "thank God that He saved me before I went very far down."[129] Another active member of the Johannesburg Gathering was J. Ord Armstrong, a bank clerk who had "belonged to the Wesleyans: but I always had a longing for a Gospel with more life and reality in it."[130] And then there was the Welshman, Henry Mordred Powell, a teacher who persuaded his wife to give up the "hot paraffin panels" she wore to alleviate her pleurisy (Powell recalled instructing her: "no wonder God did not answer; off with those things") and she was immediately delivered.[131]

Leading a church that now featured both Boer and British members in roughly equal numbers, the Bryants explicitly framed their work in Johannesburg as promoting racial reconciliation between the two formerly warring white "races." On the eve of their departure, Dowie instructed Bryant to "remember that Africa is in a transition state, and every kind word you can to say to heal the bleeding hearts you must speak."[132] He emphasized that as an American, Bryant could position himself in Johannesburg as "absolutely without entanglements . . . [and] be in a strong position to both Boer and Briton."[133] Bryant himself drew strong links between the reality of divine healing, on the one hand, and the possibility of reconciliation between Boer and Briton, on the other. He reflected that in the New Testament days it had been divine healing, carried out by Christ himself, that had unified formerly estranged Jews and Gentiles in a common cause: "Christ's ministry among the sick . . . brought Gentile and Jew together at his feet. The value of Christ's ministry among the sick lay not in the fact that men exchanged health for disease but in the fact that race prejudice and bigotry were broken down, and humanity partakers of a common woe came together to partake of the common cup of blessing which Jesus holds out to all alike . . . and it was Christ's power to heal the sick through prayer that first drew Briton and Boer to my ministry."[134]

For many of Johannesburg's Boer and British citizens in the postwar period, Dowie and Bryant's teachings profoundly resonated with their own contemporary concerns about white unity. Zion Gatherings sprung up in Johannesburg and its satellite towns on the Rand, including Germiston and Krugersdorp, as well as in Pretoria and Rustenberg.[135] Shortly after the

Bryants' arrival, the newly hired Zion Tabernacle on the corner of Bree and Smal Streets in downtown Johannesburg (this had formerly been the Presbyterian church[136]) was regularly filled with congregations of several hundred and no sitting space remaining.[137] Bryant proudly lauded that "our church in Johannesburg [was] one half Boer and one half Briton."[138] Although the war "has engendered much bitterness between the Dutch and English races," Bryant celebrated that "in our church they meet in a genuine Christian fellowship."[139] In addition to their weekly Sunday services in the Tabernacle—complete with singing from a white-robed choir—and regular "divine healing" services throughout the week, Johannesburg's Zionists engaged in a lively round of open-air preaching in the Market Square, and distribution of Zionist literature door-to-door and in the city's saloons and bars.[140] In exchange for former identities, they—in Daniel Bryant's reminiscences—"had found a standard they now loved more than their national colours . . . the blood-stained banner of the Cross . . . Briton and Boer had clasped hands at the Cross of Christ."[141]

British and Boer Zionists in Johannesburg also took encouragement from a related element of Dowie's teachings. Zion's espousal of divine healing and promotion of bodily well-being naturally complemented the contemporary bio-medical project of populating Johannesburg with a new breed of strong "Afrikanders"—the best of both British and Boer races.[142] A healthy reproduction rate and a settled family life were thought to facilitate a local white population loyal to empire. Dowie's focus on pro-natalism and the sanctity of the domestic sphere resonated with these preoccupations. *Leaves'* pages displayed Transvaalers' warm reception of Zion's promise of healthy babies born safely to mothers. Mrs. Lemke of Pretoria "gave up doctors, drugs and devils," and found God blessed her with the safe deliverance of a child.[143] Mrs. George Muloch, also of Pretoria, reported to readers that "God delivered me of a beautiful little daughter, without the aid of doctors or drugs, not having one drop of medicine or doctor in the house."[144] Mrs. Jubber of Braamfontein in downtown Johannesburg "resolved to give up all medicine, bandages and sitz baths, and wait on the Lord." The result was that "six months after, I was safely and quickly delivered of a Zion boy . . . he is an excellent advertisement for Zion."[145] Female correspondents supplied photographs showcasing their neat, nuclear families, arranged tidily in comfortable parlors, featuring abundant images of fat, healthy babies.[146] In later years, Bryant looked back on his collection of photographs from Johannesburg and found the one he "prized above all others." This was a picture of the ideal Christian family: "a happy-faced woman, with her little girl standing by her side . . . her husband's face is strong and healthy, his sleeves rolled up to his shoulders, he is

Lemke Family and Baby.
Source: Leaves of Healing 17,
no. 16, 29 July 1905, 430.
Christ Community Church
Archives, Zion, Illinois.

a carpenter, with steady employment and drawing good wages. His home is one of prayer, song, love and happiness."[147]

At a time when white residents of the Transvaal were coming to view themselves as simultaneous inhabitants of both South Africa and of a worldwide empire, conversion to Zion encouraged Transvaal members to imagine themselves part of a Christian communion that extended across the world. *Leaves* was key to facilitating Transvaal Zionists' international imagination. Dowie had commanded Bryant to "lay much stress on subscription to *Leaves* . . . this brings them into close touch both with myself, and Headquarters, and the wide scope of Zion throughout the world."[148] Converts viewed their testimonies and photographs alongside those contributed by worldwide believers. *Leaves* of April 1900 featured news items by and about fellow-believers in South Africa, Chicago, Indiana, Egypt, Kansas, and Canada. In similar fashion, the aforementioned "Zion Prayer Clock" in *Leaves* showed the time in Zion Gatherings around the world, emphasizing the church's shared global prayer and encouraging believers to keep in mind international brethren at all times.[149] By featuring devotional correspondence from across the world, the magazine cultivated a sense of a global cult of devotion to Zion's values, and to Dowie. One Pretoria correspondent wrote that, unable to see Zion's founder with his own eyes in far-off Illinois, he had instead "cut out [Dowie's] photograph from

Leaves and framed it." It now hung in his front living room.[150] In another issue of *Leaves,* a correspondent reported he had named his son "Dowie Junior," underscoring the close intimacy his entire family felt with the church headquarters in Zion City.[151] Several Zionists even managed to travel to Zion City in this period, as well to other Gatherings across the world. John Taylor traveled to Zion City in 1902, en route calling on fellow Zionists in Dundee and Edinburgh in Scotland, as well as connecting in Manchester with an old Zionist friend from Johannesburg, Ernest Cosgrove, formerly of the Royal Lancaster Regiments, sent to South Africa during the war.[152] In 1905, J. Ord Armstrong, also of Johannesburg, traveled to Zion City to train as a teacher in Zion's Educational Institution.[153] Arie van Woerkom, the former Methodist preacher who converted during Buchler's days, traveled to the Midwest for a convalescent stay in Zion City's divine healing home.[154] Whether in Zion City or in Johannesburg, Dowie instructed Bryant to remind South African Zionists they were part of a single global family, nothing less than the universal brotherhood of man: "Make them to understand that there are no separate churches; that they are all branches of one great, universal church; that there are no foreign fields, no home fields, but that everywhere Zion is one."[155]

However appealing Zion's vision of a new and unified humanity was to its devotees, and however much it echoed the contemporary rhetoric of racial reconciliation, there were important ways in which it did not tally with the political project of imperial White South Africanism. For one, officials of the new South Africa increasingly showcased scientific progress—including biomedical advancement—as the hallmark of an empire built on cooperation between Boer and Briton, rather than Anglo domination.[156] But Zionists in the Transvaal—as in the American Midwest—denounced the entire medical profession as the work of the Devil. Ernest Cox reported that he "prayed that peoples" eyes may be opened to see the farce of doctors, drugs, etc."[157] In common with adherents in Chicago and Zion City, Zionists in Johannesburg cast medical doctors as ruthlessly exploitative of suffering patients, especially female ones. Mrs. Lemke described how she "suffered untold misery" as three doctors twice scraped her uterus, and "a specialist for ladies" in Johannesburg informed her that he would need to perform a "very delicate operation, which would cost us seventy guineas."[158] In fact, Zionists asserted that medicine was the opposite of science. J. Ord Armstrong, injured in the war, lamented that "all the researchers and experiments and scientists have failed to lay a single stone for a foundation on which to build a science of medicine and surgery."[159]

The imperial establishment in turn-of-the-century Transvaal was deeply critical of these views, casting Dowietes—as they were called by the press in Johannesburg—as out-of-step with a modern white South Africa. The weekly *Transvaal Critic* called Zionism "a monument to the colossal gullibility of the world's inhabitants," and compared testimonies in *Leaves* to the patent medicine announcements that filled Johannesburg's newspapers.[160] Johannesburg's wider public was particularly concerned at the much-publicized death of several Zionists, due to their refusing medicine when ill. One young Boer man, Oswald Sussens, who died of "malarial fever," all the while resisting medical attention, attracted particular consternation.[161] An editorial in the *Rand Daily Mail* denounced "Dowiesm," in particular, and divine healing, in general, as "in defiance of all laws human and divine,"[162] lamenting that Dowie's "sect continues to grow and prosper in Johannesburg."[163] Another critical editorial reminded the public of the Transvaal's recently introduced Medicine Act, and advised members of the Christian Catholic Apostolic Church in Zion "to go easy on the Divine Healing racket, for we are a highly civilized but occasionally rough people and we do a little 'laying on of hands' ourselves sometimes."[164] In an era both of the gradual professionalization of the medical establishment and of shifting definitions of empire, divine healing came to be seen as an embarrassment to white settlers eager to style themselves as progressive moderns. The following pages demonstrate how Dowie's church also came to seem outdated to another constituency: the very class of urban working-class Boers who had initially given him such ready support.

Divisions in Worldwide Zion

By 1907 Zion's cosmopolitan empire, both at home and abroad, was catastrophically unraveling. Dissent against Dowie had steadily grown. In typical evangelical fashion, and following the anticlerical example of Dowie himself, many church members were resistant to the top-down hierarchies that now increasingly characterized the Zion organization. In particular, not all had accepted Dowie's declaration of himself as the reincarnation of the biblical prophet, Elijah. Dowie's Overseer in Detroit, Michigan, reported that despite leadership "believing Dr. Dowie is filled with Elijah's Spirit . . . some of the members of my church are not yet ready to accept that statement as truth."[165] Others in the church concluded that Dowie's pretensions to unique spiritual standing were nothing less than a massive fraud. A church elder in Port Huron, Michigan resigned in 1901 and "rejoiced greatly that I am free from the deception of Dowie . . . Dowie is the greatest pretender that ever struck this earth."[166] Dissent within Zion City also existed but was easier for Dowie to clamp down on. One Mrs. Emily

Ware and her father—she a writer for *Leaves*—"refused to accept certain claims which Dowie had recently made and which they openly insisted are pagan." Their punishment was to be "ejected into the street and ordered to leave town."[167] A steady trickle of dissenters in Zion City nonetheless abandoned Dowie. In 1903, about 150 families from Zion City left to found a new Zion City in Portland.[168] Another group of Zion City malcontents headed for San Antonio, Texas, and formed a "syndicate which will buy as much farm land as necessary to support all the settlers . . . the colony will be a Zion City without the one objectionable feature—Dowie . . . no man will set himself up to be a leader there."[169]

Dowie's sickness in 1906, combined with a precarious financial situation in Zion City, provided an opportunity for a new leader to overthrow him. Zion City had been in poor economic health since 1903 with its problems growing greater each year. This was due to long-standing structural issues within the settlement. In the estimation of at least one scholar, "inadequate capitalization, too many intermediaries, unwillingness to use outside resources, Dowie's willingness to pay overscale wages and his determination to honour dividends on Zion City stock regardless of earnings' were all contributing causes."[170] Dowie's sickness—he suffered a stroke in 1905—combined with the financial crisis gave his right-hand man and Australian Overseer, Wilbur Glenn Voliva, the opportunity to depose him in February 1906. Yet no sooner had he done so than Voliva established himself as an even more autocratic leader than Dowie. Once he had declared himself the church's new General Overseer—and with a sick Dowie exiled to his house in Zion City—Voliva used *Leaves* to inform Zion members in the United States and worldwide that he was their new absolute chief: "I am the chosen leader of the Lord and I have been commanded by God Almighty to lead his people of Zion."[171] Centralizing all power in his hands, Voliva passed a proposal granting him life tenure, and the right to appoint his successor.[172] Soon after, Dowie died in March 1907, and was widely labeled a madman (largely on the basis of his controversial "Elijah Declaration") by a hostile imperial press in South Africa, and by his own followers in the United States, many of whom now openly criticized Dowie's excesses.[173] An important exception to this general loss of confidence in Dowie was the church's African American membership, which almost entirely remained loyal to the beleaguered prophet. This was perhaps a sign of appreciation for Dowie's progressive stance on racial matters. A local newspaper from the neighboring town reported that "Dowie's church [as opposed to the Voliva-led majority] is now the church of the colored people. Almost to a man the colored people have stuck to the former first apostle."[174] At Dowie's funeral in 1907, one African American Evangelist Slater spoke "of the affection his race felt for Dr. Dowie . . . words are inadequate to express the express who have for our beloved leader."[175]

Although Voliva had declared himself Zion City's leader, in fact his claim to authority was even more contested by independent-minded rebels than Dowie's had been. Critics argued that Voliva's "one-man" rule was antagonistic to Zion's fundamentally egalitarian character. Overseer Piper, leader of the Chicago church, led the anti-Voliva fight, preaching "there is no basis for the tyrant, either in Scripture or history."[176] The Philadelphia church compared Voliva to the dreaded "Pope of Rome," a boogeyman figure who personified the triumph of a tyrannical individual over Scripture and conscience. Philadelphia sent thousands of pamphlets to Zion City demonstrating Voliva "rivals the Pope of Rome . . . such narrow-minded bigots as he have burned men at the stake, and he would do the same to make his rule supreme."[177] Dissent spread to the Northwestern states, with congregations in Portland, Seattle, and Vancouver revolting.[178] These groups soon fractured into multiple independent Zions. By "overwhelming vote," Cincinnati's congregation voted both to secede from Voliva, and to start their own local Zion church. For Cincinnati's Overseer, forming an independent Zion church was the God-ordained exercise of his conscience: "it was for me to either surrender my liberty, or do what I believed to be right and stand the consequences."[179] Within Zion City, too, independent Zion churches emerged, obedient to the promptings of their religious consciences. In 1907, *Zion City News* reported "religious leaders, like mushrooms, spring up overnight in Zion . . . we count not less than seven of these."[180] Many retained the name of Dowie's church, or a close variation, styling themselves as faithful heirs of the original Zion. The largest dissenting church—its name, the Christian Catholic Church in Zion, omitting the word "Apostolic"—also dubbed itself the "Independents," based on the principle of individual conscience in religious matters, and founded their own similarly named publication, *Zion City Independent*.[181] The church recalled the much-respected Daniel Bryant from Johannesburg to lead the congregation, aiming for a newly democratic mode of organization and governance, and argued Zion had financially collapsed because it "had rested entirely upon the personality of our leader."[182] Leading the Independents Bryant advocated a church with a "clearly defined constitution,"[183] a self-governing machinery that would endure the loss of an individual leader,[184] and—above all—guided by the Bible rather than a personality.[185]

In the Transvaal, too, many repudiated Voliva's leadership, underscoring the key role that the worldwide church could play in affairs in Zion City.[186] In fact, even before his return to the United States, Bryant had led disaffected Johannesburg Zionists against Voliva, who judged Zion City's new leader equally autocratic to Dowie in his ambitions for "one-man rule." In 1907, Bryant and the Johannesburg church had produced a local version of *Leaves of Healing,* labeling it the "South African Edition, Johannesburg," and pointedly making no mention of Zion City's new self-proclaimed leader, Voliva.[187] Moreover, in the immediate aftermath of the coup, Johannesburg Zionists—many of whom, as we have seen, were in these years British and English-speaking—considered especially objectionable Voliva's presumption that "an American [could] rule over the colonies of the British Empire" (the Scottish-Australian Dowie, of course, had been a British citizen, although he had taken an American passport in 1904).[188] Maintaining frequent correspondence with Bryant now located in Zion City leading the dissident Independent church, Johannesburg's Zionists continued their meetings in the Bree Street Tabernacle. But in this chaotic postcoup period, and amid confusion about the state of the church in North America, numbers of Zionists in South Africa severely declined. Government officials reported that "since the death of Dowie and the scathing exposures of the system [Zionists'] influence and numbers have been diminished."[189]

Within this vacuum, a new religious influence grew. A key dissenting group that would be influential in both Zion City and in Johannesburg was emerging under the auspices of the new Pentecostal revival. Between 1904 and 1906, a series of revivals occurred within transnational Holiness, Higher Life, and divine healing networks concentrated in Wales, Australia, India, and the United States. These individuals sought to recapture what they considered to be the preeminent outer sign of inner spiritual sanctification—glossolalia, or the ecstatic practice of speaking in the heavenly tongues of the angels, as described in the New Testament account of the Feast of Pentecost.[190] Already primed by Dowie's teachings regarding personal holiness, several of Zion City's residents traveled west and became leading figures in one of the main Pentecostal revivals of the day, centered in the Apostolic Faith Mission in downtown Los Angeles.[191] Via these intermediaries, as well as through the widely circulating print periodicals of the revival, Pentecostal teachings took root in Zion City. They rapidly became a locus of resistance to Voliva, who fiercely opposed the new teachings regarding "the Baptism in the Holy Spirit," and the "insane ecstasies" produced by speaking in tongues, pronouncing that "men and women go wild . . . [and] end up so physically debilitated as to give the demons a chance to reincarnate themselves."[192] But many Zion adherents did not agree with Voliva. Charles Parham, one of the major North American Pentecostal leaders, considered Zion City such a promising site for recruits that in 1907 he erected a large tent for revival meetings on the outskirts of the city.[193] Hundreds soon defected from Zion to Pentecost, with a local newspaper commenting that "the rapid, recent growth of the [Pentecostal] Apostolic Faith Mission . . . now claims the attention and sympathy of many of our best people."[194] In 1908, Daniel Bryant, recently returned to Zion City from Johannesburg to lead the new Independent church, himself became a devotee of the Pentecostal revival, regularly welcoming prominent Pentecostal pastor William Durham from Chicago to preach to his anti-Voliva congregation.[195]

In tandem with rebels in Zion City, and in particular, the influential Daniel Bryant, the dissenting Johannesburg church soon also embraced the new Pentecostal teachings. A key figure was John G. Lake, a former deacon of Dowie's in Zion City who participated in Apostolic Faith Mission meetings in Los Angeles in 1906.[196] In 1908, Lake and several associates arrived in Johannesburg—coming via Zion City—as independent Pentecostal missionaries.[197] Lake's close associations with Zion City, and the interest many in Zion City, including the much-respected in Johannesburg Daniel Bryant, had displayed toward Pentecost meant that many of Johannesburg's Zionists accorded "an open-hearted welcome" to Lake's teachings.[198] Lake and his associates initially held services both in the Zion Tabernacle on Bree Street, as well as in the private homes of Zion's membership in both Johannesburg and Pretoria.[199] Soon, almost all of South African Zion, including its most prominent and active members, had received the Pentecostal "Baptism of the Holy Ghost"—or the ability to speak in ecstatic tongues.[200] The advent of Pentecost brought a great number of new members to the church. At a service in Johannesburg in 1908, twenty-six new members were baptized in the Spirit, "most of them speaking in unknown tongues, some interpreting."[201] Initially, Johannesburg's spirit-baptized Zionists viewed the Apostolic Faith Mission's (AFM) Pentecostalism as a complementary variation on Dowie's teachings rather than as a break with them. Deacon Lemke from Zion's Gathering in Pretoria, himself newly spirit-baptized, highlighted the interchangeability of "Zion" and "Pentecost" in this period in Johannesburg in his comment that "nine-tenths of the blessed ones [those baptized in the "Spirit"] are Christian Catholics [Zionists]."[202] The wider public also perceived the distinction between these religious groups as a negligible one. The local press interchangeably referred to "Zion Tabernacle" as a name for Johannesburg's AFM organization, and journalists likewise referred to the AFM's new members as "Brothers of Zion."[203]

However much they initially perceived themselves as aligned with Zion, in fact these dissenting Johannesburgers soon distanced themselves from the older internationalist values of Zion as defined by Dowie. The context was a growing local antagonism toward imperialist jingoism and a corresponding rise in Boer nationalism. The government's racial reconciliation projects had by no means been entirely successful. Boer anti-imperial sentiment persisted, particularly given the persistence of anti-Boer propaganda in the English-language press.[204] The idea of Boer-English reconciliation based on mutual respect for the different cultures and languages turned out to have little backing from many Anglophone scholars and writers. Natal politician and imperialist ideologue George Heaton Nicholls summed up the mood of the day: "we had gone about talking of a South African nation which would consist of English and Dutch, but at the back of our minds we had supposed that they would talk English. We aimed at Anglicization."[205] Many Boers came to feel that Botha's optimistic talk about Union and reconciliation between the two white groups had come too soon. Barry Hertzog, a former Boer general during the war, articulated this growing sentiment. For Botha, English and Afrikaners could exist as a single, harmonious current, but Hertzog poke of them as flowing in two streams, side by side.[206] Anti-imperial tensions were brought to a head by the Union Government's entry into World War I on the side of the Allies. General Koos de la Rey—a famous *Bittereinder*[207] during the war—led a Rebellion against Botha and the Union Government.[208] In 1914, Hertzog founded the National Party in Bloemfontein, the Orange Free State capital. The Party explicitly aimed at freeing South African from an imperial relationship, instead nurturing a burgeoning sense of Boer nationalism. The growing Afrikaner working-class—located in suburbs such as Vrededorp—would become a key constituency in support of Hertzog's ethnic nationalism.[209]

This new mood of Boer ethnic nationalism easily converged with Pentecostals' stress on the importance of local, regional affiliations. Dowie's church had portrayed itself as a worldwide movement, strongly rooted in the Midwestern Zion City as its physical and spiritual headquarters yet at the same time deeply invested in the worldwide Gatherings that signaled the ushering in of the universal brotherhood of man. Connections and correspondence between Zion City and these international Gatherings was key. By contrast to the centrality of Zion City, one of the key characteristics of the new Pentecostal revival—not only in Johannesburg, but around the world—was its highly decentralized nature—even more so than Zion—and the absence of a single physical headquarters in the United States, or indeed anywhere else. In keeping with this decentralized logic, Lake and his associates emphasized the Johannesburg AFM's financial and institutional independence from a worldwide organization, naming the organization the Apostolic Faith Mission of South Africa.[210] Their periodical, *God's Latter Rain,* proclaimed they were an autonomous outfit, loosely linked to the global movement but ultimately independent: "we are the Apostolic Faith Movement of Johannesburg, South Africa, which is included in the great worldwide Holy Ghost Revival which has taken its impetus from the Azusa Street Mission, Los Angeles, California."[211] And while the *Leaves* had emphasized Zion's global character by displaying letters from across the world, Lake's *Latter Rain* featured only South African correspondence, emphasizing their local character. Further underscoring its territorial rootedness, *Latter Rain*'s first issue carried a "history of the movement in South Africa," and featured sections in Dutch.[212] Although initially allied with this separatist movement, Bryant and leading Independents in Zion City soon denounced Johannesburg Pentecostals' increasing autonomy from the United States and from the worldwide Zion church: "They said, 'Let us cut ourselves off from those who have brought disgrace upon us, and let us go forward with our own work.' I loved South Africa passionately but South Africa was not big enough for my spirit when cut off from my brethren . . . our fellowship must be a worldwide fellowship because Jesus said 'Go ye into the world.' "[213]

In its new Pentecostal incarnation, Johannesburg's Zion was also changing its membership composition, returning to its earlier prewar roots. In the immediate postwar years, it had had had a mixed Boer-British membership, but by 1908, Pentecostal Zion in Johannesburg was increasingly constituted by a new class of Dutch urban poor.[214] John G. Lake and his colleagues had begun work in the city during the closing days of the severe 1906–1908 depression, which had particularly affected Boers' employment prospects. Lake reported on the "intense poverty" of early Boer Pentecostals in Johannesburg, noting "you cannot keep a shilling in your pocket when you meet hungry women and children every day."[215] The doctrine of baptism in the Holy Ghost accompanied by Dowie's older stress on divine healing, both of which advocated believers' possession of unparalleled spiritual power, seem to have held a particular appeal for this constituency. As historian David Maxwell has noted, amid a pervasive culture of white poverty, alcoholism, and crime, the abstemious moral codes of Pentecostalism, deeply entrenched in the movement's Holiness roots, established a new white working-class "counter-society" in Johannesburg, within which devotees "reordered their social life . . . discipline[ed] their speech and sexuality, and adopted a puritan work ethic."[216] There was indeed a correlation between Johannesburg's poorest areas, on the one hand, and the most vigorous work of the AFM, on the other. The inner-city district of Vrededorp—the site of labor militancy among the Afrikaner poor—was also a site of vibrant AFM activity. Vrededorp, Lake reported, "has seen some of the most miraculous healings."[217] Contemporary opinion interpreted Pentecostalism's popularity among this group by citing the supposedly innate preference of unlearned Boers for magical remedies. A journalist attending an AFM service at the old Bree Street Tabernacle in 1909 commented the congregation was mainly "illiterate South Africans," susceptible to divine healing because of poor education and superstition: "here were women from Vrededorp, Braamfontein and Fordsburg who in their heart of hearts believe there is no internal medicine like the ordure of goats and Cape Dop [alcohol]."[218] Indicating the rapid shift of Pentecostal Zion (now increasingly known as the AFM) from a mixed membership to a largely Boer constituency, in 1916, a city official estimated that "all the European workers of the AFM are South Africa born and mostly of Dutch descent."[219] The first AFM census carried out in 1926 recorded that for over 12,000 of the overall membership of 15,000, their home language was Dutch—increasingly coming to be known as Afrikaans.[220]

Influenced by the broader surge of Boer nationalism, these working-class Pentecostals in Johannesburg were increasingly repudiating their internationalist Zion origins. By about 1910, the name Zion was no longer being used interchangeably by members of the ever-larger Apostolic Faith Mission. This was also the year in which the AFM printed its own baptismal certificates, which omitted any mention of "Zion," and used the name of their own denomination on official documents for the first time.[221] This shift away from Zion was partly attributable to the admittedly Anglophone imperial character of the Zionist church in Johannesburg—this despite the best efforts of Dowie and his deputies to cast the organization as a universalist, cosmopolitan home for Boers and Britons alike. Pro-imperial commentators had already cast the war as a race conflict between industrious, modernizing Anglo-Saxons and backward pastoralist Boers who, according to the *New York Times,* represented "the barbarism and despotism . . . of the dark ages."[222] In like fashion, by the early years of the war, Dowie was no longer lauding the pastoral values of the "Netherlandish race." Instead, the *Leaves* bemoaned the Boers' "ignorance": "they do not know much . . . their ignorance is appalling. They have very few books and do not care to read."[223] Boer women were cast as sexually immoral; they had "most shamefully prostituted themselves [during the war] . . . displaying "absolute lust."[224] According to Dowie, Boer men were naturally bloodthirsty, trained to kill from youth for pleasure.[225] Dowie also attacked the Boers on the basis that they were out of step with the progressive, paternalistic values of the British Empire, which "establishes everywhere the equality of every man under the law."[226] By contrast, the Boers were brutal oppressors of other races: "You say it was their country. It was no such thing. They came and took it from the Kaffirs. They flogged, murdered and enslaved the Kaffirs."[227]

Thus despite the universalistic aspirations of the church, the truth was that Dowie's opinions, as well as the views of its top leadership in South Africa, were flavored by jingoistic imperial superiority. While Dowie celebrated the cosmopolitan diversity of Zion, in fact the one true universal language of the world for him was none other than English, the tongue of empire. Dowie reminded Bryant that "it is better for the Boers to drop their Dutch and teach their children the English language, which is far more comprehensive." Dowie's hope was that the Boers' "hybrid language . . . will soon pass away."[228] Furthermore, despite his instructions to Bryant to "bind the wounded hearts" in Johannesburg, Dowie's view had in fact been that the necessary fate of the Boers was incorporation into the British Empire. Indeed, despite much public sympathy for the Boers in the United States, American politicians such as Theodore Roosevelt were still convinced that it was Britain's manifest destiny to rule lesser races.[229] Dowie's own views tallied with these. Although he sympathetically named the Boers a "crushed people who had lost their national independence,"[230] Dowie also concluded they had committed a sin of great hubris in defying the empire.[231] Dowie's view of empire was ultimately a pragmatic one, perceiving it as necessary for the maintenance of international peace and thereby a force that mitigated against all-out warfare—the latter the true sin in the eyes of the deity. An early prewar editorial in *Leaves* remarked "it is safe to say that there are 500 million today who are sitting in peace and with prosperity against that great British flag . . . the Royal lady who sits on the throne has constantly cast all her power upon the side of peace, peace, PEACE!"[232] As such, Dowie highlighted the "absurdity" of the Boers who "defied an empire of 500 000 000 people."[233] Boer destiny was imperial assimilation: "God in His Providence has designed that the late Boer Republics shall become part of the British Empire until "He Has Come, Whose Right it is to Reign."[234]

In the context of a working-class Boer revolt against the Anglicization policies undergirding white South Africanism, the Anglophone values of Dowie's worldwide church seemed increasingly ill-fitted to the popular mood. By contrast, the Pentecostal AFM seemed more sympathetic to the growing mood of ethnic nationalism. The AFM's official line—consonant with the position of many early generation of Pentecostals across the world—was to remain detached from explicit political involvement, including military service in World War I.[235] AFM adherents had links to both the Boer Republicanism of General de la Rey, and to the ethnic nationalism of Hertzog's Nationalist Party. AFM Executive Council minutes of 1914 mention AFM "brothers" arranging a visit to the Republican general, while Barry Hertzog's wife was a life-long member of the AFM in the town of Bloemfontein.[236] Hertzog attended the Dutch Reformed Church, but when news of his wife's Pentecostal baptism was scurrilously chronicled in the daily newspapers, he refused to criticize her "commitment to the Lord."[237] And within the AFM, Boer converts found a church willing to sanction their burgeoning sense of ethnic nationalism as divinely ordained. Pentecostal emissary John G. Lake, for example, admiringly commented that his Boer converts "intensely love the traditions of their race."[238] The heart of the "race," however, was not language or culture, but rather the "spirit of faith" that historically animated the Dutch settlers in the Cape. Protestant Huguenots, "the early founders of South Africa . . . came to Africa for Jesus' sake, to escape persecution of the Catholics, came in the power of God, were baptized in the Holy Ghost." In the AFM's work among the Boers, the Huguenots' "children," "the touch of God through the Holy Ghost is causing the old faith flame to burn" again.[239] Further indicating the mutually symbiotic relationship between Pentecostals and nationalists, while new Dutch-language newspapers publicized the nationalist cause and inserted the plight of the *taal* [tongue] into the public sphere, they also simultaneously chronicled AFM activities.[240] One of the first members of the AFM was a Mr. Schumann, who in addition to having the "demons of drink" exorcised from him by Lake, was also the editor of *Die Transvaler* . . . an independent secular Dutch paper with a weekly circulation of 5000." In 1908 Schumann's paper featured a four-page religious supplement on the AFM.[241]

Perhaps most important, the Boer character of the AFM increasingly defined itself against the racial cosmopolitanism of Zion. This was true with regard to the Zionist church's progressivism on the Boer-British "racial" question, and it was especially true with regard to what was known as the "native question"—the role of nonwhite peoples within the modern Transvaal Republic and within the new Union of South Africa as a whole. One of the linchpins of Boer nationalism was the protection of white jobs against cheap black labor, a goal increasingly thought to be achievable only through thoroughgoing racial segregation.[242] Yet the AFM's status as a protector of white supremacy was not immediately obvious. English-speaking public opinion worried that the AFM's practices of Baptism in the Holy Spirit might have politically undesirable effects on South Africa's black population, unloosing in them religious passions that might have more broadly subversive effects. A *Rand Daily Mail* editorial noted the "most grave feature of the spread of the [AFM] is its attitude towards the native races," reporting on the "terrible danger" of "extraordinary scenes among the Kaffirs . . . whole congregations have fallen prostrate and spoken with tongues."[243] It was indeed the case that Johannesburg's former Zionists viewed Baptism in the Holy Ghost as equally available to all, regardless of race. However, this period also witnessed an increasing racial segregation in AFM church life. Lake publicly supported the government's racial policies, admiringly comparing segregation to America's stance toward Native Americans: "the policy [was] in harmony with our American policy of segregation of the Indian tribes."[244] Lake also criticized the naïveté of foreign missionaries who arrived in South Africa with misguided notions of social equality, brandishing "brand new American ideas to teach to the natives." Lake cautioned that according an equal status to black converts was a grave error: the "African native is very different to the American Negro . . . he is a heathen."[245]

Johannesburg's AFM-Zion members soon came to entirely eschew Dowie's advocacy of mixed worship conducted without a "colour-line." As early as 1908, the AFM's committee decided "the baptism of Natives shall in the future take place after the baptism of White people."[246] By 1909, segregation was complete: "in future, the baptism of Whites, Coloured and Natives shall be separate."[247] In 1917, the AFM Executive Council declared that "we do not teach or encourage social equality between Whites and Natives . . . we wish it to be generally known that our White, Coloured, and Native peoples have their separate places of worship."[248] By 1944, the official policy of the AFM was that "the mission stands for segregation. The fact that the Native, Indian or Coloured is saved does not render him European."[249] The transformation of this Holiness-inspired group of Transvaal urban evangelicals was now complete. Originally participants within an early twentieth-century internationalist movement that promoted racial "blending" as a forerunner of the Kingdom of God, by the middle of the same century this group now identified itself part of an organization that emphasized the divine mandate undergirding ethnic particularity and linguistic and cultural nationalism.

CHAPTER FOUR

Zion's Egalitarian Promises in the Transvaal and Orange River Colonies, South Africa

Elijah Lutango was a sharecropping farmer in the rural district of Harrismith in the Orange River Colony, a territory under British rule since the Boer defeat of 1902, and part of a broad swathe of arable land known as the Highveld. Formerly a Methodist lay preacher, Lutango—in common with thousands of other black Africans resident on the farms of the Highveld—joined Dowie's church in the early years of the twentieth century. Like many others the world over, Lutango was drawn to the church's promise of divine healing and full spiritual and bodily restoration. Alongside divine healing, one aspect in particular of the church's ministry in South Africa impressed Lutango. This was the insistence of the church leadership—both in Zion City and in South Africa—that the hallmark of the Kingdom of God was the unhindered fraternizing of white and black people. Lutango's testimony, printed in *Leaves of Healing* in 1905, marveled that in the work of the Christian Catholic Apostolic Church in Zion, black and white worked closely together in egalitarian and collaborative relationships. Lutango observed that such free mingling of the races was largely unknown in other churches in South Africa: "in all Africa such love has not been known. They do not have it any of the churches." Moreover, those in South Africa had as their guiding light the example of Zion City in America, considered by many black South Africans to be a shining beacon testifying to the promises of God that his people would be one in every way. Truly, in this church Lutango felt that he had finally found the "brotherly love which is needed between the white and black who profess to love the Christ." In contrast to the other churches—and including his own former Methodist denomination—Lutango knew that in Dowie's church the order of the day was "the True Love which does not separate brethren because of difference in the colour of their skins."[1]

Zion's cosmopolitan evangelicalism had only a limited lifespan among white adherents. This chapter shows how and why Zion's adoption by black African farmers of the South African Highveld proved far more enduring. This was a class facing intense social, political, and economic stress as racial segregation and territorial segregation accelerated in the years after the South African War. White "racial" unity had been sought at the expense of the region's non-white population. Against this harsh backdrop, a class of progressive and self-consciously modernizing African farmers found in the Christian Catholic Apostolic Church in Zion a deeply countercultural organization that proclaimed the equality of all races. Furthermore, a key component of the identity of the rural black elite—and one under threat by the imperial government's suppression of black advancement and education—was the assertion of their own superiority in relation to their less educated African compatriots still supposedly mired in "heathen" tradition. In the northern hemisphere, as well as in white circles in South Africa, divine healing was increasingly viewed as out of step with medical progress and learning, but this first generation of black Southern African Zionists recast divine healing as a technique for announcing their status as progressive educated "moderns." Affiliating with Zion meant decisively breaking with the older order of health and healing represented by traditional healers, chiefs, and local patriarchs. At a time when divine healing was struggling to gain adherents elsewhere in the world, African converts succeeded in reinfusing new energy and significance into this evangelical Protestant tradition. Their employment of prayer for their bodily ailments asserted blacks' status as coequals with civilized men and women the world over, of all races.

Yet in these agricultural regions of South Africa, as in the city of Johannesburg, Zion's success as a cosmopolitan project was limited. Following Dowie's death in 1907, the church in South Africa became increasingly stratified along racial lines. Many black adherents found they were better able to enact the egalitarian promises of Zion by breaking away from American and local white figures, and instead forming independent Zion churches that stressed black leadership and autonomy from white missionaries. Instead of the older vision of the church of a cosmopolitan crossroads of the nations, these reformist strata of Zionists now began to experiment with an alternative set of contemporary ideas regarding black solidarity and racial self-reliance. Amid the failure of imperial powers to deliver multiracial citizenship, many African elite (including early Zion converts) were invoking self-consciously Africanist identities. This chapter charts this complex interplay between cosmopolitan theology and racially in-flected thinking that characterized the first-generation of early twentieth-century black Zionist converts in South Africa. As is evident at other points in the story of the People's Zion, Zion's evangelical values were not expressed within a vacuum. Instead, the challenges faced by black Zion cosmopolitans during these years exemplify the complex accommodations and compromises these radical idealists were compelled to make.

Race, Empire, and Ethiopian Christians

The last years of the nineteenth century were a period of growth for a small section of African peasantry on the South African Highveld. This was a stretch of inland plateau that encompassed the city of Johannesburg as well as some of the region's most productive farming land.[2] The discovery of precious minerals in Kimberley in 1871 and on the Witwatersrand in 1886 had given new outlets to rural black farming populations who now found themselves well positioned to produce and supply foodstuffs to the booming new cities.[3] On paper, the legislation of the Boer Republics militated against African economic flourishing; Africans could not own land in either the Or-ange Free State or the Transvaal. But in practice, the fragility of the relatively recent white agricultural economy, combined with greater African farming skill and labor surpluses, meant that some black producers still found modest opportunities to thrive.[4] In both Republics (especially the Free State), sharecropping—or "farming-by-the-halves" whereby Africans farmed a section of a white farmer's land and gave the latter a portion of the yield—became the dominant economic relationship. Sharecropping generated profits for talented African farmers, and its effect was to produce a small class of semiautonomous farmers who increasingly viewed themselves as a new black elite in their pursuit of individual landownership and the accumula-tion of capital.[5] The South African War was particularly devastating for black Africans on the Highveld; however, this hardship brought some ben-efits through the higher wages Africans earned in this period as well as in profits earned from farmers' food production for the troops.[6] And after the cessation of hostilities, many Africans took advantage of the brief lifting of restrictions on black land ownership in the Transvaal to invest their earnings in land purchase.

This small rural elite expressed great confidence in the British Empire. Many hoped that British victory over the Boers meant Africans would now become full members of an empire that positioned itself as a color-blind worldwide federation, promising equal standing to all subjects who embraced its progressive values. Indeed, this class had long sought to style itself as civilized moderns, detached from the traditional order and striving to transcend older ethnic and tribal identities.[7] The universalizing message of nineteenth-century Protestantism was particularly important in the formation of their progressive, aspirational ethos. Mission societies' message of Christ's redemptive death for all—regardless of race, class, or gender—was appropriated by many Africans in their wider search for racial equality.[8] These intertwined ideals of Christian fraternity and imperial citizenry were especially prevalent in the Cape, with its promise of franchise and equality for all subjects of the British Empire. These ideas were also espoused by Africans in the Transvaal and Orange Free State: Methodism's emphasis on self-improvement and personal holiness was particularly successful in this arable region.[9] Christianity and education, moreover, were intimately intertwined, with missionaries equipping converts with the skills to read the sacred scriptures, resulting in many black farmers undergoing several years of mission school education.[10] Many black sharecroppers were firm believers in the power of education to make Africans the equals of Europeans; many invested in building schools on their own land, hired African teachers at their own cost, and carved school desks for their children.[11]

In the aftermath of the war, however, the aspirations of these black elite were deeply under threat. In fact, their position had already been in deterioration by the end of the nineteenth century, due to a devastating succession of drought, rinderpest and other epizootics, as well as escalating pressures against African "squatting" on white farms. Small struggling farmers—usually of Boer background and in desperate need of African labor to make ends meet—had long been hostile to black competitors.[12] Although repressive laws designed to suppress the flourishing of the African peasantry had existed since the middle of the nineteenth century, in reality, the financial balance of interests meant these were inconsistently applied, despite a widespread racist rhetoric that decried the "indolent" prosperous African farmer.[13] But after the war a series of political and economic developments changed all this. The victory of Afrikaner political interests—in particular, the coming to power of Het Volk in the Transvaal in 1907 and the concessions made by the British to Boer leaders in the 1910 Union of South Africa[14]—turned the tide in favor of small-scale Boer farmers, rather than British-born absentee landowners. A decisive factor in the long-coming demise of the African peasantry was the intervention of the imperial government in the agricultural sector. Policy was now geared toward the creation of a British settler farming community, viewed as key to South Africa's flourishing within the empire.[15] Large amounts of money poured into white-owned farms, giving greater urgency to the necessity of limiting the autonomy of African sharecroppers by forcing them into disadvantageous labor tenancy arrangements. The infamous 1913 Natives Land Act both reduced the land available for African purchase to less than 10 percent of the country's territory as well as abolished sharecropping. Both changes reflected the contemporary goal of tightening white landlords' grip over black tenants.[16] Far from ushering in the hoped-for race-blind polity, as Britain sought strategic compromises with disaffected Boers, imperial rule on the Highveld in fact meant increased great strictures on black social and economic mobility, and the formation of a new South Africa aligned with white interests at the expense of nonwhites.[17]

In the Transvaal Colony (formerly the Transvaal or South African Republic), the decade after the war saw greater limits placed on the autonomy and wealth of black farmers. In Wakkerstroom, a large district of the eastern Transvaal (especially known for its sheep and cattle farming[18]), the early twentieth century was more broadly perceived by Africans as a time of exceptional suffering. Poverty and starvation was prevalent due to drought.[19] Rinderpest and the seizure of African stock during the war had decimated livelihoods. Many Africans were still waiting for imperial compensation for their devastating losses.[20] The complaint of one Wakkerstroom farmer, Muneli Ngobese (later a convert to Dowie's Christian Catholic Apostolic Church in Zion), was typical: "The Dutch soldier commandeered my horse. The English burned my house. I put in a claim for horse and home when peace came, but the English told me they had nothing to do with the Boers taking my horse and they were not paying for the houses they had burned."[21]

The Natives Land Act of 1913 designated Wakkerstroom as one of the few areas with several African-owned freehold farms included in the "Schedule of Native Areas."[22] Some of these—farms such as Driefontein and Daggakraal—had been purchased immediately prior to the Act's passing by the farsighted Native Farmers' Association of South Africa, an organization established by black lawyer and later president of the African National Congress, Pixley ka Isaka Seme. Amid a climate of land evictions and grave fears for the future, the purpose of the Association was to purchase land that could then be carved up and sold off to African smallholding farmers.[23] For those not lucky enough to possess one of these properties, Africans in Wakkerstroom district were permitted to squat on farmers' land. In return, they worked the land for several months annually, and paid rent. It was a system designed to squeeze maximum labor out of black tenants for labor-hungry white farmers. The British government collected £2 annual tax, a device to compel Africans to work further for employers. Tenants considered idle were ejected, as were tenants in excess of five families, in order to achieve what officials considered "a better distribution of labour."[24] White farmers used techniques of intimidation, including beatings and sexual violence.[25] The same Ngobese cited above commented that "our sorrow is that we live on land rented from the white man. We pay him rent but we have little peace."[26] Underpinning this exploitation was a racial ideology that cast Africans as intrinsically inferior and best-suited manual work. African self-improvement was therefore discouraged. Government officials and white farmers disapproved of "book learning" for Africans, believing industrial education of more use—although "it is not intended that [natives] should be made proficient enough to compete with European artisans."[27] Aspirational Africans in Wakkerstroom protested their second-class citizenship by arguing their education advanced them beyond "tribalism." Samuel Zungu, a Methodist preacher in the district, cited his education in pleading with the state to "exempt [him] from carrying passes and suffering under the general disabilities to which men of his colour are subjected."[28]

Conditions in the postwar neighboring Orange River Colony (formerly the Orange Free State) were even more repressive. Unlike in the Transvaal, Africans were not even permitted to own land. Two "native locations" existed—Witzieshoek in the east, and Thaba 'Nchu in the southwest—under nominal control of chiefs and tightly administered by government officials.[29] As in Wakkerstroom, most Africans lived in some form of share-cropping arrangement, working a portion of the white farmer's land annually in return for grazing space for their herds. Similar to the Transvaal, the postwar years saw a repressive clampdown on African independent economic activity. As elsewhere, white agriculture was going through a phase of state-driven "increased development," which meant "there is little doubt that demand for native labour has grown."[30] Yet everywhere white farmers complained of the shortage of African labor,[31] something they attributed to Africans' economic independence as sharecroppers, the high wages and compensation they had received during the war, and reluctance to take on poorly paid work that they were in no need of.[32] Calls to enforce legislation limiting black sharecroppers' wealth abounded. To better regulate the supply of black labor, Africans' movement throughout the colony was extremely constricted. Draconian "Pass Laws" reduced African mobility both without and inside the colony, with heavy fines and jail time exacted for those traveling without documentation.[33] Educated Africans loudly complained. Harrismith town was the second largest town in the colony, with a population of 8,300, including 3,924 "coloured" inhabitants, and its "Native Vigilance Committee"—composed of members of the town's black elite such as schoolteachers and religious ministers—lamented "this law is a yoke that we cannot bear the demands of . . . the pass law threatens our welfare as people and places us men, women and children in a dangerous position."[34] Africans who had hoped imperial rule would encourage black advancement expressed severe disappointment. The African Methodist minister Rev. Kumalo had "looked forward to the British occupation of this land to grant us greater freedom . . . to aspire to better and higher things, and to bring us out of barbarism and make us worthy citizens of the British Empire." But the reality was sadly different. In writing a petition to the British governor of the colony, Lord Selbourne, Kumalo "regretted to inform your Excellency that we [the black people] are today hindered to a greater extent than ever."[35]

Influenced by these wider trends, white Christian missionaries were also retreating from former more racially progressive stances. Rather than regarded as the intrinsic equal of Europeans—given, of course, correct tutelage to lift them up out of "barbarism"—Africans were now increasingly viewed by missionaries as fundamentally inferior to the ruling Anglo-Saxon race.[36] Profound tensions resulted between black Christians and white missionaries. Foremost among African grievances was missionaries' reluctance to ordain Africans as ministers, despite the foundational understanding of most missions that the goal was transition to "home rule."[37] While an earlier generation of missionaries invested in African ministerial training, by the late nineteenth century Eastern Cape missionary J. Davidson, for example, could state that "a native is not made fit to occupy the position of a missionary in charge of an old station with its schools, finances and relations to the European community."[38] Throughout the new colonies of South Africa, African Christians complained about discrimination in many aspects of church life, including receiving a fraction of the salaries of white counterparts, and having no allowance made for supporting their wives and children.[39] Missionaries even seemed to be reneging on their former commitment to educate Africans to a level of full equality with Europeans. Rev. Goring was a Congregationalist missionary in the Orange River Colony; in 1905, he reported to Native Affairs officials in Bloemfontein that "manual work must go with or before mental instruction,"[40] while a Lutheran missionary in the same Colony noted that "as missionaries we do not think it advisable to make Africans big scholars."[41]

Confronted by the intransigent refusal of whites to think in terms that transcended racial difference, some African Christians became more concerned with promoting black solidarity. In 1884, the Methodist minister Nehemiah Tile in the Cape split from the Wesleyans, and formed the Tembu Church, with Ngangelizwe, the chief of the Tembu, as its head. Far from representing a narrow ethnic particularism, the Tile Church drew in members beyond the Thembu chiefdom, including the neighboring Transkei.[42]

A further example was the formation on the Witwatersrand in 1892 of the Ethiopian Church, an organization founded by another former Methodist minister, Mangena Mokone. Mokone appealed to "Ethiopia" as one of the few independent African states and invoked its ancient indigenous tradition of Christianity autonomous of European missionaries.[43] Further Africanist Christian institutions of this period were P. J. Mzimba's African Presbyterian Church, and Simungu Shibe's Zulu Congregational Church, both founded in 1898, also on the Witwatersrand.[44] Many of these "Ethiopian" Christians formed alliances with the worldwide black diaspora. Mokone's church made contact with the black African Methodist Episcopal (AME) Church in the United States; both organizations shared a common interest in uplifting black people through strategies of economic uplift and racial self-reliance. A lively two-way traffic of African and North American clergymen ensued between South Africa and the United States, and the AME church quickly spread across the Transvaal and Orange River Colonies.[45] In the years after the war, Africanist religious organizations sprang up elsewhere in the Transvaal and in the Orange River Colony. In Wakkerstroom, former Methodist preacher, Joel Msimang, inaugurated the Independent Wesleyan Church, a church that stressed black leadership and allied itself to the AME Church in the United States.[46] By 1911, the Witzieshoek Location in Harrismith had, in addition to four churches under European control, ten other churches that were entirely African-led and which proclaimed themselves "Ethiopian."[47]

The refusal of blacks to accept a subordinate role with respect to the white race lay at the heart of this program, a fact that was perceived by white farmers and the colonial administration with great anxiety. Ethiopian preachers in the Transvaal were reputed to teach that "having learnt the way of salvation from the white man . . . [we are] now the equal of the white people, and therefore why should [we] look to them for assistance, as being equals [we] are quite capable of acting independently."[48] Anecdotes were darkly cited in support of the observation that "Ethiopianism" in the Colony meant that "natives are now less respectful and less amenable to the influence of Europeans than hitherto."[49] Indeed, the writings of AME American officials were quite definite that black and white races should not intermingle. The AME *Voice of Missions,* published in the United States and circulated in South Africa, proclaimed that "if the Anglo-Saxon cannot mingle his blood by wedlock with the aborigines of the country which he grabs, why does he not keep his feet in England on the fenders of his hearth?"[50] Anxiously surveying these publications, officials in the Transvaal and Orange River Colonies felt justified in their views that the American-derived AME church espouses "anti-Anglo Saxon comments" and held dangerous "pro-African independence statements."[51] Wakkerstroom's farmers bitterly complained that "alien" preachers in the area were "using the Cloak of the Gospel to preach the equality of the races" to their black tenants.[52]

However, this increasing shift toward black Christians renouncing fraternity with whites was not a seamless development. For one, significant tensions existed within these transatlantic black Christian alliances. African Americans continued to espouse racist hierarchies, with "ignorant" black Africans viewed as lower down the evolutionary ladder than black Americans.[53] Africans accused Americans of relegating "the men of this country to secondary place."[54] Moreover, many Africans in the Transvaal and Orange River Colonies continued to value the concept of a multiracial fraternity of Christians. One Methodist preacher—Rev. Joel Goronyane from Thaba 'Nchu—aspired for the full equality of the colony's races ("I do not like there to be two laws, one for the white and one of the natives"), and was critical of Ethiopian Christians precisely for the fact that they repudiated this ideal: "I think the people [white and black] ought to work together, that is why I do not agree with the Ethiopian movement."[55] One Rev. Brander separated from the American AME church due to a dispute over finances. But he had also come to aspire for greater racial harmony between whites and blacks—a goal that he found the AME church had little interest in—"When we are educated, we can be united with the white races and we can be one with the whites all over."[56] Despite its disappointments, the notion of empire continued to be invoked by Highveld Africans as a realm where race and ethnic identity were transcended by the imperial citizenry that was the right of all educated and civilized people. It was in precisely these turbulent years—a period characterized by the uneasy coexistence of idioms of both multiracialism and Ethiopianism among the Highveld's African Christian farmers—that Dowie's Christian Catholic Apostolic Church in Zion first made its appearance. That the Midwestern church—with its notions of the equality of all, regardless of class or race—was so successful in the Transvaal and Orange River Colonies was testimony to the continued appeal of universalistic ideals among the contemporary black elite.

Building Zion on the South African Highveld

Two local white Zion members were pivotal to the dissemination of Dowie's teachings to Africans across the Highveld: Pieter Le Roux and Edgar Mahon. Le Roux, discussed in the preceding chapter, was the missionary to African communities for the Dutch Reformed Church in the eastern Transvaal district of Wakkerstroom. Despite its evangelical leanings, and the fact that many in its upper echelons practiced divine healing, the Dutch Reformed Church had "serious objections" to disseminating these teachings among Africans.[57] Even Le Roux's mentor, Murray, worried that divine healing would appeal to Africans primarily as an efficacious technology, rather than as part and parcel of the Christian Gospel, thereby "distracting [Africans'] attention from more essential things." At the heart of their objection was the racist charge that Africans were irredeemably "materialistic . . . and understand so little of [Christianity's] fundamental truths."[58] But Le Roux was unable to comply with a racial demarcation of divine healings. As one who could "personally bear witness of this 'happy tiding'" he could not "remain silent about this any longer."[59] Prompted by his reading of *Leaves,* Le Roux began to exchange letters with Dowie in Zion City from 1900.[60] In 1903, Le Roux resigned from the Dutch Reformed Church and enlisted as a member of the Christian Catholic Apostolic Church in Zion, ordained by Dowie as a local South African missionary.[61] Le Roux's descendants remember the subsequent painful alienation of the family from the local Boer community. Evicted from the Reformed parsonage and spurned by local families, the only accommodation they could find in Wakkerstroom was a disused *spookhuis,* a crumbling house thought to be haunted.[62]

The second missionary involved in the circulation of Zionist teachings among African farming communities was a former Salvation Army captain, Edgar Mahon. The Mahon family had migrated from Ireland to Manchester in the 1860s, and from there, in the words of Mahon's great-grandson, "that's when they took the boat to Cape Town." Once in South Africa, they became transport riders, conveying people and goods from the Cape to the diamond fields of Kimberly. And as soon as gold was discovered in Johannesburg, the family relocated their family there, transport riding between the Cape and the Witwatersrand. They also started a saloon in the working-class suburb of Fordsburg.[63] Soon, thanks to the evangelistic activities of the Salvation Army among white Johannesburgers in precisely such working-class areas, the entire family converted, renounced their saloon work and committed themselves to the temperance cause.[64] Mahon now supported himself as a transport-rider (a common occupation for working-class whites in the city[65]), and also undertook unpaid missionary work for the Salvation Army among African communities. During a missionary trip to Natal, Mahon fell ill with lung sickness. Johannes Buchler— Dowie's first official representative in South Africa—was a pivotal figure in introducing Mahon to Zion, for Mahon was married to Johannes's sister, Joey Buchler, whom he had met while at the Salvation Army training base in the Cape.[66] Buchler visited the Mahons, carrying Dowie's literature, and successfully prayed for Mahon's healing; as he recalled, "*Leaves* changed them right inside out and upside down, it knocked all theory and all the theology out of them."[67] Greatly inspired, Mahon began to teach divine healing to his African audiences. But the local Salvation Army opposed this (perhaps also due to a particular dislike of Dowie himself[68]) leading to Mahon's resignation from the Army. Mahon went on to work as an independent missionary in the Orange River Colony, where he and his family were housed on the farms of sympathetic local white evangelicals (one of these was Walter Puttrill, a Methodist[69]) while he preached divine healing to Africans on the surrounding farms.[70] The Mahons were besieged in Ladysmith during the war, but by 1903 returned and bought a small farm, which they named Hillside, near Harrismith town. Very shortly afterward, Mahon applied for membership within Dowie's Christian Catholic Apostolic Church in Zion.[71]

Initially, Dowie had envisioned the church's presence in South Africa as largely concentrated among white communities. As he frequently reiterated in the pages of *Leaves*, this part of the continent was "White Man's Africa" due to the significant number of European settlers.[72] His instructions to the Bryants on the eve of their departure for South Africa only briefly touched on their evangelistic work among Africans, merely commenting that racial segregation should have no place, and giving equal prominence to Johannesburg's South Asian population as he did to its African one: "I have not spoken regarding the African but I wish you especially to understand that Zion has no colour line. There are many Indians traders there too . . . no matter what they may be, the church and place of meeting is open to all."[73] Yet by 1904, the year of the Bryants' arrival in the Transvaal, the work of Le Roux and Mahon—both active in thriving evangelistic and pastoral ministry among black farming communities—alerted Dowie to the possibilities of this huge demographic of potential converts. Throughout the winter months of 1904, Daniel and Emma Bryant traveled several times to Wakkerstroom and Harrismith to visit the African Zion Gatherings founded by Le Roux and Mahon. While in Johannesburg they had congregations numbering several hundred, they discovered to their astonishment and delight that open-air divine healing services and baptisms in the Highveld farmlands were regularly drawing in close to a thousand Africans.[74] By late 1904, just several months after the Bryants' arrival in Johannesburg, Dowie was triumphantly celebrating that "the Everlasting Gospel [will] win the hearts of many thousands of dark-skinned children of God."[75]

More than mere crowing over numerical success, in targeting the region's black population, Dowie was also seizing a new opportunity to promote the church's distinctive message of egalitarianism beyond the borders of the United States. He had already proclaimed that "oppressed, sin-stricken and disease-smitten Ethiopians in thousands have found a refuge in Zion . . . in Zion City they have come into their rights and privileges as in no other place on earth." Now there was a chance to extend the open welcome of the church to "the great dark Continent of Africa, the Scriptural Ethiopia."[76] African American residents of Zion City may also have viewed the recruitment of black members in South Africa with particular interest, perhaps discerning an opportunity to uplift their brethren on the African continent. For example, African Americans in turn-of the-century Zion City were keenly aware of the worldwide dimensions of black identity. Several residents were proponents of the "Back to Africa" movement of the late nineteenth century. These were the controversial ideas promoted by the AME Bishop Henry Turner, among others, that black America would be reinvigorated and the continent of Africa uplifted by African Americans' return to their ancestral continent.[77] African Americans in Zion City seized upon these ideas. For example, Richard Williamson, a waiter in Zion City's Hospice, was organizing a "colonization scheme . . . the object is to take a large number of coloured people to Liberia."[78]

Alongside the efforts of Mahon and Le Roux, Zion's remarkable spread in the Highveld was also the result of the work of a large cohort of African preachers. In 1903, after Le Roux's move to Zion, hundreds of his black Dutch Reformed congregation in Wakkerstroom embraced divine healing with him, including his most senior preachers who gave up medication for themselves and their families in favor of prayer.[79] Many of this first generation of African Zionists exemplified the self-improving values of the small rural elite. Although very few Africans owned land in Wakkerstroom (in 1905, out of 246 farms in the district, only one was black-owned[80]), many of the first black Zionists had either managed to purchase land in surrounding districts or were reasonably secure sharecroppers. The Swazi-descended Daniel Nkonyane, for example, was a senior preacher within Le Roux's Wakkerstroom congregation as well as a prosperous local land-owner. He owned 300 acres of land in the nearby Utrecht district in Natal, a three-hour horse ride from Wakkerstroom, which he visited at regular intervals throughout the year. The property had extensive crops and fruit orchards.[81] Much of the success of Dowie's church in this region seems to have been due to Nkonyane's charismatic and powerful leadership. Oral tradition has it that early members of the church in Wakkerstroom affectionately called Nkonyane *Ugodo oluhlala abafundisi,* or "the log upon which the church ministers rest," reflecting the widespread perception of his presence as deeply authoritative.[82] Another prominent former Dutch

Reformed church member who converted to Zion with Le Roux was Muneli Ngobese, who rented five acres of land near Wakkerstroom town. Through his bountiful crops, he reported he was able to make a generous living from what he cultivated.[83] Africans in the Orange River Colony could not own land, but here too the first African Zion leaders connected to Edgar Mahon were drawn from the ranks of the small farming elite. Mahon's right-hand man was the respected local sharecropper Elijah Lutango, a former lay preacher in the Methodist church, a "clear thinker and a wonderful preacher who was widely known and honoured by whites as well as blacks," in Mahon's estimation.[84]

In addition to being landowners and small-scale farmers, many of the first generation of black Zionists were also fervent believers in the values of education and learning. On their Highveld tours, the Bryants noted that many of Le Roux and Mahon's black associates were "cultured and some are well-educated and possess exceptional intellectual power."[85] One of the earliest Zionist preachers in Mahon's early days was the educated Peter Bhengu, who spoke excellent English.[86] Joseph Khumalo was a convert from the Harrismith district, and also "spoke English with a beautiful accuracy." He had been a local Wesleyan preacher for fourteen years, and a schoolteacher for fifteen.[87] Education and Christianity were also intimately intertwined for Elijah Lutango; his testimony recounted how after his conversion "the ambition of his life was now to learn to read that wonderful book, the Bible." After many obstacles, and by help of a spelling book and a Zulu Bible, he mastered the basics of literacy. His son, Micah, would in later years act as Edgar Mahon's secretary, doing his Zulu and Sotho correspondence.[88] Even those early Zion leaders who were not formally educated nonetheless recognized and sought to capture the power of literacy. The prominent Daniel Nkonyane could not read, although he knew many Bible passages by heart.[89] In a striking photographic portrait of Nkonyane and his family, published in *Leaves,* he clasps a large black-bound book in one hand—surely a Bible—an implicit acknowledgement of his respect for the intertwined values of education and Christianity.[90]

The joint efforts of these white and black Zionist emissaries met with great success among African residents of the Highveld. By the end of 1905, Le Roux, Nkonyane, and Ngobese had baptized 5,000 in the Wakkerstroom area.[91] Nkonyane and Ngobese, in conjunction with a man named Fred Luthuli, soon oversaw thirty-five places of Zion worship with forty-six under-preachers and six church buildings.[92] By the middle of 1904, within a thirty-mile radius of the small town of Volksrust (near Nkonyane's farm), Le Roux counted "1000 native Zulus who are obedient to the teachings of Zion."[93] Zionist preachers reported similar success in the Orange

Daniel Nkonyane and Family. *Source: Leaves of Healing* 18, no. 111, 30
December 1905, 315. Christ Community Church Archives, Zion, Illinois.

River Colony, baptizing scores from 1904 on. By 1907, Zionism had
topped an official government list of churches in the Harrismith Location.[94]
Dowie's teachings appealed to a diverse stratum of Africans. The church
in the Transvaal Colony drew relatively elite, educated converts out of
mission churches such as the Dutch Reformed Church as well as from the
Methodists. A similar picture was true of the Orange River Colony: here,
Zion convert Matthias Mabutyana had been a Methodist schoolteacher,
while Timothy Mabuza also defected from the Methodist church, bringing
with him a small band of followers.[95] Although the leadership of the movement seems to have been dominated by the African Christian elite, some
among the rank and file were entirely new to the Christian faith. Dowie's
teachings thus also appealed to so-called traditionalists, those who did not
belong to any Christian denomination, either European or African-led, and
who had had little previous exposure to missionary education. Mahon
reported on the "great mixed crowds" who attended services at his farm;
there assembled "heathen in their skins, some civilized but not Christian-

ized, as well as members of other churches with heads full of wrong teaching."[96] Moreover, Christian Catholic Apostolic Church in Zion doctrines traveled beyond the farmlands of the Highveld to reach Africans in the mining compounds of Johannesburg. A lively traffic between farms and mining metropolis (it was usual for African family heads to send at least one of their children to periodically work on the mines) aided in the transmission of divine healing practices and resulted in a small band of African Zionists on the Rand alongside the white congregation. In 1905, Daniel Bryant reported that a "young brother engaged in native work [on the Rand]" counted "that thirteen were born into the Kingdom" at a recent Zion service.[97]

Though not discounting the pull of individual figures such as Nkonyane or the well-respected Elijah Lutango, by all accounts it was the offer of divine healing that made the Christian Catholic Apostolic Church in Zion so attractive to these farming communities. For one, in promoting divine healing, Zion preachers such as Nkonyane and others were simultaneously tapping into deeply felt contemporary African concerns surrounding health and sickness. Both divine healing and African diagnosticians of this period were willing to view sickness and health not merely as physiological matters, but as profoundly spiritual conditions. Broadly speaking, popular African thought on the early twentieth-century Highveld held that while some illnesses stemmed from natural causes, there were also certain bodily afflictions that resulted from spiritual causes.[98] The nefarious interventions of witches or sorcerers could precipitate these misfortunes. Ancestors, too, who considered their living relatives to be neglecting their duties toward them, could also visit their displeasure on the living by precipitating bodily suffering.[99] It was the role of ritual specialists such as herbalists (*izinyanga*) and diviners (*izangoma*) to diagnose and cure manifestations of evil as well as to identify ancestral discontent. In this way, these experts provided a vital service in protecting not only individual bodies but society as a whole from malignant ill-wishers.

Moreover, the vast majority of contemporary churches were only casually interested (at best) in the supernatural causes of sickness; however, in Dowie's church, Africans found an organization willing to draw links between the interconnected realities of spiritual and bodily health. Africans had long expressed frustration that established churches refused to admit that disease was the result of ungodly interventions. In early twentieth-century South Africa, as in the United States, much official church teaching affirmed that sickness was the will of the deity and merely to be accepted with forbearance. Thus Zion preacher Elijah Lutango commented that "the Gospel was preached previously, but the people did not get healing for their bodies [because] the Devil made the pastors say that diseases come from God."[100] Yet in Dowie's church, converts found an organization willing to validate local views on sickness and health as uncannily parallel to the teachings of the church. As early as 1899, Johannes Buchler had observed that "the Kaffir's theology is far more correct than the theology of [most] Christians. This man believes that when his cattle dies, or he gets sick, that this is caused by an evil spirit."[101] And if Dowie's teachings had the edge on its Christian competitors in this respect, they also arrived in South Africa during a period when indigenous healing therapies were increasingly in disarray. The Transvaal's anti-witchcraft legislation of 1904 undercut diviners' powers to diagnose and treat sickness and attack witchcraft; new laws criminalized "any person who pretends to exercise supernatural powers," and led to the widespread perception among African communities that they were without credible spiritual defense.[102] "Native Doctoring," as it was called, was also illegal in the Orange River Colony, with colonial administrators reporting that they prosecuted "very numerous cases."[103] In 1908, for example, one Fred Setice was committed to trial for "practicing as a doctor" by administering "pounded herbs for bodily pains."[104]

Divine healing—which could operate without official condemnation yet paralleled indigenous healing in its emphasis on the supernatural—was greeted with huge enthusiasm by these communities. In the Wakkerstroom district, divine healing rapidly became the most popular aspect of Zion's work; Le Roux reported that "as soon as [Africans] see divine healing . . . they unquestioningly accept it."[105] In the Orange River Colony it was a similar story; Mahon commented that "I long ago found out that what everybody wants to know is: 'Do people really get healed by prayer?' "[106] New Zionists emphasized the act of healing was not merely bodily repair, but rather "snatching [the people] out of the hands of Satan," as one African preacher put it.[107] Zionist evangelists reported remarkable success in freeing people from "the devil in them who does not want God's work to prosper."[108] Reports of astounding miracles circulated widely. Daniel Nkonyane was said to have even raised from the dead a woman whose body was already in an advanced state of decomposition.[109] In the Christian Catholic Apostolic Church in Zion, unlike in the vast majority of other churches active in the region, Africans found new spiritual resources that claimed to penetrate the underlying causes of affliction. One old woman, healed through prayer from "chronic consumption," said that "the Missionaries have always told me about a God I have never been able to find, but now I have God in my heart and I have found the Christ."[110] Despite their principled determination to separate from white-led churches, black Ethiopian Christians in this area also found Zion's intertwined bodily and spiritual cures hard to resist.

Mahon reported a "young Ethiopian minister who was sick and asked for prayer . . . This is a great come down for our friend to come to a white man for prayer, as the Ethiopian teaches independence from the white man."[111]

But it would be a mistake to think that converts prized Zionism merely as a Christian variation of indigenous healing therapies, or that these Africans who laid on hands and prayed for healing considered themselves as "baptized" versions of a diviner or herbalist. To the contrary, divine healing was widely understood by practitioners of this period as a technique of modernizing self-improvement, part of the broader repertoire of African progressiveness that characterized the aspirations of the black elites who led the church. For all divine healing's resonance with indigenous health theories (in particular, its argument that sickness was the work of nefarious spiritual agents), adherents knew its bodily disciplines were strictly exclusive—all faith must be placed in the Judeo-Christian God alone. This was a spiritual discipline that detached Africans from local loyalties, setting them on an entirely different trajectory to one mapped out by indigenous concerns. A Zionist preacher in Wakkerstroom "gathered all the people together and explained the truths of Zion." Immediately they "took down all their medicine charms as a token from that day on they were going to live for God alone."[112] Zion believer Fred Luthuli from Wakkerstroom preached the necessity of renouncing local therapies for divine healing's superior cures: "a woman who had been ill for a long time was treated by the native doctor. When I came to her the woman told me that the doctor could not heal her, and we threw her medicine out."[113] Whatever the deeply felt continuities with existing cosmologies, in this period conversion to Zionism was cast—both by black and white Zionist church workers and by ordinary members—as a decisive break with older religious systems. Embracing divine healing meant cutting oneself off from one's ancestors. No longer could a Zion convert make sacrifices to their ancestral spirits, for example. Samuel Molapo, a Zion convert from Harrismith, described the intense spiritual tussle involved in renouncing belief in ancestors for reliance on God: "It means so much more for us natives to become Zionists than white people, because the white man believes in God and Jesus Christ, but we only believe in the spirit of our ancestors . . . it is very hard for us to give up this belief and accept the other."[114]

Zion's codes of holy living also prescribed other disciplines that strove to detach Africans from existing loyalties to traditional values. Divine healing meant breaking allegiances to traditional healers as well as to ancestors, but it also had radical consequences for female converts' loyalties to husbands, fathers, and brothers. African patriarchs in districts such as Wakkerstroom and Harrismith were expressing increasing anxiety about female autonomy in these years.[115] Insecurity of land tenure undermined males' control over their homesteads and families, and many young people—both women and men—were escaping parental authority by seeking work in towns and cities. A 1911 article on "Native Behavior" in Harrismith lamented that "older natives are in despair as they have no control over their children, the women won't work at their kraals and the boys won't herd [cattle] but prefer to loaf in town."[116] Many older males of the region viewed Dowie's church as yet another force eroding patriarchal authority. For one, Dowie strictly forbade alcohol, something that was drilled into converts in South Africa and in the United States. But the communal brewing of beer by women for their husbands was integral to the maintenance of African conjugal relationships. One woman who embraced Dowie's teachings decided to cease brewing for her husband, even though she would "be considered to have lost love for [him]." But the woman "remembered the words of Jesus—'Who loveth Father and Mother more than me is not worthy of me'—and folded her hands for wrong-doing [i.e. refrained from wrong-doing]."[117] Divine healing's socially divisive consequences—including women's absences at all-night prayer meetings—were accused of undermining traditional marital responsibilities. One husband declared himself opposed to Zion "on account of the separation it makes between the people." Against her family's wishes, a woman went for baptism at a Zion meeting. Enraged, her male relatives arrived "with sticks and shields, their eyes flashing fire and their hearts full of rage."[118]

Meta Budulwako's testimony is in many respects a typical narrative of those African women who sought the self-improving, modernizing disciplines of Zion. Her story also illustrates the difficulties encountered by female converts who transferred their loyalties from their families to the church. Although the child of traditionalist parents, Budulwako had been sent to a Lutheran mission school near Wakkerstroom at the age of fifteen where she learned to "read the Bible in my native language," and where she became a member of the Lutheran church. After leaving school, Budulwako, like many women from the area, entered into domestic service at a white household in Wakkerstroom. But she found that there she became very ill: "my stomach could not bear any food, even a mouthful of water caused severe pain and swelling . . . my breath was so short that breathing was almost impossible. I also suffered from female trouble." At the same time, a local family of African Zionists took Budulwako into their home while she convalesced from her sickness; it is not surprising that they "advised [her] to ask for prayer" and to renounce medicine. Although skeptical about the efficacy of prayer, Budulwako "consented to having prayer said for me as I could see death was near." Visited also by Pieter Le Roux

Meta Budulwako. *Source: Leaves of Healing* 25, no. 25, 8 October 1904, 860.
Flower Pentecostal Heritage Centre, Springfield, Missouri.

who regularly laid hands upon her—an indication of white Zionists' willingness to breach contemporary taboos regarding racial interaction—the
young woman began to improve. Impressed by what she took to be the evidence of prayer's efficacy, Budulwako decided to set her old life behind her:
"as soon as possible I sought the Zion minister [Le Roux] and made a full
confession to him." But Budulwako's family were staunchly opposed to her
conversion to Zion. Perhaps her brief mention that they were "heathens . . .
who knew nothing of the Word of God" is an indication that they wished
her to consult local healers for her predicament. Budulwako, however, was
undeterred by this familial hostility; her loyalties were now transferred
from her elders to God and to Zion: "my people are against me . . . but I am

determined by the grace of God to be true to Zion, no matter what others may say or do."[119]

Divine healing's bodily disciplines set converts such as Meta Budulwako at odds with their families, their communities, and their traditional healers. It also engendered conflict with their white employers. Formerly some employers in the Wakkerstroom area had paid African workers in tobacco (one of the major commercial crops of the district), now Zion tenants objected on the grounds of Dowie's ban on smoking: "the master would threaten them, but 'no' was the answer . . . [they] used to be slaves of drink and tobacco. Glory to God."[120] Farmers objected to Zion preachers on their farms, complaining tenants absconded from work to attend church.[121] Zion convert Johann Gobesa was denied a pass to travel and preach, for he had already "been warned off a good many farms."[122] Le Roux reported that Wakkerstroom farmers "turned [Zionists] out of their livings . . . and threatened them with imprisonment for refusing to take medicine."[123] In the Harrismith district, local authorities categorized Zion as "unsettling to the native mind."[124] Mahon reported that white farmers worried divine healing's large meetings that drew Africans from around the district would spread disease, as well as "bring undesirable characters to the neighbourhood." As in the Transvaal, farmers refused to give their employees the necessary passes to attend meetings, in a largely unsuccessful bid to thwart their religious practice.[125]

In opposing Zion, white farmers of the Highveld correctly perceived the subversive truth that this Midwestern church stood for progress and equality for all, regardless of race or class. Although white opinion in the Transvaal and Orange River Colonies was highly unsympathetic to education for Africans,[126] considering it gave Africans ideas above their status, Dowie instructed Bryant to "embrace every opportunity of teaching these poor people to read and write."[127] Zion in South Africa, as in the United States, believed in education and schooling as essential aspects of the self-improvement of working people, regardless of race. By 1905, there were seven Zion schools in the Wakkerstroom area, with seventy-six pupils, one opened by Nkonyane on his farm with classes taught by the young convert, Meta Budulwako, to whom he paid a small salary.[128] In the same year, the Harrismith district counted three Christian Catholic Apostolic Church in Zion schools, all founded by sharecropping families who had converted to the church. The three schools were entirely self-supporting, charging students three shillings per household per month, and having between seventeen and forty-three pupils at any given time, both male and female. In contrast to the government's views on the desirability of manual training, no industrial skills were taught by two of the three schools, which instead focused on students learning reading, writing, and arithmetic.[129] Reflecting the long-standing commitment of this farming class to education, black Zionists welcomed the prospect of progress represented by Zionism for their youth: "we grew up in the dark . . . we had no school and no teaching. But we do not want our children to be the same."[130]

Schools and the renunciation of medicine were integral components of this new community of Zionists, but belonging to the church also meant refashioning members' leisure time. Mahon started a small choir composed of church members that performed in local venues around Harrismith and its locations. The choir seems to have been influenced by the inspirational canon of African American spiritual music, songs replete with imagery of the Israelites being "lifted up out of slavery." Indeed, some even commented that the style of the singing recalled the well-known African American Jubilee Singers who had toured the region a decade ago. Harrismith's newspaper commented of the Zion choir that "the vocal performance of these dusky nightingales vies with those of the famous Jubilee Singers." As Robert Vinson has pointed out, the Jubilee Singers—who represented the "talented tenth" of black American society—were much talked about by African elite during their South African tour as models of black success and uplift. Their stirring performances of hymns were taken as "inspirational evidence that access to Western education, Christian piety and entrepreneurial capitalism could transform blacks into first-class citizens in a racially inclusive society."[131] For the singers of the new Zion choir in Harrismith, this aspirational ethos of black progressiveness was undoubtedly one they shared with their more famous colleagues. In addition to education and choral hymnody, however, they also added divine healing to the disciplines enjoyed by civilized moderns the world over. But white opinion in Harrismith was unsympathetic to these aspirations. Despite the local journalist's evident enjoyment of these "dusky nightingales," municipal authorities nonetheless drew the line at the "Zion Choir" performing at the town's annual Agricultural Show, declaring it "not fitting" to have a black choir appear for the entertainment of the white crowds.[132]

But it was Zion's explicit advocacy of the mingling of the races that was perceived as especially threatening to the codes of white settler society. In an era of increasing restriction of African aspirations toward equality with whites, Zion's inclusivist ethos and Dowie's insistence that there be no "colour bar" in religious matters was warmly welcomed by black converts. In his testimony for readers of *Leaves,* Harrismith Zion convert, Elijah Lutango, observed that prior to the arrival of the Christian Catholic Apostolic Church in Zion in the Orange River Colony, the "Gospel was preached and people received it, but there was no fellowship between the whites and

the blacks . . . they were never one in the love of the Lord."[133] But in
Dowie's Zion, Lutango found "the True Love which does not separate
brethren because of difference in the colour of their skins."[134] For Lutango
as for many others, a Christianity that adhered to racial demarcations fell
sadly short of the overarching dimensions of the Full Gospel.[135] The practical implications of this cosmopolitan theology were profound. Throughout
the Transvaal and Orange River Colonies, Zionist preachers such as
Nkonyane, Lutango, and Ngobese worked in unusually collaborative and
egalitarian relationships with their white superiors. Unlike other white-led
mission organizations which were increasingly dragging their feet over African ordination, the Christian Catholic Apostolic Church in Zion followed
a policy that "natives should be ordained to the office of deacon, evangelist etc."[136] Although this was certainly an aspiration shared by Dowie and
Bryant, it also seems to have been an opinion shared by local white Zionists, especially Edgar Mahon, who lamented the style of his Dutch neighbors who had "the Bible in one hand, the whip in the other, the whip being
used in preference to the Bible." Instead, Mahon proclaimed his own practice was to eschew "the whip, and to actually shake hands with the natives
and sit at meals with them."[137] Services were attended by both whites and
blacks, a highly unusual phenomenon for churches in towns such as Wakkerstroom and Harrismith. A "Magic Lantern slideshow of the Life of
Christ" organized by Mahon largely drew a black audience, but "several
white people were also much interested."[138] In Harrismith as well as Wakkerstroom, Bryant baptized largely black groups of converts, but often there
would be several white Zionist converts also taking their place to be immersed in a river or lake.[139] These public displays of multiracial piety
deeply shocked whites of the area. A reader of the *Harrismith Chronicle*
snidely marveled that "a priest [would] prevail upon a white woman to be
immersed three times in icy cold water for the benefit of assembled kafir
converts."[140] Dowie had founded Zion City as a healthy haven from Chicago's corrupting influences; African converts similarly sought to establish
a sanctuary within which they could be insulated from the segregated logic
of the outside world. Indeed, as the contemporary purchase of farms in the
Wakkerstroom district by the Native Farmers' Association suggests, this
was a wider goal shared by many other Africans of the period. Zion members, too, longed for land and the autonomy it brought. Bryant reported
to Dowie that black converts craved land within which they could freely
build the new world of Zion, and within which they could practice their
religious disciplines unmolested. They wanted "to go to some place in
South Africa over which the Zion flag floats and which is kept clean by
strong Zion hands, and where white, black and yellow alike can live and

love one another, and labour in perfect peace together."[141] Le Roux similarly recognized that Zion "peoples' one desire is to have a Zion City in their own country, where they can live and serve God in peace."[142] To this end, in 1903 Le Roux leased land in the Wakkerstroom district and applied to officials to build a church and school and settle fifty families "for the spread of Christianity" on it.[143] But white officials refused the application, stating they "discourage[d] the gathering together of large numbers of natives on particular farms."[144]

Zionists in the Harrismith district were no more successful when Mahon pursued similar attempts to inaugurate a dedicated Zion settlement. In 1902, he unsuccessfully applied to the Secretary of the Colony for financial support to start "a practical self-supporting mission farm."[145] Denied dedicated land, these Zionists used existing farms to build up small self-sufficient communities of believers. Daniel Nkonyane, for example, aspired to build a Zion church on his 300 acres of land in the neighboring Utrecht district.[146] His plans were thwarted by the opposition of the white-run Methodist church and the local magistrate. Nonetheless, there were a "good few" Zion people living on Nkonyane's farm, and he was glad to say that "everybody in the area comes to church upon my land."[147] In 1903, Edgar Mahon purchased a farm in the Harrismith district—Kalkoenkrantz— as his old property at Hillside had become too small to hold those who congregated for divine healing services.[148] He also ensured that the permitted number of five African sharecropping families resident on his farm were all church members. In this way, Mahon's farm, like Nkonyane's, provided a small foothold for local Zion families to carve out a living.[149] Ever ambitious, Dowie even toyed with an inverted "Back to Africa" experiment. This was his briefly lived idea of inviting black converts from South Africa to take up residence in Zion City, finding there a safe haven of racial cosmopolitanism, and adding their labor to the collaborative enterprise of building the Kingdom of God on earth. "I have been thinking it would be splendid for me to bring to Zion City four or five thousand of our African converts from South Africa, where they have been cruelly and shamefully treated by the British government . . . shall we not have that kind of City where we can bring the varied races of earth to labour and work together?"[150]

In contrast to white South African Zionists, no black Zionist of the early twentieth century that we know of undertook the long journey across the ocean to Zion City. Nonetheless many African converts possessed a keen sense of their membership of this worldwide multiracial church. Converts such as Lutango spoke of Zion City as a beacon of hope, a city as well as an abstract ideal that infused divine justice and equality across the entire world. Lutango mused that "Zion City spread her light so quickly over the whole earth and among all nations, until it also lighted up this dark country . . . this light having spread with great rapidity among us blacks."[151] African members' affinity to and connection with Zion City and to Dowie was continually stressed. Bryant reported that converts' "faces beamed with delight" when "we told them of Zion City . . . we told them how the General Overseer . . . had sent his special love to them."[152] In 1904, Bryant gave a public lecture on Dowie and Zion City to assembled believers in the Wakkerstroom area, complete with "stereopticon views" of the utopian settlement.[153] African listeners were "delighted and said [they] had now been across the sea to America and had seen with [their] own eyes the things of which [they] had been told."[154] Further exemplifying this sense of strong connection to Zion City was the attentiveness with which African Zionists followed events in Zion City, Illinois. Once the Bryants had returned to Zion City in 1908, African Zionists perceived the couple's continued childlessness with great sympathy. Lutango recalled their continual prayer for the Bryants: "it became a burden to us on our hearts and many of our Zion gathering never left off praying to God about this matter." When the news finally arrived in South Africa that Emma Bryant had given birth to a son, "we were drunk with joy. All the Zion gatherings were very glad and greatly stirred . . . May God be praised!"[155]

Predictably, the local white population expressed considerable outrage at the cosmopolitan ideals of Dowie's church in their midst. It is true that some authorities saw Zion's racially integrated worship as evidence that this was not an anti-European, "Ethiopian" church that sought to claim "Africa for the Africans" and to ensure "no white man will be seen in Africa, everyone [will] be killed."[156] Although disapproving in principle of multiracial fraternity in religious matters, some officials nonetheless took Zion's racially mixed services as practical evidence of the good will black converts felt toward the white race. In 1904, Daniel Bryant held a large baptismal service in the river on the outskirts of Wakkerstroom town during which 150 people, including several whites—some of whom were members of Le Roux's own family—were immersed in the river's waters. While the local Wakkerstroom Magistrate disapproved of these "Yankee notions" of baptizing in frigid water, he was reassured this was not "politics under the guise of religion"—for at least "white people went through precisely the same discomfort."[157] For the most part, it seems that interracial intercourse was a large part of why local white opinion was so hostile to the work of the Christian Catholic Apostolic Church in Zion. In 1903, weekly newspaper the *Transvaal Critic* criticized Dowie for allowing testimonies and photographs of white and black converts to be featured side by side in *Leaves of Healing,* citing with indignation a printed letter in the magazine from a "kaffir."[158] In the conservative environment of Harrismith, Mahon's racially progressive stance caused especial outrage among his farming neighbors. He declared it was the mixed composition of church meetings on his farm that "has very much upset some of our Dutch neighbours . . . [they were] so enraged they decided to cut us right out of their society and reckon us as one with the natives."[159] Indeed, this perception that Mahon, as a white man, did not maintain the proper racial hierarchies may have lain behind the barbed comment of the British Commandant of Witzieshoek African reserve who, in refusing Mahon permission to conduct church work there, commented that "to my mind, Mr Mahon is not the class of man that is required for native work."[160]

However, the extent to which black and white Zionists existed in racial harmony should not be exaggerated. For all Dowie's rhetoric, and despite the personal progressiveness of individuals like Edgar Mahon, many white Zionists were ambivalent about incorporating blacks into the church as equals. Despite the fact that white missionaries, their families, and a handful of sympathizers worked closely with African Zionists on the Highveld, the bulk of white Zionists in urban Johannesburg and a handful of other cities seem to have had little interest in pursuing Dowie's ideal of a multiracial fellowship. It is true that a Mrs. Ward of Kimberly reported to the readers of *Leaves* that her congregation stood not only for the reconciliation of the white "races" but also of the solidarity of whites with blacks. Using language that echoed Dowie's own words, she wrote: "we love British and Boer and Kaffir alike, for we have all one Father, one Savior and one Guide."[161] There is little evidence, however, that this was a view more widely shared among white Zionists. For many whites, Zion's cosmopolitanism was largely realized in their pursuit of fraternity between the Boer and British white "races." Indeed, even Zion's white missionaries reiterated racist views of the period that Africans' role was fundamentally to provide labor to settlers. Le Roux, for example, praised Zion's capacity to "civilize" Africans, but it was the transformation of "unreliable" Africans into trustworthy servants that he particularly emphasized in his letters to readers of *Leaves.* He boasted that "in Zion the raw native becomes a honest and conscientious labourer who loves to do right . . . all the white people want Zion natives as their servants."[162] Even Bryant, Dowie's own emissary to South Africa, at heart believed missionaries among Africans in the Transvaal and Orange River Colonies should still maintain a "proper" distance from their converts. Thus Bryant praised Le Roux for not "adopting that fatal and foolish practice of 'being a Zulu with the Zulus' . . . [he has] strictly maintained the dignity of [his] own natural refinement."[163] Perhaps

Wakkerstroom Baptism. *Source: Leaves of Healing* 15, no. 25, 8 October 1904, 857. Christ Community Church Archives, Zion, Illinois.

this was an indirect criticism of Edgar Mahon's greater willingness to fraternize freely in his own home with black church members. And in common with missionaries of all denominations, and despite the rhetoric of black ordination, Le Roux still scrutinized his black preachers for signs of an unwarranted independent ministry, or any activities that suggested the influence of Ethiopianism. When his assistant Muneli Ngobese renewed his

preacher's certificate at the local magistrate's office without Le Roux's knowledge, the latter complained to officials that allowing this degree of autonomy "was somewhat risky, as a native might get away from his minister, and yet continue to have his permit renewed."[164]

Pieter Le Roux, in particular, appears to have been viewed with skepticism by his black church members, some of whom perceived him as still promoting the racially exclusive values of Boer society in general and the

Dutch Reformed Church in particular. Lucas Zungu was an early convert of Le Roux's from Wakkerstroom, and was first appointed by Le Roux as a local and subsequently a head preacher in the Christian Catholic Apostolic Church in Zion in the district. But Zungu found it impossible to advance to the higher rank of evangelist. While he was confident that the American "Rev. Daniel Bryant was keen and willing to appoint us as evangelists," he suspected that "Bryant was influenced by the Rev. Le Roux not do so ... Mr Le Roux had seceded from the Dutch Reformed Church which church is strongly opposed to ordaining Native ministers." Like Dowie, Zungu considered racial segregation in the realm of religion unacceptable; as he recounted in later life: "that Church at that time would not have native ministers or evangelists ... why colour distinction in church affairs! Absolutely intolerable!" In 1907, Zungu departed from the Christian Catholic Apostolic Church in Zion and started a new organization, which he named the African Christian Baptist Church of South Africa. The inclusion of "African" in its name reflected his concern with black autonomy in church life.[165] Zungu was one of the first of this generation of African Zionists to express outrage over the existence of a color bar within the church. After Dowie's death in 1907, and with the increasing influence of the local Pentecostal AFM, many more black Zionists would express profound disquiet about the rapid growth in racialized thinking within the church in South Africa.

The Collapse of Cosmopolitanism

The previous chapter described how, in the aftermath of Dowie's death in 1907 and the arrival of the Apostolic Faith Mission in Johannesburg in 1908, South African members of Zion accepted the teachings of Pentecost. While this was true of white Zionists on the Witwatersrand, Pentecost was also warmly embraced by many African Zionists, at least initially. Le Roux was the most prominent advocate of Pentecost among the white Zionist community; in 1915, he was elected president of the Apostolic Faith Mission in South Africa, a position he held until shortly before his death in 1943.[166] It was also he who acted as the main conduit for introducing the doctrine of the Baptism of the Holy Spirit to his black congregations in the Transvaal. Le Roux reported great interest among black Zionists in Pentecost: "the crowds flowed in, hundreds were saved and baptized in the Spirit ... the presence and power of the God was more real and evident and lives were endued with real power."[167] The first run of 10,000 baptismal certificates printed by the AFM in 1910 had 5,000 in Dutch and

English, 2,500 in isiZulu (spoken in Wakkerstroom), and 2, 500 in Sesotho (spoken in Harrismith), numbers that confirmed the Pentecostal movement's popularity with Africans as well as Boers and English-speakers.[168] Moreover, many of the most prominent of the black Wakkerstroom leaders joined Pentecost, including men such as Daniel Nkonyane and Fred Luthuli.[169] As with the reception of Pentecost within white Zion in Johannesburg, there was initially a great deal of fluidity between the two organizations. For example, in 1909 it was agreed by the AFM and the Christian Catholic Apostolic Church in Zion that they would mutually recognize the authorizing documents held by black preachers within the sister organization.[170]

Wakkerstroom believers were open to the new teachings, whereas Zionist figures in the Harrismith district in the Orange River Colony largely remained aloof from the Pentecostal revival. Edgar Mahon was personally skeptical of the new teachings, referring to the Baptism in the Holy Spirit, and its accompanying gift of speaking in tongues, as mere "sham and excitement."[171] Meanwhile, although initially accepting of the new doctrines, Daniel Bryant in Zion City had come to feel similarly critical, regarding the ecstatic display of tongues as "disorder, noise, the violation of everything taught in the Word regarding church life." By 1909 he had concluded that "I do not have to roll on the floor, nor scream nor disturb the public, nor make a fool of myself to bring myself to where God can bless me."[172] These two anti-Pentecost groups—one in South Africa, one in the United States— formed a new alliance: Mahon along with Elijah Lutango, his coworker in the Harrismith district, linked their churches in South Africa to the reformed "independent" Christian Catholic Church in Zion started by Bryant in 1909. Denouncing the excesses of Dowie's authoritarianism and self-aggrandizement, Bryant's new Christian Catholic Church in Zion committed itself to restoring the essentials of Dowie's original message of divine healing ("the original tenets of the faith as practiced in the beginning by Dr. John Alexander Dowie") and in the process, repudiated both Pentecost and the leadership of Voliva.[173]

In the meantime, conflict began brewing between white Pentecostal leaders in the AFM and those African members within it. Tensions were especially evident in the Wakkerstroom district. As the last chapter showed, the predominance of Boer figures within the AFM, combined with the rise in a racially exclusive ethno-nationalism, began to militate against the racially mixed worship recommended by Dowie. An early debate within the AFM had revolved around the practice of "holy kissing" between blacks and whites in Zionist congregations. The practice was inspired by Paul's command for believers to "greet each other with a holy kiss," and is still in use among some older white AFM members in South Africa today.[174] But displaying the increasing antagonism toward multiracial fraternizing, in 1914 the Executive Council of the AFM condemned the practice as "inexpedient," recording its "strong disapproval" of blacks and whites interacting in this way. "We do not teach or encourage social equality between whites and natives," the Council concluded.[175] Shaking of hands between whites and blacks was also a major concern; by the beginning of the 1920s, the Committee had prescribed that "European Overseers and Workers in charge of the Native work should teach the native never to be the first to offer his hand to a white person, or to approach them first in public places, but to wait until the white man made the first advance."[176]

Racial tensions within this new post-Dowie incarnation of the Zion church began to play out in other ways. Prohibitions against mixed fraternizing were accompanied by increased powers given to white Pentecostals and diminished autonomy for black members. A "Native Council" was formed to represent black members, yet half of the Council still consisted of white members, and every decision the Native Council made had to be approved by the all-white AFM Executive Council.[177] The first nine elders of the AFM in Johannesburg elected in 1913 were entirely white.[178] White leaders such as Le Roux—now based in Johannesburg as a prominent leader of the AFM[179]—attempted to clamp down on black practices considered to be unscriptural or unsuitable (or perhaps merely contrary to the views of white leadership). Nkonyane, now emerging as the strongest African leader in Wakkerstroom, believed in taking scriptural narratives literally as templates on which to build every aspect of ritual life. The Book of Revelation, for example, told Nkonyane that God's faithful wore white robes. Soon, many were wearing snowy surplices for their worship. A group of Wakkerstroom Zionists withdrew for a three-day fast broken only by their ritual drinking of milk. They did this because it had been prescribed in Paul's letters to the Corinthians and Hebrews.[180] Le Roux severely disapproved of these innovations, and attempted to restrict them, feeling Africans' scrupulousness displayed a legalism akin to Roman Catholicism.[181]

Many of the Wakkerstroom congregation—disgruntled at a loss of autonomy in a formerly egalitarian ministry—began to reassert their identity as members of Zion, strategically invoking its progressive promises for African people. Even during the brief years that the Wakkerstroom congregation linked itself to the AFM, it had clung to the name of Zion as a symbol of all that they stood for and prized, its "teaching of a clean life and of divine healing."[182] In 1910, the AFM conceded this, noting "the natives deem the name of Zion so essential that this portion of the Mission shall be known as the Zion Branch of the Apostolic Faith Mission."[183] Soon, however, many came to feel that the incompatibility between Zion and Pentecost was simply too great to continue even in this limited alliance. The key disagreement was over black Zionists' desire for greater self-determination in religious matters. In 1914 a meeting was arranged between Le Roux and 220 old Zion converts in the small Eastern Transvaal town of Ermelo, around seventy miles north of Wakkerstroom. Le Roux attempted to persuade the group to remain within the AFM.[184] But black Zionists used the meeting to formally repudiate the AFM and to assert their loyalty to Zion City in North America, a symbol of the cosmopolitan values that Pentecostals such as Le Roux were now seeking to erase. At the close of the meeting all but seven chose to remain in Zion.[185] Fred Luthuli, an early convert from Wakkerstroom, spoke on behalf of the group to Le Roux asserting Wakkerstroom Zionists' determination to remain free from the unwelcome control of Le Roux and other AFM leaders. He invoked "Zion" as their guiding light, not the local rule of Pentecostal leaders who operated according to a racialized logic: "we are still Zion people . . . there is only ONE Zion and that has its headquarters in Zion City . . . We cannot turn away from it for our hearts are full of Zion . . . we follow no *man,* we follow Zion."[186] Several independent Zionist churches emerged from this Wakkerstroom rupture, with one of the most subsequently famous being Elias Mahlangu's Zion Apostolic Church (his use of both "Zion" and the "Apostolic" from the Apostolic Faith Mission indicating the intertwined Zion-Pentecostal identity of these years, and the influence of Pentecostalism upon early twentieth-century Zionists).[187]

Despite these challenges to Dowie's universalistic church, there was during this period a Zion center that still flourished in the Orange River Colony. This was the work conducted by Edgar Mahon, operating in conjunction with seventy African coworkers and ministering to thousands of Africans on the farmlands of the Colony and of the neighboring British Colony of Basutoland. Disillusioned with the Pentecostal revival, Mahon's church positioned itself as loyal to the new reformist Christian Catholic Church in Zion led by Daniel Bryant.[188] For his part, Bryant strongly believed in the importance of American Zionists continuing to support missionary work in South Africa, especially in the context of disarray and disunity in Zion City. In 1910, he preached a sermon to his congregation stating that "we need a world work to preserve Christian unity . . . there is nothing that will preserve the unity of the church like a world vision followed by a world work."[189] The next year he proposed that the church assume the responsibility of sending Mahon $1,400 a year in order "to set Elder Mahon free from the need of supporting himself so he could better serve the Lord."[190] By 1917, one-half of the American church's tithes were sent to the South African branch of the Christian Catholic Church in

Zion.[191] The first missionaries—two young, unmarried women named Ethel Thorpe and Myrtle Sisson—were sent out in 1912; Sisson had formerly been Bryant's stenographer in Zion City and was enthused "by an ardent missionary spirit."[192] More missionaries followed over the years, with three single women from Zion City arriving in the 1920s, and a married couple in the 1940s.[193]

Despite the odds, this reformist Zionist church in the Orange River Colony under Mahon continued to be inspired by Dowie's ideals of racial equality. The church's ability to maintain their cosmopolitan horizons was largely due to the fact that the long-standing dream of a South African "Zion City" was realized. In 1913, the year of the Natives Land Act, the support of the American church meant that Mahon was able to purchase a large farm named Mooigelegen, of which a 200-acre portion was entirely dedicated to Zion's work (this portion was named Etembeni, or "Place of Hope") with a church, lands for converts to farm, and a school.[194] The mission and the school continued to attract African converts who were drawn by its promise of self-improvement and progressiveness for all, regardless of race. One of the most outstanding examples of the opportunities that Zion still offered to its African converts was the story of a young woman, Eva Khumalo, who had completed her teaching training at Lovedale School in the Eastern Cape, a bastion of the black elite of the day. She then gave up a position as headmistress of a Wesleyan school in Natal to teach at Etembeni. In 1913 Khumalo wrote to the readers of the *Zululand and Basutoland Missionary* (the periodical started by Bryant's church in Zion City, largely for the purpose of fundraising for the South African church) that she "thanks God for the progress of our little school in this country where a native is said to be too low to be educated . . . we hope for great things, that this school may be the means of uplifting the native races of South Africa."[195] Another example of the mission's commitment to education and professional advancement for its African members was its investment in her brother, Fortescue Khumalo, who "has taken two years of normal training beyond the grammar schools, and is now teaching at Amanzimtoti Institute near Durban."[196]

Underpinning their promotion of education for black converts was the church's continued commitment to the solidarity of a human family that transcended racial division. In 1914, Mahon celebrated "that those who dwell on our farm, white and black alike, are one family in the Lord," and told of a black stable boy "who lay at the point of death with rheumatic fever and who was healed through the prayer of our white workers, who prayed for him just as earnestly and tenderly as they would have done for a white worker."[197] For some years, black and white continued to freely mingle in church and outside of services. Mahon reported on long evenings spent with his native evangelists at his home "where we spoke of things pertaining to the Kingdom, sang hymns and before parting just before midnight spent a season in prayer."[198] All of Mahon's family members were engaged in missionary work, and they too, enacted what they held to be the fraternity of the human family. In 1921, Mahon's twenty-eight-year-old daughter, Evaline, took up residence in a remote mountainous area of Basutoland as a Zion missionary, sent there largely on account of her being fluent in Sesotho and able to efficiently evangelize. The colonial authorities of the area "consider[ed] it most undesirable that a young woman be living alone in the Maluti mountains surrounded by Natives." But Mahon and members of the church retorted that she was not alone, "for she is never without two or three native female companions, and one woman always occupies her sleeping hut with her."[199] Black converts too seemed to perceive the mission's unusual characteristic in this regard. One Zion worker, Deacon Mabula, was amazed that he sat alongside a cart with a white man (this was Mahon) and that "when we outspanned he would not let me lead the horses to water or do any work or open any gates . . . I do not understand this, I can only say that God is softening the hearts of the people who were so hard on us."[200] Further evincing the countercultural direction of the mission in this period was the fact that—as in Dowie's day—missionaries' activities continued to arouse the ire among their conservative white neighbors. One Hester Eksteen volunteered at the mission's school to teach spinning and weaving; "her friends are amazed she is teaching kaffirs, and Free State school officials are aghast at her outrageous conduct in giving natives the benefit of her training."[201] In 1918 Mahon reported that local white farmers "have many times tried to frighten the natives by telling them that the police are going to put a stop to this work . . . but I told the white people they might as well try stop the wind as stop the Spirit of God working in either black or white."[202]

But even this bastion of Zion cosmopolitanism was not immune to the wider changes occurring in society. As the century wore on, white workers in the church increasingly displayed conservatism where they had previously been liberal. Changing perspectives on education are a good barometer of these shifts. Alongside the emphasis on academic education, from an early date the mission's school also began to promote the value of manual or industrial education for its black converts. By the end of the 1910s, a "Manual Day" on Tuesdays had been introduced to the school, where girls were taught cooking and other forms of housework, and boys instructed in carpentry. In 1919, the Zion City schoolteacher-missionary Ethel Thorpe wrote an opinion piece for the American magazine where she concurred with the opinions of Dudley Kidd, a prominent South African advocate of racial segregation, that "while book education seems to close the mind or open it in a distorted fashion, industrial work has an excellent effect."[203] By 1929, the mission declared to its supporters in the United States that "manual work was stressed."[204] In part, this was a strategic move in the hopes of gaining much-needed financial support for its schools from a government long in favor of industrial education for Africans and heavily suspicious of "book learning." But fragments from missionary correspondence and reports suggest that staff genuinely concurred with the racist view that Africans were innately suited to industrial rather than academic education.[205] Students lamented these changes, with boys rebelling against "sweeping the floors," and students still intent on pursuing higher education. In 1926, a young Etembeni student Jacob Nhlapo defiantly affirmed that "there is still room for more knowledge in me and I am determined to fill it up."[206] Manual work was done by the students, but reluctantly. A 1928 government inspection of the mission's school regretted to note that "as regards the farm work, it is generally felt that the boys look upon it more as a task than as learning something useful for later life."[207]

The career of Elijah Lutango, Mahon's long-term coworker, offers a further illustration of these developments. Lutango had become increasingly ground down by the harsh administration of the Orange Free State Province toward Africans (formerly the Orange River Colony). As Zion City missionary Myrtle Sisson correctly commented, the laws of the province "were constantly framed with no other purpose than to keep the black man down."[208] At the end of 1913 Lutango relocated with his family to neighboring Basutoland as a missionary for the Zion church there. His reason: "he was unable any longer to cope with the injustices of the Dutch farmers in the Free State."[209] By 1921, Lutango—now in Basutoland—had enlisted as a sympathizer of the South African National Native Congress. As the main platform for African elite's calls for political representation in this period, the nationalist policies of the new organization must have resonated with Lutango's frustration at the ever-lower ceiling placed on black aspiration both within and without the church. Lutango now also began preaching about the importance of black autonomy in church matters.[210] Edgar Mahon undertook an emergency trip to Basutoland to bring Lutango back into the fold: "to try and rectify errors made by our old-time warrior."[211] Mahon's efforts were to no avail, and in 1922 Lutango seceded from the Christian Catholic Church in Zion in South Africa to form his own independent Zionist church, taking many of his followers with him. His son, Micah, remained loyal to the white-led Zionist church for another decade, but by 1934, he too had severed his connection with Mahon and

Bryant, being the leader of a "deeply laid plan to withdraw the church as a whole from white missionaries." White staff commented that many who joined his revolt who were "led on with ideas of native advancement, and some speculated that Micah was inspired by the ideals of the period's popular labor movement, that he had been "drawn into the net now called the Industrial and Commercial Workers' Union."[212]

The careers of the Lutango father and son suggest that by the interwar years, the positions of Ethiopian and Zionist Christians were not, after all, so distant from each other. In these ever-more repressive decades, the educated black elite of South Africa's farming lands increasingly lost faith in white-led Zion's ability to maintain fidelity to the radical promises of Dowie's church. Faced with the collapse of Christian cosmopolitanism in early twentieth-century South Africa, and the rise of ethnically inflected Pentecostalism, many Zionists pursued similar courses to their Ethiopian colleagues. As white Christians would not accept them as equal brethren, they instead committed to religious paths that espoused the virtues of black African autonomy and self-determination. Yet at no point did these reformers renounce their loyalty to the values and identity of Zion. Their independent, black-led churches still almost entirely identified as Zionist organizations, and continued to prominently incorporate the name "Zion" into their institutional nomenclature. Most of these schismatic reformers viewed their rupture from Zion City and from white Zionist missionaries as fulfilling—rather than repudiating—the egalitarian values of their Christian faith.

CHAPTER FIVE

Sectarian Creativity and Populist Prophets in Interwar Johannesburg

IN THE INTERWAR decades of the 1920s and the 1930s, a popular new phenomenon arose in Johannesburg. These were the hundreds of Zionist churches that rapidly sprouted up in the city. Many were very small with only a handful of members and met in a tiny room in an inner-city slum or in a borrowed space in a mining barracks; others grew to be large and influential city churches with branches across the country. Most of these new churches were led by young men with little or any formal education or theological training, many of whom had never previously led a church. Some had broken away from existing Zion denominations to found a new church; others simply started their own Zion organization from scratch. All claimed to work by the inspiration of the Holy Spirit (reflecting the growing influence of the Pentecostal revival across South Africa), and professed themselves directly anointed by God to correct the excesses and errors that existing denominations had fallen into. Many criticized the African Christian elite of Johannesburg—including the older luminaries within the Zionist movement—and argued that the only true qualification of a religious leader was the guidance of the Spirit rather than education, worldly esteem or clerical seniority. Increasingly, these charismatic young figures came to style themselves as divinely appointed "prophets" rather than officials vetted by the religious establishment. These youthful reformers and their hundreds of new churches found wild popularity among Johannesburg's black population. Although these populist prophets were deeply disapproved of by the city's established churches, Zion and otherwise, these antiestablishment developments fueled a period of major growth for Zion in Southern Africa.

Great bursts of sectarian creativity were not new to the Zion tradition—for example, the very many churches that emerged in Zion City, Illinois after Dowie's death—nor to Protestantism more broadly. Indeed, the unregulated emergence of new denominations reflects the individualistic and subversive characteristics that define the Protestant tradition. A recent history of Protestantism identifies at least three major eruptions of this kind since the tradition began: in Germany of the 1520s, England of the 1640s and the United States' Holiness revivals of the nineteenth century.[1] Johannesburg of the interwar decades arguably deserves its place among this chronicle of international Protestant sectarianism, given the hundreds of churches that exponentially arose in these years, and the many thousands of individuals caught up in this ferment of denominational innovation. Yet—in line with a broader hesitation to interpret Zionists as legitimate representatives of the Christian tradition—scholars have been reluctant to consider the institutional fragmentation of Zion that occurred in these decades as part of an international Protestant tradition of sectarianism. Instead, Zionist schism in Southern Africa has been taken as evidence of the primacy of African culture. Bengt Sundkler and others argued that "tribal differences . . . [were a] powerful disintegrating force"; "tribal prestige" meant certain factions refused to be under the authority of rival ethnic constituencies, so broke away to start a new church.[2] This chapter instead situates the denominational proliferation of this period as a pivotal moment within a wider evangelical narrative of conscience-driven Christianity, reformist critique, and institutional schism.

Zion sectarianism emerged in the context of a much broader mood of antiestablishment turmoil in Johannesburg. Historians have argued that the repressive South African state and economic depression combined to produce "a failure of black political imagination" in interwar Johannesburg, portraying black politics—largely in the form of the African National Congress—as "passive and inert" throughout the 1920s and 1930s.[3] Yet as older avenues to black social mobility closed off amid segregation, African residents of the city were experimenting with radical new ways to flourish. Congress may have failed to find a mass following in this period but in turning to revolutionary political movements such as Marxism, socialism, and anarchism, some of Johannesburg's Africans were debating the relevance of hitherto established social consensuses regarding hierarchy, decorum and propriety, and the role of ordinary working-class people in relation to the black elite who dominated Congress.[4] Yet by only examining politically inflected activism we risk obscuring the large areas of black life where intense struggles over power and authority were also being fought. In particular, interwar Johannesburg was a milieu of energetic religious debate and contestation—a dynamic exemplified by the very many new Zionist churches that sprouted up as vehement critiques of established ways of being "Christian." Fierce arguments were taking place across the city over who could rightfully lead a church, what the role of formal qualifications in ministerial formation was, who were the correct leaders of the people—both within churches and in the outside world—and what counted as legitimate spiritual authority. Middle-class mores of hierarchy, rank, and prestige were constantly up for grabs in the court of public opinion, and a wave of youthful reformers were overturning and redefining previously accepted concepts of propriety in religious affairs.

In particular, this chapter explains how these decades witnessed a new Zionist critique of the value of literacy and learning. An earlier generation of African Zionist converts had prized education precisely for its subversive qualities. In a context where the white state restricted Africans' access to learning on the grounds of supposedly intrinsic racial inferiority, Zion's affirmation of education for all had profoundly egalitarian implications. Yet several decades later, a widespread perception arose among youthful Zionists that their church leaders had lost their spiritual zeal in becoming overly allied with "respectability" as defined by the secular world, and most of all, as exemplified in the prestige their leaders awarded to school and seminary qualifications. Youthful reformers felt something vital to the spiritual life had been obscured in this emphasis on secular degrees and certificates. Triggering a characteristically evangelical cycle of internal debate and regeneration, young Zionist prophets now assigned new meaning to education. Rather than a challenge to the restrictive racial logic of the white state, education was now aligned with the values of an elite snobocracy of middle-class Africans who conflated learning and piety. In antiestablishment terms that could have been used by Dowie in Melbourne of the 1870s, or in Chicago of the 1890s, these early twentieth-century urban prophets argued that true Christians were legitimated by God alone and that not only was education unnecessary, but that its acquisition could even hinder genuine piety. In addition to charting the sectarian proliferation that emerged in the interwar period, this chapter thus maps out a further important shift occurring within Southern African Zion during these years. This was Zion's dramatic transformation from a relatively small organization patronized by a literate African farmer class into a sprawling and decentralized black urban movement dominated by youthful, largely uneducated, and independent-minded reformers.

Education and Johannesburg's Black Urban Middle Classes

The first decades of the twentieth century saw extensive African migration from rural areas to South Africa's cities. While the city of Kimberly received a great many new African residents in this period, nothing could equal the scale of black migration to Johannesburg. The gold mines of the Witwatersrand had been drawing workers of all races from Southern Africa and further afield since the 1880s. By the interwar period, the growing secondary industries of the city were evermore hungry for labor, as were domestic households for servants. Between 1911 and 1921, the city's African population increased by 7% in the case of men and by a whopping 50 percent for women.[5] Between 1921 and 1936, over 100,000 more African residents arrived to the city, an overall increase of 94 percent in its black population.[6] A range of rural factors pushed people out of the farmlands into the city for employment, these included growing land dispossession such as we have already seen at play in the Orange Free State and the Transvaal, increased taxation, and a series of devastating animal epidemics and drought.[7] Against this backdrop of agricultural dispossession, the wages available to Africans in the city were a great draw.[8] Urbanization also provided new opportunities for autonomy, especially for urban African youth, who as wage earners in the city were able to pursue their own projects of social mobility independently of rural elders. This was also the case for young African women who, migrating to the city in greater numbers after the First World War, found freedom from gerontocratic rural hierarchies, unwanted marriages, and an overall deteriorating quality of rural life.[9] Despite rapidly increasing rates of female migration, in terms of absolute numbers, cities in the period under study in this chapter were still mainly male preserves; in 1936, only 11 percent of African women lived in urban areas.[10]

These were also the decades of a rise in a small African urban middle class. Many of the city's residents were unskilled men housed in compounds and barracks attached to gold mines who stayed in Johannesburg for work contracts of several months or even years, and then returned to their rural homes. But the interwar period did also see the rise in a permanently urbanized African class, one housed in the city's residential areas rather than on the mines themselves. Moreover, Johannesburg's urbanized African classes were disproportionately drawn from the ranks of the rural elite described in the last chapter, being squeezed off the land for all the reasons discussed there. These were the "well-educated professionals and artisans drawn from mission stations and mission reserves . . . South Africa's 'talented tenth.'"[11] There was, however, significant variation within this category, which included the better-educated professionals such as teachers, clergy, clerks, interpreters, nurses, municipal workers but also small business owners and petty commodity producers such as shoemakers, cobblers, tailors, clothes menders, peddlers, hawkers, carpenters, tinkers, builders, and wagon makers.[12] Johannesburg's black elite was thus populated by Oxbridge-educated lawyers such as Pixley ka Isaka Seme and Saul Msane, vice president of the South African Native National Congress as well as editor of its official newspaper organ, *Abantu Batho*.[13] But it also included the less exalted clerks, teachers, and municipal workers, many of whom are recorded in Mweli T. D. Skota's *Who's Who* of 1932, such as one D. M. Denalane, an interpreter in Johannesburg's Native Affairs Department, and later chief clerk at the Robertson Deep Gold Mine Compound.[14] The ideal, moreover, for women of this class was that they pursued lives of "devout domesticity," occupying full-time roles as homemakers, wives, and mothers.[15] Members of this class tended to live in townships and locations such as Alexandra, New Clare, Nancefield, and Sophiatown (where Africans could purchase land) or in inner-city slums where rooms in yards could be rented.[16]

Johannesburg black petit bourgeoisie society displayed a lively and diverse Christian culture with high rates of church attendance. In the 1930s, an observer of inner-city black culture noted that "practically all the natives . . . belong to a Christian church."[17] As on the Highveld, Christianity promoted an aspirational ideal for Africans that embraced notions of individual progress, economic independence, and an elusive notion of civilized progress.[18] Church-run institutions such as *manyanos* (women's groups) and the regular "church teas" for fundraising purposes gave rise to new forums for associational networks in the city, as well as acted as crucibles for the formation of urban identities characterized by middle-class respectability. The most important denominations among the city's Christian elite were the historic and white-led mission churches such as the Methodists, Anglicans, and Lutherans. A former resident of Sophiatown recalled how the area "seethed" on Sundays with "the great mass of people on their way to church," largely to the Anglican mission, the largest church in the area with 2,000 communicants.[19] But other types of churches also flourished. By the late 1940s, the popular North American African Methodist Episcopal Church claimed to have 7,000 full members on the Rand.[20] A number of local independent Ethiopian-style churches also espoused the gradualist values of elite respectability and claimed many middle-class black members. The prominent Bantu Methodist church, for example, had 3,000 members on the Rand while the African Congregational Church had more than 2,000.[21] The dividing line between Africans linked to the older and prestigious white-led mission denominations and the new class of Ethiopian ministers was a permeable one. Both were inspired by similar values of black progress via civilized respectability. In 1923, the city's Director for Native Labour reported that "the relationship between the two classes of churches would appear to be good and I am informed that certain of the better class of ministers of native separatist churches are on occasions invited to preach in European controlled churches and vice versa."[22]

For all members of this urban class, Ethiopian or otherwise, the civilizing value of education was a key article of faith. Many had had formative years at famed missionary-run schools such as the Methodist Healdtown School in the Eastern Cape or the American Board Ohlange Institute in Natal before their arrival in the city.[23] These experiences decisively shaped their opinions regarding the transformative value of education for individuals, and for the black community as a whole. Johannesburg's black middle classes had an unshakeable confidence in education's ability to move people from "barbarism" to "civilization." One J. J. Nduma wrote to *Bantu World* (a leading black middle-class periodical) in 1933 that "education is a royal road to a city of gold and opportunities . . . education is the root of genuine growth in the individual and national vigour and strength."[24] Literacy was seen as key to the progress of Africans into broader fraternities of civilized moderns. According to the *Bantu World*, "our political liberation, our social status, our economic strength, our mental growth and our spiritual wealth all depend on the extent of the literacy of our great numbers . . . words—books—are the Alpha and Omega of progress."[25] Inspired by this vision, Johannesburg's black petit bourgeoisie made great sacrifices to educate their children,[26] buying books and newspapers despite financial strictures.[27] The proliferation of correspondence schools and night schools across the city in this period is also evidence of the general high regard for education's transformative power.[28] The 1920s was the decade when libraries and reading rooms for Africans sprouted up across the city as well as a lively newspaper press, with publications such as *Abantu Batho* (1912), *Umteteli wa Bantu* (1920), and *Bantu World* (1932) forming the tastes and opinions of the city's middle classes. These publications frequently featured articles on the value of education, celebrating the attainment of degrees, certificates, and school prizes as key markers of black success.[29]

Equipped with both Christianity and education, these elite members considered themselves modern African individuals, embracing the best of the old ways while moving forward to progress and modernity. An opening issue of *Bantu World* compared "emancipated Bantu who lives the life of civilized man, taking tea at a well-appointed Bantu Club" with the old African who "lived in semi-barbarism eating his mealiepap with a wooden spoon out of a clay pot."[30] A self-conscious shift away from older linguistic and ethnic identities was key to many in this class. Rejecting narrow ethnic affiliation, *Bantu World* published articles in a variety of languages—Zulu, Xhosa, Sesotho, Setswana, and English—embodying the determination of the modernizing African middle classes to be united not by language or ethnicity, but by common participation in modernity.[31] Middle-class Africans joined associations in the city on the basis of voluntary participation within a shared community of progressiveness, rather than prior ethnic or linguistic links. Johannesburg's elite Bantu Men's Social Club, for example, emerged as a focal meeting point for middle-class Africans, offering debating, lectures, and amateur dramatics.[32] An American patron of the club observed that "any mention of tribal loyalties is deprecated, and English is fostered in belief that a common language will help merge Natives of different tribes into a Bantu nation."[33] Moreover, in the battle against "heathenism," the remedy for tribalism was of course none other than education: "with mighty weapons we arm ourselves; education, religion follow in our rear; woe to thee o Tribalism!"[34]

It follows from all of this that the city's middle classes had a strongly felt sense of their own superiority, of the wide gulf between themselves, on the one hand, and the vast bulk of uneducated black South Africa, on the other. In 1911, the first national census calculated that only 6.8 percent of all Africans in South Africa could read.[35] The number of literates remained a small minority well into the twentieth-century; by 1936, only 12 percent of a total African population of 6.6 million were literate, and most of those in the cities.[36] Educated Africans saw this as a great setback for the progress of the race in South Africa; a 1940 editorial in the *Bantu World* maintained that "it is clear that most of our ills and disasters spring from the existence of illiterate, blind, emotion-controlled masses who cannot read and reason for themselves."[37] Elite members spoke frankly of their uneducated compatriots as an obstacle to the development of the race. An earlier 1932 article in the *Bantu World* had lamented that "as long as the bulk of the masses cannot read or write, so long will they be a menace to the welfare of the community. No community can progress above its most backward class . . . it is only through the uplift of its backward classes that South Africa will benefit."[38] Although the city's middle-class Africans tried to live as new and progressive moderns, unhindered by "tribalism," they recognized that most of the country still lived enmeshed in the old ways. Newspapers contained numerous laments about the "sting" of tribalism; *Umteteli wa Bantu* grieved that "we Bantu are cut up into a thousand and one tribes through family feuds."[39]

A major component of black middle-class identity was thus their perception of themselves as the self-appointed leaders of the people. Where most
of their compatriots were unenlightened, it was their responsibility to provide tutelage and guidance. The duty of the middle classes was to educate
their "uncivilized and heathen compatriots": as *Bantu World* put it, "the
problem of illiteracy is universal and urgent. Everywhere leaders of thought
and action are fighting desperately in the battle between illiteracy and salvation, for illiteracy is death . . . it is the race between salvation and
chaos."[40] The necessity of middle-class leadership was widely discussed in
this period. According to a *Bantu World* editorial of 1933, "the scarcest
thing in the world is not diamonds or platinum . . . It is effective leadership,
a true leader must possess loyalty, education, alertness, decision, enthusiasm and reliability."[41] Few figures symbolized the aspirations of the
black middle class to uplift their people as much as that of the teacher and
the religious minister, two of the most common professions for the urban
elite.[42] Teachers would impart the sacred good of education to the masses.
More than mere providers of information, teachers were those "who can
be the uplift or the downfall of their people . . . his voice reaches far and
wide, he is a man highly respected."[43] Although many women found themselves shut out of the formal labor market on the Rand, teaching was one
of the few professions open to black females. Charlotte Maxeke was perhaps the most famous example of this; as a graduate of the African American Wilberforce College she returned to Johannesburg in 1901 where she
and her husband opened schools in the East Rand of Johannesburg and
northern Transvaal.[44] Teachers imparted civilization, progress, and learning,
whereas ministers taught their congregants the lessons of self-discipline and
a Christian code of morality: "the Bantu preacher must uplift the people
by constantly teaching them the value of vital lessons without which his
people cannot prosper, with them they will advance and become a great
and noble race."[45]

Despite these lofty goals, conditions in Johannesburg severely constricted
the ambitions of this self-improving class. For one, the city's municipal administration was ambivalent about permanently urbanized Africans, expressing the period's racist views that towns were destined for European
residency while simultaneously being constrained by mining capital's need
for proximate black labor.[46] This resulted in an uneasy official tolerance of
urban Africans mingled with chronic underprovision of life's necessities.
The Johannesburg municipality passed draconian Pass Laws and bureau-
cratic legislation rendering Africans ever vulnerable to expulsion from the
city on account of faulty paperwork.[47] As was the case in the rural areas,

racial segregation began to permeate every aspect of urban society during these years. Even the small number of Africans holding "exemption certificates" on the grounds of their education and overall "civilized" status—the cream of urban black society—were vulnerable to official harassment, perhaps especially so, falling victim to racist dislike of educated Africans. Despite the fact that the possession of an exemption certificate entitled the bearer to be out at all hours, "the holder could be stopped by a policeman, even one with half his education and possessions, and asked in rude language where he is going at night . . . any cheap jack European can tell you to *Voetsak*[48] with it in your possession."[49]

Middle-class Africans were also severely constrained financially. Black skilled and semiskilled workers in Johannesburg received dramatically lower wages than white counterparts, and combined with the high cost of living, the average Rand African could barely make ends meet.[50] The aspiring middle classes were therefore highly insecure, often blending imperceptibly into the ranks of more humble working classes.[51] One African "respectable" woman lamented that despite her ambitions for a better life, she has "to stand here day after day and kill myself washing."[52] Living conditions in the city were dire, compounded by the administration's failure to provide affordable housing for Africans. Inner-city slum yards in Fordsburg, Ferreirastown, Marshalltown, and City and Suburban proliferated; these were areas where landlords charged extortionate rents for tiny rooms.[53] Despite their desire for respectability, poorly paid clerks, interpreters, teachers, craftsmen, shopkeepers, and ministers of religion lived in the city's worst parts alongside the unemployed, criminal, and destitute.[54] Small-scale producers and artisans—who made up the vast majority of the black middle classes—were also losing their livelihood in the interwar period, faced with competition from factories, poor whites, and British manufacturers dumping cheap products for the African market into the country. Bootmakers and cobblers were a particularly struggling constituency.[55] Even the teacher—the prized profession of this demographic—was increasingly under threat, with professionals retrenched and their salaries dramatically slashed, indeed, almost halved during the Depression of the 1930s.[56] In 1928, a black head teacher's monthly wages were ten pounds and ten shillings; three years later, in 1931, head teachers were paid six pounds ten shillings.[57] Class sizes grew immensely during this period, further putting strain on teachers.[58] With the latest cuts on teachers' salaries how could they—the *Bantu World* demanded—"maintain a standard of respectability in keeping with the dignity of their profession?"[59]

The gradualist values of the black middle classes were also challenged by a growing wave of populist radicalism sweeping Johannesburg. Many educated Africans had long been linked to the African National Congress (renamed, in 1923, from the South African Native National Congress), an organization that advocated the progressive, gradual inclusion of literate Africans into a multiracial franchise.[60] Congress was concerned with eradicating racial segregation and establishing equality of opportunity through the gradual uplift and development of the black people, rather than advocating for a dramatic overturning of the social order.[61] Yet by the late 1920s, it had become clear that this moderate approach was of little practical value. Congress' anti-pass laws campaign had failed, its pleas for parity of education had been disregarded by the government, and the economic color bar had if anything been intensified.[62] At the same time as these disappointments were occurring (and more probably than not in response to them), a more defiant swell of working-class activism arose across the country. Trade union movements such as the Industrial and Commercial Workers' Union (ICU) became highly popular organizations based not on the old elite hope of gradual recognition with the eventual attainment of education and progress, but on organized labor's radical demands for immediate transformation of the economic order. Populist leaders and activists were, by and large, drawn from the ranks of the petit bourgeoisie. Many ICU leaders were members of the rural elite based in freehold property and mission reserves who had firm identities "as children of God, readers of books and citizens of Empire."[63] Yet it was precisely this constituency that experienced extreme material constraints and downward social mobility, and for whom invoking the uneducated, unskilled rural proletariat as a force for transformation seemed an increasing attractive option.[64] Unlike their more moderate middle-class counterparts, they were vocal critics of white missionaries' work. At the ICU's annual conference of 1925, its president exhorted the audience that for "Christ's sake, tell the Europeans to keep their white Jesus, and let you have your own land which they took from you."[65]

Many black middle-class commentators were scathing in their denunciation of this new strand of radical populism.[66] Congress luminary Richard Selope Thema asserted that "class hatred would bring forth endless strife"; the only hope for South Africa was continued striving for older ideals of multiracial cooperation.[67] But middle-class Africans found themselves increasingly outnumbered by those who rejected the hoped-for multiracial franchise of a future South Africa and emphasized a future vision of black advancement via racial solidarity as well as class allegiances. Many joined Marcus Garvey's transnational Universal Negro Improvement Association (UNIA) and worked for "Africa for the Africans."[68] Some radicalized branches of Congress in its Johannesburg offices collaborated with the

UNIA's agitation against low pay, high prices, pass laws, and the color bar. Yet the mainstream of the city's African elite continued to denounce Garvey's popular radicalism as both undesirable and unattainable, thinking Garveyism would create overreliance on international blacks and antagonize an already hostile white government. In 1920, *Umteteli wa Bantu* cautioned its readers against the lure of "racial bitterness"; it would be "lunatic to be influenced by impossible ideal of all Black Africa."[69]

During the 1920s, a further populist development occurred, one that was also perceived by the Christian middle classes as a grave threat to civilized society. This was the dramatic proliferation of black-led churches in the city. The emergence of new churches was not in itself an entirely new development. As the previous chapter showed, the turn of the century had seen the birth of dozens of Ethiopian organizations across South Africa. Despite being radical in their calls for black leadership, many of the Ethiopian churches nonetheless continued to espouse the gradualist, moderate values of the city's elite. Many ministers were educated in leading missionary schools across the country and many continued to see themselves as the natural leaders of the uneducated masses. By the 1920s, however, a very different crop of churches had sprung up, largely from within the ranks of the Zionist churches and heavily influenced by the Spirit-infused theology of the new Pentecostal Christianity. Claiming to be acting on direct instructions from God, this new batch of leaders considered education entirely unnecessary and proclaimed that the true man of God needed no worldly qualifications—the sole anointing of the Holy Spirit was more than sufficient.

"Many Mushroom Organizations Spring Up in Johannesburg"

The division, however, between the new populist wave of Zion churches and the African Christian establishment was not absolute. For some time, early twentieth-century Zion churches in Johannesburg had continued to reflect the gradualist values of the city's black middle classes. Most early Zionists continued to affirm their commitment to the old ideal of multi-racial cooperation between Christians, working closely with white Zion figures still active in South Africa. In 1913, Wilbur Glenn Voliva, besieged by clerical rivals such as Daniel Bryant at home, revived a branch of the Christian Catholic Apostolic Church in Zion in Johannesburg. In 1913 Voliva appointed a white Johannesburg Zionist from Dowie's era, the Welshman Henry Mordred Powell, as his representative.[70] Funded by

Voliva, Powell resecured the old Zion Tabernacle on Bree Street that had until then been occupied by AFM Pentecostals.[71] Many old African Zion leaders from Wakkerstroom disillusioned with Pentecost reaffiliated themselves to Zion. Both Daniel Nkonyane and Muneli Ngobese submitted applications for readmission in Voliva's revived Johannesburg Zion Church in 1913.[72] A key figure in the new Zion in Johannesburg was the Mosotho Paulus Mabiletsa, a long-time member of the church since 1905, drawn in during Mahon's large evangelistic drives in Basutoland to Zion's baptism by immersion, which Mabiletsa approvingly deemed "in accordance with the scriptures."[73] The educated Mabiletsa was one of Voliva's "most successful native preachers" in Johannesburg. He acted as the church's clerk and was also the pastor-in-charge of the Zion Tabernacle on Smal Street which he ran with his wife, the latter being ordained by Powell as a Deaconess.[74]

During the 1910s, education still continued to lie at the heart of Zion's identity in Johannesburg, as it had done on the Highveld. The Zion Tabernacle doubled up as a night school for church members (run by a Mrs. Matlanyane in conjunction with Mabiletsa's wife).[75] Other Zion churches and schools rapidly sprung up over the city. By 1914, a "native" branch of over forty members was established in Jeppestown—with an attached nightschool—while a branch opened in Ophirton, a working-class suburb southwest of the city, led by a Mr. Stegman, a "carpenter by trade and a well-known man among the colored people."[76] Even those rival Zion organizations hostile to Voliva continued to prize education as an integral component of the spiritual life. Edgar Mahon—whose rival Christian Catholic Church in Zion in the Harrismith district professed loyalty to Daniel Bryant in Zion City—soon opened a branch in Germiston location east of the city.[77] This church was led by Walter Hadebe, a teacher who had been "healed of insanity and his one daughter of fits."[78] As the educated owners of a three-bedroom house, the Hadebe family exemplified the self-improving values of the educated elite. Originally from Basutoland, Hadebe had converted in the days of Mahon and Lutango's large-scale proselytization in that country, and had married a young woman who had taught in one of the first Zion schools.[79] Described by Mahon as a member of a "wonderful Christian family," Hadebe's eldest daughter, Grace, taught school subjects in the bedroom and living room of their house to almost one hundred children who gathered for instruction.[80] Although their next-door neighbor was a lively informal bar with "beer-drinking and boisterous talking," the Hadebe family entertained themselves at night by singing Zion songs in their home for church members (indeed, many of these musical pieces were their own compositions).[81]

Moreover, even after they had severed their ties with the American headquarters in Zion City, most of Johannesburg's early black Zionists maintained their faith in the intertwined values of education, respectability, and progress. In 1915, Voliva—besieged by financial troubles in Zion City—failed to send rent for the Johannesburg Tabernacle. The building's owners took furniture in lieu of payment, chronicled scurrilously by the city's newspapers.[82] Zion's Johannesburg leadership were unhappy they were still paying tithes to North America, but receiving little from Voliva, not even a building for their meetings.[83] Mabiletsa was the first to secede from Voliva, forming the new Christian Apostolic Church in Zion (the removal of "Catholic" indicating his was a different church to the American one). Mabiletsa declared his new church entirely independent of Zion City, informing Johannesburg's native commissioner that "any outside interference with our Zion churches would be totally unnecessary and intolerable."[84] It soon grew to be one of the largest black-led churches on the Rand, with a membership of approximately 5,000 by 1925.[85] The profile of Mabiletsa's deputies reflected the membership of aspiring yet struggling educated middle classes. David Rankos a preacher in Mabiletsa's church was an employee of the city's municipality;[86] another preacher was Obed Zwane who was a "soft goods hawker, but stopped because of sore feet as he used to walk a lot."[87] By 1934, the church opened a large branch in Alexandra Township, the headquarters of its operations. Reflecting church members' aspirations for middle-class respectability, at the opening, Mabiletsa preached that "it is good to have a habit of building and dwelling in good houses because even in the coming life we will dwell in good houses."[88] Mabiletsa's church was famous for its school in Alexandra Township, "one of the very few schools for Africans on the Rand," with classes going right up to Standard VII, as well as schools in the small towns of Daggakraal and Amersfoort in the Transvaal for rural members.[89]

John George Phillips was another early Zionist leader in the city whose life and career exemplified his belief in the complementarity between Christianity and education. Phillips had arrived in Johannesburg from Nyasaland (today Malawi) in 1904, the first generation recruited by the Witwatersrand Native Labour Association to work on the Rand.[90] Phillips—named after the Anglican priest had who baptized him—reflected the self-improving values of many Nyasa mission-educated men of this period.[91] Phillips's daughter, Jane, recounted that her father "was educated at the headquarters of the Universities Mission of Central Africa . . . he had good progress in all his studies, but particularly distinguished himself in the study of the Bible . . . he was always head of the class."[92] Like many men of his class and background, Phillips styled himself as a self-conscious modern, free of

Christian Catholic Apostolic Church in Zion African Preachers, Johannesburg. *Source: Leaves of Healing,* 14 February 1914. Christ Community Church Archives, Zion, Illinois.

traditionalism and the past. Jane wrote that although "the Rev. John G. Phillips was the son of a Chief and by rights his successor," her father decided to "turn from these honours to the greater glory of preaching the Everlasting Gospel."[93] Once on the Rand, Phillips became a clerk at Crown Mines, an occupation reserved for those with education.[94] He soon succumbed to a respiratory condition—a common ailment among Nyasa migrants in the city—and found that he had "a very weak chest and suffered much . . . no medicine did him any good." Although a devout Anglican, he came across tracts that taught "Divine Healing," and went to Pastors [John G. Lake] Lake and Tom [of the AFM]." Jane tells how "these brothers prayed for him, with the Laying on of Hands, and he got wonderfully healed."[95] Briefly allied with Voliva,[96] by 1920, Phillips had, like Mabiletsa, grown weary of Voliva's heavy tithing demands on the Johannesburg congregation, complaining "seven shillings a month is too great a burden for native people in their poverty, with taxes and school fees and school books, clothing, rent and food."[97] He also disagreed with Voliva's grandiose authoritarianism, remarking scornfully that Johannesburgers were not impressed by "American methods of boasting."[98] Phillips instead asserted his loyalty to the Gospel alone and its improving effects: "as preachers we are all out for the preaching of the Gospel which makes men and women honest, moral, clean, industrious, of good report."[99] Phillips established a new Zionist church, the Holy Catholic Apostolic Church in Zion.[100] By 1924, it had 700 adult members in Johannesburg. As with Mabiletsa's organization, Phillips's congregants styled themselves as part of the respectable African middle classes. An elderly present-day member of the church remembers his father would tell him that in the days of John George Phillips, male members were expected to wear black suits with ties to church: "You were supposed to be a gentleman in the church with your tie! You were supposed to be a Westerner!"[101]

Educated Zionist ministers such as Phillips and Mabiletsa moved easily among the best of black Christian society. Mabiletsa, for example, sent his son, Phillip, to Fort Hare—the leading African educational establishment of the day—to work toward a BSc, where his teachers praised him as "a young man of exceptional intelligence with a special bent for the Sciences."[102] Mabiletsa's new Zion Tabernacle in Alexandra was regularly patronized by luminaries of black society; a 1936 service featured one of the wives of Zulu regent Cyprian ka Solomon as well as the mayor of Alexandra and leading business owner and political leader, E. P. Mart Zulu.[103] Then there was Zionist minister T. Mwelase, one of the few in Johannesburg still loyal to Voliva, and who was a respected local figure in his community, chairing rate payers association meetings in Sophiatown.[104] Phillips, Mabiletsa, and other Zionist leaders frequently preached at the pulpits of the most prominent Ethiopian organizations. Phillips, for example, was invited to perform the ordination for Andrew Zungu, founder of the much-respected Congregational Church of South Africa, while Walter Ndebele's church was lent the building of the African Congregational Church for its own large services.[105] Further suggesting Zionist leaders' good standing within these elite circles, *Bantu World*—a chronicle of the black middle-classes—regularly reported on the doings of these figures; announcing in its news-about-town section, for example, that the "Rev. Matthew Koza of Germiston [Phillips's senior minister] paid a flying visit to the Eastern Native township on business."[106] Mabiletsa's activities were also a frequent presence in these pages,[107] and in fact, during the 1930s, he acted as a seller and agent for *Bantu World* in Alexandra.[108] Skota's *African Yearly Register*—the index of black luminaries of the interwar period—listed in its pages the "leading native ministers" of the day, and included Rev. Walter Ndebele of the Christian Catholic Church in Zion.[109]

Not all Zionists in Johannesburg were as sympathetic to the values of the African Christian establishment. In the same period that saw the growth of Mabiletsa and Phillips's churches, an entirely more populist element began emerging within Zion. Older Zionists espoused the elitist confidence that education marked them out as natural leaders. Yet another strand existed within Zionist thought that argued God's work was carried out wherever the "Spirit bloweth" and denounced those who assumed education and training qualified them to be religious leaders. This attitude became even more pronounced in the Pentecostal movement of the early twentieth century, active in Johannesburg since 1908 in the form of the AFM and a host of other Pentecostal churches that subsequently cropped up in mining barracks. This was, after all, a tradition that in North America initially established no standard of education as necessary for ordination in any of its major denominations. And in the 1920s, a Pentecostal minister in England commented that the only preparation needed for ministry was a miraculous "upper-room experience."[110] In South Africa, Pentecostal-inspired arguments soon erupted in a falling-out between Mabiletsa, in Johannesburg, and Daniel Nkonyane in the Transvaal. Nkonyane—who had left the AFM in protest of the racism of white leaders—briefly allied himself with Voliva's revived Zion. After Mabiletsa broke away from Voliva, Nkonyane was one of many Transvaal Zionist figures who linked himself with Mabiletsa's new church. But tensions began to brew between the educated Mabiletsa and the Transvaal church leader who was unable to read or write. The issue at stake was Nkonyane's growing commitment to Pentecost, and the belief that the Baptism of the Holy Spirit conferred the ecstatic experience of speaking in tongues upon true believers.[111] Mabiletsa vehemently disagreed with the Nkonyane, attempting to clamp down upon the latter's promotion of the doctrine. The dispute came to be cast as a conflict between "spirit" and "education." An oral tradition in Nkonyane's church today holds that the "literate and highly educated" Mabiletsa manipulated his learning to oust Nkonyane from leadership. By the 1970s, and still reflecting wariness of the ambivalent value of education, Nkonyane's church members remembered that "Mabiletsa took advantage of his position as church clerk to delete Nkonyane's name from the records, replacing it with his own, and he also took over the church funds."[112] Nkonyane now struck out on his own, founding a new church named the Christian Catholic Apostolic Holy Spirit Church in Zion and with the inclusion of "Holy Spirit" signifying Nkonyane's conviction that the Spirit trumped Mabiletsa's learning. By the 1930s, Nkonyane's rival church had a thriving branch on the Rand, based also in Alexandra Township, and led by a relative, one Abraham Nkonyane.[113]

Across Johannesburg, a wave of similar Spirit-fueled disputes broke out between older established Zionist ministers and their junior subordinates. Although diverse in content, these arguments all revolved around the tension between an established ecclesial hierarchy and the revelatory pronouncements of a Spirit-inspired individual. One of Phillips's junior preachers was Obed Ndhlela, a shoemaker, who came to strenuously object that Phillips "wore boots during the ministration of the Holy Eucharist," contravening Ndhlela's understanding of Scriptures' injunction against shoes in holy places.[114] Ndhlela split from Phillips and formed a new church, which he named the Bethesda Zion Apostolic Church of Africa, situated in the African freehold area of Johannesburg named New Clare, and which banned shoes during its services.[115] By 1921, the church numbered several hundred members, and held services in Ndhlela's tiny room in New Clare which served as bedroom, workshop, and church; Ndhlela's clerical garb sat side by side with his boot-making tools.[116] Despite his own status as a breakaway minister, Ndhlela himself was aware of the danger of independent-minded secessionists claiming inspiration from on high; his new church constitution of 1921 mandated the necessity of "canonical obedience which binds against schisms."[117] But this secessionist soon had to himself contend with unruly individuals within his congregation who appealed to their direct revelation from the Spirit. One of these schismatic figures was G. Masopha, who claimed that inspiration from God had ordered him to break away from Ndhlela: he "sat and prayed and came forth with the name of this different church . . . the Galatia Apostolic Church in Zion."[118] Walter Ndebele was also subject to similar breakaways. In 1924, one Mahlangu founded the Congregational Apostolic Evangelical Church. He had decided to leave Mahon and Ndebele's Christian Catholic Apostolic Church in Zion because it "baptised in houses [not in rivers], renounced Apostles' teachings and traditions, misinterpreted the testament and divorced it from the rest of the Bible."[119]

These dissenting figures exemplified a growing sense in interwar Johannesburg that "education" and "Spirit" need not always ally. As one Dlamini wrote to the *Bantu World* in 1933: "some people say that the word of God can be realized through education. But that is wrong. It only by the Spirit that the word of God can go well."[120] Most of the new Zion church founders were without either education or ministerial training. Albert Madi, the founder of the Christian Apostolic Faith Church in Zion—a 1931 breakaway from Mabiletsa's organization—was a tailor.[121] Obed Ndhlela was a boot-maker. George Khambule, also a founder of a new Zion church in 1919, worked underground on the mines, and had only minimal reading and writing skills gleaned from attending a night school.[122] Instead of appealing to their years of education, these figures were grounding their legitimacy on a divine mandate rather than on secular qualifications. This contemporary juxtaposition of "spirit" versus "education" was evident in the religious career of Edward Lion, a Zionist minister of Johannesburg in the 1920s. Born in Peka, Basutoland in 1880,[123] the young Lion aged twenty made his way to Johannesburg where he was employed in a hotel as a cook before becoming a popular preacher in the Pentecostal AFM and eventually in the 1920s, the founder of his own church, the Zion Apostolic Faith Mission Church.[124] As Lion announced to government officials: "I have no papers, I was appointed by God."[125] A Zionist interviewed by Lutheran missiologist Bengt Sundkler in the 1940s similarly contrasted divine appointment versus worldly "papers," announcing that, although he had started his own church, "I was never ordained for that work." The basis of his authority was a "Voice" that said, "I will put the *Umoya* [the Holy Spirit] into thee, because thou hast received a Heavenly Ordination."[126]

Claiming a divine mandate offered new opportunities to figures who ordinarily struggled in the Rand's socially and economically stratified environment. Appealing to the Spirit enabled the minimally educated to claim religious rank previously reserved for only the formally trained and qualified. The inspiration of the Holy Spirit could also create space for female leaders. Although the vast majority of church founders of this period were men, a handful of women also claimed that the Spirit directed them to form churches. One of the most famous female church founders was Christiana Nku of Evaton, located south of Johannesburg. A member of the AFM, throughout the 1920s, Nku spoke of receiving heavenly visions of the Temple of Jerusalem on Mount Zion. "Ma Nku"—as her followers called her—understood this to be a model of the new church she should found, and broke away from the AFM to inaugurate the St. John's Apostolic Church. By mid-century, it was one of the largest Zion-Apostolic churches on the Rand, with tens of thousands of members.[127] The inspiration of the Holy Spirit could also usher in new financial opportunities for those who struggled to make ends meet. Junior ministers within established churches— including Zionist organizations—often received little or no pay. By contrast, a church founder could expect to receive tithes direct from their followers, which they were under no compulsion to hand over to either white or black supervisors. Skeptical commentators inferred from this that church founders were motivated by their desire "to gain a livelihood without physical toil."[128] In the cash-strapped milieu of black Johannesburg, this type of entrepreneurial clericalism could pay off. Whatever the size of the church, heading one's own denomination meant the founder accessed congregants' tithes, usually eking out a relatively stable living.[129] In 1920, adult members of most Christian churches were expected to contribute two shillings per month, including a contribution toward the minister's salary.[130] By the 1950s, a study of a Johannesburg African location noted the relatively high earnings open to ministers of "the African independent churches," observing that ministers received additional income from baptisms, funerals, weddings, and special fund-raising functions.[131]

An older generation of Zion ministers responded with great alarm to this populist profusion of unauthorized new organizations. Some churches, like Mabiletsa's, even tried—seemingly without much success—to enforce a uniform standard of education and training for ministers. The mid-twentieth-century constitution of his Christian Apostolic Church in Zion stated: "all persons being male requiring to be called into ministry shall pass an examination in Scripture and Scripture Knowledge and History."[132] T. Mwelase, who led the Johannesburg Zion church loyal to Voliva, angrily wrote to *Bantu World* denouncing those "people who call themselves Zionists while they are not . . . they are not taught and they shame us in the sight of other churches . . . [we] do not consecrate a pastor who is not trained." In contrast to these unschooled reformists, Mwelase identified himself as a properly qualified representative of Zion City headquarters: "I had three years training and then I was ordained a pastor. After the training I asked permission to start a church for the blacks and I was permitted."[133] The Mahon-controlled Christian Catholic Church in Zion also attempted to distinguish their organization—which operated according to a strict Dowie-era hierarchy of deacons and evangelists—from the numerous new Zions. By 1933 Edgar Mahon was lamenting that "unfortunately many of our break away fanatical natives call themselves *amaZioni,* which would make it appear them belong to us . . . but we have no connection of any kind with them."[134] By 1946, Mahon's son, Alfred, took the drastic measure of changing the name of the church to entirely renounce any connection with "Zion" and its populist connotations. The church's fundraising literature noted how the "self-appointed prophets . . . brought the name of Mr Mahon's mission into disrepute and caused no little embarrassment." From henceforth, then, the Zion church in South Africa loyal to Bryant in Zion City was called the Mahon Mission.[135]

The ministers of an older Zion tradition were deeply disapproving of these populist reformers, and Johannesburg's broader African Christian establishment also reacted with consternation. The eruption of independent religious activity upended their conviction that it was only those with education—that is to say, themselves—who were qualified to lead the masses and to occupy the hallowed position of a religious minister. One *Bantu World* correspondent asked, outraged, "who can explain the Word of God without any knowledge in him just by depending on the Spirit?"[136] At a Methodist conference in Johannesburg in 1932, African clerical luminaries such as Z. R. Mahabane and A. Mtimkulu dubbed the profusion of independent churches as the "blind leading the blind," their leaders were merely "ignorant men." Suggesting the fiery Pentecostal flavor of much of the new style of preaching, these elite lambasted the "mediocre types of sermons bristling with hell fire . . . fall[ing] short of the mentality of the educated Bantu."[137] Throughout the 1930s, African newspapers increasingly bemoaned the "insult from untrained preachers who frequently frighten us about death, telling us to repent so that we may not go to hell . . . but who can hardly read or write yet want to lead."[138] Whereas these church founders claimed their organizations' names had been directly given to them by God, educated Africans snidely criticized their innovations as ignorance. One Inkhabela wrote in to *Bantu World* angrily inquiring whether "it [is] the spirit that is not supported by education which brings about so many denominations that have such funny names that even dogs laugh at them?"[139] In the opinion of many, the sacrosanct profession of the "ministry"—a top professional aspiration for African elite—had become a laughing stock. It was further "cheapened" by the aspirations of unqualified pretenders who invoked the "Spirit": "this noble profession has become nothing more than quackery among the Bantu."[140] Inkhabela asserted: "religion without education has no dignity."[141] Seth Mokitimi, chaplain of leading Anglican college Healdtown, disapprovingly cited his "doubt and foreboding" at this profusion of sectarian, unregulated religion: "the ministry has a low standard of literacy and they receive no training . . . great multitudes in this fold get very little teaching."[142] European missionaries were as skeptical—or even more so—as the black Christian establishment of these ecclesial pretenders. Prominent Johannesburg American Board missionary, Ray Phillips, dismissed these figures' aspirations to religious leadership, noting that Zionist so-called Archbishops were those who had the Spirit and little else besides this. According to Phillips, they merely "graduated from work in the compound, obtained a collar from somewhere, put it on back to front, and 'How do you do, Archbishop!'"[143]

Much of the fear surrounding Spirit-fueled reformists stemmed from a contemporary incident known as the "Bulhoek Massacre." In April 1921, over one hundred adherents of the Eastern Cape cleric Enoch Mgijima—founder of the new "Israelite" church after his split from a North American black Holiness denomination—were gunned down by the state for refusing to vacate territory they claimed had been given to them by God. The Israelites were convinced that Mgijima was a latter-day biblical prophet, and that their small patch of land in the Eastern Cape was God's new holy city.[144] Deeply alarmed at the massacre, the black intelligentsia issued warnings to the wider public about the threat of schismatic "religious fanatics" who led followers to disaster. Leading African Christian spokesperson D. T. T. Javabu wrote in Natal paper *Ilanga lase Natal* that "the Israelite leadership has shown a remarkable misreading of the Bible, a fault due to little education."[145] An editorial in the same newspaper cautioned its readers not to follow the mistake of the Israelites, and imagine scripture to be "literally" true. Do not "imagine yourself to be a latter-day Ishmael,"[146] its readers were advised, nor make the mistake of "unsophisticated rustics" who believed "that people must worship on the model of Israelite patriarchs."[147] Lack of education on the part of these church leaders could have disastrous consequences. A 1921 *Umteteli wa Bantu* article dubbed the Israelites "dangerous fanatics" who practiced "weird rites" and "oppose themselves to the forces of law and order."[148] Another editorial of 1925 opined that disaster would result from following the Spirit rather than the laws of the land: "the main trouble with native unorthodox sects is that they regard themselves as above human law . . . the Israelites refused to move from Bulhoek when ordered to do so."[149]

Union government officials concurred with these assessments of the dangers of populist Christian movements. The Bulhoek Massacre embodied the administration's worst fears about Christianity's subversive potential, and prompted a government inquiry into independent black-led churches throughout the Union.[150] In 1926, the Native Churches Commission published its recommendations for state policy. After Bulhoek, they knew well that "occasionally really dangerous men will secure the control of these groups as did Mgijima in the case of the Israelites, and trouble will follow."[151] The commissioners recognized "the duty of the Government to endeavor to check the spread of doctrines and practices which might be harmful to the community."[152] To this end, the commissioners recommended that churches that existed independently of European supervision, and whose ministers could not prove a certain level of educational qualification, would henceforth be barred from a range of privileges. These included the right to erect church buildings and schools as well as the ability of church ministers to act as marriage officers, to purchase communion wine, and to access much-needed concessions for railway travel.[153] By imposing these restrictions, the commissioners hoped that individuals would be deterred from founding their own Zionist and Apostolic churches.

The measures designed to repress the independent proliferation of these evangelical and Holiness-style black churches proved unsuccessful. In 1925, the year before the publication of the report, a Methodist missionary in Johannesburg had pointed to the existence of "65 such bodies [separatist churches] most purporting to have their headquarters on the Rand,"[154] while in the same year another commentator reported on the "many mushroom organizations which spring up and die in the back streets of Johannesburg."[155] By 1938, government officials estimated that there were 320 "schismatic" black-led churches in the Union of South Africa.[156] In the 1940s, Sundkler's study estimated 350 "Bantu independent Churches" in Johannesburg alone.[157] Most churches were very small, with only a handful of followers beneath the church founder, but a few boasted memberships into the thousands—or even, as in the case of Ma Nku, tens of thousands.[158] The numerous "scores of queer little native sects in Johannesburg"[159] (as one European commentator dubbed them) mostly chose complex names that simultaneously displayed their joint Zionist and Pentecostal-Apostolic Faith Mission heritage as well as confounded establishment notions of "correct" church names. Two typical examples from these years were the Apostolic Heaven Church in Zion and the Apostolic Messenger Light World Church in Zion.[160] In 1933, *Bantu World* observed that the often "long and unwieldly" names of the "multiple religious sects" of Johannesburg frequently included the words "Apostolic" and "Zion" in their titles, giving the "bewildering" examples of "Unto the Church of God Apostolic Jerusalem in Zion" as well as the "Zion Holy Apostolic Church Nation of South Africa."[161] Sundkler, in the 1940s, similarly observed the "bewildering" preponderance of Churches calling themselves with the names "Zion," "Jerusalem," "Apostolic," "Full Gospel," "Pentecostal," and so on."[162]

Critics attacked Zionists for their unruly disrespect of hierarchy and education, but mostly they were outraged by these figures' monopoly over the city's popular healing economy. It is true that the respectable Zion churches of Mabiletsa and Phillips had long stressed the need to renounce biomedicine in favor of divine healing. Yet the emergence of the new figure of the Zion "prophet" as a dedicated healing specialist was a distinctly new development of these years. Claiming to be inspired directly by God, these individuals could often accumulate significant reserves of personal power. For the precarious middle-class elite of these years struggling to shore up their reserves of authority, the charismatic healing prophets were a further blow to their status as leaders of public opinion.

Doctors and Prophets, Education and the Spirit

Health and sickness were ever-present concerns for Africans living on the twentieth-century Rand. Cities such as Johannesburg made Africans of all classes quite literally sick. For those living in the inner-city slums, poor sanitary provisions, and overcrowding in residential areas caused typhoid, typhus, and smallpox, leading to inflated infant mortality rates. City health officials labeled Johannesburg's slum districts "nurseries of infection".[163] Those working and living in mines and compounds also faced grave dangers. Throughout the twentieth century, miners were beset with risks of silicosis and deadly accidents.[164] One miner described how "you expect death to occur at any time in your daily work routine."[165] Mining compounds, too, left much to be desired, being dark, unsanitary, crowded, and especially bleak in the cold winter months. Regular reports on compound accommodation found them "unfit for human habitation" with inadequate provisions of food.[166] Dangerous working conditions and poor living circumstances meant the death rate of workers on the Rand was so high—pneumonia was one of the main killers—that by 1913 labor recruits from Central Africa were banned because they were too susceptible to death and disease.[167] Despite these dire conditions, formal medical provision for Africans, both within compounds and outside in the African-occupation areas of the city, was very scarce. Very few mine compound hospitals had trained doctors working within them, and the reputation of these establishments was such that the general perception of them was that the chances of leaving alive were low.[168] Throughout the 1930s, African readership newspapers lamented the acute shortage of doctors among the "Bantu population."[169]

It was also the case that many Africans of interwar Johannesburg did not place their entire trust in biomedical cures alone. As had been the case in nineteenth-century Melbourne, a lively informal health economy flourished in the city. A range of healing therapies addressed not only the multiplicity of physical ailments besetting its residents, but also offered cures for unemployment, love troubles, and other misfortunes. Although biomedicine largely restricted its purview to physiological ailments, this more populist realm conceived of health in the broadest possible terms, embracing psychological, spiritual, and social aspects as well as physical components. As was also true for the city of Durban in this period, the anonymity of urban living in Johannesburg precipitated widespread fears about witchcraft, and the threat of "unfamiliar people [who] could be potentially carrying or administering dangerous *muthi* [medicine]."[170] In the 1930s, the ethnographer Ellen Hellman indeed found that in Johannesburg "a belief in *abathakathi* [sorcerers] is far from dying out," and that women in inner-city slum yards gave as evidence "the noise made at night when witches walked over the corrugated iron grooves of their rooms."[171] Amid a climate of anxiety precipitated by the social pressures of urban living, the ministrations of herbalists able to offer talismans or protective medicines against witchcraft were greatly valued.[172] Hellman found a "constant demand for the services of the *inyanga* and his medicines" in the inner-city slums.[173] Herbalists also had a booming trade in mining compounds; in the large Jubilee and Salisbury mining compounds, for example, there were in each at least "ten traders in native herbs . . . iguana skins to lay on rheumatic parts of body, wild board fat to contest poisons, lion's liver to make the consumer brave."[174] A history of Alexandra Township has even suggested that far from the scarcity of biomedical provision being lamented as a lack, many residents of Johannesburg were skeptical of the efficacy of "white" medicine, intentionally withdrawing themselves from clinics and hospitals and instead seeking out the services of diviners and herbalists to combat witchcraft.[175]

The city's popular healing practitioners were far from pristine traditional experts transplanted untouched to the city from rural areas. Instead, these therapists evidenced a complex coexistence of old and new medicine, with European, African, and Asian healers drawing from an eclectic mixture of medicines and treatments of different provenance and periods. A "native herbalist" in Johannesburg sold not only traditional remedies, but also "modern synthetic remedies." When queried about why he sold aspirin, he replied, "we have got to keep up to date."[176] In like fashion, European chemists also offered non-Western medicines; shops located in the inner-city slums offered mail order potions promising cures for impotence, unemployment, chest pain, and love troubles.[177] There was, for example, the popular "Benoni Herbalist," who had clients visiting from across the Rand, and the inner-city storekeeper who along with foodstuff sold his customers bottles of "Davis Pain Killer" for coughs and chest pain.[178] Medicine and other forms of therapeutic treatment in interwar Johannesburg exemplified a fluid, complex admixture of African, European, herbal, bio-medicinal, and magical registers; a bricolage of different healing therapies reflecting the cosmopolitan composition of the city itself. Many of the city's healers hailed from far lands. John Chavafamira came to the city in the 1920s from eastern Zimbabwe, borne along by a Manyika migrant network that sought work in waitering and domestic service. Once in the slum yards of Doornfontein, Chavafamira established himself as a popular inyanga; indeed, it was the far-off provenance of his therapies that established his reputation as "more efficacious than those of Zulu or Sotho [*inyangas*]."[179]

Johannesburg's black elite viewed these informal health practitioners with great disfavor. For them, medical development along scientific lines was a hallmark of their faith in the value of education in helping Africans attain equal status with Europeans. Severe white opposition existed to training blacks as full doctors; however, the city's African elite took the handful of trained black doctors as a powerful symbol of the progressiveness of their race, a sign that blacks' capabilities were equal to Europeans, and a precursor of hoped-for full integration in society. In 1932, *Bantu World* asserted that the "eight Bantu doctors [in the country] are proving that in the field of science the black man can hold his own."[180] A 1934 full-page spread celebrating "African pioneers in the Medical Field" such as A. B. Xuma, S. M. Molema, and Roseberry Bokwe lauded that these are "men who by their ability, integrity and determination proved that African [can] master the science of medicine."[181] The tiny handful of African men who managed to qualify as doctors—usually by training in Britain or the United States, although the first cohort of black doctors graduated by Wits in Johannesburg in the early 1940s[182]—represented the highest level of professional and social prestige for the black middle classes. Many doctors also went on to occupy leading roles in political and public life, key examples being Xuma and Molema who respectively served as president and secretary of the Congress in the forties.[183] Although almost no African women trained as doctors in this period, the nursing profession was a prestigious one for female members of the petit bourgeoisie. In 1932, *Bantu World* asserted that recent nursing graduates "have heaped honour on the Bantu Race . . . proving their value and worth to the Race."[184] A nursing sister, one M. T. Dwane, was a member of the black aristocracy, being the daughter of clergyman Rev. Dwane who had founded the Ethiopian Order (a black Ethiopian-inspired breakaway from the Methodist church that eventually affiliated itself to the Anglican Church in South Africa). After training as a nurse at Lovedale Institute, she qualified as one of the first black nurses in the Transvaal and worked at hospitals in mining compounds as well as for the Johannesburg City Council as a nurse in the Klipspruit location.[185]

The black middle classes hoped that the figure of the doctor would supersede the diviners and herbalists who were still so popular among their compatriots. *Umteteli wa Bantu* lauded that black doctors showed the people the difference between "the efficacy of white medicine and the shame of black mystery . . . the superstition on which the witchdoctor and herbalist have thrived is fast losing its hold on Bantu people."[186] A 1934 letter to the editor asserted "it is only qualified doctors who would help to suppress the superstition that is the cause of slow development, and in the way of Christian progress."[187] Like doctors, nurses were seen as vanguards of progress and civilization for the black community, "deal[ing] intelligently and authoritatively with witchcraft and other superstitious ideas of diseases . . . the grossest and most cruel things in heathendom."[188] Throughout the interwar period, *Bantu World* and *Umteteli wa Bantu* ran numerous articles on the importance of gaining scientific knowledge about healthcare, information that these figures hoped would in time trump "superstition." In 1920, *Umteteli* started a regular series named "Health," whereby it enlisted the services of an "eminent doctor of medicine with unusually varied experience in the treatment of tropical diseases" to present in simple terms information on "the great scourges which afflict humanity."[189] From 1939, *Bantu World* featured its own column by "the Doctor" who advocated that "it is essential that the African people should know how to preserve their health, and that knowledge can only be secured by men who have studied the structure of our bodies and how they function." Like the figure of the teacher or the religious minister, a doctor was considered a learned expert whose possession of knowledge enabled them to guide, lead. and instruct the masses, over and against the superstition proffered by the "native witchdoctor." A series of articles on the stomach, bowels, liver, infectious diseases, and various medicines followed, urging Africans to study and absorb the lessons of bio-medical knowledge: "to read these articles aloud, say on a Sunday evening after church."[190]

But the "backward" diviner and herbalist were not the only foes of bio-medical hegemony in this period. In this era of exponentially multiplying Zionist churches, the new figure of the Zionist reformer was also increasingly rivalling the authority of doctors and nurses. The divine healing services of these new churches were quite different to those of an earlier period. For one, Zion services of the first generation of believers had been orderly occasions, marked by nothing more exuberant than hymn singing and prayer. For example, early Zionists on the Rand during the teens held sober "tea parties" on Saturday evenings in the Zion Tabernacle.[191] These events, which levied a small fee from attendees, consisted of tea, cake, and vigorous hymn singing.[192] But a decade later, the laying-on of hands for healing prayer became increasingly ecstatic, a reflection of the influence from the Pentecostal AFM. R. R. R. Dhlomo leading member of the city's African intelligentsia, and assistant editor of the *Bantu World*, wrote a regular column under the pseudonym of "R. Roamer."[193] His columns cast disapproving jibes at the unrestrained emotive quality of the services of the city's new Zionist churches, lambasting the "*amaziyoni* of local fame . . . [who] shriek with emotion and fling themselves to the ground."[194] New Zionist preachers were accused of subverting social and religious propriety, creating an indecorous cacophony of religious zealotry: "[they] wake us up every Sunday morning at 5am shouting, dancing and singing in different tunes, consigning us to perdition when we do not wake up and follow them."[195] A description of a healing service carried out in a Johannesburg branch of Daniel Nkonyane's Christian Catholic Apostolic Holy Spirit Church in Zion in the early 1930s described how members "danced wildly, singing simultaneously in multitudinous musical keys . . . filled with the wind [Holy Spirit]."[196] Healing services could even last all night, to the horror of their neighbors, as was the case of one service of the Christian Apostolic Church in Zion reported in late 1933.[197] Most of these new Zionist churches met informally in a room or two in a township or in a mining compound or barracks, but the larger services were often held in the open-air to accommodate the multitudes who gathered for healing prayer. By the 1940s, an empty stretch of veldt, or countryside, adjacent to Alexandra Township became the site for "hundreds to congregate on Sunday afternoons, laying healing hands on the sick."[198] Wemmer Pan, a lake in the inner city, not only featured baptisms by full immersion, but also lively healing services on the banks of the water.[199]

In addition to its more Pentecostal ecstatic flavor, the new wave of Spirit-filled Zionist churches differed from their predecessors in other ways too. In an earlier stage of the church's life—both in South Africa and in the United States—it had been considered normal for all believers to lay on hands and pray for the healing of others. However, during the interwar years and beyond, the notion that only those particularly inspired or directed by the Holy Spirit were qualified to lay hands on the sick became commonplace. This, then, was the era in which a differentiation in labor emerged between the preacher or evangelist—who read and interpreted Scriptures to the congregation—and the healing prophet (*profethi*)—who relied solely upon the inspiration of the Spirit.[200] One example of this increased prominence in healing services given to those who claimed to be Spirit-filled—rather than educated—was the career of Emmanuel Tsotetse, born in 1918 in a rural farm in the Orange Free State, who went to Johannesburg as a young man in the late 1930s. He worked as a messenger for a chemist's shop, and in this period also joined the Holy Catholic Apostolic Church in Zion, that was led by one Cornelius Hlatshwayo (who had broken away from Matthew Koza, who led the church after the death of John George Phillips in 1936). Tsotetse and his wife (a further example of the egalitarian opportunities afforded for women in this new populist incarnation of Zion) both rapidly became famous within the church as prophets, renowned for their marvelous spiritual powers in laying hands on the sick. By the 1940s, the bishop of the Holy Catholic Apostolic Church in Zion, Cornelius Hlatshwayo, would seldom pray for healing for his congregants, focusing instead on preaching the word, and it was the prophets Tsotetse and his wife who were entrusted with the difficult business of healing prayer.[201] Another fragment of evidence similarly suggesting a new differentiation of labor between literate preacher and Spirit-inspired prophet is a *Bantu World* account of a service of the Christian Apostolic Church of God in Zion in Alexandra Township in 1933. The journalist listed the different church officers who attended the service, making it clear the "prophetic" office was a distinct rank, expanding the range of official roles as conceived of by Dowie: "they had an all-night service to pray for somebody who was sick . . . evangelists, prophets, elders and many church members were gathered."[202]

Inspired by the Spirit, this new wave of prophets claimed to receive direct guidance from God regarding individual misfortune or sickness. Frequently, the prophet discerned the cause of the illness as none other than witchcraft. At the service covered by the *Bantu World* mentioned above, the journalist found that one "Evangelist Matthew" began to "prophecy, saying that the sick lady was bewitched by her relative, a light-coloured one."[203] A decade later, in the 1940s, Sundkler observed a near identical process whereby the prophet leading a Zionist healing service for a sick woman divined that someone in the congregation had slipped a bottle of "poison" into her food.[204] If the Spirit told prophets the cause of a disease, then it also gave them the cure. Often, these were highly detailed procedures, revealed directly to the prophet by the promptings of the Spirit, and containing specific instructions the afflicted should follow. Evangelist Matthew thus recommended that "the sick lady must be immersed in a drum of water together with two wooden and steel rods. It was said that the rods meant she will bear a son."[205] It was in this period that prophets also began to frequently carry messages from the Spirit to congregants that healing would occur if certain garments or articles of dress were worn. American missionaries from Zion City still active in South African—largely in the form of Mahon's church—were critical of these practices, seeing them as evidence of the "Africanization" of divine healing. One disapprovingly commented on "a certain independent native church" in the Germiston location that "believes the Holy Spirit speaks to them and commands them apart from the Word of God." The "cures" given to people by the church's prophets were "that you must always wear some white garment, even if only a dirty white handkerchief tied around the head."[206] Sundkler similarly observed around the same time that "in all healing activities there will be some prophesying about the colour of sash or cord that the patient should wear to get rid of the illness."[207] Uniforms and sticks also became commonplace items in Zion churches of this period. Nkonyane, one of the earliest of the Spirit-filled Zionists, informed his congregants that "each person should carry one stick . . . branches of the tree could be bent into different forms, and it would be the Holy Spirit which would determine the shape of the stick."[208]

Doubtless, in addition to their reliance on the Holy Spirit, these popular prophets were drawing on older idioms of healing circulating the city. Many parallels can be drawn between the prophet who received instructions from the Holy Spirit, and Johannesburg's popular diviners who claimed guidance from their ancestral spirits. Indeed, as was the case with American missionaries from Zion City, the opinion of other contemporary commentators was that the new influx of Zionist prophets was a lightly Christianized version of traditional healing. Bengt Sundkler, conducting research in the 1940s in Zululand but also in Johannesburg, argued that "prophesying is divining, in a supposedly Christian form." He noted that diviners underwent a process whereby they were "called" to the profession by their ancestors (often the "call" manifesting as an illness). Zionist prophets of this period also spoke of the way they had been "made sick," yet this time "by the Holy Spirit" (*uyaguliswa uMoya*).[209] Others called to be healing prophets spoke of the Holy Spirit descending on their shoulders and upper back, much as the ancestral spirits did to an individual whom they were beckoning to their service.[210] Diviners both "smelled out" the cause of the sickness as well as prescribed medicinal cures for its remedy, and so did the prophets. Older-style Zionists concurred with Sundkler, denouncing the new prophet-centered healing mechanisms as nothing but traditional medicine in a new guise. One of Edgar Mahon's African preachers in the Christian Catholic Church in Zion lamented a young woman in Johannesburg whom their older-style Zionist church had lost to a populist prophet who had instructed her to tie "a woollen green string around her body . . . [they] teach her this string will watch over her while she is trusting and waiting for an answer to prayer." This Zionist and his coworkers fruitlessly tried to persuade her of the "folly of trusting this string," arguing it was nothing more than a variant of the cures prescribed by a diviner: "we tried to show her this string is in place of medicine used by native women when they want children."[211]

Yet it would be overstating the case to argue that Zionist prophets were a seamless continuation of indigenous healing therapies. This new generation of urban divine healers was deeply critical of the expertise of traditional healers, just as they were of the supposed "knowledge" of biomedical specialists such as doctors. While popular prophets clearly elided languages of divine healing and ancestral-guided healing, these Christian healers were still convinced that the Holy Spirit's powers far exceeded those of the ancestral spirits who assisted their diviner and herbalist rivals. Prophets considered the scale and scope of the Holy Spirit (*uMoya*) to be far larger and more efficacious than the narrow confines of regional ancestral spirits.[212] This perception seems to have been reflected in popular opinion. Often a prophet working by the inspiration of the Holy Spirit was consulted as a powerful last resort in cases where a diviner had failed. Moreover, there is evidence of Zionist prophets attempting to publicly and dramatically convert diviners to Christianity, believing "their" Christian Holy Spirit was capable of trumping diviners' minor ancestral spirits.[213] Many Zion leaders and prophets, moreover, explicitly forbade congregants not only from using Western biomedicine but also from consulting traditional healers who claimed to have powers to diagnose and cure witchcraft. The constitution of the Holy Catholic Apostolic Church in Zion—dated 1936—stated in its opening paragraphs that church members were not only prohibited to "partake in dancing, revelings [*sic*] and things of heathen custom for these are included in the flesh," but were especially "forbidden to have anything to do with witchcraft in any form."[214] While by the 1950s some Zion churches had relaxed the prohibition against biomedicine (in large part due to pressure from the state), the prohibition on consulting diviners or using any form of traditional medicine remained strictly enforced. The Johannesburg-based Bishop Ramampona of the Apostolic Nazareth Galalee Church in Zion ordained that members of his church "cannot take medicine, only the white man's medicine." Alternatively, the Nations 12 Apostolic Nazareth Church in Zion prescribes "no medicine, only white doctors," whereas for the Zion Combination Church of South Africa Christian Catholic Holy Spirit Church in Zion it was "no medicine, not even white doctors allowed."[215]

In leaning on the Holy Spirit in this fashion, these prophets were also explicitly pitting their healing practice against those within the congregation who possessed education or learning. As it turned out, the Spirit appeared to uniquely favor those with no formal learning. At an all-night healing service in 1933 of the Christian Apostolic Church of God in Zion in Alexandra Township, it was pronounced by one of the leaders that "those who would like to lay hands on the sick should be examined through the Spirit to see if they qualify," starkly stating that "the educated would not be qualified."[216] Someone even added a note to the effect that "the educated people will not be resurrected during the time of the Resurrection." Not all were in agreement with this hardline stance. One Mr. Simelane started to question the prophet's exclusion of the educated, inquiring "about the verses that they read, and that the educated people will not be resurrected, where was that written?"[217] But leaning on their claim to be inspired by the Holy Spirit, prophets attempted to silence any who disagreed with them, often by threatening to exercise their superior spiritual powers against them. When the sick woman in Evangelist Matthew's service refuted that she knew a relative of such complexion said by Matthew to have cursed her, he replied "I am a prophet from long ago, if anyone refutes my prophecies I curse them."[218]

Leaders of the more established Zionist churches in the city were greatly
perturbed at prophets' denunciation of educated ministers. Current-day
Zionist minister Godfrey Maseko recalled that his grandfather led a Zion
church from the family home in Sophiatown in the 1930s (probably linked
to T. Mwelase, for the church was one of those that remained loyal to Voliva). Maseko recalls how family tradition has preserved a memory of his
grandfather denouncing those illiterate prophets who claimed to be receiving visions directly from God. These were those who claimed "this uniform came through a vision, that dress came through a dream, those leaders
had dreams or God came to [them] in a vision and showed [them] this piece
of cloth, that was white with blue or red, with stars and the moon." In contrast to these "wild" claims, Maseko's grandfather's church—just like the
organization under the educated John George Phillips—wore respectable
suit and ties to services, eschewing the revelatory uniforms and garments
recommended by prophetic individuals.[219] Similarly, an elderly present-day
member of Phillips's church remembers how his leaders of the mid-century
would often denounce the "virus of uniforms" spreading through the city;
"uniforms" here were shorthand for the Spirit-inspired revelations prophets
claimed to receive: "God said we must wear this! God said we must wear
that!"[220] Older Zionists were sure that dubious claims to visionary experience were no guarantee of religious orthodoxy. In 1934, T. Mwelase, still
loyal to Voliva, wrote to *Bantu World* reminding readers that "Our Lord
Jesus gave the warning in Matthew 7:15–23, 'Watch out for false prophets.
They come to you in sheep's clothing but inwardly they are ferocious
wolves.'" Mwelase went on to say that the original fathers of Zion in
South Africa did not claim to be prophets, and they did not heal via special
messages they received from the Holy Spirit. Their Zion founders merely
laid hands on the sick and prayed, quietly and soberly, without claiming
special revelatory experiences: "Overseer Bryant did not hold a stick or go
bare footed . . . all the heresies we see here are not from Zion . . . I am
against this Zionism which contradicts what we learned from Zion."[221]

    Though the Zionist establishment denounced prophets as heretics, Jo-
hannesburg's African elite interpreted prophets' growing influence in the
city as a troubling new variation of African "superstition." Many saw the
contemporary figure of the Zion healing prophet as a dangerous fanatic,
leading his gullible and ill-informed flock to certain death. In 1934, R. R. R.
Dhlomo wrote a short story set in Johannesburg that had as its centerpiece
a desperately ill woman whose husband called for the ministrations of "the
Shepherd of Mount Zion." The story recounts how the Zionist congregation descended on the house, "dressed in spotless white . . . they sang lustily,

[swayed] in maddened joy of religious enthusiasm, sat round the woman in a circle, while their leader—the self-proclaimed "prophet"—placed his hands on her head muttering blessings in an unknown language . . . his eyes were blood red and raving." Dhlomo's story ends with the husband swayed by the prophet's delusions, and tragically maintaining that "medicines and doctors are signs of our faithlessness and rebellion to God" at the very moment that his wife dies.[222] Dhlomo's short story was a commentary on the dangers of the unregulated, popular Christianity of the day, and of the dire consequences linked to the absence of rational thought and proper education among religious leaders. Dhlomo's negative assessment of Zionist prophets seemed confirmed in public opinion when in late 1937 smallpox broke out Johannesburg, including on a Germiston factory floor, leading the city's health officials to order compulsory vaccination of all employees.[223] Several refused and were fined for their stance. During their court appearances, they stated to the Magistrate that "[their] religion did not allow [them] to be vaccinated and [they] had a special message from God telling [them] not to undergo treatment."[224] In the eyes of the black press, those who claimed to receive "special messages from God" in fact "threatened the interests of the health of the whole nation . . . Africans will be well advised to submit to vaccination as it is the only way to prevent the spread of terrible disease."[225]

Some critics went a step further, arguing that Zion healing prophets were religious charlatans seeking to enrich themselves at the expense of a gullible public. A letter to the *Bantu World* in 1933 bemoaned false shepherds who "ate the fat" of their flocks: "when tired of work they simply buy collars at the nearest shop and begin to form Independent churches . . . they are deceiving people by not teaching them the right Doctrine or even a sip of education. They are false ministers, eating the fat of the flock but not giving the flock the right pasture."[226] *Marabi Dance,* novelist Modiwe Dikobe's fictionalized account of his childhood in Sophiatown in the 1920s, features a Zionist prophet "Reverend Ndhlovu." A migrant worker from Northern Rhodesia who began life as an illiterate worker on the Rand, Ndhlovu restyled himself as a prophet of the "Apostolic Faith Church of Zion," by falsifying an ordination certificate and beginning an extravagant faith healing career that involved swindling large amounts of money out of Sophiatown's gullible residents for his healing services.[227] Dikobe's narrative portrayed prophecy as religious entrepreneurship; while these "prophets" may claim to be inspired by God, Rev. Ndhlovu was in fact an unscrupulous charlatan. In the estimation of the middle classes, these religious frauds ruthlessly preyed on "the uneducated and backward Bantu; it was "the ignorant native who has absorbed more religion than his brain can hold who falls prey to the wiles of the pretender."[228] Critics from the petit bourgeoisie African classes of the city lamented that these "leaders are out for self—glory and little else. Hence the absurd nomenclature and extravagant titles of these churches and their headings."[229]

By the end of the 1930s—despite the early convergence between Zionists and the African Christian establishment in Johannesburg—significant differences characterized these two groups' divergent values. Where the Christian establishment valued education, training, knowledge, hierarchy, procedure, and decorum, the new Pentecostal-inspired Zionist schismatics and prophets prioritized inspiration, revelation, spontaneity, and ecstatic displays of the Spirit. Contemporary commentators and subsequent generations of scholars have cast these differences as a juxtaposition between the supposedly innate characteristics of "European" versus African" religious styles. In fact this was a fundamentally theological argument carried out between Johannesburg's African Protestants about rival modes of religious legitimacy and authority as sanctioned and authorized by church tradition, Scripture, and the Holy Spirit. This debate was not restricted to only African Protestants: the enduring evangelical tension between institutional unity and conscience-driven diversity had also characterized the Zion tradition in both Australia and in the United States, as well as the evangelical movement more broadly. The next chapter further explores this interplay between unity and diversity, catholicity and fragmentation, cosmopolitanism and difference. As the century progressed, many youthful Zionist reformers turned aside from the difficult business of establishing schismatic groups, and instead addressed themselves to the equally challenging task of building up and holding together vast transregional congregations. In this respect, then, even these independent-minded prophets were expressing their continued fidelity to Dowie's vision of Zion as a unified community of the faithful that transcended nation, ethnicity, and language.

CHAPTER SIX

Cosmopolitanism, Ethnicity, and Migrant Labor Networks in Southern African Zion

O N 2 5 M A R C H 1 9 3 2, a large and festive event took place in the Witwatersrand town of Springs, one of the Johannesburg-area mining settlements that sprung up in the late nineteenth-century along the rich seam of minerals that made up the gold reef. This occasion was the opening ceremony of a new church building for Elias Mahlangu's Zion Apostolic Church, a structure of which the *Bantu World* report on its ceremonial opening commented "how beautiful it is!" The building was made up of "black bricks, had twelve pillars and twelve big windows . . . it is 41 by 39 feet." Adding to the celebratory feel of the day, a cow and three sheep were slaughtered to feed the "many people" who attended the event. Perhaps the most noteworthy aspect of the meeting, however, was the diverse character of the international crowd of believers who gathered to celebrate their new church building. In addition to the coterie of ministers from Johannesburg, the *Bantu World* reporter marveled at the far-flung origins of many who attended. There were Zion Apostolic Church people from across the Union of South Africa, from Johannesburg and the Transvaal but also from the neighboring Orange Free State, and from coastal Natal. Members, moreover, had traveled to the event from outside of the borders of the Union, undertaking several-day journeys from as far away as Swaziland and "Mashona," or southern Rhodesia. The day's proceedings were a microcosm of the transnational, ethnically diverse composition of Mahlangu's church. Headquartered on the Rand, Mahlangu's organization was one of the largest and most geographically diffuse Zion churches of this period, with congregations scattered throughout much of Southern Africa.[1]

The very many new Zion churches brought into being by the charismatic young church founders and prophets of interwar Johannesburg were innovative experiments in ethnic and linguistic cosmopolitanism. The highly stratified world of the mining compounds categorized and divided workers into groups predicated on ethnicity, language, and geographical provenance, whereas Zionist churches in the city, drawing on Dowie's older rhetoric of universalistic cosmopolitanism, rejected this style of ethnic-linguistic demarcation. And while white colonial states across the region were attempting to govern by categorizing Africans into fixed territorial-ethnic identities, Zionists continued to insist Christians should form solidarities transcending narrow classifications. Thus amid the ethnic enclaves of mining compounds—and frequently existing in tension with them—there sprang up isolated clusters of Zionist cosmopolitanism; churches that presented a dizzying variety of languages and ethnic groupings and which self-consciously styled themselves as bringing into being a new and unified African Christian people. These experiments in religious cosmopolitanism did not remain confined to the city. As migrant laborers, church founders and laity alike were great travelers, frequently moving back and forth between the city and their homes elsewhere in the Union or in neighboring Colonies. Their migratory routes became the conduits through which the internationalist values of urban Zionism traveled across Southern Africa. Migrant missionaries transmitted Zion's radical messages of loyalty to God far and wide, convening constituencies throughout the region that, rather than looking to local chiefs and elders as their authorities, instead referred themselves to their church's headquarters in Johannesburg—and ultimately to God himself.

But Zionists found the contemporary environment to be uncongenial to their pan-ethnic aspirations. In general, this was a period characterized by an increasing segmentation of identity along ethnic and linguistic lines; indeed, one scholar has noted that these years were marked by the "resurrection, redefinition and remobilization of ethnic identities."[2] Far from being solely attributable to white rulers' efforts to establish more repressive governance (a "divide-and-rule" strategy exemplified in the South African apartheid state's attempts to create segregated ethnic "homelands" where it hoped all nonwhites would eventually reside), the flourishing of ethnic identities in this period was pioneered by a more complex cast of actors. These included the architects of white-led states but also featured traditional African chiefly authorities and early black nationalists. Beleaguered black elite—struggling with both white repression and popular discontent from African communities—discerned in the so-called creation of tribalism an opportunity to solidify their own status as the natural customary leaders of the people.[3] The 1920s through the 1940s saw regional ethnic projects emerge among Zulu leaders and intellectuals as well as in the neighboring

British protectorate of Swaziland, both areas with strong historical traditions of monarchical and chiefly power.[4]

This chapter shows how these developments had profound consequences for Zion churches across Southern Africa. The hostility of white states to Zionists' efforts to enact a border-crossing cosmopolitanism meant this highly mobile constituency of Christians continually struggled with official efforts to thwart their activities. External pressures such as these meant that forming allegiances with ethnic politicians could have beneficial consequences for Zionists' ability to move freely and worship unhindered. Zion in Swaziland, for example, became explicitly allied with promoting the institution of the Swazi monarchy and Swazi cultural values. The evangelical cosmopolitanism of Zionists in this period was thus by no means a seamless project, and espousing universalistic commitments was not an inevitable outcome of conversion to the descendants of Dowie's church. Amid great external pressures from white-led states and a range of societal constraints, believers were compelled to invest in more locally grounded expressions of their faith. The nativist mood of the day made it difficult to live as the pure cosmopolitans many Zionist believers sought to be. Instead, pragmatic compromises and alliances with ethnic politicians were pursued. As the earlier chapters have already shown, this tense dynamic between cosmopolitanism and ethnicity is a frequently recurring one in the story of Zion in Southern Africa and North America. Zionists' efforts to craft a cosmopolitan fraternity of believers has seldom been supported—at least not for very long periods of time—by the broader worlds of the nineteenth and twentieth centuries.

Cosmopolitans in the City

Johannesburg's migrant mining culture propelled heterogeneous groups of people from across Southern Africa into new proximity with each other.[5] In the 1920s, a resident of Doornfontein—an inner-city slum yard—recalled that "the residents were mixed as the league of nations."[6] Another commentator from the early 1930s observed that the downtown Ferreirastown area, another working-class suburb, was filled with "all nationalities—poor whites, Syrians, Chinese, Indians, Malays, natives, half-castes."[7] Yet such diversity did not always equate with actual cosmopolitanism. For many who found themselves in the city in this period—especially those resident in the mining barracks—ethnic identification became an important route to flourishing and security. Doubtless this was in part the product of a deliberate strategy of divide and rule on the part of mine officials who encouraged

division along ethnic lines, hoping that cleavages—not infrequently
leading to bloody "faction fights"—would mitigate against workers' collective action.[8] But leaning on ethnic networks was also important for these
migrant workers, living in grim, single-sex hostels and compounds, placed
amid strangers who spoke unfamiliar languages. Surrounding oneself
with compatriots from a home area could be enormously comforting.
Northern South African Pedi migrants on the Rand, for example, accessed
jobs and accommodation through "sticking together," both "en route to
work and at their place of employment." Many burial societies in mining
compounds, acting as forms of self-help associations or funeral insurance,
were also predicated upon ethnic lines.[9] Migrant criminal networks newly
formed on the Rand also assisted with buttressing ethnic identity; urban
gangs were formed according to ethnic and linguistic affiliation. The mid-
twentieth-century Zulu-dominated Ninevites, the Sotho "ama-Russians,"
and the Mpondo Isithshozi all reinforced regional and linguistic solidarity
and assisted migrants with negotiating the hard world of mining compounds and hostels.[10]

Affiliation to a Christian community also reinforced migrants' ethnic affiliations. The older and more established mission societies in the city—of
which there were around twenty in 1923, including Anglicans, Presbyterians, Catholics, Wesleyans, and Congregationalists[11]—had founded their
Rand organizations in response to the needs of church members from specific rural regions who had migrated to Johannesburg for labor. The goal
of urban mission societies was "to follow up and shepherd Church members who left their rural areas for the mines," in the words of Ray Phillips, the American Congregationalist missionary on the Rand.[12] Many
missionary societies concurred with government officials regarding the
moral dangers of "detribalization" amid urban conditions, and viewed a
strong ethnic identity as the antidote to the social ills caused by the dis-
integration of "tribal" society."[13] Missionaries' role as translators of
local languages was here relevant. As Patrick Harries has pointed out
with regard to the Swiss Presbyterians working among Mozambicans on
the Rand in the early twentieth century, it was precisely missionaries who
were responsible for codifying in written form the local Ronga and Thonga
languages of Mozambique, which became almost a "church lingua
franca."[14] There were also strong correlations between ethnic identity and
affiliation to a particular mission-run church such as Methodism, Catholicism, or Anglicanism. In the 1950s, an investigation of "separatist churches
in mining hostels" revealed that a largely Basuto residential hostel had a
"deep attachment to the Paris Evangelical Mission or the Roman Catholic
Church," whereas the minority Batswana population largely belonged to

the London Missionary Society, and the tiny Xhosa group were Anglican or Methodist.[15] Several decades later, a survey undertaken in Soweto showed "the distribution of membership of churches is very closely linked to the distribution of tribes residing in a particular area . . . various native areas are served by different missionary groups, migrants from the native areas to Johannesburg probably turn to the church they knew in their home area."[16]

Alongside these efforts to prioritize geography, language, and ethnic kinship, there were efforts to pioneer more expansive allegiances. This was the era of burgeoning nationalist consciousness embodied in the African National Congress's determination to unite the black people of the country into a single unified constituency. But pan-ethnic nationalism struggled to develop a unified mass membership. Beset by chronic organizational weaknesses and lack of funding, Congress increasingly struggled to contain local factions and feuds, and the splintering of the organization along ethnic lines. By 1933, the Transvaal branch of Congress was split into a North Sotho Kgatla/Pedi group, on the one hand, and a Nguni collection, on the other.[17] Toward the end of his life, Sol Plaatje, a founding member of the South African Native National Congress, lamented "the failure of our race to unite, and that the demon of tribalism is still the great stumbling block to our unity."[18] Although ethnic divisions characterized the leadership of the Congress, its vision of multiracial cosmopolitanism could hardly be said to appeal to the rank and file of South Africans. Its membership numbers peaked in 1918–1919, at the time of miners' unrest in Johannesburg, and this consisted of only 3,000 paid up members in the Transvaal, meagre numbers probably reflected in other countrywide branches. Members were largely drawn from the ranks of middle-class professionals such as teachers, clerks, and municipal workers; it largely failed to establish itself as a mass organization and struggled to gain popularity amid the compounds of the migrant mining world. For many migrant laborers, tight-knit forms of sociability predicated on language, culture, and geography continued to feel more meaningful than the disembodied, unrealized notion of the "nation" upon which they had very little tangible purchase.[19]

But where pan-ethnic nationalism failed to gain popular currency, new forms of Christianity proved successful in creating more cosmopolitan horizons. This was especially true of the newer evangelical Holiness and Pentecostal organizations active in the city. A key moment of this strand of piety was believers' radical renunciation of their sinful past before their triumphant possession of a sanctified future; to achieve the hoped-for perfected state, believers had to confess and repent of all prior evil doing.[20] For those who made decisive breaks with their pasts in accessing a new future defined by sanctified holiness, it was but a natural step to also imagine themselves also severed from older affiliations of tribe and geography. The older Protestant and Catholic mission organizations of the city tended to conduct their work along ethnic lines; these radical Holiness groups sought to transcend ethnicity in inaugurating the new Kingdom of God. In contrast to the Swiss Presbyterian missionaries who focused their energies almost exclusively upon migrants from Gazaland (Mozambique), the evangelical Compounds Mission reported an extraordinarily diverse catalogue of converts. In 1913, Nigel station on the Rand listed: "11 Basuto converts, 22 Zulus, 10 Batonga, 10 Shangaans, 8 Bachopi, 8 Swazis, 6 Matabele, 2 Pondos, 1 Xhosa and 1 Mdonje."[21] Holiness evangelists explicitly taught their converts the Kingdom of God erased ethnic distinctions. In 1921, a Compounds Mission evangelist at the Langlaagte Deep Compound illustrated his sermon by drawing a huge wheel in the sand of the open compound where his listeners were congregated, explaining that "this circle is South Africa, in the centre is Johannesburg. Each of these spokes is a line leading to Johannesburg, here are Shangaans, Bachopi, Batswa, Bathonga from the East, Zulu and amaTonga from the South East, amaBaca and amaPondo from the South, amaXosa, ama Fingo from the South West, Basuto and Bachwana from the West." This pedagogical display illustrated the place of all people in the Kingdom of God where "true happiness is found alone in Jesus Christ,"[22] reminding converts that prior ethnic affiliations were subordinate to believers' new identity as followers of Christ.

Advocating the radical renunciation of the past was also a feature of the many new Zionist churches active among migrant mine laborers. In 1913, there were three Zion Tabernacles belonging to Voliva's church in the Reitfontein, City Deep, and Crown Mine sites (all using large halls granted by sympathetic mining authorities), while more informal Zion services as well as night schools were held within personal rooms in more than ten mining compounds across the Rand.[23] Every Sunday afternoon, open-air evangelistic services were conducted by one Amos Vilakazi in Johannesburg's Market Square, which "thousands of native labourers from the gold mines" attended.[24] Other evidence also suggests Zionist churches drew many followers from the highly international milieu of migrant laborers on the mines. Obed Ndhlela's Bethesda Apostolic Church in Zion, for example, was reported by city officials to "[have] a strong following among mine natives."[25] John George Phillips also preached extensively in the compounds, and was lucky enough to be awarded a meeting room by mining management; "the Compound Managers gave them a big room where they held meetings . . . hundreds of native men were converted through these meetings."[26] Other Zionists, of a less educated, elite background than Phillips, and themselves resident in compounds simply held services in their own personal rooms.[27] Moreover, the line between compound and city was far from a hard and fast one. Many miners traveled off premises during weekends to attend services in nearby locations and townships in the residential areas of the city, looking for opportunity to mingle with brethren who resided in more permanently urbanized spaces. Amid the municipality's effort to strictly regulate Africans' movement, the technicalities of leaving the compound for an overnight service in town could result in trouble for the devout. A police raid of a small house in Germiston Location in the early morning hours of a winter's night in August 1918, found nine Zionists inside "holding a service . . . everyone were mine employees, and had no permit from their respective mines to be away." They were all charged and found guilty with contravening pass laws.[28]

A handful of Zion churches on the Rand appear to have been organized along ethnic lines. A glance at the authoritative list of black-led churches in South Africa compiled by Bengt Sundkler in 1945 reveals that some Zionist organizations did style themselves as catering for believers of particular geographical, linguistic, or ethnic origins. Sundkler's count included the Holy Zion Apostolic Zululand Church in South Africa as well as the Zion Apostolic Gaza (Mozambique) Church of South Africa.[29] Also along these lines, a 1944 health report on Alexandra—which painted an invaluable picture of the mundanities of daily life in the township—mentioned a Basutoland Zionist Church that was noted for displaying a "universal hostile attitude to any person outside of the community."[30] Some Zion churches on the Rand sourced their ministers from their far-off home areas, appearing to prefer one of their own background and language to minister to them. In 1928, Shangaan preacher, Jack Taju, was invited by a Gazaland congregation of Zionists at City Deep Compound in Johannesburg to "take over the congregation," which he accepted, traveling from Gazaland to the Rand to assume his new position as pastor to the congregants of the church.[31]

However, the large majority of Zion churches eschewed these ethnic designations, instead turning to the universal grammar of international Holiness Christianity. Sundkler's list, for example, also shows that permutations and combinations of "Apostolic," "Zion," "Pentecost," and "Spirit" were far more common in church names than were specific geographic or ethnic designations. Predicated on their common identity as children of God, Zionists' gatherings in Rand compounds and barracks as well as in locations and townships were linguistic and ethnic melting pots. Elias Mahlangu's Zion Apostolic Church, with its headquarters on Main Street in downtown Johannesburg, and which held services in compounds throughout the Rand, was composed of members who were Swazi, Zulu, Ndebele,

and Northern Sotho.[32] Mabiletsa's church in Alexandra Township in its
large new building, present also in numerous mining compounds across the
Rand, had not only Sotho preachers working within it but also Zulu,
Xhosa, Tswana, Swazi, Shangaan, and Nyasa ministers, as well as a colored
(mixed-race) preacher of unknown parentage.[33] The Nyasalander John
George Phillips' church boasted a great following of Shangaan members—
from present-day Mozambique—and his right-hand man, one Matthew
Koza, was from Gazaland. In addition to this mingled Shangaan-Nyasa
membership, Phillips' church also had very many Sotho and Zulu adherents.[34] Rev. Maseko—who led a church loyal to Voliva—was a Swazi
who had migrated to Johannesburg for work; after his death, the church
was led by one Marapula, a builder from Malawi. In general, Maseko's
grandson recalls how the church in those days was constituted by "lots of
migrant workers from Malawi . . . all living in hostels."[35] These examples
are drawn from the most prominent Zionist churches on the Rand; a similar pattern of ethnic heterogeneity also marked out less illustrious organizations. The New General Apostolic Church in Zion of South had been
started by a former preacher under Mabiletsa, a Xhosa man from the
Eastern Cape named Sturrman who had married a Zulu woman when he
moved to Johannesburg. He broke away from Mabiletsa's church to found
his own organization, typically "after he saw the name of his new church in
a dream." Sturrman's Rand congregation consisted of Xhosa, Sotho, Zulu,
Shangaan, Swazi, and Pedi members, and services were held in multiple languages, including Zulu, Sotho, and Xhosa.[36] Linguistic heterogeneity was a
prominent feature of these polyglot gatherings. The same Emmanuel Tsotetse who became famed for his healing skill was also a proficient interpreter, translating preachers' sermons from isiZulu to his own native Sesotho
for the benefit of Basotho congregants in the church.[37] Mahlangu, head of
the Zion Apostolic Church, had no need of a translator in his services, for
he was a skilled linguist able to preach in many different languages. Mahlangu's son remembered "Father used to know almost all the languages—
Venda, Shangaan, Pedi, Sotho, Tswana, Zulu, English, Afrikaans. He was
very good at Afrikaans."[38]

Moreover, while most Johannesburg Zionists had by now detached
themselves from the white North American Zionist church, this did not
mean they rejected the older vision of Zion as a cosmopolitan gathering.
Examining the constitutions and founding charters of Zion churches of this
period suggests the persistence of modes of thinking that sought to transcend the parochial and the nativist. Mabiletsa's constitution of the mid-
1930s proclaimed his organization was not for a specific ethnic group but
for the entire "race of people within this sub-continent of South Africa . . .

the indigenous people [who] are sitting in darkness."[39] The constitution of Edward Lion's Zion Apostolic Faith Mission Church aimed to "show them of Basutoland, of the union of South Africa, and throughout all the coasts of South Africa and territories that they should repent and turn to God."[40] Another charter invoking a broad sense of belonging was Obed Ndhlela's Bethesda Zion Apostolic Church constitution of 1921, which was both pan-African and cross-continental in its aim "to preach the word of God among all descendants of Ham,"[41] thereby also identifying the continent's African people as continuous with a biblical race. Titus Msibi was an early convert to Zionism during the days of Mahon's activities during the South African War.[42] In 1931, he was one of the many ministers who founded his own Zionist church on the Rand, naming his organization the Congregational Catholic Apostolic Church of Zion in South Africa. In contrast to the pan-Africanism of Mabiletsa's constitution, Msibi's new church's charter went a step further. It asserted that God's sovereignty summoned the entire world—not just the people of the continent—into a community of believers: "the bedrock of [our] faith is that all nations and peoples of this world must in one accord raise their unanimous voice of praise to God, the Father, Son and Holy Ghost."[43] Daniel Nkonyane's Christian Catholic Apostolic Holy Spirit Church in Zion similarly echoed this Dowie-era tradition of cosmopolitanism. Using language that could have come straight out of early editions of the *Leaves of Healing,* Nkonyane's constitution asserted, "We the church believe in the Universal Brotherhood of all man without distinction of race, creed, sex, caste, colour, caste."[44]

Putting this cosmopolitan theology into practice, Zionist migrant laborers detached themselves from ethnic networks and proclaimed themselves as marked by radically different loyalties. These acts of solidarity were delineating the contours of a new community of people on the Rand, cutting across ethnic divisions and drawing in fellow members as brothers in the family of God. Titus Ndhlovu was a migrant worker to the Rand who hailed from Manica Province in current-day Mozambique, an area of heavy labor recruitment abutting Rhodesia and the northern Union. Ndhlovu, a devout member of Zion, remembered that in the mining compounds the Zionists were increasingly living as a distinct group, aloof from the ethnic politics and divisions of the "non-believers": "separated from the non-believers . . . [Zionists] were attributed their own dormitory . . . there they would sleep as well as holding their own services."[45] This was not just true of the Zionists; across a wide range of denominations, Holiness Christians in residential barracks on the Rand disliked immersion among nonbelievers and feared the corruption of the outside world. A preacher of the evangelical Compounds Mission regretted "converts have to sleep amidst noise and profanity and the opposition of some thirty to forty heathen" in a dormitory. He noted his relief that "some Compound Managers have seen fit to give the Christian boys rooms to themselves where they can study, sing and pray."[46] Although Zion workers sought to sleep in the company of fellow believers—rather than with men from their home regions as many others did—they also united with brethren to form networks of assistance and mutual support. A further instance of the mobilization of religious identity was the consolation afforded to sick or dying Zionists in mining compounds who were visited by "brothers" belonging to the church as opposed to kinsmen or compatriots from their home areas.[47]

New Zion identities offered converts much needed material support. This was the case more broadly with other evangelical networks. In the same period, and mirroring the mutual assistance offered by the city's ethnic "homeboy" networks, a Holiness preacher on the Rand started a church "for the purpose of collecting money to give proper burial to natives who died friendless on the mines."[48] In like fashion, Meshack Hlatshwayo, bishop of the Holy Catholic Apostolic Church in Zion in the 1940s, would assist with securing employment for church members who migrated to Johannesburg from rural areas (largely from the Wakkerstroom district, where his church had a large following) as well as lean on his contacts in the municipality to procure the necessary permits for church members to work in the city.[49] All this helped with finding employment and defraying city costs. Church networks also provided ready-made forms of sociability. Zulu and Sotho migrants to Johannesburg during these decades were well-known for their a capella *isichatamiya* and *kiba* singing groups that performed in mining hostels on weekends, providing entertainment as well as a sense of shared identity.[50] A tantalizing fragment of evidence suggests that Zionists in mining compounds were similarly making use of their leisure time, but in the interests of cementing the bonds of church fellowship rather than ethnic identities. Emmanuel Tsotetse—the multifaceted prophet and translator—was also a talented singer, who together with a few other young men from his Zion church, would regularly perform church songs at hostel events over the weekends.[51] Sociability, entertainment, cultural production, and relaxation were thus all brought into the orbit of one's identity as a member of a Zion church.

These new people of God were not always welcomed by their ethnic countrymen on the Rand. Some migrants felt that Zionist compatriots betrayed their ethnic obligations. One example of this was the Mozambican Titus Ndhlovu. As a worker and resident of the large ISCOR steel factory, Ndhlovu experienced considerable conflict with his countrymen in the residential barracks, largely on the grounds of his hardline stance against invoking ancestors in sacrificial rituals as many of his compatriots continued to do on the Rand. When the compound manager investigated the cause of the tension, he was informed by ISCOR residents that "Ndhlovu reproves everything, he even forbids the Christians to follow their ancestral traditions . . . he claims the only way is the Bible." At Ndhlovu's ordination ceremony as a Zion evangelist he was given the new name of *Sigwaba Inkana* ("Driving by Force" in isiZulu) for he knew he would have to "preach this Gospel by force" in the face of stiff opposition from his fellow countrymen on the Rand.[52] Evangelical Christians on the Rand were more broadly perceived as reneging on the social contracts that made compound life bearable. The periodical of the Compounds Mission reported that at the Nigel compound, south of Johannesburg, one convert was ceaselessly persecuted by his "drunk roommates." This was because, postconversion, he refused to make his required monetary contribution to the weekend "feast of pig and whisky." Outraged, his roommates "tore up his books, broke his slate and insulted him," even locking him in a room.[53]

In certain respects, these pan-ethnic spiritual solidarities found common cause with other contemporary endeavors to transcend the local. A handful of Zionist ministers—especially the elite representatives of "old" Zion—were linked to the pan-ethnic nationalist organizations of the city. The founder of the Zion Apostolic Church, Elias Mahlangu, was a "Congress Man"—that is, a member of the African National Congress—something his son recalled "caused Father much trouble with the authorities."[54] Against the wishes of his father Cornelius, the bishop of his church, the young Meshack Hlatshwayo of the Holy Catholic Apostolic Church in Zion was also heavily involved in Congress politics, although he renounced such activities when he took over the church in the 1940s.[55] Thanks to its heterogeneous migrant population, Johannesburg also became a crucible for the nationalist movements of neighboring countries. Early Malawian nationalism, for example, was forged amid the networks of Nyasa migrant laborers, churchmen, writers, and intellectuals who found themselves on the Rand during the interwar period. A handful of Nyasa Zionists were involved in these initiatives. The founding charter of the Nyasaland Native National Congress listed none other than John George Phillips as one of its inaugural members, while J. P. William Longwe was both the secretary of Mabiletsa's Christian Catholic Apostolic Church in Zion, and also one of two founders of the Nyasaland Congress in 1912, closely working alongside Phillips.[56] A smattering of evidence, moreover, suggests that a few involved in Zion were also interested in the transatlantic pan-Africanism represented by organizations such as Garvey's Universal Negro Improvement Association. A small number of African Americans in the city were active in Johannesburg's Zion (unfortunately almost nothing further is known about this constituency), suggesting the appeal of the church to a broad stratum of black figures preoccupied with issues of racial uplift and self-help. One of these American figures was a Mr. Graham, a hairdresser, who gave "his spare time to bless the people of his own colour in Africa," being particularly active in the Ophirton branch.[57]

The majority of believers on the Rand held their overarching goal as the establishment of the Kingdom of God, understood by them as detached from the secular polity of the nation-state. Most Zionists on the Rand therefore distanced themselves from formal involvement in nationalist politics, and steered clear of activities that could be interpreted as subversive of political authority. Indeed, this stance was in no small part responsible for Zionists' survival and growth over the twentieth century; European officials across the region may have disliked aspects of Zionist worship, but they correctly perceived a fundamental truth: "that [independent churches"] vitality is not drawn from anti-European sources."[58] Along these lines, one Rev. Mazibuko's Apostolic Messenger Light World Church in Zion avowed that "no anti-European political propaganda will be conducted in our church."[59] Edward Lion instructed his following to obey officials—"let every soul be subject to higher powers, for all powers are ordained of God"[60]—whereas Matthew Koza of Phillips' Holy Catholic Apostolic Church in Zion ordered followers to "give unswerving loyalty to the Government . . . any rebellion against higher powers, either in church or state, is forbidden."[61] Johannesburg Zionists of this period seem to have been content to "render unto Caesar what was Caesar's"; their main interest was not agitating for greater rights for black people. Echoing Dowie's earlier prohibition, some churches explicitly forbade members from union membership because the people of God were not to form solidarities with worldly causes. Despite their leader's involvement with Nyasa nationalism, Phillips' church constitution affirmed "we firmly believe that the people of God should have no connection with labour unions, secret societies, or any other organization or body, wherein there is fellowship with unbelievers and are bound by oaths. We are exhorted to be content with our wages."[62] An intriguing exception to this prohibition was Mahlangu's Zion Apostolic Church, which on the aforementioned inauguration of their new church building in Springs invited "the Industrial and Commercial Workers' Union . . . they came with a lot of enthusiasm."[63] But for the most part, Zionists were pursuing nothing less than the establishment of God's Kingdom on earth, a polity that entirely disregarded not only ethnic identities but also the territorial borders that nationalists were attempting to delineate in this period. Instead, Zionists sought to forge explicitly internationalist communities, pan-ethnic entities that tended to straddle, rather than be contained by, national borders.

Extending the Kingdom of Zion

Johannesburg's cosmopolitan Zionists ensured their message spread far and wide across the region. Indeed, all Christian groups on the Rand had long recognized the unique potential of the city's mobile residents for disseminating Christianity across the subcontinent. After a sojourn in the city, transient migrants tended to not only take their earnings home with them but also the teachings of the Gospel. The missionaries of the Apostolic Faith Mission recognized that "Johannesburg as a missionary centre holds a position quite unique in South Africa . . . those who are converted to Christ here carry the Gospel to their homes and the calls from there come faster than we are able to meet them."[64] American Congregationalist missionary, Ray Phillips, noted "how strategic Johannesburg is for reaching the whole African sub-continent . . . these young men will go back to heathen villages of far corners of the land . . . there, the seed that is sown here will bear fruit."[65] Examples abound of outward-bound evangelistic movements from the metropolis to towns, cities, and farmlands across the region. More often than not, labor migrants would act as missionaries to their own home areas, relying upon ready-made connections and their existing linguistic expertise. For example, a Mozambican laborer at the City and Suburban Mine, David Mlambo, was converted through the Compounds Mission. In 1914, Mlambo "felt a strong call to work among his own people in Gazaland, Portuguese territory . . . taking his wife and children, and financed by voluntary contributions, he undertook the long and arduous journey and preached the Gospel there for two years."[66]

A similar centrifugal mechanism facilitated Zion's dissemination from the Rand outward across Southern Africa. The large Zion Christian Church first entered Bechuanaland (present-day Botswana) through a returning migrant from the Rand. This was a man named Motsisi Ralefala, who had driven a taxi in Johannesburg—during which period he also converted to Zionism—before returning home in 1933. Bearing "letters" from Johannesburg that testified he was a "bonafide priest," newspaper *Bantu World* told how Ralefala was hailed in his home town of Mochudi as the one "who went east [i.e., Johannesburg], was baptized there and returned, full of the Bible."[67] Once home, Ralefala organized a following of Zionists

among his own Bakgatla people, and even led a pilgrimage from Bechuanaland to Moria—the Zion Christian Church (ZCC) ritual center several
hundred miles north of Johannesburg—the following year.[68] A similar
dynamic carried Zion further north to Nyasaland (present-day Malawi).
In 1919, colonial officials reported "two Nyasaland natives recently returned from the Rand with Preachers' Certificates issued by the Christian
Catholic Apostolic Church in Zion, and signed by a Mr. John George
Phillips."[69] The Zion Apostolic Church of Elias Mahlangu focused its
missionary efforts on Northern Rhodesia (present-day Zambia)—due to
the large numbers of migrants from Northern Rhodesia who attended
Mahlangu's church in Johannesburg. Samuel Moyo from Port Jameson in
Rhodesia worked on Johannesburg's mines between 1913 and 1917, and
was during this period also ordained a minister in Mahlangu's Zion Apostolic Church. Upon departing for home in 1917, Moyo was charged by
Mahlangu with starting a branch of the church in Northern Rhodesia
among his compatriots.[70] One of the conduits by which Zion arrived in
Swaziland was through the Makhubu family, who were migrant workers
in Johannesburg, and who brought news of John George Phillips' church
back home with them to Swaziland in 1944.[71] In addition, there were the
homeward-bound migrants to areas within the borders of the Union itself,
many of whom carried Zion's teachings home upon completion of their
contract.

Regional mining metropolises other than Johannesburg were also important in Zion's spread across the subcontinent. The town of Musina, located on the border between South Africa and today Zimbabwe (then
Southern Rhodesia), drew in substantial amounts of migrant labor to its
coal, iron ore, copper, and diamond mining industries. In the 1920s, a contingent of young men from Machaze district in Mozambique's centrally situated Manica Province traveled there for a period of work. Once in Musina,
they were converted to Voliva in Zion City's Christian Catholic Apostolic
Church in Zion led there by another Mozambican, Paulos Moyana. Johannesburg's influence, however, was still indirectly felt in Musina. Moyana had
joined the small church loyal to Voliva in Johannesburg in the mid-1920s. In
later years Moyana worked on the mines in Musina and started a branch of
the church there. Men such as Noah Sithole and Amon Chikoti were sent by
Moyana from Musina home to Machaze in Mozambique as "pioneer evangelists." Once they had prepared the ground, Moyana—now independent
of Voliva, and bishop of his own Zion denomination in Musina—visited
the area to baptize the many new converts.[72] A few other instances similarly testify to evangelistic conduits that bypassed Johannesburg. A major
route by which Zionism reached the north of Mozambique was via net-

works with Nyasaland, rather than through Johannesburg. Zacarias Muiambo, a leader in the present-day Mozambican Igreja Zion Apostle em Moçambique (Zion Apostolic Church of Mozambique) notes that "most people of the northern region [in Mozambique] still talk about one Dingiswayo Mutetwa, who preached and planted the Zion Church in Malawi, from which some of the Mozambicans received it and brought it home."[73] (This might be the same Dingiswayo appointed "Overseer for Rhodesia" in 1923 by a Johannesburg branch of the church loyal to Voliva in Zion City.[74])

Young urbanites fanning out from Johannesburg and from other centers of migrant labor found their radical message of detachment from older loyalties was warmly received by many at home. For one, Zion's faith-healing cures, procured by these young evangelists from the city, were viewed as decisively superior to anything on offer from local specialists. In Mochudi, Bechuanaland, *Bantu World* reported peoples' marvel when Ralefala healed the sick—this former taxi-driver evidently being considered a prophet of great spiritual power. Instead of using medicines, he merely sprinkled supplicants with salt water—also in some cases fanned by a piece of holy cloth or paper[75]—as he prayed for them: "Miracles indeed! The sick no longer go to hospital. They say that the medicines there do not heal as they are surpassed by Zion's salt water."[76] At a large meeting in 1938, it was reported that Ralefala—dubbed by the people as "God's servant"— "healed people of eye ailments, sores, madness, blood infections." He also prayed for "those who had lost things," particularly poignant in this area of heavy labor migration to the Rand, including "many women whose children had left home for work were prayed for to have their children return."[77] Many in Mochudi seemed to understand Zion as a movement that broke the dreaded power of the witches' craft in their district. A 1939 account of the healing of two mentally ill people concluded that "witchcraft is judged and stopped with all might by God's servant,"[78] while another newspaper report celebrated that "spells and potions are cast out in Jesus' name" at these large Zionist evangelistic meetings.[79]

In Gazaland, too, adherents viewed Zion as a modernizing force that broke the power of traditional diviners. Zacarias Muiambo's history of his own denomination, the Igreja Zion Apostle em Moçambique, remembers that before the coming of Zion to Muchaze district in the 1930s, many considered that a certain Nyasa witchdoctor named Muchapi exercised great power over the region. Yet after Sithole and Chikoti brought Zion's teachings to the area, "those possessed by evil spirits dedicated themselves to Jesus, and evil spirits were cast from them, the demonic clothings burnt, the drums and other objects destroyed . . . witch doctors handed over their charms to be burned."[80] For those in Muchaze joining Zion meant renouncing faith in traditional healers as well as in ancestral spirits: "they accepted that whenever they got sick, only the laying on of hands by church elders in the name of Christ was sufficient . . . they could not consult the lot casters [diviners]. Even the ancestral ceremonies had ceased in the minds of believers."[81] And as in Johannesburg, loyalty to Zion meant embracing its progressive disciplines. Sithole brought not only divine healing to his home district of Muchaze, but also literacy, for he had learned to read and write on the mines. His new converts greedily seized on this as an integral part of Zion's fashioning of new selfhood; his nephew, Titus, "could not read but was eager to learn how to read the Bible." Sithole taught the young boy "the vowels," and Titus stayed awake at night studying the primer reader book his uncle had brought from South Africa, along with the teachings of Zion. Soon, Titus found that "God performed a miracle . . . from there on he was able to read the Bible as he wished, and he could no longer separate himself from it."[82]

By teaching converts to repudiate traditional healers and ancestral spirits, as well as embrace the possibilities of literacy, these urban evangelists came into conflict with chiefs and elders across the region. By the early twentieth century, chiefly power in the Union and surrounding territories had been severely eroded.[83] By the 1920s, industrialization and urbanization meant generational and gender disputes were a source of anxiety for early twentieth-century chiefs, with tensions exacerbated by the rise of class-based political movements in the late 1920s, and in particular, the Industrial and Commercial Workers' Union (ICU).[84] Chiefs faced recalcitrant and increasingly politicized subjects resistant to the legitimacy of traditional law and older codes of respect. Despite their deliberate erosion of the institution of chieftaincy, the Native Affairs Department nonetheless viewed chiefs in the Union as a bulwark against politicized Africans, and attempted to calcify chiefly authority into "traditional rule" (seen most fully in the Native Administration Act of 1927). But the decline of chiefs' standing with their subjects continued, as did the rise to power of headmen, or *izinduna*, who often were able to gain the popular legitimacy chiefs perceived as appointees of the government lacked.[85] Even the relatively privileged chiefly elite of Zululand—their monopoly on cattle contrasted with commoners' reliance upon migrant wage labor[86]—found their powers significantly reduced.

Chiefs complained Zionist evangelists from the city undermined their already weakened authority. In teaching their subjects the disciplines of Holiness Christianity, these troublesome young preachers and prophets were encouraging people to subvert social decorum and to rupture with the past—chiefs were preeminent guardians of both. In Gazaland, for example, the popular reception of Zion was tempered by the fierce opposition of traditional male elders. In Muchaze, families of Zionists such as Titus Ndhlovu bitterly complained to their chiefs that their convert relatives were dividing the family and displeasing their ancestral spirits by refusing to pay them homage: "when our ancestors want to bless us there is no way [for them to do so], the family is not marching together." In at least one case, a chief intervened in an attempt to force Ndhlovu to "follow the instructions" of his family elders.[87] This was a pattern evident across the whole of Southern Africa. In the 1930s, Chief Isaac Molife of northern Zululand complained to the Magistrate about the "strange conduct" of the Zionist-type prophet George Khambule, recently arrived back in the region from Johannesburg, highlighting particularly his "determination to follow strict rules concerning pollution and purity."[88] In Bechuanaland, the former Rand taxi driver, Motsisi Ralefala, while finding huge success in his preaching and healing (one gathering in Mochudi had more than 1,300 attend; "heads as far as the eye could see"[89]), found that he also incurred the hostility of the region's chiefs, who felt their authority profoundly undermined by the disciplines of Zion. A meeting of all the chiefs of the Bechuanaland Protectorate with the resident commissioner in 1957 found all speaking with a common voice: "Chiefs were unanimous that Zionists were a subversive influence on tribal life. They preached loyalty to God alone and did not recognize temporal authority."[90]

Chiefs were particularly concerned at how Zionists "dislocated family life, as women of the faith refused to obey husbands"—in the grim assessment of a contemporary colonial official.[91] Across Southern Africa, twentieth-century chiefs' already fragile authority was predicated on obedient female subjects domiciled at home.[92] Complaints that Zionists disrupted proper codes of respect between husband and wife had long dogged the transmission of the faith across the region. Councilor Mmothi Pilane, an adviser to a Mochudi chief, confessed himself perturbed in 1940, on account of the fact that the returned migrant Ralefala's Zion church was "breaking up family life—the husband or wife or children belonging to different denominations." He gave an example of his own niece, who had joined the church, and had now left her family since her conversion to go and live in Pietersburg, the site of the church's ritual headquarters.[93] Correctly perceiving that allegiance to Zion weakened adherents' loyalty to local authorities, elders worried that Zion in Bechuanaland subverted order, respect, and public decency. One chief even speculated that "Zionists indulged in sexual orgies and contributed to the moral delinquency of the youth."[94] White officials were entirely in agreement with chiefs on this point. The district commissioner of Kanye, Lobatse in Bechuanaland reflected darkly on the spread of pernicious teachings from across the border in South Africa: "This so-called religion which has its origins in the Union has now spread into Bechuanaland, and every village where it exists there is nothing but chaos, the sanctity of families has been broken, and no peace, harmony and good government exists."[95]

Authorities also objected to the free movements of these urban evangelists around the region. Through traversing the capacious borders of God's land, cosmopolitan Zionists disregarded chiefs' efforts to regulate and police their territories amid a context of African land dispossession and the destabilizing effects of mass labor migration, particularly of the youth. In 1944, Paramount Chief Mshiyeni in Zululand complained to government officials that Zionists "come from afar whom we do not know, and say they are Messengers of God. We don't know these people . . . no person should preach until he has reported himself to the Chief, who will question him and ascertain his standing and character."[96] Officials of the Union and of surrounding colonies held similar views to chiefs and elders about the undesirability of itinerant evangelists crisscrossing the country. The 1926 Native Churches Commission had recommended that "unrecognized" African ministers be withheld the railway concessions usually available to clergymen, a move doubtless intended to restrict black evangelists' mobility. Anxious communications flew back forth, not only between Natives Affairs employees across the Union of South Africa, but also between officials in Johannesburg and Pretoria and administrators in Swaziland, Bechuanaland, Rhodesia, Northern Rhodesia, Basutoland, and Nyasaland. Intercolonial officials banded together—largely unsuccessfully, it seems—to block Zionists from South Africa from crossing the border into Bechuanaland; to "stop any more Zionists entering the territory, and attempt to rid the territory of Zionists who had illegally emigrated over the past years."[97] As in Bechuanaland, officials in Northern Rhodesia also refused entry to preachers they considered suspect. In 1923 Samuel Moyo—originally of Port Jameson, Northern Rhodesia, and having spent some years working on the Rand—was also barred to the colony as a newly returned preacher in Mahlangu's Zion Apostolic Church on the grounds that "he does not come under European control."[98]

But despite these considerable obstacles, many Zionist Johannesburg-based churches successfully possessed networks of believers across Southern Africa. The free flow of migrant laborers across borders proved impossible for both chiefs and white officials to effectively police. Phillips soon had a substantial following in Mozambique ("I have a very great work in Gaza"[99]) as well as—as he informed the Director for Native Labour in Johannesburg—"throughout the Transvaal, Orange Free State,

Natal, Zululand and Basutoland, with preachers in charge of every gathering, numbering altogether some thousands of numbers."[100] By 1940, Phillips's successor, the Mozambican Matthew Koza, was seeking approval from Swaziland authorities to introduce the church there.[101] Mabiletsa's upwardly mobile church appears to have been unusual in not only having congregations, but also owning church property—buildings and schools—across the Union of South Africa, as well as in German-ruled South West Africa.[102] The older dream of establishing self-contained Zion cities across the region continued. In 1932, Mabiletsa's Christian Apostolic Church in Zion purchased a farm outside of Wakkerstroom from the Native Farmers' Association of Africa. The land was used to host regular meetings of the church, including delegates from the city of Johannesburg.[103] Edward Lion's Zion Apostolic Faith Mission Church was similarly cross-regional, boasting members primarily in Basutoland, but also in Natal, Zululand, Orange Free State, Portuguese East Africa, and Bechuanaland.[104] Moses Muteto of the Christian Catholic Apostolic Church in Zion, headquartered in Johannesburg, had two deputy overseers to supervise the main branches of the church—one was Dingiswayo in Northern Rhodesia, the other was his overseer for the branch in Portuguese East Africa, a Jeremiah Koza.[105] Although most of these are examples of large and successful Zionist organizations, migrant labor networks meant even the humblest Zion church on the Rand boasted an international membership. William Mkize, head of the tiny Zion Apostolic New Jerusalem Church based in Benoni, applied to the Swaziland authorities in 1937 to visit his "small congregations" in the southern Swazi towns of Mankanyane and Sihlute.[106] The miniscule Galatia Apostolic Church in Zion, founded on the Rand in 1939 and with only fifty members twenty years later—"mostly labourers, but also with two teachers"—nonetheless operated in the "West Rand, Swaziland, Basutoland, Bechuanaland."[107]

Estranged from local elders, Zionists across Southern Africa now looked to their church headquarters in Johannesburg as the locus of their cosmopolitan identities as Christians. In the 1940s, Sundkler reported Zionists across the Union took great pride in the fact that the "Golden City was the see of their church"; it was a "matter of prestige" to claim "our President lives in Johannesburg."[108] Geographically disparate believers were reminded of their common identity as Zionists—an affiliation counter to loyalty to elders and chiefs—by the frequent visits ministers from Johannesburg paid to outlying branches across the subcontinent. Indeed, many ministers more often supervised at the regional level than at church headquarters in the city. Elias Mahlangu's son remembered him as "widely travelled," describing how in overseeing branches across the subcontinent, he frequently journeyed to "Rhodesia, Swaziland, and many other countries in Southern Africa, to the other main cities in South Africa and also to Natal and Zululand." Sometimes such itinerancy could be hazardous. His son recalled: "once when he went to Rhodesia, he was stranded and almost run over by elephants before I sent money for his fare back home."[109] John George Phillips was also a frequent traveler, especially to Gazaland. In 1924, he undertook a journey not only to Lourenco Marques, the capital, but also north up the coast and inland to "Gijan, Chibuto, Shonwene, Chai Chai, Belen Maria, Sabie and from the latter place to make my return to Lourenco Marques."[110] Extensive travel was also undertaken by Johannesburg's Zionist ministers within the Union. Jeremiah Maduna, head of the Christian Catholic Apostolic Church in Zion, announced to the Secretary of Native Affairs in 1936 that "I am on a long journey to all places among our people of this church."[111]

Frequent visits enabled city leadership to be present at key moments, symbolizing the close ties between headquarters and regional branches across Southern Africa. The purpose of Phillips's 1924 visit to Gazaland, for example, was to ordain a successor to the position of a "principal preacher" who had recently died.[112] Sometimes not only the minister but also the congregation from Johannesburg headquarters would descend on a regional branch for a special celebration. At the Mochudi branch in Bechuanaland of the Zion Christian Church, a "big celebration" was attended not only by local believers, but by "groups from Pretoria and Johannesburg [who] travelled by train and by car . . . there were also Zionists from Rhodesia in attendance." Alienated from traditional authorities and family elders, Mochudi Zionists were pioneering novel cosmopolitan modes of being. Songs were sung at the meeting "praising Jehovah and the Messiah," one celebrating Zion's eclectic fellowship by proclaiming that the "nations are entering . . . the sound is so moving and the drums are so amazing."[113] Zionists from the city regularly visited brethren in the Transvaal's Wakkerstroom area, a regional locus of Zion activity that historically rivalled Johannesburg in significance. In the 1940s, Emmanuel Tsotetse and other young men in the Holy Catholic Apostolic Church in Zion would regularly cycle from their homes in Pimville, Johannesburg to the small town of Amersfoort near Wakkerstroom—160 miles from the city—to visit the rural brethren. The advantage of cycling was that these young urban proselytizers would invariably be invited to spend the night on the farms they passed through, and hence yielded more time to converse and spread Zion's message. There they would spend the evening, holding prayer and healing services.[114]

Literature produced by the church headquarters in Johannesburg and widely distributed across the region performed a similar function. These documents affirmed Zionists' membership not of fixed ethnic and territorial polities but of transnational Zion. Two Rand migrants who returned home to Nyasaland possessed "Preachers' Certificates . . . signed by a Mr. John George Phillips of Grahamstown Street, Johannesburg."[115] Stephen Mavimbela and Andrew Zwane in Swaziland carried certificates signed by Daniel Nkonyane in Charlestown, over the border in South Africa, thus proclaiming their origins as a South African church.[116] However diverse and fragmented Zionist churches were, all certificates were remarkably uniform, bearing the name of the church, the name and address of its General Overseer and the instructions that the evangelist or preacher was authorized by headquarters to "preach the Gospel, pray for the sick, bury the dead."[117] Many surviving certificates from this period also bear the imprint of a "credo" from Dowie's era: "Zion is the Full Gospel of Salvation from Sin, Healing from Disease and Holy Living through the Power of the Indwelling Holy Ghost, by whom the Sons and Daughters of Zion are being prepared for the Coming of Zion's King."[118] The circulation of these certificates marked out believers as sons and daughters of "Zion's king," not subjects of chiefs. Uniform was also important in this regard. This was the period when many Zionist churches pioneered the use of distinctive dress, the details of which had been revealed to the church's prophet in a dream or revelation. As well as a sign of prophetic revelation, a distinct uniform worn by all church members across the subcontinent proclaimed its wearers' membership in a transnational organization cutting across local affiliations.

Further sustaining these cosmopolitan identities, most churches had regular conferences where regional branches visited Johannesburg for a gathering of the entire church. The frequency of these meetings ranged: the Apostolic Holy Messenger Church in Zion had a General Meeting every year in Sophiatown,[119] whereas the Bethesda Zion Apostolic Church of Africa only met in its entirety in New Clare once every three years.[120] Mabiletsa's church met annually in Alexandra Township for its great "Zion Synod." It was considered an honor to represent the regional church at headquarters' conference. Asa Mmango, born in 1936 near Wakkerstroom, remembers how his father and other men who belonged to Mabiletsa's church vied for selection to travel to Johannesburg's "Synod." Those selected had to collect donations from the congregation to cover their long train journey to Alexandra Township.[121] In case of Nkonyane's church, with its powerful base in the Transvaal, the large annual conference occurred in the town of Charlestown near Wakkerstroom, not Johannesburg. The church met there for a large Easter Service; believers from Johannesburg, the rest of the Union, and neighboring countries streamed to attend. A Swazi minister, Soul Sibandze, remembers how his father and other men would travel for days on foot from Swaziland to Charlestown, an arduous journey that included hiking over a large mountain range.[122] In 1939, *Bantu World* reported that Nkonyane's "big meeting" in Charlestown had 940 attendees (many from Johannesburg); the following year over 1,000 people attended. Signifying the importance of the Rand as a hub of the church alongside Charlestown, these meetings were jointly led by ministers both from Johannesburg and from Charlestown.[123] Conferences could last several days to a couple of weeks; the General Meeting of the Christian Catholic Church in Zion in Sophiatown in 1915 would "last about ten days and [would have] natives coming from the Orange Free State, Natal and various parts of the Transvaal."[124]

Important business occurred at these large annual meetings, including the appointment of church officials and the inauguration of new buildings.[125] But these meetings were also occasions for fiery, spirit-filled preaching and worship, reminding believers across Southern Africa of the meaning of Zion, the Kingdom of God. The *Bantu World* advertised Mabiletsa's upcoming annual Synod meeting ("it's on the lips of everyone belonging to the Flag of the Most High"). The newspaper announced that the Rev. Mdlalose's (invited to be a key speaker) verbal skill and preaching acuity would powerfully convene the assembled "nations": he "who is like a buffalo running through a forest; he shouts so loudly that all the nations answer and come into Zion . . . [he is] a person who can both talk and sing, everything that comes out of his mouth is sweet." All the Synod's speakers, the article went on, would "shout without tiring that righteousness is seen by God alone." Meetings such as Mabiletsa's and others were inaugurating new forms of pan-ethnic spiritual solidarity. These gatherings invited participants to imagine themselves part of an expansive continent-wide community: "the Cathedral where all the Zionists of this church from South Africa meet, other groups also gathering from German South West Africa and East Coast Africa." Ultimately, membership of this entity was not defined by ethnic, regional, or even national characteristics, but by loyalty to Zion. The article tells us that Mdlalose's final words to the congregation were: "Come back Children, says God, I will take you one by one from the nations and bring you to Zion."[126]

Perhaps the most successful example of Zion internationalism was a church whose headquarters were not in Johannesburg at all, but outside the small town of Pietersburg in the north of the Union. This was Engenas

Lekganyane's ZCC. Engenas Lekganyane was born in the northern Transvaal around 1880, and as a young man moved to Johannesburg seeking employment. There, he became an evangelist within the Pentecostal Apostolic Faith Mission.[127] At some point, however, Lekganyane joined Elias Mahlangu's breakaway from the AFM.[128] Around 1920—in a typical schismatic move—Lekganyane broke with Mahlangu on the basis of the latter's use of white robes and staffs—which Lekganyane objected to—and instead affiliated his small following to Edward Lion's rival Zion Apostolic Faith Mission, soon being named bishop for the Transvaal.[129] Around 1925, Lion named "Elder E. B. Lekganyane" evangelist over the Pietersburg area.[130] However, in the same year Lekganyane seceded from Lion (possibly due to Lekganyane's second marriage, for Lion prohibited polygamy[131]) and started his own organization, the Zion Christian Church. Within a decade, the ZCC had become an important player on the regional Zionist scene. In 1925, the church had 926 adherents. Ten years later, this had doubled to 2,000, and by 1942, it had 22,487 members, with 55 congregations in South Africa but also in Zimbabwe and Bechuanaland.[132] By 1954, the membership was 80,000.[133] Lekganyane's powerful organization owned property across Southern Africa. For example, in 1953, a farm of 3,000 morgen in the Tuli Block (a narrow strip of land adjacent to Zimbabwe and South Africa) was bought by Lekganyane to settle 2,000 Bakgatla Zionists on.[134]

Much of the ZCC's success stemmed from the fact that its headquarters were not in Johannesburg. Greater access to land outside of the city meant Lekganyane could lift the institution of the annual conference to an entirely new level. In 1930, using donations raised from followers he bought three large farms thirty miles from Pietersburg, which he named "Zion City Moria," reflecting the longstanding desire of Zionists—in Africa as in North America—to possess land dedicated to a sacred cause (Moria referred to the biblical mountain where God appeared to King David).[135] Although Mabiletsa's church grandly referred to its meeting place in Alexandra as a "Cathedral," the vast majority of Zionist leaders in Johannesburg had only a cramped church building or an unused classroom for their conferences. By contrast, the spacious Moria offered sweeping amounts of land for members across Southern Africa to undertake pilgrimage to. Moreover, Lekganyane's new Zion City was an easy bus ride from Johannesburg. In 1954, a *Drum* reporter noted during the Easter meeting forty-six buses hired at £80 brought thousands of pilgrims from the Rand.[136] By the 1950s, three times a year—at Easter, Christmas, and the Jewish New Year in September—tens of thousands visited the church for several days to a few weeks, there to be blessed by Lekganyane's curative prayers.[137] Lekganyane's reputation among his followers suggests the great heights of authority to which a prophetic reputation could propel an individual. Prompted by a carefully crafted and tightly controlled canon of oral and written stories of healing miracles, the church came to view Lekganyane as a deeply holy man, indeed almost a deity in the eyes of many. A prominent ZCC historian, a man called Lukhaimane, said of his leader: "he was a messiah who came to deliver his people from bondage, he was a prophet for his followers."[138]

Zion and Ethnic Nationalism

Despite the success of Zionist leaders in unifying their region-wide followers via new pan-ethnic spiritual solidarities, significant tensions did disrupt these projects. As the century progressed, regional politics increasingly came to the fore across much of Southern Africa. These developments were part of a complex strategy on the part of traditional political authorities to preserve power as the incursions of colonial states into African affairs extended. Moreover, during a period of growing black political discontent—exemplified in the rise of the Industrial and Commercial Workers' Union throughout the 1920s and 1930s—African chiefly elite discerned an opportunity to preserve their influence by casting themselves as the "natural" leaders of African communities.[139] This was especially the case with regard to the British Protectorate of Swaziland, as well as in Natal and Zululand, regions within the Union of South Africa undergoing a powerful resurgence of Zulu cultural nationalism centered in the Zulu monarch, Solomon kaDinuzulu, and which attempted to rehabilitate "traditional" customs.[140] For example, in the 1920s, the "Zulu National Congress"—later renamed Inkatha yeZulu—was started by members of the Zulu royal elite, and had set as its goal the economic betterment of the Zulu nation, including the creation of farming cooperatives and land-buying syndicates. The monarch was key to this: Inkatha took its name from the mystical grass "coil" of the nation, *iNkatha*, thought to hang from the roof of the king's residence. As such, it represented the significance of the Zulu royal family in knitting its people together, suggested by the tightly bound-up grass coil.[141]

These ethnic politics undermined Zionists' efforts to present themselves as a cosmopolitan gathering of Christians. One such instance—much publicized in the press of the day—was a Zulu walkout from Elias Mahlangu's Johannesburg-based Zion Apostolic Church.[142] Mahlangu's large church was characteristically diverse in its ethnic composition, as well as geographically diffuse. In 1927, government officials estimated the church had

9,000 members in 120 centers across Southern Africa.[143] Mahlangu's right-hand man was a Sotho, the Rev. Mokoena, and to oversee the church's Durban branch in Natal Mahlangu commissioned a Tswana deputy, Rev. Seheri.[144] But ethnic Tswana-Zulu disputes soon fractured the church. One of Mahlangu's ministers in Natal was Ezra Mbonambi, a traditionalist Zulu figure who had close ties to a number of local chiefs.[145] Newly appointed to Durban, the Tswana minister, Seheri, soon accused the Zulu Mbonambi of financial mismanagement.[146] Mahlangu traveled down from Johannesburg to resolve the issue, but the meeting ended in disarray when a fight broke out between Seheri and Mbonambi's supporters—Tswana and Zulu, respectively—leading to the arrest of forty individuals after what both church members and government officials referred to as a "faction fight." Tellingly, this was the contemporary label for interethnic conflict.[147] Mbonambi bitterly accused Seheri of "dividing the people into factions" and reminded Seheri that he carried no legitimacy in Natal among the Zulu people: "Bechuanaland [the Tswana region] is a far-off country."[148] In the recollection of Mahlangu's son, Seheri soon left Natal, defeated by this tide of Zulu cultural nationalism, and "went back to Botswana [Bechuanaland] to lead his people there."[149]

The ethnic conflict splintering Mahlangu's church soon spread to the Witwatersrand. Mbonambi in Durban maintained that far-away Johannesburg headquarters—and its Sotho leader, Mahlangu—had no authority over the regional Zulu branch.[150] Mbonambi's polemic against Johannesburg-based Mahlangu was carried out in the pages of Natal's isiZulu-language newspaper *Ilanga lase Natal*, where Mbonambi referred bitterly to the unwelcome interventions of Mahlangu's Rand church in local Zulu affairs: the cosmopolitan "crowds of Johannesburg are notorious in Durban for slandering my name . . . and defaming my reputation." Mbonambi informed the readers of *Ilanga*, the Zulu public of the 1920s, that he—by contrast to the "crowds of Johannesburg"—was not hungry for power or status. He insisted that he was merely acting as loyal guardian of the spiritual interests of the Zulu people: "I am not claiming the Presidentship [of the church], but I desire that the people of my land shall be saved from their sins."[151] Eventually the dispute was resolved by Mahlangu's strategic decision to divide the church into a "Transvaal Section," under himself, and a "Natal Section," under Zulu control and led by Mbonambi and a Zulu Rev. Nxaba. Mahlangu earnestly hoped that, although the unity of Zion had been splintered, nonetheless "the blessings of the Lord Jesus Christ will lead us on the right path."[152] These sorts of problems were not confined merely to Mahlangu's organization. Zulu ethnic factionalism also appeared within Mabiletsa's large church, where one of Mabiletsa's most senior ministers was the Zulu Rev. Mdlalose, with links to the Zulu royal family. Mdlalose came under much pressure from the Zulu membership of the church on account of the fact that "he owed allegiance to a Sotho leader, Mabiletsa who took Zulu money and gave it to the Sotho." Mdlalose and Mabiletsa eventually reconciled these tensions by opening a bank account in Durban that ensured Zulu congregants' donations stayed in the region, rather than be remitted to the Sotho Mabiletsa in Johannesburg.[153]

Perhaps the most significant instance of the fraught interplay between ethnicity and evangelical Christianity was the emergence of a Swazi Zion in the 1930s. This was the result of a Swazi secession from Daniel Nkonyane's South Africa-headquartered Christian Catholic Apostolic Holy Spirit Church in Zion. Nkonyane's church was situated in Charlestown, twenty miles from Wakkerstroom, within the broad corridor of the eastern Transvaal that, along with Harrismith to the west, was the historic home of Zion on the Highveld. This region had also—until the end of the nineteenth century—been part of the neighboring Swazi Kingdom, and so consequently had a great deal of Swazis living and working in the area; indeed, Nkonyane himself was of Swazi descent.[154] In 1895 the formerly independent Swaziland had become a protectorate of the Boer Transvaal Republic (much against popular Swazi sentiment) and following the Boer defeat of 1902, was administered as a British protectorate by the British, with the Swazi monarch retaining nominal power as a paramount chief. By 1914, Swaziland lost almost two-thirds of its territory to the Transvaal, part of a controversial "re-scheduling" of land available for African occupation under the British administration and in keeping with the government's broader efforts to limit African landownership and to drive Swazis into employment in the labor-hungry mines of the Witwatersrand.[155]

Zulu and Swazi members of Nkonyane's Charlestown-based church initially experienced little difficulty in conceiving of their congregation as a seamless pan-ethnic unity. Fluid movement between the Union and Swaziland was a defining feature of this region, with many important Swazi proselytizers possessing extensive South African connections. The story of one of Nkonyane's earliest Swazi converts, Johanna Nxumalo, offers insight into the permeable Zulu-Swazi identities dominating Nkonyane's church in this early period. Nxumalo was born in Swaziland in 1890 to a prominent Christian family, the Nxumalos (her brother, Benjamin, would be involved in founding meetings of the South African Native National Congress), and attended the prestigious American Congregationalist girls' school in Inanda, outside of Durban, South Africa. In 1907, Nxumalo started teaching at a Congregationalist school in the small town of Groenvlei, an easy distance from Charlestown (it was during this period that she discovered

Nkonyane's church). Yet alongside her South African ties, Nxumalo was also closely linked to the Swazi monarchy: she was the sister of Lomawa Nxumalo, the main wife of the Swazi regent, Bhunu V, and mother of Sohbhuza, who would become paramount chief of Swaziland in 1921. In 1913, Nxumalo was baptized by Daniel Nkonyane and, in a rare example of missionary enterprise by an unmarried woman, Nxumalo was commissioned by Nkonyane to be his first missionary to Swaziland, where she "began preaching, praying for people, prophesying and receiving followers."[156] Nxumalo was thus a missionary who also inhabited a prophetic role, indicating the opportunities that could open up for women who claimed the inspiration of the Holy Spirit in their independent activities.[157] In about 1960 her husband recalled of Johanna—now dead some thirty years—that "she had the Spirit to a high degree." She appeared to have received revelations instructing her to use veils and sticks in her healing prayer. Her husband recalled: "she prophesied with veils and then followed it up with sticks . . . yes, she trusted the sticks would help the sick."[158]

The careers of other individuals also exemplified the cross-cultural and cross-linguistic processes by which Nkonyane's Zion church was carried to Swaziland. Andrew Zwane, for example, brought the faith home to Swaziland after a period working as a laborer on Johannesburg's mines and later in Charlestown itself, where he joined Nkonyane's Christian Catholic Apostolic Holy Spirit Church in Zion.[159] There was also Stephen Mavimbela, originally a Methodist preacher stationed in Barberton in the Eastern Transvaal, an area of considerable Swazi settlement.[160] By around the mid-1920s, now back in Swaziland, Mavimbela received the gift of the Spirit and, much to the consternation of his Methodist superiors, started speaking in tongues. Hearing of Nkonyane's Pentecostal Zionist church across the border in South Africa, Mavimbela traveled to Charlestown and was there appointed a minister within Nkonyane's organization (since 1921 named the Christian Catholic Apostolic Holy Spirit Church in Zion), having resigned from the Methodist church.[161] Mavimbela worked closely with Andrew Zwane tirelessly evangelizing the length and breadth of Swaziland, as well as with his wife Elizabeth Mavimbela, who was renowned as a "very powerful preacher . . . sometimes my grandmother would be preaching to the whole congregation, men and women, and my grandfather Stephen would be in the congregation listening to her." While his wife's talents were as a preacher, Stephen Mavimbela—like Zwane—was considered a Spirit-inspired prophet, capable "of just putting his hands on you and then you are healed."[162] A descendant of Stephen remembers the Mavimbela family home became renowned as a local center for faith healing: it was "like a hospital! We had no place to sleep, so many patients were living at our place."[163] For about a decade, these thriving Swazi branches remained loyal to Nkonyane's church headquartered in Charlestown, across the border. Through Nkonyane's Swazi overseers—primarily Mavimbela and Zwane—Swazi Zionists sent regular tithes to Nkonyane in Charlestown. They also traveled long distances by foot to attend the annual Good Friday service at Charlestown, well as regularly received Nkonyane on his frequent visits to his congregations in Swaziland.[164]

Yet Swazi Zionists' loyalties to Nkonyane in South Africa were soon riven by tensions. In sharp contrast to Zionists' troubled interactions with chiefly authorities in other regions of Southern Africa, many Swazi Zionist leaders enjoyed close relationships with the Swazi royal family, a fact largely to do with the elite backgrounds of early Zion proselytizers. Johanna Nxumalo's sisterly link to the Queen Mother meant that when the latter suffered from poor eyesight, Daniel Nkonyane was invited to pray for her at her residence in Swaziland, restoring her sight, and thereby securing future invitations to attend her and other members of the royal family.[165] Nkonyane's other Swazi evangelists were themselves close to royal circles. Before his career as a Methodist preacher, Mavimbela had been a warrior, part of the regimental age group linked to Bhunu, the father of the paramount chief of Swaziland, Sobhuza II.[166] As a talented prophet, Mavimbela is remembered to have divined the existence of dangerous, harmful "medicine" placed in the thatched roof of the royal residence by an ill-wisher, something that further increased Zionists' standing in royal circles.[167] Further suggesting the cordial relationship between Zion and the Swazi monarchy is the fact that from the 1930s on, a strong following of princes from the royal kraal in Swaziland would undertake the journey across the border to South Africa to "kaNkonyane" (Nkonyane's place) for the annual Good Friday service.[168]

Most all, it was the Swazi paramount chief, Sobhuza himself, with whom Zionist leaders enjoyed a warm relationship. Sobhuza's sympathy for the Zionists needs to be interpreted in the context of the ethnic-cultural revival programs he undertook during this period, part of his broader determination to preserve Swazi "culture" against European and missionary influence. An unsuccessful deputation to London in 1923 that attempted to have the controversial 1907 Land Partition reversed led Sobhuza to view cultural revival—rather than territorial integrity—as key to avoiding Swaziland's entire assimilation within the Union of South Africa and wholesale subjection to its racist legislation.[169] The king and his advisers were also concerned at what they perceived as the breakdown of Swazi society by the extensive youthful labor migration to the Rand and the corresponding demise of chiefly and traditional authority. The 1920s and 1930s were decades during which Sobhuza—together with the Zulu monarch, Solomon kaDinuzulu—attempted to rebuild the prestige of the monarchy. His plan was to revive old monarchical rituals such as the annual rain-making *Incwala* ceremony as well as the regimental age-grade system *imibutho,* which required men to serve the paramount chief for a period of time at one of the palaces. Promoting supposedly ancient Swazi values was key to this project. Christian missions' provision of Western-style education increasingly came under fire from Sobhuza for "causing the Swazi scholar to despise Swazi institutions and his indigenous culture."[170] Within a broader climate of burgeoning ethnic nationalism and antimissionary sentiment, the wildly popular faith-healing Zion churches seemed to Sobhuza a laudable example of a Christianity capable of operating entirely independently of European control. A distinctly Swazi church would undergird the broader project of ethnic nationalism. Indeed, Sobhuza had long dreamed of instituting a "Swazi National Church," telling Swazi religious leaders in 1939 that "England has its Church of England, Germany was represented abroad by its German [Lutheran] mission. So we in *Ngwane* [Swaziland] ought to have a Swazi Church and a Swazi Cathedral."[171]

Moreover, for Nkonyane's deputies in Swaziland, an alliance with a powerful local patron seemed an expedient route to gaining protection from hostile colonial authorities. In common with believers across Southern Africa, early Zionists in Swaziland experienced considerable opposition from colonial administrators as well as European missionaries, the traumatic memory of which is still preserved in the traditions of all the major Zion churches in the country. While officials objected to the itinerant ways of these religious cosmopolitans, hostility also arose due to a perception of Zionists as subversive of authority in their propensity to secede from established denominations. In 1937, a British official in Swaziland noted with consternation that "any person who joins the sect can gather a congregation and start of church without reference to any higher authority." This was deemed a "potential source of trouble among the natives" as religious subversion could possibly translate into political dissent.[172] As elsewhere, officials also worried that Zionist prophets undermined male elders and chiefs' authority by attracting female converts into their orbit. Sensitive to this, figures such as Stephen Mavimbela took great precautions during their evangelistic journeys to "never enter the homestead if only the wife of the homestead was at home. He would ask them to come out and pray under a tree. So everything is correct." Yet despite these measures, many women "would want to follow Mavimbela after he prayed for them . . . sometimes the husbands were angry."[173] Chiefs were warned by colonial administrators that Zionist misconduct in "seducing" young girls away from their

homes should be reported to them immediately.[174] Swazi Zion bishop, Soul
Sibandze, recalls that at "that time the white man said these Zionists are
no good, they must be cast out, they are taking wives from peoples'
homes."[175] Local European missionary organizations, most of all the
powerful Nazarene medical mission that ran a large hospital in the town
of Bremersdorp (today Manzini), also put pressure on the colonial government to clamp down upon the activities of the "lunatics . . . who prayed
in the mountains" and repudiated the power of biomedicine in favor of
prayer.[176] While Swaziland officials stopped short of outright banning, they
nonetheless recommended local regional commissioners to conduct interviews with "leaders of this sect . . . calling upon them to produce relevant
literature" in order that the teachings of Zion could be carefully scrutinized
for evidence of political intent.[177] As in neighboring South Africa, sites for
schools and churches were immensely restricted privileges.[178]

The fragile status of Zionists in Swaziland meant the local patronage of
the Swazi paramount chief outweighed the protection of a transnational
religious leader across the border in Charlestown—one held in no high regard by colonial authorities. By the 1930s, Sobhuza had publicly invited
beleaguered Swazi Zion churches to come under his protection. In a famous speech to church leaders he proclaimed that Zionists were *tinhlanhla
tami* ("my very own crazy ones"), thus turning on its head the common
criticism that Zionists' claim to be inspired by the Holy Spirit meant they
were "mad."[179] A common saying among Swazi Zionists, still in use today,
is that "as a hen does to its chicks, so the King protected us under the wing
of his arm from the British."[180] In 1937, both Zwane and Mavimbela severed links with Daniel Nkonyane in Charlestown and styled themselves as
independent Swazi Zion churches enjoying the patronage of King Sobhuza II.
Bishop Soul Sibandze recalls how the King ceremonially collected Zwane
and Mavimbela's ordination certificates issued by Nkonyane and dramatically tore them up, proclaiming them null and void "because the names on
them were in South Africa." Sobhuza is then said to have ordered the issue
of new certificates bearing the name "the Swazi Christian Church in
Zion . . . because the King had now become leader of their church."[181] In
1940, Sobhuza established the church's new headquarters at his royal *kraal*
(homestead), Lozitha, to symbolize its standing as the national church of the
Swazi people. The church's documentation from this time on proclaimed
that the church's headquarters were at "Lozitehlezi, the Royal Kraal."[182]
Moreover, all tithes were now kept in the country, instead of remitted to
Nkonyane across the border as had been the case prior to 1937.[183]

A handful of Zionist churches in Swaziland continued to maintain links
to Johannesburg-based organizations, preserving the original transnational

character of the movement. By the 1930s, Obed Ndhlela's Bethesda Zion Apostolic Church in Africa established branches in Swaziland, while Mabiletsa's Christian Apostolic Church in Zion was also represented there, claiming a membership of 4,064 people under local Swazi preacher Marko Mtetwa.[184] Although the new Swazi Christian Church in Zion experienced numerous secessions over the following decades (in quintessential Zion style), the new churches that emerged after the 1930s (what Sundkler called Swaziland's "unruly army of numerous competing prophets"[185]) all were alike in one important respect: they styled themselves as local national organizations, loyal above all to the Swazi paramount chief. In return for the protection and patronage of Sobhuza, Swazi Zionist churches were willing to lend spiritual legitimacy to the monarch, casting his reign over the nation as divinely mandated. In the early 1940s, the annual "Good Friday" service was instituted whereby Zionist leaders such as Mavimbela and Zwane would be hosted by the King at his royal kraal to lead the nation in prayer and praise with the Royal family visibly presiding. Much of the point of this new Easter celebration was that, being situated in Swaziland, it explicitly displaced the centrality of Nkonyane's South African meeting in Charlestown, which Swazi Zionists were now forbidden from attending.[186] An even more powerful religious validation of ethnic nationalism was also evident in the willingness of Zionist leaders to begin offering prayer and benediction at Incwala—an event that other missionary-led churches in Swaziland typically denounced as pagan ritual directed at ancestral spirits in the interests of procuring rain.[187] The mutual approbation of Zion and the monarchy was displayed in other ways too. Zionist leaders in Swaziland drew upon a biblical grammar of divinely ordained kings to argue for the legitimacy of the Swazi monarchy. In the 1950s, the decade before Swaziland's independence from Britain, the then-leader of the Swazi Christian Church in Zion of South Africa published rousing praises of Sobhuza II in the national newspaper, *Izwi lamaSwazi:* "My God bless our Swazi King . . . May he grow so old that he will have to walk stooping . . . Sobhuza is like Solomon of old in wisdom and his father, Mbandzeni I [a nineteenth-century Swazi king] compares with Moses of old in Israel."[188] Indeed, by the 1950s the Swazi Zionist churches had become one of the main platforms for pro-independence, pro-monarchical thought in the country, providing a platform for nationalists' to criticize missionaries' importation of a foreign, especially "European" Christianity into Swaziland. In this polemical context, the typically Zionist disciplines of faith healing, abstention from alcohol, tobacco, and pork, and "indulging in frequent prayer meetings sometimes lasting through the night"[189] were strategically recast as quintessential Swazi as well as deeply evangelical.

This alliance between Zion leaders and ethnic patriots was never an entirely seamless one. There were areas where Swazi custom—increasingly celebrated as an intrinsic component of the new nationalism—was felt even by this ethnically leaning constituency of Zionists to be incompatible with their commitments to Holiness-Pentecostal Christianity. Polygamy was one of the major areas of dispute. By the time of his death in 1982, Sohbuza II had taken over seventy wives; polygamy was a cornerstone of Swazi society and part of the monarch's efforts to form strategic alliances with important families throughout the nation. But monogamous marriage was integral to the Protestant Christian worldview of many Zionists. Bishop Maziya, an elderly senior leader within the contemporary Swazi Christian Church in Zion summed up his church's uneasy tolerance of the practice: "it is true that some of us are polygamous . . . nonetheless, it is a violation of our procedure. It leads to conflict and strife, we are expected to have one wife."[190] Perhaps the greatest tension in this alliance between Zion and the royal establishment was felt with regard to ancestral spirits. Swazi monarchy was undergirded by the connections between the living and the dead. The King, and the entire Swazi nation, felt themselves to be continually guided by those relatives who were deceased. The Incwala, for example, prominently involved prayers of thanksgiving from the nation to their ancestors for blessing them with good crops and harvest.[191] For some Zionists, this could be easily elided with their own institution of prophecy; many came to believe that ancestral spirits, along with the Holy Spirit, were instructing them in their visions and prophecies. But over the course of the twentieth century, and commensurate with a surge in antimonarchical sentiment in Swaziland, a growing number of youthful Swazi Zionists came to feel this approbation of ancestral spirits to be a profound betrayal of the evangelical values of Zion. The next chapter examines the efforts of a certain reformist group of Swazi youth to realign Zion with what they considered to be a more biblical variant of Christianity. Zion, this group of youthful reformists believed, needed to renounce its commitment to local religion and to the institution of the monarchy, and to bring itself once again into accordance with the universal tenets of Zion, the Kingdom of God.

CHAPTER SEVEN

Youthful Reformers and the Politics of Bible Schools in the Kingdom of Swaziland

ON A SLEEPY SATURDAY MORNING in the middle of 2016, about fifty or so young and middle-aged adults, including myself, gathered in a large classroom in the center of the town of Manzini (formerly Bremersdorp), Swaziland's second largest city. These were working men and women, and many were engaged in full-time church ministry, mainly in various Zionist denominations. But they were also, for this duration of this day at least, students. They had assembled for a full day of classes on various aspects of the Christian Bible. One Sunday a month, over a four-year period, they would gather at this same venue for a day of study. At the end of the four years, if they had attended the requisite number of classes as well as handed in all the homework assignments, they would be in possession of a much-valued diploma from an organization known as Zion Bible College.

Once everyone had settled into the tightly packed rows of plastic chairs and studiously drawn out their Bibles and notebooks, the three teachers—one white North American missionary, funded by an organization descended from the original Zion church founded by Dowie in Chicago in 1896, and two Swazi Zionist ministers—asked the class to turn to a chapter in the Old Testament Book of 1 Kings. This was a text that dealt at some length with the role of kings and prophets in the nation of Israel. After asking a member of the class to read aloud from Chapter 14, with the rest of the class carefully following, the teacher—a well-known Zionist called Jerome Sangweni—began to talk students through the key themes of the extract, taking his cue from a typed-out set of study notes. The class was a balance of top-down instruction and dialogical participation. Sangweni moved slowly through the text, verse by verse, explaining how the story described the prophet Ahijah foretelling the overthrow of the king, Solomon, and the ascension of a rival figure, Jeroboam.

Sangweni was frequently interrupted by class members requesting a clarification of the meaning of a certain verse, wanting to be sure they had grasped the sense of it for their own personal spiritual edification. At one point, a lively debate on the topic of prophecy broke out. The parallels between ancient Israel and Swaziland, both possessing a rich economy of prophets and kings, had not gone unnoticed. One student, a young woman active in her Zion church as a Sunday School teacher, claimed that the time of godly prophets—as described in their reading of the Old Testament—had long passed, and that the elderly prophets who today dominated their Swaziland Zion churches were "false ones." Others vehemently disagreed. Sangweni stepped in and offered some reflection. His advice to the students was this: return to the text of the Bible, and study carefully all descriptions of prophets. Once they had understood the true scriptural meaning of a prophet, they would then be in a better position to evaluate their own Swazi prophets in the here and now.[1]

This chapter draws together many key themes of the story of transatlantic Zion. For one, recent developments in Swaziland evince the most recent cycle of reform to grip this ever-changing religious movement, a regeneration that has profoundly destabilized the reign of charismatic prophets who became so powerful in Zion churches throughout the twentieth century. In their seemingly unqualified support for the institution of monarchy, for Swazi custom and for the virtues of gerontocratic, patriarchal authority, Zionist prophet-led churches in Swaziland are typically seen as resistant to progressiveness, to democratic reform in the Kingdom, to youthful dissent, and to outspoken female members.[2] This chapter shows that the time-honored evangelical pattern of subversive dissent from youths toward their spiritual elders was nonetheless well and alive in many of these churches. The Southern African Zionist tradition of the last thirty years has been subject to considerable internal debate and transformation. Invoking the enduring evangelical impulse toward reform, since the 1970s, youthful Zionists in the Kingdom of Swaziland have engaged in vocal criticism of their elderly church leaders, and especially of the male prophets who exercise such powerful sway in many Zion congregations.

In mounting these criticisms, the institution of the Bible School has become an all-important resource for youthful reformists of the prophetic tradition within Zion. This calls to mind a further major theme in the transatlantic history of Zion—believers' invocation of the egalitarian resources of Christianity to overturn the power of religious elite. Early believers in Melbourne, Chicago, and Johannesburg mobilized the new practice of divine healing to subvert the authority of a recently professionalized medical class, whereas in late twentieth-century Swaziland it was the symbolic power of education—and in particular, of biblical literacy—that was used to skewer the authority of largely uneducated prophets. Zion traditionalists eschewed religious education in favor of direct inspiration from the Spirit, whereas this new generation of young reformers argued that training in the Word of God—portrayed by them as an open book, accessible to anyone with the desire to learn—is the single necessary characteristic of a godly leader. Youths and women usually excluded from positions of leadership within Swazi Zionist churches now declare themselves empowered to oust elderly male prophets. Bible education has become an important weapon in a fiercely fought gerontocratic and gendered contest over religious orthodoxy, legitimacy, and leadership. In the Witwatersrand of the interwar period it was the "Spirit" that emerged as a democratic, leveling force, but some eighty years later, it is the reverse: now learning and education provide spiritual mobility to hitherto disempowered elements within the country's Zionist community.

This chapter also underscores the enduring interest of Zionist believers in forming cosmopolitan religious communities that transcend race, ethnicity, language, and geography. Most scholars maintain that contact between American and African Zionists entirely disappeared in the aftermath of Dowie's death, and the subsequent splintering of the movement in the United States and Southern Africa. The Bible Schools discussed here are a reminder of the fact that, while it is certainly the case that the profusion of prophet-led independent Zion churches was largely autonomous of North American Zionists, there persisted important and hitherto unstudied pockets of transatlantic exchange. American Zionists' offer of subsidized scriptural education, and African Zionists' enthusiastic reception of this, illuminates how and why transatlantic Christians have continued to value communion with fellow believers across the ocean.

Struggles between Elders and Youths

By the time Swaziland obtained its independence in 1967, the character and composition of the country's Zionist churches had profoundly transformed. Zionist churches of the 1930s were populated by youthful subversives, male and female migrant laborers who undermined the African Christian elite's monopoly over clerical power. By the 1970s, however, the leadership of Zionist churches in Swaziland was dominated by elderly men,[3] with women and younger members largely excluded from leadership.[4] In the 1970s, in a Swazi branch of Daniel Nkonyane's Christian Catholic Apostolic Holy Spirit Church in Zion the average age of a minister was sixty-seven,[5] while in both Swaziland and South Africa it was the norm for only older married men to assume leadership in a Zionist church (marriage being an indication of seniority).[6] In addition to this increasingly elderly, male demographic, this was when Zionism's power base shifted to the countryside. Scholars collecting data in the 1970s confirmed Zionist churches were predominantly in rural settings with scarce representation in Swaziland's towns.[7] Another change was Zionists' growing reputation as the church for the poor and uneducated—admittedly a trend that had been discernible even in the interwar years. In contrast to elite figures such as Paulus Mabiletsa, Walter Ndebele, and John George Phillips on the Rand, a study conducted in the 1970s found that most Zionists in Swaziland had education only "between Grade 1 and Standard II," while another counted that only one in eight ministers had any theological education.[8] One contemporary Zionist's memory of the church in the 1960s was that "the majority of ministers were not educated, [they] had gone up to maybe primary school level."[9] Simon Mavimbela, grandson of the famous Swazi prophet, Stephen, commented: "we Zionists [were] willing to go to poor, dirty people."[10]

The other important shift in these years was that the prophet became an increasingly powerful figure in many congregations. This was the period when a prophesying practice known as *siguco* became a regular component of Zionist healing prayer in Swaziland as well as elsewhere in Southern Africa. Siguco was a fast, rhythmic, danced, or run prayer-circle in which believers perambulated in tight circular form, singing, praying, and speaking in tongues, as they went, overseen by the prophet of the congregation and usually with the individual desirous of healing prayer in the center. The dynamic movement of the prayer-dance was thought to encourage the Holy Spirit, thereby enabling the prophet to freely and volubly prophesy about the cause and cure of the sickness they (usually he) was presented with.[11] Siguco was undoubtedly one of the most popular features of Zion churches during these years, with many attending to enjoy the impressive display of prophetic power. Siguco thus offered a space within which individual prophets could expand their influence relative to the wider congregation. Siguco did have precedents; several Swazi Zionist ministers recall from their elders that siguco was practiced in the days of the church founders of the 1930s, but as "quite a sedate practice" that involved slow prayerful walking rather than the "wild spinning" of the 1970s when "the older generation passed away."[12] One Swazi Zionist minister remarked "*siguco* came much later . . . during our fathers' times the old Zionists were not doing much of this, this siguco started very, very late."[13] Another minister dated the practice to the late 1950s.[14] Others speculated that siguco's origins were far-flung and exotic, imported into Swaziland via the labor networks of the Rand from Botswana or even Malawi.[15]

In Swaziland as well as the region more broadly, this was also the era in which prophets became more explicit in their invocation of ancestral spirits in divining their cures. In an earlier period, and in keeping with the ethos of Zion as a modernizing movement demanding rupture with past beliefs, Zion prophets and ordinary believers were reluctant to admit reliance on ancestral spirits, although doubtless this did occur, if patterns in Christian denominations across the spectrum are any indication. But undertaking research in Soweto in Johannesburg in the 1960s, the anthropologist Martin West found many Zionist prophets freely admitted their reliance on both ancestors and the Christian Holy Spirit. In one church, thanksgiving services were held for "the healing gifts of their Senior Prophet . . . and to the Prophet's shades [ancestors] and also to God for the work of the Prophet."[16] Mozambican Zionist minister Zac Muiambo confirms this was when invocation of ancestors became more common, disapprovingly remarking "it was in the 1960s, 1970s that these things started with a kind of prophet that appeared and then the church started to be crooked . . . these prophets started to say, yes you must do something for your ancestors. People were turning back to the old system, where you mix up ancestor worship with the church."[17]

This trend was particularly evident in Swaziland (perhaps compounded by Swazi Zionists' historic openness to Swazi "custom") and nowhere more so than in the case of the Jericho Zionists. Founded by a former migrant worker to Johannesburg who broke away from Andrew Zwane's Swazi Christian Church in Zion to found his own organization in 1951, the Jericho church grew into the country's largest Zionist church with around 30,000 members by 1990.[18] Eliyasi Vilakati was the son of a convert to the Pentecostal Apostolic Faith Mission in the southern district of Mankanyane—perhaps his Pentecostal background primed Vilakati for the visionary quality of the church he would found. While working as a truck loader at a factory in Johannesburg in the 1940s, Vilakati received visions instructing him to return to Swaziland and start a new church. His Jericho church was characterized by a focus on prophecy and the ecstatic possession by the Holy Spirit, with one minister announcing in 1978 that "Jericho is a church of the spirit! Amen! The things of this church come from above."[19] But Jericho was also a church of ancestral spirits, with prophets invoking the guidance of their relatives during the whirling of the siguco and recommending church members pay homage to their ancestors to improve their lot in life. Indicating the respect "Jerichos" accorded to deceased family, Vilakati stated in the late 1970s "I do not see how you can be a Christian if you do not respect the traditional customs. Even those who are dead should be respected and we should have feasts together with them."[20]

Afforded regular opportunity for displaying their divinatory gifts during siguco, prophets became increasingly influential figures, wielding considerable authority over the congregation and even appointed church officials. Prophets were always a small but powerful minority; most Zionist churches had only 4 percent of the congregation renowned for these abilities.[21] And in keeping with broader demographic trends, this tiny spiritual elite was largely composed of older men, many with little or no education.[22] Some prophets also occupied leadership positions such as bishop, minister, or evangelist, although this was not necessarily the case, as a prophet's gifts were sufficient to place him in a position of authority regardless of formal appointment.[23] Thus what had begun its life in the mining hub of the Witwatersrand as an antihierarchical impulse contesting the authority of clerical elite and the African Christian establishment, now propped up enormously powerful and older, largely male, individuals. Suggesting the large reserves of authority available to those who claimed inspiration both from the Spirit and from their ancestors, Jericho church founder Vilakati once stated that "I progress through prophecies . . . Jehovah said I am greater than all people on the earth."[24]

In particular, these older male prophets were renowned and feared for their ability to "see" into people's private affairs. Many Swazi Zionists of this period spoke of their anxiety of being "outed" by a prophet, particularly fearful of the accusation of witchcraft leveled against them by an all-seeing figure. A journalist for the country's daily newspaper, the *Times of Swaziland*, recalled his childhood memories of the early 1970s. It was a time when nightlong funeral vigils—a cornerstone of Zionist religious life—were dominated by prophets exposing figures whom they accused of causing the death of the deceased: "just before dawn some men possessed with the powers to cast out demons would take the floor by pointing at suspected witches and remove magic potions they said were responsible for the death of the child."[25] Such accusations of witchcraft, leveled by powerful prophets, could result in catastrophic violence; the murders of those suspected of witchcraft were, and are, common in Swaziland.[26] Prophets could force other types of public confessions too, often with disastrous consequences. One man in the Catholic Apostolic Church in Zion in Dameseku, near Manzini, was almost killed by church members after a prophet reported he had stolen con-gregants' goats from their gardens.[27] Prophets were not above using their reputation as powerful seers for personal gain; some charged high fees. In the Jericho church in the 1970s, congregants strove to differentiate between true prophecies and the fact that "prophets can make up prophecies to tell lies about other members," often to score points in ongoing disputes or rival-ries.[28] Prophets could also use their powers to manipulate sexual relation-ships; it was a common perception of prophets that they "misused the Spirit" by claiming female congregants should visit their homes for prayer alone.[29]

This prophetic elite found further influence through their alliance with political powers beyond the orbit of the church. The country's indepen-dence from Britain in 1968, if anything, consolidated the paramount chief Sobhuza II's power. As early as 1959, the colonial government had broached the issue of introducing constitutional development with Sobhuza. Sobhuza "moved quickly to pre-empt the development of mass-based political par-ties" by vesting control over Swazi custom, law and land in the figure of the monarch and in his conservative circle of advisers, the Swazi National Council. This repressive move meant Sobhuza was soon faced with a pro-liferation of new political parties agitating for multiparty democracy, as well as a powerful labor movement resulting in widespread unrest in 1963. Faced with the alarming prospect of ceding power after independence, the monarchy once again drew on the resources of cultural nationalism to position the institution of the king as integral to an independent Swazi-land. In 1964, Sobhuza formed the Imbokodvo National Movement as the political wing of the Swazi National Council, denouncing new political parties as "foreign, divisive and hostile to Swazi tradition, of which he was not only guardian but the unchallengeable interpreter."[30] In the elections of 1967, the Imbokodvo Party swept to power, which was the result, as the historian Hugh Macmillan suggests, of political intimidation and sustained ethnic mobilization.[31] New legislation put pressure on foreigners who imported "un-Swazi" ways (this directed at the labor movement, many of whom hailed from South Africa). As in the 1920s, the performance of the *Incwala*—the annual rain-making ceremony led and directed by the king—was also given increased prominence, and siSwati became promoted as a language (replacing isiZulu) in the postindependence school curric-ulum.[32] Shortly after independence, the King acted decisively to secure his absolute control. In 1973, Swazi parliament voted to suspend the constitu-tion, and handed all power to the king who instituted a "traditional" system of governance. All political parties were banned and democracy declared "un-Swazi," a situation that persists today.

The elderly male prophets and ministers of the country's Zionist churches became key allies of the monarchy in crafting and maintaining the legitimacy of "traditionalist" rule. As we have seen, in the 1930s Zionists and Sobhuza entered into a mutually beneficial relationship; Zionists giving spiritual support to the king's ambitions to codify Swazi tradition in a bid for independence from Europeans, and in return, receiving the monarch's patronage, especially useful in the context of the colonial era. By the 1970s, Swazi Zionists' sanction of the "traditional" order was even stronger. Their willingness to invoke ancestral spirits in their worship, a linchpin of Swazi religion, was evidence of this. In the turbulent transition to independence, Zionist churches continued to play a key role in assuring monarchical rule, with "bus loads" of Zionists going to the polls to vote for Imbokodvo candidates in the crucial election of 1967.[33] After Sobhuza's declaration of a State of Emergency in 1973, suspending the Constitution and banning all political parties, Zionist leadership strongly came out in support of monarchical rule, deeming it in keeping with Swazi "tradition" and the divine order of things. Jericho leader, Eliyasi Vilakati, used his sermons to remind believers the King was divinely ordained: "it is good to respect your King, for even in heaven we shall not be equal, we shall still be made to stand around our kings of the earth."[34] Throughout the turbulent 1970s, the Incwala was a display of royal power, and an opportunity for Zionists to demonstrate loyalty to the King. Each year, the leaders of all major denominations urged members to attend the Incwala as a show of support for their monarch, and prophets and ministers maintained a visible presence as key dignitaries.[35] Rumors circulated, moreover, that royal figures relied on the powers of prophets to eradicate political enemies. The *Times* made oblique allusions to this murky alliance of political and prophetic power: "a well-known Zionist who 'smells things' [i.e., a prophet] equals power in this country . . . prominent and powerful people will visit the Zionist to be told who is bewitching them . . . can you think of one single person who got well known countrywide for talking the 'adakadabra' language who was not seen walking through the corridors of power?"[36]

But by the end of the 1980s, Zionist elders and royal elite were increasingly confronted with recalcitrant youth. A younger generation of Swazis began to oppose the authoritarian rule of the monarchy and called for the newly crowned Mswati III to revoke the state of emergency introduced by his father, and reintroduce banned political parties. Some speculated this swell of youthful resistance was inspired by political change in South Africa as it became clear that democratic elections would take place there in the early 1990s. It was also inspired by other world events such as the dissolution of the Soviet Union in 1991, taken by Swazi youth as a clarion call for democratic reform in their own country.[37] But dynamics internal to Swaziland were also responsible for the emergence of youth-based resistance. By the 1990s, the demographic composition of the country meant Swaziland had become a youthful nation; in 1995, 60 percent of its population was under twenty.[38] While this youthful population was increasingly educated and urban-based,[39] it was also beset by severe problems. Along with a high rate of youthful unemployment, youthful HIV diagnoses took off in the 1990s, with 10 percent of the country declared positive in 1993, and one in four teenagers infected by 1994.[40]

This youthful generation articulated their anger against the political order by vocal activism. SWAYOCO (Swaziland Youth Congress) was formed as the youth league of the banned political organization PUDEMO (Peoples' United Democratic Movement), and regularly demonstrated—albeit often dispersed violently by police—calling for "the freedom of our people from the ruthless minority that exploits, divides and sucks from the poor the least that they have."[41] Moreover, this was also when labor movements successfully organized. In 1996, trade unions shut down the country's labor force for one week.[42] The University of Swaziland was the hub of much youthful political activism, repeatedly closed throughout the 1990s for political demonstrations and even raided by the army in 1990 resulting in the severe injury of students.[43] Swazi youth became increasingly outspoken in their perception of being failed by the monarchy and the entire gerontocratic political establishment. Elders retaliated, maintaining young protestors should "stay out of politics," for "governing a country was too much of a job for the youth . . . go to any country in the world and you will never find it governed by the youth."[44] Ever loyal to the monarchy, elderly Zionist leadership denounced political activism as "un-Christian,"[45] and declared multiparty democracy was "evil" as the majority of people could always be trusted to "make the wrong choices once allowed to choose," citing the example of the popular choice of Barabbas for release from crucifixion instead of Jesus of Nazareth.[46] And while youth bombarded government with calls for action on the HIV-AIDS crisis, Zionist leadership declared the use of condoms not only "unSwazi" but also "an abomination to God." Youths' call for sex education in schools was criticized on the grounds that "students should not be taught lessons meant for adults."[47]

Zionist elders and prophets were also facing increased youthful recalcitrance within their churches. Elders bemoaned the unwarranted independence and disrespect shown by youth. In the 1970s, youthful fashions such as bell-bottoms and shorter skirts for women were lambasted by Zionist preachers in their sermons.[48] A 1978 sermon by Jericho Church in Zion

founder, Eliyasi Vilakati, delivered to his congregation at Mankanyane—
by now a region of particular Zionist strength—reprimanded the youth for
lack of respect for elders: "something is happening at the bus terminals, [it is]
very bad, the young ones push the elders aside as they enter the bus, they
sit down and expect the elders to stand . . . [when] young people forget respect for elders . . . these is no blessing in these things."[49] Even more dis-
turbing, Jericho church elders found many young men were beginning to
claim prophetic powers—abilities that had formerly been exclusively commanded by senior members of the congregation.[50] By the 1980s, young
Jericho men were famous for their formidable displays of spiritual power
while in a state of possession, including ferociously roaring like lions,
speaking in tongues, and violently exorcising evil spirits.[51] This led to frequent conflicts between elders and youths. As one elder reported in the
1980s, "the older members can control their spirit because they have been
in the church longer and have more experience regarding power, the spirit
comes on younger member and they don't see anything . . . this does no
useful work until it is settled by the spirit of the older members."[52] Seniors
criticized what they perceived as youths' unskilled and poorly disciplined
use of these powers, lamenting "what does a young person know? I don't
like these prophets because they destroy families, when we're sick we run
to these prophets and they lie to us."[53] Despite these protests, Jericho elders
found themselves dislodged from their accustomed positions. Vilakati's
prohibition against polygamous marriages, for example, was effectively
out-weighed by youths' preference for this martial arrangement.[54] It was
common during Jericho services for elders to expel youths from the church
building for their noisy displays of the Spirit, but youths merely moved
outside and "then the church will be carrying on with two different pro-
grammes . . . it is chaotic, it causes confusion in the church."[55] Other
youthful Zionists, however, responded to gerontocratic pressures in a very
different way. While Jericho youth appropriated prophecy for their own
ends, others began to question the very legitimacy of prophecy as a Christian practice.

boSindisiwe

The backdrop was a wider Christian revival that swept Swaziland in the
1970s. This revival was strongly tinged by "charismatic" Christianity; a
new iteration of Pentecostalism that spread from established Pentecostal
denominations such as the Apostolic Faith Mission to influence worship in
a range of Protestant denominations. As with the older forms of Pentecos-

talism, the new Charismatics celebrated the gifts of the Spirit, yet did not insist this would necessarily manifest through speaking in tongues and healing miracles.[56] These decades witnessed the explosion of international Charismatic and broader evangelical activity across sub-Saharan Africa, often disseminated by American and British evangelists in conjunction with local staff.[57] By the 1980s, while Zionists were still the largest Christian group in Swaziland with 25 percent of the population, evangelicals now constituted 17 percent of Swazis, and the North American Pentecostal Assemblies of God was the fast-growing denomination.[58] Swaziland's churches were now divided into three associations: the Council of Churches representing historic denominations such as Anglicanism, Catholicism, and Methodism; the League representing Zionist and Apostolic churches, and the Conference of Churches constituted by the Protestant evangelicals, and whose denominations largely represented the new Charismatic-flavored revival. In the ten years between 1984 and 1994, the third of these—the evangelical-Charismatic Conference—had by far the highest growth rate at 104 percent.[59] Many of these newer organizations emphasized work among the youth. Interdenominational evangelical organizations such as Campus Crusade for Christ, Scripture Union, and Swaziland School Christian Fellowship preached in schools and in colleges. Visiting evangelists from South Africa and across the continent, as well as from as far afield as South Korea, a hotbed of evangelicalism, toured the country's schools, held tent revivals in rural areas, preached on radio and television, and disseminated Christian literature.[60]

This new youth-focused evangelical revival differed from prophet-controlled Zionist spirituality in important ways. Zionists stressed the unique powers of prophets in mediating God's will (and the desires of ancestral spirits) to the congregation, whereas new evangelical churches emphasized above all the necessity of obtaining "salvation." Salvation was the typically evangelical doctrine that sinful individuals were redeemed by the death of Jesus Christ on the cross, that this blessing was accessed only by an individual's conscious acceptance of Christ as their "Lord and Savior" and that once accepted, an individual stepped into a life of unparalleled spiritual power. Prophecy required the expertise of the Spirit-inspired individual to guide the congregation, whereas the salvation doctrines of evangelical organizations were highly egalitarian. These teachings stressed spiritual empowerment consequent on being saved—or "born-again"—was equally available to all, even the most humble believer; furthermore, that salvation was entirely unreliant on mediating figures between the individual and God such as a prophet. A further feature of evangelical churches of this period was their renewed commitment to the Judeo-Christian Bible as the literal, inspired Word of God. One example of the new churches stressing salvation was the popular Alliance Church in the country's capital, Mbabane. Led by a young Rev. Sandile Dlamini, the church had a high growth rate of 20 percent per year. Its membership was mostly drawn from a youthful, professional, upwardly mobile demographic, and stressed in its teachings "getting people saved in big numbers," with church members encouraged to go public places such as hospitals and bus ranks to spread the message of salvation, freely available for all.[61]

As suggested by the example of the Alliance Church, fervent evangelistic work was crucial to this new swathe of churches. After all, according to evangelicals of this period, the flipside of individual salvation was eternal damnation for those who refused it. Campus Crusade, active in schools and colleges, disseminated badges, stickers, and flags among converted Swazi youth bearing the words "I found it." When asked what had been found, the wearers were meant to simply reply: ""New life in Jesus Christ."[62] A glance at the letters section of the *Times* reveals salvation devotees frequently pleading with the general public to accept Christ. One Jabulani Nkambule urged readers to "just open your heart and say 'God I am a sinner, please forgive me, I request you to lead me in the new life until I reach heaven.' "[63] Another exhorted his fellow Swazis to "believe in Jesus . . . you will be delivered from bondage and find freedom and life."[64] Moreover, the notion that salvation was immediately available to anyone in the church regardless of rank, and that no individuals was more privileged in their possession of salvation than any other, frequently segued into an overall ethos of self-improvement and upward mobility. The youthful, educated members of these new churches found a Christianity that promised to furnish them with further qualifications and skills. Scripture Union, for example, held "leadership training courses" for the young people it targeted on campuses, stressing "Christian leadership, general management and financial management."[65] Key features of the Alliance Church were the seminars and Bible Study groups continually on offer to the congregation. Rev. Dlamini himself had attended a series of training workshops in Amsterdam—no doubt assisted by international evangelical networks of support—where he learned "about new methods of evangelism." He reported the "professional people in urban areas" who constituted his church were eager to learn more. As a result, he inaugurated "training sessions" for church members every Thursday evening after work.[66]

Zionist youth embraced these evangelical experiences of "salvation," finding a more laity-empowering version of Christianity.[67] An early devotee—and subsequently the most prominent Swazi Zionist critic of the prophetic tradition—was Isaac Dlamini, a young man from the Nhlangano area in the south. Born into a long-standing Zionist family belonging to a

Swazi branch of Mabiletsa's Christian Apostolic Church in Zion, Dlamini's early life exemplified the easy accommodation many churches made to traditional religion. Ill from childhood, Dlamini and his family took this as evidence that his ancestral spirits were calling him to be a *sangoma* (diviner), and Dlamini even embarked on training required for initiation into the profession. But by the 1970s—and reflecting the evangelical revival sweeping the country—Dlamini, now in his twenties training to be a watch maker, had a dramatic conversion experience after hearing an evangelical pastor of the Swedish Free Church preach during tent crusades around the town of Nhlangano. After being invited forward to an "altar call," Dlamini received salvation.[68] In typical evangelical fashion, Dlamini began preaching and testifying about his experience at school in an effort to persuade his peers about the necessity of salvation.[69]

Another important Zionist figure who had a salvation experience was Jerome Sangweni, also from Nhlangano, and who had grown up in the Swazi Christian Church in Zion (the branch originally led by the prophet Andrew Zwane). Dlamini had found salvation in a rural tent crusade, whereas Sangweni was exposed to evangelicalism while living in the northern Swaziland sugar mill town of Mhlume. Although unsuccessful in his efforts to secure employment, Sangweni did find that the cousin he was living with in Mhlume was "a saved person" who invited him to attend services at "a big, interdenominational fellowship" run by the "Soldiers of the Cross" (a salvation-focused ecumenical movement). In contrast to his Zionist church where services centered on the revelatory utterances of the prophet during siguco, Sangweni found this new evangelical fellowship prioritized the democratic uplift of all laity through the experience of individual salvation. Thus Sangweni's own conversion experience came after hearing someone preach on the classic text of empowerment and spiritual triumph, Luke 1:37—"for with God nothing shall be impossible." After being invited forward for an altar call, Sangweni remembered how he "prayed and thanked God for saving me . . . I had felt God's hand on me."[70]

Another prominent Zionist who had a transformative experience was Meshack Dlamini, a civil servant within the Ministry of Agriculture whose professional status reflected the increasingly educated profile of those Zionists who gravitated toward evangelicalism. Dlamini was introduced to this brand of evangelical piety by his brother-in-law in Mbabane who had founded an independent evangelical church. Dlamini remembered his brother "brought out his Bible and preached the Word of God for an hour . . . the key message was that I must be born again . . . I got saved after realizing I was living a sinful life, and I went home from the bondage of sin."[71] Women in Zionist congregations seemed especially open to the new teachings. Excluded from leadership positions by male prophets, female Zionists may have found they had much to gain from the egalitarian doctrines. Dlamini recalled the "saved ones" in his church were largely "young ones . . . but mostly it was the women, from the very beginning it was the women. The men later followed."[72] One example of such a woman was Xolile Tshuma, who grew up in the Swazi Ephillipi Christian Church in Zion and later "became a Christian by listening to preaching in a [nearby] church . . . I am now saved by Christ."[73]

These figures found senior leadership in their churches—especially prophets—reacted with hostility to their enthusiastic testimonies about emancipation from sin. They were scornfully dubbed *boSindisiwe,* or "the saved ones," by their church's leadership, a label they came to wear with pride. Jerome Sangweni remembered, "if you could mention being saved in our Zion meetings, you would really feel that you had spoiled everything." He continued with sharing his testimony, but found "I was the most hated person, after I had testified in church, the whole service would change and they would oppose whatever I said, indirectly but with hostility . . . out on the homesteads [in the rural areas], they would talk bad things about me."[74] Isaac Dlamini also found that when he preached to his Zion church about salvation, "someone would start a long song that would discourage him to go and sit down."[75] Reflecting the generational struggle implicit in these dynamics, his church elders told him "they didn't want to be told what to do by the young boy, Isaac."[76] Meshack Dlamini found the senior leadership of his church so perturbed at his talk of salvation that they called a special meeting of all the elders before whom Dlamini was required to "explain himself."[77] Some born-again Zionists were even ejected from their churches by elders unable to tolerate their salvation preaching.[78]

Elders especially objected to what they perceived as youthful arrogance in claiming a superior state of salvation. Saved youth were heavily critical of elders' prophetic practices, especially the institution of the siguco and the invocation of ancestral spirits. Evangelicalism taught converts to draw sharp delineations between their old lives as sinners and their new existences as saved Christians. Prophets' invocation of ancestral spirits seemed unacceptable.[79] Saved Zionist Nhlanhla Magongo remembered how "guys who got born-again used to hit hard among the Zionists, and the Zionists started hating them . . . the born-agains said everything the Zionists were doing was wrong."[80] Many Zionist elders objected to being berated by holier-than-thou youths. Erickson Dlamini, now bishop of the Zion Apostolic New Jerusalem Church, remembered how his elders angrily asserted no young man could claim "perfection": "they would say to me, 'you cannot be saved, when you are killing ants as you move around, how many ants have you killed this morning? How can you be saved while you are still in this world?'" Elders tried to reason with Dlamini by likening the spiritual path to a journey through crocodile-infested waters, arguing that "if you say you are saved, it's like you are saying you've already crossed all the rivers with crocodiles in them, yet you can still be grabbed by a crocodile and you may not reach heaven."[81] Older Zionists delighted in finding evidence of continued sin in those who claimed salvation, arguing this gave the lie to their hubristic claims. Nhlanhla Magongo remembered "it wasn't that easy to say you were born-again as they would scrutinize you, check every corner of your life, if you fell into a sin, they would make sure you knew about it."[82] Simon Nzima, a pastor in the Jericho Zion church who found his salvation during Scripture Union meetings at his high school, related to me how after being born-again, elders would rebuke him and other youthful boSindisiwe by reminding them "no one can be saved while they are still alive . . . to say you are saved is sheer arrogance."[83]

Elders worried that newly empowered boSindisiwe would upset the stratified hierarchies around which Zion churches—and Swazi society more broadly—were structured. Elders objected not just to youths' claims to superior spiritual standing, but also to their increased education, wealth, and professional attainment. Erickson Dlamini, who attended college and later became a civil servant in the Department of Labor, remembered how tension arose with his elders not just because he claimed salvation, but also due to his education and social aspirations. At the occasion of his wedding, Dlamini planned the ceremony in a hall at the technical college he was attending. His church leaders objected to this as an unwarranted display of his education, preferring Dlamini be married in the humble mud and stick building where church services were held at home. In the end, his Zion elders refused to attend the ceremony in the college hall.[84] Saved Zionist women, moreover, undermined the male-dominated hierarchies of the church. Although conservative Zionists argued women with independent careers could be dangerously subversive (prominent Bishop Samson Hlatshwayo pronounced that "women who earn more than their husbands deny them sex"[85]), many saved women pursued active ministries promulgating the new teachings. Isaac Dlamini worked in close collaboration with his wife, Elizabeth, who organized and trained women in their Zion church. Indeed, it was only because of Elizabeth's support, Erickson Dlamini reckoned, that Isaac managed to survive the hostility of his leadership.[86] Another saved Zionist woman, related to the Mavimbela dynasty and known as "Reverend Mavimbela," is today famous for her itinerant street preaching. "A lot of people are now coming to her," in the words of her relative, Stephen Mavimbela.[87]

More broadly than threatening the balance of power in Zion churches, elders feared that boSindisiwe were venturing into the dangerous territory of criticizing monarchical rule. There was some truth to this. Isaac Dlamini, for example, broadcast sermons on a local Christian radio station during which he would subtly criticize the pro-monarchical stance of Zion elders by reminding listeners that the imperative to follow Jesus was greater than loyalty due to any earthly king.[88] Some new Zionists took it a step further, foreswearing attendance at the Incwala on account of the event's invocation of ancestral spirits.[89] Other saved Zionists engaged in outright defiance of the political order. During the labor unrest of the 1990s, striking textile workers sung "gospel songs from the Jericho and Zion churches" as they marched.[90] Solomon Mvubu, a saved minister within the Holy Catholic Apostolic Church in Zion, was also active in the banned Ngwane National Liberatory Congress, one of the political organizations calling for democratic reform.[91] The outspoken Rev. Mavimbela is on record in the national newspaper as "mustering the courage to inform His Majesty the King at the Good Friday service that the country's power brokers have not yet seen the Lord and their souls are not clean." In a "hoarse tone," she exhorted the monarchy, before an audience of thousands, to "open their hearts to the Lord for them to see salvation."[92]

Many of this new generation of Zionists soldiered on within their congregations, attempting to introduce reform despite opposition from elders. Undoubtedly, many were inspired by the prospect of bringing salvation to their unenlightened Zion brethren. Although he underwent "severe persecution," Isaac Dlamini had a visionary experience whereby God directed him to preach the Gospel to people wearing "blue and green Zionist gowns" (the color of his church's uniform). For this reason, he considered it his duty to remain a Zionist.[93] Another saved Zionist and an electrician by training, Simon Nzima, related to me a vision: "he had the light, but he should not flee with the candle to the electricity, but should stay in the darkness."[94] Many of these boSindisiwe soon found they gathered a cluster of like-minded young people around them in their churches, many young women. Jerome Sangweni, despite being hated by the elders, found great consolation in one such group. While frustrated within their own Zion churches, they would frequently partner with non-Zionist members of evangelical churches in Nhlangano to "go and preach in the homesteads, maybe hire a school hall to preach and maybe once a year we'd have a revival campaign."[95] Isaac Dlamini, the oldest figure within this group of saved individuals, became a mentor figure, advising on how to negotiate the difficulties of introducing salvation-centered teachings to resistant prophets. Both Nhlanhla Magongo and Jerome Sangweni remember regularly visiting Dlamini in his small watchmaker's shop in downtown Manzini, seeking his counsel on spiritual matters.

For many boSindisiwe, and in keeping with broader evangelical doctrines, the Bible was their legitimating manual. Under fire from repressive elders, an experience of education in a Bible School was a symbol of their new status as born-again Christians and a means to legitimate themselves in the face of opposition. Yet many struggled to access theological education due to financial constraints but also due to most evangelical seminaries' negative perception of Zionists as "syncretistic" Christians. The prospect of Bible School, however, became more possible with the assistance of North American missionaries linked with Dowie's original church. Eager to reestablish themselves in Southern Africa, and after many years of absence, churches in Zion, Illinois, were once again looking with interest to their Zionist brethren across the ocean.

New Ways of Doing Mission

For many decades after Dowie's death in 1907, Christians in Zion, Illinois viewed their brethren in Southern Africa with discomfort and embarrassment.[96] The profusion of independent prophet-led Zionist churches were considered highly unorthodox by American Zion missionaries in South Africa, most of whom were by the 1930s working with the Mahon-led Christian Church in Zion.[97] Moreover, its quest for recognition from the state—and their need for assistance for their schools—caused the Mahon's church to distance itself from the "hundreds of self-styled prophets who gathered little groups of followers around themselves."[98] To the strict evangelicalism of the mission, Zionists' ecstatic Pentecostal piety seemed a distasteful mingling of the old and the new. American and South African mission staff surmised that prophets masqueraded as indigenous diviners and herbalists, mingling their healing practice with "witchcraft and superstition."[99] In 1933, Edgar Mahon informed Natal's Native Affairs Department that "unfortunately many of our break away fanatical natives call themselves amaZioni, which would make it appear they belong to us. But we have no connection of any kind with [these] wild, white-robed AmaZioni."[100] By 1946, church leaders in Zion City, in conjunction with missionaries in South Africa, changed the South African organization's name from the Christian Catholic Church in Zion to the Mahon Mission. The Mission informed its supporters in the United States this was to avoid confusion with the "numerous little Native Sects . . . with ridiculous names, headed by self-appointed prophets . . . and [who] brought the name of Mr Mahon's mission into disrepute and caused no little embarrassment."[101]

American missionaries felt little zeal to reform Zionists' errors, only lamenting they themselves were frequently confused with "Zion" because of their historic links to the movement: "many of the people say they have heard queer stories about us, thinking we were with the group of people here who beat their drums, sing, march, and carry on all night."[102] Indeed, of the numerous churches that constituted North American Zion by this point, the only activity among independent African Zionists was the supply of church literature (baptismal and ordination certificates, tracts, pamphlets and old issues of *Leaves of Healing*) by a South African member of Voliva's church in Cape Town—one Arthur Mellor.[103] Yet beyond this, Mellor as a representative of Voliva's church in the region offered little to South Africans. Its detached stance toward the hundreds (by the late 1960s, probably thousands[104]) of Zionists across Southern Africa was shared by church leadership in Zion, Illinois. Carl Lee—successor to Voliva and general overseer from the 1950s to the 1970s—responded to missiologist Bengt Sundkler's inquiries about links between American and African Zion. He replied: "our Church has no contact in terms of direct missionary activity with these groups . . . these 'White Robers' in South Africa in no way reflect the general teaching or theology of the Christian Catholic Church here at Zion, Illinois, [they] have a strong emphasis on the ecstatic . . . and we know they have moved considerably away from the original teachings of missionaries sent by Dr. Dowie."[105]

This is not to argue that churches in Zion did not take their missionary duties seriously. In 1920 Daniel Bryant's church in Illinois with which the Mahon Mission was affiliated, changed its name from Christian Catholic Church to Grace Missionary Church, believing the latter name more fitting because we are "highly missionary in our activities . . . the great missionary field in Basutoland and in the South Africa states among the coloured races has become a heritage of this church."[106] Although Voliva's only missionary representative in South Africa was Arthur Mellor, his church supported missionaries in the Native American Navajo Nation, Japan, and the Philippines.[107] Moreover, by the late 1970s, churches in Zion, Illinois were coming to gradually express interest in conducting missionary work among independent black-led Zion churches in Southern Africa. This shift can partly be explained by the rapidly changing perceptions of what constituted legitimate missionary work. The success of anticolonial independence movements across the world underscored the ambiguous relationship between Western mission agencies and European imperialism. From the

1950s, worldwide Christians increasingly accused Western missionaries of racism and paternalism, many considering their continued presence in the non-Western world inappropriate in a postcolonial era. In 1974, at a meeting in Lusaka, the All Africa Conference of Churches issued a block on Western missionaries and money sent to Africa, reflecting the widespread conviction that foreign assistance created undesirable dependency and stifled African leadership.[108]

Responding to this shift in mood, Western missionaries across denominations and geographic areas, including evangelicals in North America, became increasingly self-critical regarding the links between missions and colonial domination. Anxiety about the missionary enterprise had been well and alive in missionary circles at least since the turbulent 1970s, the era when independence movements swept Africa. The Lausanne Movement (1974) and the Commission on World Mission and Evangelism (1961) were key voices. Both addressed themselves to reconceptualizing mission in a postcolonial age. Inspired by popular evangelist Billy Graham, the Lausanne Movement brought together Evangelical Protestant leaders from across the world to pray and reflect with a sense of "penitence by our failures," critically reflecting on how the theology and practice of Christian mission was tainted by an "imperial" past.[109] There was intense self-scrutiny of how Christian mission had historically allied itself with imperial and colonial regimes; "a turning toward past colonial alliances to prophetically indict such systems of power and a turning away from the lure of such hegemonic practice."[110]

Many within evangelical circles in the United States now looked for new ways of doing mission. The influential British missiologist, Andrew Walls, read on both sides of the Atlantic, was a vocal proponent for a dialogical agenda for mission in a postcolonial world. Walls asserted the need for a radical rupture with old "modes" of mission: "the [imperial] crusading mode and the [postcolonial] missionary mode are sharply differentiated means of extending the Christian faith . . . The [imperial] crusader may first issue his invitation to the Gospel but, in the end, he is prepared to compel. The [postcolonial] missionary, even if his natural instinct is to desire compulsion, cannot compel, but only demonstrate, invite, explain, entreat and leave the results to God."[111] For many within North American evangelical circles, in keeping with this newly dialogical mood, definitions of mission expanded to include humanitarian assistance and development work rather than a sole focus on proselytization. Along these lines, The Evangelical Alliance Mission (TEAM)—one of the largest interdenominational evangelical mission organizations active during this period—states on its website that "we work holistically to see churches have a broad impact across societies and cultures, with initiatives in evangelism, education, health, anti-trafficking, community development, agriculture, disaster relief and creation care."[112]

A further development during this period was a surge in interest in the so-called "Independent churches" of sub-Saharan African, both among academic missiologists and practitioners of mission. Across Africa, Pentecostal-inspired, black-led popular Christian movements were now taken by missionaries, missiologists, and theologians as evidence that Christianity could exist independently of Western supervision. The Aladura churches of West Africa (themselves with indirect roots in Zion City via the influence of the Philadelphia Faith Tabernacle, an early twentieth-century breakaway from Dowie's church[113]), the Roho in Kenya, and above all the Zionist and Apostolic churches in Southern Africa, were hailed as instances that demonstrated Christianity did not necessarily have to be wedded to Western culture. This is not to say that missiologists and missionaries were uncritical in their assessment of these independents; many lamented that Zionists had strayed from orthodoxy Christianity due to their import of elements of indigenous culture, especially ancestral worship. One South African scholar of Zionism, G. C. Oosthuizen, even dubbed independent church movements in Africa "post-Christian."[114] But despite these assessments, many evangelical-minded missionaries hailed independent churches as largely positive examples of inculturated, indigenous Christianity. Whatever their drawbacks, these churches offered Westerners fresh opportunities for doing mission in the new and enlightened mode. It was less about American churches converting "heathen pagans" into replica models of Western Christians, and more about American churches drawing alongside sister organizations, developing leaders, and providing theological training to these largely uneducated constituencies, all the while self-consciously respecting their distinct cultural values.[115]

Church leadership in Zion increasingly came to perceive it as greatly serendipitous that the most famous of all the independent churches—the Zionists of Southern Africa—were profoundly intertwined with their own history. Contact between church leaders in Zion and G. C. Oosthuizen only confirmed this. In the early 1980s, visiting Chicago to conduct research into the roots of Zion in the United States, Oosthuizen contacted the Christian Catholic Church in Zion and stayed in the home of Grant and Barbara Sisson in Zion, influential members in the Christian Catholic Church (this was the branch that had remained loyal to Voliva, led by Lee in the 1970s). The Sissons, moreover, had a long-standing interest in the Zionist churches of Southern Africa. Grant's aunt, Myrtle Sisson, had been the first missionary sent in 1912 by Bryant's church to work with Edgar Mahon.[116] During this visit, Oosthuizen shared his publications on Zionists in

Southern Africa with the Sissons and others, as well as explained that the Zionists were in need of training, especially theological education, to correct their syncretistic leanings.[117] Shortly after, in the early 1980s, the Sissons and other leadership visited the Mahon Mission in South Africa, then under the leadership of Edgar Mahon II (grandson of the original Edgar), and were taken on a tour of independent Zionist churches. Oosthuizen acted as guide for this expedition, taking the Sissons to witness a Zionist baptism on Durban beachfront. Grant Sisson and Roger Ottersen—then general overseer—were greatly moved, describing how on hearing that the white Americans were from the "Christian Catholic Church in Zion," one Zionist on the beachfront demanded "'where have you been all this time?' [This] was the challenge of [our] lifetime . . . we just felt like we had a burden on our shoulder now, it just emphasized the need to get people to go to South Africa and be part of what is a great work."[118] American Zionists felt a pressing responsibility to provide assistance to these churches historically linked to them, and who now seemed so lamentably far from evangelical Christianity. Ottersen recalled: "several said to us, 'we know we are not worshipping in the proper manner, but we have had nothing to go by and no one to teach us.' I was unable to think of a good answer for these men."[119]

These developments—a shift toward a more dialogical mode of missions and a new postcolonial appreciation of indigenous Christian movements—meant churches in Zion, Illinois came to see the *amaZioni*—as they called them—a promising new mission field. In 1986, Ottersen's church sent a young Zion couple, Tim and Luann Kuehl, as "the first Christian Catholic Church missionaries to serve in Southern Africa with the AmaZioni people, under the auspices of the Mahon Mission."[120] Luann was born and raised in Zion, a third-generation descendant of Italian carpenters who had settled in Zion in 1905.[121] Tim's parents had been TEAM missionaries in Japan; he had attended TEAM short-term courses as well as completed a short missionary course with InterVarsity Christian Fellowship while at University.[122] In 1989, a South African couple Richard and Geraldine Akers were the next addition, both having been active in the South African Baptist Missionary Society and their appointment reflecting the Mahon Mission's close links to Baptist organizations in South Africa.[123] Greg and Carlene Seghers (Carlene, like Luann, a third-generation Zion resident) joined the mission in 1993.[124] In 2000 a new organization was formed (positioning itself independently of the Mahon Mission), named Zion Evangelical Ministries in Africa (ZEMA).[125] The organization grew rapidly, not least because of its success in the evangelical missions-funding world of the USA. A visit from an academic missiologist from Moody Bible Institute in Chicago in the mid-1990s led the latter to declare the project "the greatest open door in contemporary missions." Word about ZEMA rapidly spread through North American networks of funders and missionary personnel.[126] From the early 2000s, ZEMA began to partner with large mission organizations such as TEAM, who supplied seconded missionaries.[127] In 2002, ZEMA expanded from South Africa into neighboring Swaziland, via the efforts of a North American couple, Bruce and Carol Britten.

ZEMA missionaries represented conservative evangelical Protestantism: its website lists biblical inerrancy and the penal substitution of Jesus Christ as key doctrinal beliefs. The organization's goal in Southern Africa was to "make the amaZioni more soundly biblical in their beliefs," and in the process to reduce the syncretistic practices they considered to contravene evangelical Christianity.[128] Despite ZEMA's uncompromising attitude toward these fundamentals, its personnel in Swaziland and South Africa reflected newer attitudes toward best missionary practice, including a cautious respect for African Christians' "culture." ZEMA's theory of missions was considerably influenced by its missionaries' reading of a 1989 study by British Baptist missionary, Harold Froise, who with his wife, Marjorie, worked among Zionist leaders in South Africa. Froise's research argued for a more culturally sensitive missionary engagement with Zionists.[129] He advocated the need for missionaries to divorce themselves from older modes of missionary work that had estranged black Zionists from the mother church in the United States: "since paternalistic attitudes have been criticized as one of the most prominent reasons for the existence of the independent churches, a method of learning together is contemplated."[130] Froise listed "pitfalls to avoid for missionaries," most around insensitivity to cultural difference, including a realization that "African culture revolves around the spirit world . . . denying its existence and ridiculing the fears of Africans can only lead to alienation."[131]

From the start, then, ZEMA in Southern Africa was characterized by a deliberate accommodation of cultural "difference." The pioneering missionary couple, the Kuehls, spent a year in intensive isiZulu language study upon arrival in South Africa. The next missionary couple to arrive in the country in 1989, Greg and Carlene Seghers, spent their first two weeks living in a rural Zulu homestead. As Greg put it: "that was what our missionary internship had recommended to us, to get out, away from the English language environment and to get right in with the families and with the culture."[132] Although all were adamant there was major work to do in "bringing Zionists to trusting in Jesus alone for their salvation," rather than in their ancestral spirits, emphasis was placed on respecting the nonharmful "cultural" aspects of Zionists' worship. All missionaries were adamant their goal was not to turn Zionists into American Christians. According to Luann Kuehl, "our ultimate goal is not to change the Africanness . . . we love African worship."[133] Mike McDowell, ZEMA's director until 2014, commented "we have been very cautious not to interrupt African culture because we think that's something that needs to remain within the Zionist movement . . . we don't want to discourage the distinctly Africans things that they do like robes, drumming or dancing . . . if you take that away, they won't be amaZioni anymore, they'll be Western in their orientation."[134] ZEMA missionaries also prioritized friendships with Zionists—what the new school of mission theory dubbed "relational mission." Echoing the multiracialism of Dowie's era, Greg Seghers commented that late-apartheid South Africans "couldn't believe a white guy was going to sleep in a black man's bed . . . so you began to see there was a way of gaining mutual respect and trust as you broke down the walls."[135]

ZEMA emphasized biblical education as a means to foreground the fundamentals of evangelicalism—but also as a route to realizing a culturally sensitive mode of missionary work. Missionaries considered Zionists' overreliance on what they considered to be the less desirable elements of culture—especially continued allegiance to ancestral spirits—was due to lack of knowledge about what God mandated in the Bible. Contemporary Zionists, they concluded, had not sufficiently developed a personal knowledge of the Scriptures. Ensuring that African Zionists received "sound biblical teaching" became something of a mantra of the mission. The first step was a Bible correspondence course used by ZEMA missionaries, built around a short booklet written in Zion, Illinois, "This We Believe." Missionaries soon felt dedicated face-to-face teaching sessions were required, so throughout the 1990s the idea arose of developing a Bible Study curriculum taking place in locations around the region, with a focus on "training pastors" scripturally.[136]

By 1995, ZEMA missionary Richard Akers had written a four-year curriculum for what would be named Zion Evangelical Bible School. The course was pioneered in the Eastern Cape, South Africa, where the Akers were based, and then introduced to Sunbury—ZEMA's KwaZulu-Natal base near Durban—in 1996.[137] The course was guided by the notion of egalitarian access for all to biblical education. Although the original plan had been for a central teaching center, it rapidly became apparent that for working people, night and Saturday classes located in their communities made more sense.[138] Another early principle of the classes was affordability as well as presenting the material in peoples' mother tongues—courses were written in isiZulu, siSwati, and isiXhosa. Over four years, a student would complete 360 credits, with ten credits from one Saturday class and homework.[139] The ethos of the classes was to "let the Bible speak for itself," to clearly and systematically present the teachings of the Bible. The curriculum had a great deal of exegetical material with certain books of the Bible discussed in depth, verse by verse. Other sessions focused on applying biblical precepts to everyday life; Lesson 16.4.1, for example, discusses Christians' response to HIV-AIDS and is entitled "Suffering, Health and God's Judgement: A Biblical Foundation."[140] Emphasizing the exegetical, text-centered flavor of the classes, ZEMA missionary in Swaziland, Brett Miller, differentiated between teaching "of" and "about" a book of the Bible, with a strong preference for the former: "we really strongly focus on teaching the Bible and just teaching the Bible . . . where we can, we look at every verse."[141]

For ZEMA staff, Bible classes seemed a fitting enactment of the new missionary orthodoxy that long-term development in church personnel or structure should be made, rather than a fly-by-night operation. Zion missiologist Harold Froise's recommendation had been that ceding power to local leaders should be prioritized, not least because "the leadership potential in African societies is great and the New Testament model of handing over administration to local leadership early on should be encouraged."[142] In keeping with this ethos, ZEMA missionaries viewed their role in Southern Africa as time-limited, being clear that their long-term goal was to hand over to "nationals." In the words of Greg Seghers: "the exciting thing is watching Zionist co-workers that are running their own schools and making sure that what we are doing can be replicated and sustained by African brothers who are very capable of running schools."[143] Missionaries' report from the annual Bible School teachers' conference in 2014 celebrated African teachers were "becoming more active in giving feedback about the missionaries' teaching, even criticizing one missionary's exegesis of a particular topic."[144]

Another advantage, for ZEMA missionaries, of focusing on Bible education was that they could position themselves—not as promoting American-style evangelicalism—but as presenting the truths of the Bible, immutable universals for all people in all places. Thus they congratulated themselves that their classes did not constitute Americans telling Africans how to do things, but God instructing both Africans and Americans alike with the eternal truths of Scripture. Luann Kuehl described how if someone raised a difficult question in a class—for example, about the continued role of the ancestors—"you don't ever say, don't do this, or you're doing this wrong." Rather, "you can instead say, well what does the Bible say, okay the Bible says, no, that's not true. This is what is says."[145] Greg Seghers similarly used the Bible to deflect importance from his own status as American missionary. When asked by a Zionist pastor, "'what Zion City teaches about a particular subject,' Greg's response was, 'In Zion they teach you go to the Word of God, and the Word of God says.'"[146] Echoing this, Mike McDowell stated "when we observe some of their unusual and I'd have to say occult practices, we don't say anything . . . we don't openly confront them. We invite pastors and leaders to come and study the Bible together, and there are places in Scripture, like with ancestor worship and contacting the dead, that the Bible speaks to."[147] ZEMA stressed that predicaments faced by Africans had their parallel in problems in the West: "the path of the amaZioni believer and the Western believer run parallel in that we both have fears we must turn away from to wholly trust Jesus Christ . . . in a society focused on career path and financial success sometimes we are bound by fear of not having enough."[148] ZEMA missionaries were adamant that not all culture was negative. Bruce Britten, a ZEMA missionary in Swaziland in the 2000s, wrote in a book designed for Zionist students: "We say no to customs that are against the Bible. We follow the good customs of our nation, we sing in our national way, we don't sing like foreigners. We are not forced to follow foreign customs. We follow the Bible."[149]

The development of Bible education as the linchpin of ZEMA's ministry coincided with youthful Zionists across Southern Africa becoming increasingly critical of their elders. Bible Schools took off because young Zionists responded so enthusiastically to the proposal. Richard and Geraldine Akers commented, "we wanted the pastors to have some type of training, but it came out of their requests—they were saying they wanted training."[150] ZEMA missionaries encountered many youthful, educated individuals in Swaziland and South Africa eager to cooperate and who eventually became teachers and administrators in the classes. One of the prominent ZEMA figures in Johannesburg, Godfrey Maseko, recalled: "we were all young men who were enthusiastic and hard-working and the missionaries came to know us, and because of our intellectual standing we could interpret for them when they came to our churches . . . we were hand-picked as young men who would first interpret and as the years went by we were given tasks in the offices."[151] ZEMA missionaries were certain that Zionists such as Maseko greeted them so enthusiastically because they were eager to increase their biblical knowledge. Although this was true, it was also the case that the advantages gained from scriptural education were being mobilized to fight local battles—religious and social conflicts waging long before the arrival of ZEMA missionaries on the scene.

"We Must Compare What Prophets Say
with What the Bible Says"

Despite their welcome of North American missionaries, boSindisiwe in Swaziland had in fact already undertaken their own efforts to improve their scriptural learning. Attending Bible Schools locally or in South Africa was a goal of many; the Swaziland Evangelical Bible Institute and the Swaziland College of Theology, with its links to the North American Pentecostal Assemblies of God denomination, were considered the most prestigious institutions.[152] For many young Zionists, the cost was prohibitively expensive and few could afford to quit their jobs for full-time study. Jerome Sangweni was fortunate in that he found a Bible School close to his home in Nhlangano, meaning he could attend New Haven Bible School between 1996 and 1998 and still work to support his family.[153] Many also found evangelical seminaries hostile toward them as Zionists, considering their faith a syncretistic corruption of the Gospel, and usually demanding they "convert" to evangelicalism as a condition of acceptance. Isaac Dlamini, for example, was rejected from Nazarene Evangelical Seminary in Nhlangano on account of his refusal to leave his Zionist church.[154] Across the border in Maputo, saved Zionist, Zac Muiambo, found the Assemblies of God Bible School did accept Zionists, but "when the teachers taught, they're always against the Zionists. Any bad example they want to give, they say, 'don't be like a Zionist.' So people do not like to go there."[155] For both logistical and doctrinal reasons, the vast majority of new Zionists opted to study the Bible via correspondence course, either with schools based in South Africa or the United States. The All Africa School of Theology based in Witbank near Johannesburg, founded by Fred Burke, a former Assemblies of God missionary, became a popular choice. Isaac Dlamini was one of more than 500 Swazi Zionists who had completed training there by the late 1980s.[156]

Long before the arrival of ZEMA in the early 2000s, a Bible School for Zionists had historically been the goal of boSindisiwe. In its earliest form, the idea predated the boSindisiwe movement by a decade. Sundkler found that in the 1960s, a Zionist "College" was the topic of "lively debate" in the siSwati press, although the idea was eventually vetoed due to opposition from prophet-type Zionists who "pointed out that neither Jesus nor the Apostles were learned people . . . the ministry was never a vocation for which one prepared by study. It was all a matter of being filled by the Spirit."[157] Despite this opposition, by 1976, Isaac Dlamini succeeded in opening a Bible School for Zionists called Faith Bible School (perhaps this was why Dlamini became popularly known as the "Light" of the Zionist churches).[158] Dlamini received assistance from Mennonite missionaries from the USA posted in Swaziland. Harold and Christine Wenger, followed by Darrel and Sherill Hostetter in 1983.[159] Part of the Protestant Anabaptist tradition, the mid-twentieth century was the period in which Mennonites—like many Protestant denominations—had radically defined their conception of mission work. Mennonite missionaries were particularly active in West Africa in the 1950s, immediately before the withdrawal of British rule from the region. In the course of their work with African-led Aladura churches, Mennonites came to articulate a new style of missionary engagement, one that prioritized openness to cultural difference, expressed appreciation of "indigenous" expressions of the faith, and drew alongside African churches as partners rather than top-down superiors.[160] Suggesting the channels via which this new missiology influenced Mennonites in Swaziland, Darrel Hostetter's parents were posted as Mennonite missionaries to Nigeria; Hostetter himself visited them in the 1970s. Furthermore, before their posting to Swaziland, the Hostetters visited Selly Oak College in Birmingham to study the influential missiologist Harold Turner's writings, absorbing material articulating the new missiology and celebrating the opportunities presented by African independent churches.[161]

In collaboration with the Wengers and Hostetters, Dlamini crafted a way of bringing biblical training to boSindisiwe. Dlamini's wife, Elizabeth, who set up the mobile school with him and taught classes, recalled "[Isaac] said he wanted to help the Zionists because the Zionists didn't go to school or college for training as pastors, they [senior leadership] just chose you to be a pastor, no training."[162] Strategically taking into account the gerontocratic structure of Zionist churches—with power concentrated in the hands of prophets and senior ministers—Dlamini realized that inroads boSindisiwe made into Swazi Zionism depended on the support of this all-important leadership. As one early teacher of Faith Bible School, Erickson Dlamini, recalled, "if you only preach to the youth and they accept Christ, they will encounter some problems. The old people up there will think this is just a youthful innovation and it's uncalled for. But [Isaac] believed that if we can influence the leadership then."[163] Tailoring the class to the needs of working people with limited income, the Dlaminis decided on a mobile-school approach, traveling throughout the country to hold classes in local communities. Lungile, Isaac's daughter, remembered "our inspiration was that these people couldn't afford to come to a place to stay for a long time, some are busy, some are working, some are just farmers, so we looked for what would suit them."[164] The Dlaminis strategically held classes in schools and other public buildings, rather than in Zionist churches, so that "everyone would feel free," rather than be under the disapproving gaze of senior leadership.[165]

They built up a team of teachers, and the multiracial composition of the teaching team—Hostetter working alongside Isaac Dlamini and others—recalled Zion's older tradition of cosmopolitanism. Yet it did not always sit well with the formal emissaries of Zion in South Africa. Darrel Hostetter remembered how shocked he and Isaac were when they visited the Mahon Mission in the late 1980s, and were startled to find "all the white leaders were staying at one place . . . all the African leaders at another . . . Isaac and I insisted that I [Darrell] needed to be with our Swazi pastors and where they were sleeping and eating."[166] Financial instability, however, long plagued the organization and after the time of Dlamini's sudden death in 2002 the school had closed.

It was around this time that ZEMA began to work in Swaziland. An American couple, Bruce and Carol Britten, were key figures in ZEMA's expansion into Swaziland. The Brittens were long-term residents of Swaziland, having arrived in 1967 as self-funded missionaries to teach at a local Christian high school, Franson Christian High (Bruce was a science teacher). By the 1990s, they had come across ZEMA and "got hooked" on the idea of providing biblical education to Zionists. In 2003, they started as ZEMA missionaries, although funded by TEAM, opening the first Bible School in Swaziland.[167] Armed with an authorizing letter from Christ Community Church in Zion, Illinois, the Brittens approached the League of Churches—the umbrella organization for Zionist and Apostolic churches—for permission to start a school aimed at Zionists. Although the League's leadership was dominated by older conservative ministers, they agreed to Britten's proposal, perhaps seeing the way the wind was blowing in terms of the preferences of a younger generation but also having in mind a prophesy of the deceased King Sobhuza II, that Zionists should have their own ministerial training institution.[168] The Brittens started the first school in Mbabane, meeting in a school there, and expanded to Manzini, Nhlangano, and then throughout the country; today there are thirty-three schools across Swaziland, most meeting in school or church buildings.[169] The Brittens were surprised at the quick response. Bruce had warned Carol in advance of the first class to expect only "2 or 3" students; instead, they found a class of thirty-six.[170]

The Brittens formed alliances with key figures in the youthful generation of salvation-professing Zionists. Isaac Dlamini had passed away several months before their arrival, but they discovered other leaders among the boSindisiwe movement who could assist them. One was Nhlanhla Magongo, a keen Faith Bible School participant, who met the Brittens at the country's annual Good Friday service in 2003. Magongo recalled Britten invited him to help with rendering the teaching material into siSwati: "Bruce said, 'I'd love you to help me with the translation.' As the work expanded he asked me to help him full time, with grading books, translating the lesson notes from English to siSwati, helping Bruce at Easter Meetings with interpretation, encouraging some Zionist pastors to come to the Bible School."[171] Another important early contact was Jerome Sangweni who, with his qualification from New Haven Bible School in Nhlangano, became a primary Bible teacher alongside Britten. Britten recalled that: "I found out that this *Babe* [Father, a respectful term for older men] Sangweni already had a degree in the Bible, as far as I knew, he was the only Zionist who did . . . so I had a long talk with him. About what he believed concerning the Bible compared to what I was teaching. There were some differences but nothing vital, so he became the first Swazi teacher."[172] Also on the original teaching team was Dr. Busa Xaba, a leading educator and administrator both at the University and in the Ministry of Education, and Isaac Dlamini's son, Sifiso, who had obtained a theological degree in South Africa. As one graduate of the classes commented, the four of them made a dynamic teaching quartet: "Sangweni, Bruce, Sifiso, and the late Xaba! Eish! Abraham Busa Xaba, the late! Sho! Sho! Those four, they were solid teachers."[173]

The first generation of Zion Bible School students found it a transformative experience to be surrounded by like-minded young people, all struggling with alienation from their church elders. The classes began to constitute a network of reformed Zionists cutting across institutions, forming powerful new solidarities that transcended denominational loyalties and affirmed believers' common identity as saved Christians. Meshack Dlamini, part of the pioneer class in Mbabane in 2003, recalled it was his "first time to study the Bible." He heard from another Zionist pastor "there is a white man who has started a school in Mbabane," and that the fees were low, so decided to go along. He found a group of similarly minded Zionist pastors as well as women who taught Sunday School. For Meshack and for many in the pioneer class, it was a novel experience to find others "in the same boat." He remembered that in "this first class, we became like a family," forming bonds across institutions that endure to the present day: "even now if I have a service, who should I contact to come and preach and help me here and there, they help me a lot, really, like a support group."[174] Sipho Masilela, who attended a class on the Swazi-South African border, in the small town of Jeppes Reef, similarly commented that one of the most powerful aspects of the classes had been "it gives the social networking amongst other pastors, and even with those who are teaching us, and then you're able to ask even things that you think you ought to know, and then when they explain it from the Bible, you start to understand."[175]

Most of all, those who attended these classes found the teaching departed from established Zion ways of reading and interpreting Christian scriptures. ZEMA missionaries were convinced the Bible was not valued in Zionist churches, diagnosing this as the cause of the doctrinal error they considered to have crept into Zionism. In fact, the Bible lay at the heart of all Zion services, although it was used in a radically different manner to what evangelicals considered proper. The vast majority of Zionist leaders and prophets were not educated (let alone possessing a theological education), and for many, a fluent reading of the entire Bible was beyond their grasp. Limited literacy led to distinctive ways of using the scriptures. Solomon Dube, who grew up in the Swaziland branch of the Christian Apostolic Church in Zion, remembered how in his church it was said "the priest used to be given 'eyes' only for the service, he would open the Bible and read the text, he finishes that, he cannot read anything anymore . . . but when it's time for the service he can read again, by the Spirit."[176] Considering themselves enabled to read by the Spirit—rather than by secular literacy—Zionist leaders developed a mode of exegesis that selected individual texts in a fragmentary fashion, almost mosaic-like, and rather than reading entire chapters or stories, they extracted particular verses they felt directed to by the Spirit. These fragments would be read aloud by the leader once, then repeated by the congregation, and then their spiritual meaning explained, usually by reference to a prophetic revelation that had led the preacher to that particular verse, and which required considerable explanation and decoding.[177] One Jericho minister in the late 1970s explained this was a form of exegesis that centered on the leading by the Holy Spirit: "anyone who wishes can go to a Bible School. But what is important to us is that we know how to read the Bible for the Spirit helps us to read the Bible and preach . . . the Spirit explains all the verses in the Bible and what they mean."[178] This style of biblical exposition grounded authority in the Spirit-inspired individual; without the benefit of their revelation, the Bible was a mysterious, visionary text that remained a closed book to the congregation. With the interpretation of the prophet, however, the esoteric spiritual meaning of the Bible could be unpacked.

In contrast to this prophet-mediated textual practice, students found at Zion Bible College a radically different style of scriptural exegesis. Teachers such as Britten and Sangweni presented the text as entirely open to any reader whatsoever. The Bible they taught at the College was nonmysterious and transparent in meaning, its egalitarian riches could be understood by any ordinary congregant. Teachers stressed the "factual" nature of the Bible—solid "knowledge" regarding the will of God—enabled believers to critique the mysterious pronouncements of prophets who claimed inspiration from on high. Underscoring this, Britten told students "some people say they don't need the Bible, only the Holy Spirit . . . but we have the Bible and we KNOW. The truth is in the Bible, no matter what people say."[179] Classes also emphasized the Bible's meaning was entirely literal, present wholly within the text itself, and not in need of any type of specialized exegesis or interpretation. Vusumuzi Mkhatshwa, a student at a Mbabane class, recalled how impressed he was when teachers exhorted him "just preach the 'black' [i.e., the print on the page], just teach the Word, don't minus or add anything else."[180]

Furthermore, in many Zion churches members were expected to passively receive a mysterious text decoded by an all-seeing prophet, but in Zion Bible College students were taught to actively wrestle with the Word and make it real in their own lives. Students were encouraged to appreciate the narrative trajectory of the Bible as a whole. In contrast to the verse-focused approach of prophetic readings, students were taught—in typical evangelical manner—to see the entire sweep of the Bible as a single narrative of salvation history, beginning with the prophets and culminating in Jesus Christ. Students were guided through a carefully selected range of both Old and New Testament Books, and encouraged to look for thematic similarities connecting texts written over vast chronological periods. With the Bible established as a single, seamless narrative (sharply contrasting with the fragmented mosaic of verses prophets operated with), students were prompted to see themselves as actors within this story, and as recipients of Christ's salvation along with the biblical characters they read about. Mkhatshwa recalled one particularly dynamic sermon when Jerome Sangweni was preaching on the book of Jeremiah and roped students into the drama, allocating roles for each student, and culminating in a dramatic call for salvation: "That day! You couldn't even go to the toilet in case you missed anything! [Sangweni] took everyone into the corner and then he picked us out one by one from the corner, and then he called an altar call. That class was so powerful!"[181]

Zion Bible College students mobilized these participatory Bible-reading techniques in their own churches. After his first year of study, Meshack Dlamini disseminated the lessons he had learned among his own church members, an organization called the Church of Christ in Zion. Dlamini introduced an hour-long session before the main Sunday service that focused solely on Bible Study, reusing material he had received during Bible classes.[182] Inspired by the conviction that the Bible was the egalitarian possession of the entire congregation—not just reserved for the Spirit-inspired exegesis of prophets—Dlamini formed a partnership with the Bible Society of Swaziland. The Society supplied his church with recorded New Testament readings in siSwati as well as discounted Bibles. Dlamini played the recordings to the congregation before the service—aimed especially at those who could not read—and distributed Bibles to the remainder. He recalls this "motivated them in such a way that we saw a dramatic increase of reading and studying the Bible . . . the whole theme of the programme was based on *Kukholwa Kuvela Ekuveni* ("Belief comes from Hearing the Word")."[183] In neighboring Mozambique, ZEMA missionaries supplied discounted Bibles to women; one female missionary found "many [women] had never held a Bible in their hands before, they were amazed and had felt the Bible was only for men." She also started a literacy class so that women were able to read their new books.[184] In addition to encouraging laity to read scriptures, Zion Bible College graduates developed their own personal reading practices. Individual daily "quiet time" with the Bible was encouraged, and so was small group Bible Study during the week.[185] Pastors attending the classes were exhorted to not just pick up the Bible during their sermons and preach on whatever verse the Holy Spirit led them to, but rather to invest in intensive and thoughtful preparation.[186] Britten advised students to "spend hours studying a single chapter of the Bible" and to harness the lessons for their own lives, discounting the necessity of a prophet to interpret the text for their behalf: "pray: 'Holy Spirit empower me to obey this chapter myself.' "[187]

Equipped with these egalitarian techniques, youthful Zionists used biblical training to rebut disapproving church leaders. Britten and other teachers encouraged students to scrutinize their elders by using scriptures as the measure of orthodoxy; the Bible, in other words, had the authority to unseat powerful elders and prophets. Britten's popular book *Power of Jesus* provided students with two columns of Bible verses, one relating to the characteristics of false prophets and the other describing the qualities of true prophets. Students were advised to draw on the Bible as a guide for evaluating the actions of their leadership: "we must compare what Prophets say with what the Bible says," Britten's text instructed students.[188] Simon Nzima, a young minister within the Jericho church who completed Zion Bible College training, used his knowledge of the Bible to criticize the prophets dominating his church: "the "prophet should be someone who listens to the message of God . . . but the prophets in our church are not prophets of God. The Bible says that the time is coming whereby people will call themselves prophets, even though they are false prophets."[189] Before his death in 2002, Isaac Dlamini similarly mobilized his knowledge of the scriptures to critique the prophetic practices of his bishop. His coteacher Erickson Dlamini recalled one time they planned a Faith Bible School session on the Holy Spirit, and found they ran up against their bishop's claims to superior access to the Spirit: "our own Bishop marveled at how we could speak on this topic, when it was he himself was the true expert on the Holy Spirit . . . the Bishop exclaimed 'I know the Holy Spirit! I have prophesied!' " Dlamini described how Isaac gathered all his bravery and systematically went through biblical verses teaching the meaning of "true" prophecy to his very senior bishop: "Isaac opened his notes, and went through as to what is the Holy Spirit . . . [he said to the bishop] you cannot say that the Holy Spirit is hitting you on your back and you are screaming because you hear something, or you hear something spinning on top of your head. And the bishop said, 'What's all of this!' So really, Isaac had a tough time. But I thank God for giving us a man as brave as him!"[190]

Many Zion elders responded with great hostility toward their members' attendance at Zion Bible College. Meshack Dlamini found elders would boycott his preservice Bible class, or deliberately arrive late.[191] Others voiced their mistrust of youthful members gaining ideas above their station and growing disrespectful toward those elders. Zionist bishop Solomon Dube found the classes bolstered the pretensions of "some of our young people who think they are on top of the world and better than anybody else." Dube noted that after Bible College, "I see that they come back worse, they look down on people, they are despising of the priest and they try to confuse the people by giving rival messages." His approach was to let them attend Zion Bible College, but "when they come back, I have to unlearn them," reminding them the essence of Christianity was not "the paper" (i.e., the certificate), but its moral precepts, to "be a better person than you were."[192] Well aware of the dangers of alienating powerful church leaders, Zion Bible College instructors counseled students to practice respect for their seniors. Britten's advice to students was "work under those leaders who are older and experienced, learn from them, respect them. Of course, some older leaders are slow and stubborn. Yet we advise you: 'be patient, wise and humble. Pray.' "[193] Although Isaac Dlamini's teaching career predated the inauguration of Zion Bible College, he was attentive to these difficulties in his Faith Bible School, lamenting "if a young person goes to Bible School today . . . they come back and chase away the old ones who have so much experience. The young ones have new ideas they got at Bible School, but they haven't been disciplined. They haven't learned about the church."[194]

Many Bible-educated Zionists concluded that they were unable to work under the stultifying authority of their prophets. Some left their churches to form new organizations that stressed the importance of salvation and the Bible as an egalitarian book for all. These young boSindisiwe's conception of true Christianity was reflected in their choice of names for their new churches. Many omitted older "Zion" or "Apostolic" nomenclature replacing these with terms favored by evangelicals that stressed salvation and the Bible. Examples of new church names emerging in recent years founded by Zion reformists are The Believers in Christ,[195] Amazing Grace Church in Africa,[196] New Blessings of Salvation,[197] and Holy Bible Focused Church International.[198] Many new organizations erased practices they considered not in keeping with the egalitarian promise of salvation as laid out in the Bible. Most of all, they disowned prophecy and the ritual of siguco. All "prophetic" innovations, including the use of items of dress and the ritual application of blessed water to sick people, were banned.[199] A letter to the *Times of Swaziland* described a Believers in Christ service, with the author marveling: "you wouldn't believe me if I say they fall under the Zionist sect . . . the way they conduct praise and worship you'd think heaven has come down, they sing nicely, they dress smartly not like the other [Zionists] who you find with lots of ropes round their necks, I heard they don't attend these useless water-cleansing services [*kugeza emanti*]."[200]

Many reformed Zionist churches have emerged in Swaziland; however, in recent years even the older traditional Zion denominations have begun to display changes. Due to the large number of boSindisiwe who remained within the Zion movement, the influence of evangelical theology has gradually percolated through these churches, especially as a youthful generation of subversive "salvationists" aged and came to occupy prominent positions as seniors and elders. Jerome Sangweni is a senior Zionist who stayed within his old Zion denomination, and slowly reformed it from within, sometimes using wily strategies to do so. He chuckled as he related to me how he persuaded his congregation to relinquish siguco by relocating services to a venue with an unvarnished dust floor. The pounding of feet during siguco created such clouds of choking dust that congregation members became decidedly less enthusiastic about the dance.[201] Today, most Zion churches in Swaziland—even the prophet-centered Jericho church—recognize the value of biblical education; Zion Bible College missionary, Brett Miller, has a thriving ministry of visiting Jericho churches and welcoming ministers to Bible classes.[202] The spectacular deeds of flamboyant, Spirit-filled prophets are still regular points of discussion in the local newspaper, but also present is the disapproving commentary from senior Zionist leaders who seek to distance themselves from these "un-Christian" practices.[203]

If one listens carefully, a profound anxiety is frequently expressed that something of value may have been irretrievably lost to the Zion tradition. Many Zionists are torn about the benefits of improved education and consequent egalitarian access to the Bible. Although considered in keeping with a reformed Christianity, older Zionists nonetheless fear that much of the distinctive Spirit-filled spirituality of their faith is lost. Simon Mavimbela, grandson of the original Stephen Mavimbela, opined to me that spiritual potency had diminished since ministers started believing in education. "God doesn't listen to our prayers anymore," he lamented.[204] Indeed, as early as the mid-1990s, one senior Zionist leader had diagnosed the changes within his church. His comments make it clear how far this people of the Spirit had already traveled from their ecstatic, visionary past in their quest for education as the marker of saved Christians: "Our children are told at school that Zionists are uncivilized, so Zionist leaders have tried to accommodate their requests. Some are encouraging education. Some have even started schools themselves. Others have adopted music and choirs. People want more preaching and teaching and less prayers for the sick. But in doing so, the church stands to lose the strength of its spirituality."[205]

Afterword

Zion and Pentecost

IN RECENT YEARS Zion has experienced a gradual encroachment on its monopoly as the religion of choice for many Southern Africans. While Saturdays and Sundays across the region still see white-garbed Zionists streaming to daytime or all-night services, many carrying wooden staffs and small bottles of curative water or Vaseline blessed by a prophet, now one of the most characteristic features of urban and rural life in this part of the world is the ubiquitous presence of amplified Pentecostal preaching, a self-dubbed "apostle" booming from crackling loudspeakers their message of divine deliverance from financial and material impediments. This turn of events is noteworthy in light of the fact that much of this book has charted the phenomenal growth of Zionist churches throughout the twentieth century. Very little has been capable of slowing down the dramatic expansion of this evangelical movement across the region, including the introduction of Pentecostalism to South Africa in the early twentieth century. Despite the hostility of colonial governments and the antagonism of African political authorities, Zion's status as Southern Africa's largest popular form of Christianity has hitherto been unquestioned. Yet—if current rates of adherence to Pentecostal Christianity continue to grow—the remarkable story of the exponential growth of the People's Zion in Southern Africa might at last be slowing down, and in doing so, nearing a new chapter.

A relationship both competitive and symbiotic between Zion and Pentecost is nothing new to the history of the former. For one, the early Pentecostal revivals in the United States at the turn of the last century were closely connected to developments within Zion. Many key Zion City figures—John G. Lake among them—were involved in the Azusa

Street revivals in Los Angeles. As discussed in Chapter 3, Lake subsequently led a Pentecostal revival in early twentieth-century Johannesburg that was for about a decade largely interchangeable with Dowie's older Zion church. The new Holy Spirit-focused theology of Pentecostals, furthermore, was a close relation to the Holiness-inspired teachings of divine healing: both traditions emphasized the quest for spiritual perfection, and both Zionists and Pentecostals espoused an interest in bodily disciplines—healing and speaking in tongues—as the definitive evidence that perfection had been attained. Pentecostal teachings also shaped the charismatic prophet-centered spirituality of independent Zion African churches in the twentieth century. From Pentecost, these new Zion prophets borrowed their emphasis on the Holy Spirit's ability to directly address and instruct individual Christians. Some Pentecostal churches in the Southern African region explicitly distanced themselves from Zion, such as the Apostolic Faith Mission and the large Assemblies of God. However, in much popular practice, Zion and Pentecost tended to blend into each other. This is evident in the names of many Zionist organizations that have incorporated terms such as "Zion" and "Apostolic" side by side in their institutional nomenclature. Historically, the two traditions are best understood as coexisting on a fluid spectrum of Holiness Christianity in Southern Africa, rather than as polarized organizations espousing radically different theologies and worship styles.

Alongside these instances of harmonious exchange, fierce competition has also existed between Pentecostals and Zionists over the last century. Many believers in Voliva-era Zion City engaged in scathing polemic against the "diabolical" antics of those who claimed to have been baptized in the Holy Spirit and to speak in the tongues of angels. There were also detractors of the Pentecostal revival within Southern Africa. Many early sympathizers of the movement—both black and white—came to disagree with the Pentecostal practice of ecstatically speaking in tongues as an unseemly corruption of the true gospel. As one disgruntled group of Zionists reported to Daniel Bryant in 1909, "many of our Zion people in South Africa are sick and tired of the confusion and disorder reigning there in Pentecost."[1] African Zionists, in particular, found much to criticize in Lake and the Apostolic Faith Mission's willingness to ally themselves with the cause of white nationalism and reverted to the Zion organization, a sign of their preference for the more universalistic theology espoused by Dowie. Further disagreements between Pentecostals and Zionists abounded as the century progressed. Many of the schismatic breakaway Zion churches that emerged over the last hundred years occurred due to disagreements between senior and junior ministers regarding the exact role of the Holy Spirit in the congregation. Daniel Nkonyane's important Christian Catholic Apostolic Holy Spirit Church in Zion, for example, was formed due to the inability of Nkonyane's superior, Paulus Mabiletsa, to tolerate his junior minister's experiments with speaking in tongues.

Since the 1990s, however, more sustained tension has arisen between Pentecostals and Zionists in Southern Africa. This development is linked to the emergence of a distinctively new type of Pentecostal Christianity in the region as well as around the world. Popularly known as "Charismatic" Christianity, or "Pentecostal-Charismatic" Christianity, Chapter 7 discussed how the new movement arose as one of those moments of internal reform and regeneration that have so often characterized the worldwide history of evangelicalism. As North American Pentecostalism of the 1930s grew increasingly institutionalized and structured, by the 1960s, many second and third-generation Pentecostals began to complain the vigor of the early movement had been lost, and to yearn for renewed spiritual fervor within their churches. In keeping with the general youth-focused culture of this decade, the "charismatic" revival—as it came to be known—first took off among communities linked to university campuses and student churches. Reflecting the ecumenical nature of youthful Christian networks, one of the most distinctive characteristics of the revival was that it exceeded any denominational boundaries, shaping Christian practice in a range of denominations including the Catholic Church. This youthful generation of Charismatics had a very different interpretation of their faith than did older traditional Pentecostal denominations. Older Pentecostals had seen it as their religious duty to remain aloof from the world, renouncing a whole host of lifestyles and behaviors. By contrast, the charismatics who emerged in the 1960s and 1970s did not see things in such stark terms and were in general more willing to embrace worldly pleasures—a characteristic that would come to be significant in the Southern African context. Early Charismatics were willing to drink, smoke, dress fashionably, go out, and socialize with nonbelievers. They emphasized the ecstatic, fervent spiritual passion of the Holy Spirit, not the minute prescriptions on daily life their Pentecostal forefathers stressed.[2] Pentecostal-Charismatic networks rapidly spread across the world, including across much of the African continent, again relying on student networks situated on university campuses.[3]

As was the case with Zion, many of the new Pentecostal-Charismatic churches that consequently sprung up in Southern Africa from the 1970s on were affiliated to international organizations, and their place in the local religious landscape was, and is, as outposts of larger global churches. Believers' extensive use of electronic and digital media—including the internet but also TV and radio—were an important element in maintaining these large transnational fellowships. One of the largest new Pentecostal-Charismatic churches with huge memberships in both South Africa and Mozambique is the vast Brazilian Universal Church of the Kingdom of God, estimated to have 12,000,000 members worldwide and around 200 branches in South Africa alone. But many Pentecostal-Charismatics are affiliated to bigger transnational mother churches located on the African continent itself. These organizations stem from African initiative, and although sharing warm links with like-minded Pentecostal-Charismatics outside of the continent, operate largely independently of non-African assistance or monetary help. Nigeria, for example, is a major hub of this new Protestantism, sending missionaries and building branches across Africa and beyond. Two of the most significant new Pentecostal churches in Southern Africa are outposts of the Nigerian Church of All Nations, and the Redeemed Christian Church of God. But some of the new Pentecostal churches are genuinely local organizations, flourishing in the regional soil of particular countries. Thus in Swaziland, there is the Worship Centre, founded by a Swazi electrician turned "prophet," Justice Dlamini, as well as the Sword & Spirit Ministries, also started by a local Swazi "Apostle" acting in conjunction with his wife, "Apostleness" Thwala.

These new Pentecostal-Charismatic churches focus on believers' triumphant vanquishing of all that holds them back in every area of their lives. This optimistic stress undoubtedly echoes older Holiness themes within the Zion movement itself. While the evangelical churches of Southern Africa of the 1970s and 1980s emphasized "salvation," the new Pentecostal-Charismatic churches are characterized by the quest for what is known variously as "deliverance" or "dominion." Sword & Spirit Ministries in Swaziland, for example, states on its website that they are a church "commissioned [by God] to raise a people of dominion and influence."[4] Dominion implies mastery over obstacles in one's life. Many of these new churches have a highly developed "demonology," and a belief that every misfortune that besets a believer is caused by the influence of nefarious spirits of satanic provenance. Pentecostal-Charismatic believers usually refer to these areas of misfortune as demonic "strongholds" in their lives. But although possessed of a theology that sees the existence of evil as a considerable obstacle, this is ultimately a movement that teaches victorious triumph. Through affiliating themselves to organizations such as the new Pentecostal-Charismatic ministries or fellowships, believers express great confidence that they are tapping into the mastery that will enable them to throw off the spiritual shackles that imprison them. The annual Christmas service of the Nigerian Church of all Nations—both in Nigeria and in its outposts around the African continent including in Johannesburg—not only commemorates the "Birth of our Lord and Savior," but also "uses the occasion to unleash holy terror on the kingdom of darkness . . . mass prayer shakes the foundations of the satanical kingdom and causes commotion at the gates of hell."[5]

In particular, many of these churches are highly attuned to the "strongholds" of financial insecurity and conversely, the monetary blessings that come the way of the true believer once "deliverance" is achieved. Most of the new organizations have highly developed theologies of tithing, believing that it is only through generously giving to the life of the church and to the pastor that one—through these acts of faith—unleashes the dominion of God in one's life. At the opening of a new Pentecostal-Charismatic church in Swaziland—Divine Healing Ministries—the bishop urged the congregation to freely offer during the collection going even so far as to declare that "people should offer notes and not coins . . . if you give 5 cents you will remain a 5 cents person, so give, because it is a fact that givers never struggle for anything in life."[6] The belief in financial prosperity as the mark of a true believer has created an aspirational, upwardly mobile ethos that celebrates middle-class professional attainment, expensive cars, and luxury clothing. The good life is victoriously celebrated in many of these churches as a sign of the spiritual blessings arrived from God. One journalist dubbed the carpark at one of the region's most prominent Pentecostal-Charismatic organization, Rhema Church—dubbed by many "the most powerful church in South Africa," due to the frequent attendance of State President Jacob Zuma at services—as "the forecourt of a luxury car dealership every Sunday."[7] Similar displays of wealth are on display in Pentecostal-Charismatic churches across the border in Swaziland. In 2016 at the opening of the new "Jesus Calls Worship Centre" in Manzini, Swaziland, the local newspaper reported that the ceremony was attended by sleek, well-dressed, and moneyed devotees: "it now official, Christians are the most stylishly dressed lot! The opening of this church turned this function into a fashion showcase, the pastors and wives [arrived] chauffeured in sleek wheels."[8] But by no means all new Pentecostal-Charismatics across the region are part of the region's rapidly growing black middle classes. Many are from humble backgrounds, and for them the financial success ethos of these churches and the glamourous lifestyles of their pastors, "Apostles", and "prophets" are aspirational symbols of the blessings God can bring to the life of the true believer, and what they can themselves aspire to one day attain.

There are evident continuities between this recent crop of Pentecostal-Charismatic churches and the older Zionist movement. In addition to their shared emphasis on the power of the Holy Spirit, both Zion and the new Pentecostalism make similar connections between the intertwined significance of body and spirit. Neither Zion nor Pentecost are flesh-denying forms of Protestantism that erase embodied experience from the religious life. For both Zionists and Pentecostal-Charismatics across Southern Africa, the experience of divine healing continues to be practiced (perhaps more prominently in Zion organizations), and the belief that God decisively intervenes to repair ruined bodies informs communal and individual worship. Both movements, moreover, are dominated by idioms and themes of self-improvement, self-mastery, and the upward trajectory of a faithful believer's life. The success of these churches demonstrates that the typically Holiness and Higher-Life egalitarian theme of personal triumph for all continues to resonate in contemporary Southern Africa where many are struggling to transform their lives amid huge inequalities of wealth and privilege. There are significant instances of overlap between the movements, as there has been throughout the twentieth-century, especially in the lives of new Zionists who occasionally migrate to the new Pentecostal-Charismatic "ministries" or "fellowships," and some of whom even start their own new "salvation" churches that incorporate aspects of Pentecostal teachings. In 2006, a Pew Forum-funded survey on Christianity in South Africa found that approximately one-third of Zionists and Apostolics in the country would identity as "charismatic."[9]

There are also important differences between the two movements and their adherents. As we have seen, as the twentieth century progressed, Zionists came to be known for their status as a church of the poor and the socially marginalized. While to some extent this has been modified in the middle-class background of some of the more youthful members belonging to the new "saved" Zion organizations, it is still broadly true that Zion churches across Southern Africa are regarded as organizations for those situated on the periphery of financial security and social success. Being middle class and being Zionist are identities that, for many, sit together uneasily. New Pentecostal-Charismatics, by contrast, with their smartly dressed pastors and huge church buildings, their use of new technology such as the internet in their worship services, and their reliance on social media technologies like Facebook and Twitter, are proclaiming themselves part of a prosperous, forward-looking elite part of the growing black middle classes—whether this is in actuality or merely in aspiration. Affiliating oneself with a new Pentecostal-Charismatic church amounts to making a statement about one's social aspirations. Pentecostal-Charismatics thus regard Zionists with no small degree of scorn, viewing their humble social origins and their lack of education and advanced degrees as out of keeping with the victorious ethos of a Christian who has accessed God's deliverance. In this way, the typically evangelical rhetoric of "winning" and accessing spiritual power has taken on an important new dimension in many of the new Pentecostal-Charismatic churches, and in the context of early twenty-first century Southern Africa. Although both Zionists and Pentecostal-Charismatics subscribe to notions of triumph, in the grammar of the latter group of churches this emphasis has become tightly interwoven with notions of upward social mobility in the difficult neoliberal economy of the region, punctuated by regular financial and economic crises, devastating droughts, famines, and political instability.

Zionist leaders express a great deal of disapproval of these new churches, as well as intense anxiety that they are losing their youthful members to them. Most recent statistical surveys from several countries across the region indicate the phenomenal growth of these churches, suggesting that, taken as a whole, the new Pentecostal-Charismatics are fast outstripping the traditional dominance of the Zionist churches as the largest popular religious movement of the region. A 2006 study on Pentecostals in South Africa undertaken by the Pew Forum estimated that one third of the urban population identified themselves as adherents of the new Pentecostal movement; in 2008, a South African survey found that Pentecostals were the single largest-growing religious group in the country, experiencing a 55 percent growth rate between 1996 and 2001.[10] Data on the rapid dominance of new Pentecostal-Charismatic churches over the religious landscape suggest very similar trends in other countries in the region, including Swaziland, Botswana, and Mozambique.

Critiquing and attempting to make sense of the great success of the new Pentecostal-Charismatic churches, Zionist leaders draw negative comparisons between the authentic piety of the Zion movement and the false promises of Pentecostal pastors and prophets. Many of the ministers I have interviewed throughout the course of this book maintained that their younger members were increasingly being drawn to the new churches on account of their slick worship styles. While modern music complete with drum kits and deafening electronic amplification suggested a certain "modern" worship style, other ministers noticed that it was specifically the prosperity teachings of the new churches that attracted many of their members. Godfrey Maseko, Bishop of a large Zionist church in Johannesburg, lamented that "people are moving out of the amaZioni movement into these Pentecostal churches." Maseko's opinion was that the cause of this was that the newer Pentecostal-Charismatic churches told Zionists, "come to our church, we will bless you, you will be rich, we will heal you, you will live a wealthy life on this earth . . . people are looking for wealth in modern life."[11] Maseko and many other pastors saw this almost exclusive focus on financial blessings as a superficial corruption of the pure

Holiness teachings represented in John Alexander Dowie's church. Historically, it is true, the nineteenth and twentieth-century evangelical movements—including divine healing—displayed very little interest in financial or material wealth as a marker of piety. Other Zionist critics of the new Pentecostalism maintained their allure was only fleeting, and that its wealth-focused spirituality was hollow compared to what could be found in the Zionist movement. In Swaziland, Simon Mavimbela similarly observed that "most of the young people from the Zionists are going for the [Pentecostal] ministries now," but also stated his opinion that "some of them turn back from the ministries and come back here [to Zion]." For Mavimbela, descendent of the renowned prophet Stephen Mavimbela, the "prosperity gospel" piety of the new Pentecostal-Charismatics was thin and "play-like." True faithful ardor was found in spiritual "wilderness," far from the comfortable, corporate environs of the new Pentecostal churches and their smart, glossy worship: "the youth in time find the praying here in Zion is very strong. There in the ministries there is a lot of time that is wasted, playing music and all that. They are not like people are in the wilderness. They pray like it is play."[12]

Despite the scathing opinion of Mavimbela and other Zionist leaders, the millions of adherents of these new organizations indicate that Pentecostal-Charismatic teachings do in fact offer a powerful and deep spiritual experience for many, more than comparable to what Zion has represented for millions over the past century and a half. In a region where financial worries are at the top of the list for most, and making ends meet is a daily struggle for many households in the Southern African region, the promise of these churches and their miracle-working pastors and apostles to bring monetary blessings to the faithful are hard to resist. And while some have denounced the "false consciousness" element of this promise (echoing here the old secular or materialist critique of Christianity in Africa), in fact there is also much evidence that adherence to these churches has begun to affect tangible, practical changes in believers' lives. New Pentecostal men are encouraged to focus on saving money and investing it in their families and in the church, rather than spending their pay checks on male networks of alcohol-based socializing. Women, by contrast, find they are greatly supported by their churches and their religious leaders in their career aspirations and financial independence—for many of these churches, professional success, and financial autonomy are the characteristics of a godly woman.

Arguably, then, these new Pentecostal-Charismatic churches are occupying the populist, egalitarian space that for many decades was monopolized by the Zionist churches. As did Dowie's church to its working-class membership in Gilded Era Chicago, contemporary African Pentecostal-Charismatic churches promise their adherents that their belief in God will be accompanied by radical uplift, individual self-improvement, and personal advancement for all, regardless of worldly standing or status. While throughout the twentieth century, Zion similarly attempted, amid widespread racial segregation and political and territorial disenfranchisement, to equip those without formal power with the spiritual resources of evangelicalism, Pentecost's offers today are not so dissimilar. Its promise to twenty-first-century believers is that God is the great leveler of finances, and that good things are coming to the economically dispossessed if they only have enough faith (evident in large part through their generosity of giving and tithing to the church). Similar egalitarian themes as these have populated the history of Zion on two continents over 150 years. Many scholars and commentators as well as the general public, see only a radical rupture between Zion and Pentecost. They see the former as an old form of Christianity focused on healing, and the latter as the new modern iteration of Christianity emphasizing financial prosperity. In fact, both impulses are equally representative of the enduring power of evangelicalism to reshape the social landscape of Southern Africa in highly egalitarian ways. The popularity of both Zion and Pentecost speaks to the enduring allure of promise of Christian evangelicalism to equip very ordinary men and women with extraordinary power.

Interviews

MOZAMBIQUE

Zacarias Muimabo, Matola, Maputo, 22 June 2016

SOUTH AFRICA

Richard and Geraldine Akers, Nelspruit, 18 November 2015
Richard Akers, Sunbury, 6 January 2016
Barry and Louise Atkins, Sunbury, 6 January 2016
Nani and Mhleta Dlamini, Cape Town, 12 March 2016
Luann and Suzanne Goosens, Sunbury, 6 January 2016
Nomlindelo Hlatshwayo, Soweto, 16 June 2016
Thami Hlatshwayo, Soweto, 14 June 2016
Thami Hlatshwayo, Soweto, 16 June 2016
Tim and Luanne Kuehl, Johannesburg, 24 November 2015
Peter Le Roux, Elsa Le Roux, and Louise Vonstaden, Pretoria, 27 November 2015
Edgar Mahon III, Durban, 8 January 2016
Netta Mahon, Pretoria, 25 November 2015
Godfrey Maseko, Johannesburg, 24 November 2015
Sipho Masilela, Jeppes Reef, 4 June 2016
Elizabeth Mathonsi, Jeppes Reef, 4 June 2016
Asa Mmango, Soweto, 16 June 2016
Michael Mpande, Cape Town, 11 March 2016
Greg and Carlene Seghers, Sunbury, 18 August 2015
Andrew Sisson, Sunbury, 5 January 2016
Andrew Sisson, Sunbury, 7 January 2016
Chris Smit, Wakkerstroom, 30 July 2015
Marius and Nozipho Swart, Sunbury, 6 January 2016

Mrs. Tshuma, Jeppes Reef, 4 June 2016
Emmanuel Tsotetse, Soweto, 16 June 2016
Marie Weidelmann, Harold Le Roux, and Lynette Le Roux, Wakkerstroom,
    19 December 2015

SWAZILAND

Elizabeth Dlamini and Lungile Dlamini, Ludzeludze, Manzini, 23 June 2016
Erickson Dlamini, Motjane, 10 August 2016
Meshack Dlamini, Matsapha, 19 August 2016
Sifiso Dlamini, Manzini, 29 June 2016
Solomon Dvuba, Matsapha, 15 July 2016
Peter Kopp, Mbabane, 30 September 2016
Nhlanhla Magongo, Manzini, 8 June 2016
Herbert Mavimbela and Rev. Dlamini, Ludzeludze, Manzini, 23 June 2016
Simon Mavimbela, Mbabane, 11 July 2016
Bishop Maziya, Manzini, 15 July 2016
Brett and Evelyn Miller, Manzini, 9 August 2016
Vusumuzi Mkhatshwa, Mbabane, 17 August 2016
Jameson Mncina, Maguga, 6 June 2016
Philemon Mvubu, Manzini, 15 August 2016
Simon Nzima, Manzini, 30 September 2016
Jerome Sangweni, Manzini, 8 June 2016
Soul Sibandze, Mahlanya, 27 June 2016
Bishop K. Vilakati, Mankanyane, 30 July 2016

UNITED STATES

Bruce and Carol Britten, Akron, Ohio, 24 July 2016
Lee Deming, Zion, 23 July 2013
Jon and Lauren Emmanuelson, Zion, 3 October 2015
Daniel Hess, Lancaster, Pennsylvania, 27 September 2016
Darrell Hostetter, Lancaster, Pennsylvania, 17 October 2016
Gerry and Katy Lee, Zion, 4 October 2015
Mike McDowell, Zion, 19 July 2012
Cleburn and Alyce McIlhany, Zion, 24 March 2014
Cleburn and Alyce McIlhany, Zion, 25 March 2014
Cleburn and Alyce McIlhany, Zion, 26 March 2014
McIlhany Family (Cleburn, Alyce, Keith, Kevin), Kenosha, 26 March 2014
Mrs. Mintern, Zion, 18 July 2013
Tim Morse, Zion, 20 July 2013
Tim Morse, Zion, 21 July 2013
Tim Morse and Lee Deming, 22 July 2013
Anastase and Immaculee Nzabilinda, Zion, 19 July 2012

Chuck Paxton, Zion, 16 July 2013
Lee Paxman, Zion, 18 July 2013
Paul and Carrie Seelhammer, Zion, 3 October 2015
Greg and Carlene Seghers, Grant and Barbara Sisson, and Mike McDowell, Zion, 20 July 2012
Rose Simon, Zion, 23 July 2013
Grant and Barbara Sisson, Zion, 18 July 2014

List of Primary Sources

RECORDS IN SOUTH AFRICA

Pretoria Archives

NTS Files
1457, 1469, 1439, 1434, 1431, 1430: vol. 1–4, 1428, 1422, 1420, 1486, 1484,
1480, 1459, 1458, 1451, 1428, 1427, 118, 1486, 1485, 1483, 7265, 1498, 120,
121, 170, 688, 1472, 1473, 1474, 1477, 1461, 1478, 1479, 1480, 1481, 1482,
1483, 1484, 1486, 1487, 1488, 1489, 1491, 1492, 1493, 1494, 1495, 1496,
1497, 2757

BAO Files
7286, 7256

GG Files
179, 1575, 1574, 1571, 1550, 2198, 1958, 957, 1569

DGO Files
79, 75, 71, 77, 49, 59, 55, 56, 57, 311, 46, 48, 76, 78, 80, 82, 83, 84, 85, 86, 87,
88, 89, 90, 191, 192, 193, 194, 195, 196, 197

DG Files
1544

URU Files
1270

SNA Files
361, 144

LD Files
72

KJB Files
516, 2, 4, 5, 9, 100, 402, 403, 406, 412, 418, 462, 477, 492, 493, 504, 505, 512, 515, 516

JUS Files
31, 385

HKN Files
1/1/7

GOV Files
1209

GNLB Files
369, 363, 353, 335, 299, 216, 205, 206, 208, 238, 262, 292, 370, 371, 383, 384, 401, 41, 70, 159, 281, 309, 310, 1, 2, 4, 7, 10, 12, 17, 18, 19, 20, 22, 26, 31, 32, 33, 38, 40, 42, 52, 53, 56, 57, 58, 67, 68, 69, 71, 72, 74, 78, 83, 85, 86, 87, 88, 90, 96, 97, 100, 103, 107, 109, 110, 111, 114, 116, 119, 121, 122, 125, 126, 127, 129, 132, 134, 136, 137, 141, 142, 145, 149, 150

CS Files
709

INL
1/4/28

Wakkerstroom Magistrate Files (LWM)
3–175

Bloemfontein Archives

Colonial Office Records
216, 280, 327, 385, 536, 607, 609, 93, 414, 493

Governor Files
92, 97, 104, 135

Harrismith Magistrate Files (LHT)
2/1/1/26, 2/1/1/27, 2/1/1/28, 2/1/1/29, 2/1/1/30, 2/1/1/34, 2/1/1/37

Harrismith Muncipality Minutes (MHT)
1/4/1, 1/4/2–3, 2/1/6, 2/1/7, 2/1/8, 2/1/10, 2/1/14, 2/1/15, 2/1/16, 2/1/19, 2/1/21, 2/1/23, 2/1/25, 2/1/27, 2/1/28, 2/1/29, 2/1/30, 2/1/32, 3/1/15, 3/1/16, 3/1/20, 8/1/12

Native Affairs Files (NAB)
1, 2, 3, 4, 5, 6, 10

Miscellaneous Harrismith Records
LVR 2/3/7, LWI 2/1/1/3, LWI 2/1/1/16, ORC 332, SOO 1/1/178

Apostolic Faith Mission Archives, Johannesburg

Le Roux Diary, 1890
Red Notebook
Misc. Notebook, JG Lake related
Le Roux Diaries and Correspondence, 1920s
Le Roux Correspondence, 1896–1908, departure from DRC
Le Roux, 1939ff. material
Christian de Wet thesis on AFM
Executive Committee Minutes 1908–1914
Executive Committee Minutes 1915–1920
Executive Committee Minutes 1925–1927
AFM magazines and periodicals from South Africa, including *Trooster* and
   Comforter

Dutch Reformed Church Archives, Stellenbosch

Documents detailing resignation of Le Roux, found in Zion, Le Roux folder

Zion Evangelical Ministries of Africa Archives, Sunbury

Baptist Union Missionary Reports
This We Believe Bible Correspondence Course
CCC of Zion in Africa Constitutions
CCC of Zion in Africa Executive Council Minutes
One Hundred Years of Zion—Success and Failure—by Lyle Mahon, 1996

RECORDS IN SWAZILAND

RCS 155-37, RCS 589-40, RCS 791-36, RCS 282-1941, RCS 320-40, RCS 728-37

RECORDS IN BOTSWANA

Secretariat, Box No. 497—S.497/5/1
Secretariat 435 Box 435, S.435/3/1
Secretariat 291, S.291/18/1
DIV.COM.S.3/17

RECORDS IN THE UNITED STATES

Christian Catholic Church Archives, Zion, Illinois

Zululand and Basutoland Missionary
Mahon Mission Photo Album
Zion City History by Anton Darms
This We Believe, History and Beliefs of the Christian Catholic Church—Ottersen
Zion in South Africa Folder, Misc. Material
Zion School System—Lucille Bidille
Zion Facts—Lucille Bidille
Zion Facts II—Lucille Bidille
History of Zion—Lucille Bidille
Daniel Bryant Correspondence and Writings
Wilkinson Correspondence
Misc. Periodicals, including *Leaves of Healing, Theocrat and Visitor*
Foreign Missionary Correspondence, including with Ernest Cox
Misc. Publications and Reports
Membership Application Forms A–Z
International Divine Healing Association

Grace Missionary Church Archives, Zion, Illinois

Grace Missionary Church Minutes
Church History Scrapbooks, complied Marian McElroy
Basutoland and Zululand Missionary

Zion Historical Society, Zion, Illinois

Zion City News
Zion City Independent
The Zion Herald
Leaves of Healing (ed. J. A. Dowie)
Leaves of Healing (ed. J. A. Lewis)
Community News
A Voice From Zion (ed. Sprecher)
Zion Banner
The Theocrat
The Final Warning (ed. Voliva)
Leaves of Healing (ed. Voliva)
A Voice from Zion (ed. Crawford)
Leaves of Healing (ed. J. A. Dowie, Australian edition)

Zion Evangelical Ministries of Africa Archives, Zion, Illinois

Correspondence from Greg and Carlene Seghers

Newberry Library, Chicago

Midwest Manuscript Collection, Zion, Boxes 1–35 (including newspaper
  clippings)
Leaves of Healing (ed. J. A. Dowie), 1896–1908

Pentecostal Flower Heritage Center

Interview with Cleburn McIlhaney

YMCA Archives, University of Minnesota Library

Rand Young Men's Journal
Miscellaneous Records and Reports

ARCHIVES IN THE UNITED KINGDOM

Methodist Archives, SOAS

Reports of Wesleyan Methodists in South Africa

Salvation Army Archives, London

All the World
The Officer
War Cry
Miscellaneous Papers from South African Territory

University Library, Cambridge

Standard and Diggers News
Imperial Colonist

Archives of the School of Oriental and African Studies, University of London

Native Churches Commission Questionnaires, MS 380256

ARCHIVES IN SWEDEN

Uppsala University Archives

Bengt Sundkler Papers—Boxes 92, 95, 96, 97, 98, 99, 101, 103, 104, 106, 107,
  108, 109, 110, 111, 112, 113, 114, 115, 116, 117, 118, 119, 120, 121, 122,
  123, 124, 126, 127, 128, 130, 131, 132, 133, 134, 135, 136, 137, 138

PERSONAL PAPERS

Cleburn McIlhany papers (Zion, Illinois)
Church documents in the possession of Soul Sibandze, Swazi Christian Church in
  Zion of South Africa (Lobamba loMdzala, Swaziland)
"My Story," by Erickson Dlamini (possession of Erickson Dlamini)
Darrell Hostetter papers (Lancaster, Pennsylvania, United States)

OTHER NEWSPAPERS

Rand Daily Mail
Star
Transvaal Leader
Bantu World
Bantu Mirror
Drum
Times of Swaziland
Harrismith Chronicle

Abbreviations

AFM Apostolic Faith Mission
AME African Methodist Episcopal (Church)
BNA Botswana National Archives
CCC Christ Community Church (formerly Christian Catholic Church in Zion, under W. G. Voliva)
DNL Director for Native Labour
GMC Grace Missionary Church (Zion)
GNLB Government Native Labour Bureau
ICU Industrial and Commercial Workers' Union
NAD Native Affairs Department
NAS National Archives of Swaziland
NASA National Archives of South Africa
NC Native Commissioner
SAB National Archives Repository (Public Records of Central Government Since 1910)
SNA Secretary for Native Affairs
SNC Sub-Native Commissioner
SOAS School of Oriental and African Studies, University of London
TEAM The Evangelical Alliance Mission
VAB Free State Archives Repository (Bloemfontein)
YMCA Young Men's Christian Association
ZCC Zion Christian Church
ZEMA Zion Evangelical Ministries of Africa

Notes

INTRODUCTION

1. Christ Community Church Archives, Zion, Illinois, J. A. Dowie to D. Bryant and E. Bryant, 5 November 1903, 18–19.
2. Throughout this book, "faith healing" and "divine healing" will be used interchangeably. While "divine healing" was the contemporary term used by nineteenth-century practitioners, it is seldom heard today, in either the United States or sub-Saharan Africa.
3. See Zion Evangelical Ministries of Africa, http://www.zema.org.
4. Philip Jenkins, *The Next Christendom: The Coming of Global Christianity* (Oxford: Oxford University Press, 2002).
5. David Goodhew, "Growth and Decline in South Africa's Churches, 1960–1991," *Journal of Religion in Africa* 30, no. 3 (2000): 350.
6. Willem J. Schoeman, "South African Religious Demography: The 2013 General Household Study," *HTS Theological Studies*, 73, no. 2 (2017): 2; *Fulfilling the Vision: A Report of the Swaziland Evangelism Task* (Mbabane: Webster Print, 1995), 20–22.
7. Important recent publications on North American divine healing include Heather D. Curtis, *Faith in the Great Physician: Suffering and Divine Healing in American Culture, 1860–1900* (Baltimore: Johns Hopkins University Press, 2007); James Opp, *The Lord for the Body: Religion, Medicine and Protestant Faith Healing in Canada, 1880–1930* (Montreal: McGill-Queen's University Press, 2005); Nancy A. Hardesty, *Faith Cure: Divine Healing in the Holiness and Pentecostal Movements* (Peabody: Hendrickson, 2003).
8. But see Heather D. Curtis, "The Global Character of Nineteenth-Century Divine Healing," in *Global Pentecostal and Charismatic Healing*, ed. Candy Gunther Brown (Oxford: Oxford University Press, 2011), 29–46; Jonathan R. Baer, "Redeemed Bodies: The Function of Divine Healing in Incipient Pentecostalism," *Church History* 70, no. 4 (2001): 735–771.

9. W. E. Boardman, *Record of the International Conference on Divine Healing and True Holiness, Held at the Agricultural Hall (St Mary's Agricultural Hall, Islington)* (London: J. Snow & Co., 1885), vi, 171–175.

10. Philip Cook, *Zion City, Twentieth-Century Utopia* (Syracuse: University of Syracuse Press, 1996), 218.

11. Boardman, *International Conference,* 171.

12. Baer, "Redeemed Bodies," 762.

13. A recent survey of Zionism makes no mention of its North American origins. Joel Tishken and Andreas Heuser, "Africa Always Brings Us Something New: A Historiography of African Zionist and Pentecostal Christianities," *Religion* 45, no. 2 (2015): 153–173. An important exception is Jean Comaroff, *Body of Power, Spirit of Resistance: The Culture and History of a South African People* (Chicago: Chicago University Press, 1986), chap. 6.

14. Joel Cabrita, *Text and Authority in the South African Nazaretha Church* (Cambridge: Cambridge University Press, 2014), 5–6.

15. For a representative sample of this huge literature, see G. C. Oosthuizen, S. D. Edwards, W. H. Wessels, and I. Hexham, eds., *Afro-Christian Religion and Healing in Southern Africa* (Lewiston: Edwin Mellen Press, 1989); and James Kiernan, "Wear 'N' Tear and Repair: The Colour Coding of Mystical Mending in Zulu Zionist Churches," *Africa: Journal of the International African Institute* 61, no. 1 (1991): 27–28.

16. Lamin Sanneh, *Translating the Message: The Missionary Impact on Culture* (New York: Orbis Books, 2009).

17. Steven Feierman, "Explanation and Uncertainty in the Medical World of Ghaambo," *Bulletin of the History of Medicine* 74, no. 2 (2000): 343–344.

18. Karen E. Flint, *Healing Traditions: African Medicine, Cultural Exchange and Competition in South Africa, 1820–1948* (Athens: Ohio University Press, 2008).

19. Terence Ranger, "Religion, Development and African Christian Identity," in *Religion, Development and African Identity,* ed. Karl Petersen (Uppsala: Scandinavian Institute of African Studies, 1997), 31.

20. Frances Fitzgerald, *The Evangelicals: The Struggle to Shape America* (New York: Simon & Schuster, 2017), 3.

21. Mark A. Noll, *The Rise of Evangelicalism: The Age of Edwards, Whitefield and the Wesleys* (Downers Grove, IL: InterVarsity Press, 2003).

22. Melvin E. Dieter, *The Holiness Revival of the Nineteenth Century* (London: Scarecrow Press, 1996).

23. Boardman, *International Conference,* vi, 171–175.

24. Dieter, *The Holiness Revival,* 141–146; James Robinson, *Divine Healing* (London: Pickwick, 2011), 1:41.

25. Donald Dayton, "The Rise of the Evangelical Healing Movement in Nineteenth-Century America," *Pneuma* 4, no. 1 (1982): 15.

26. Raymond J. Cunningham, "From Holiness to Healing: The Faith Cure in America, 1872–1892," *Church History* 43 (1974): 499, 512.

27. Robinson, *Divine Healing,* 83.

28. John Walsh, "'Methodism' and the Origins of English-Speaking Evangelicalism," in *Evangelicalism: Comparative Studies of Popular Protestantism in*

North America, the British Isles, and Beyond, 1700–1990, ed. Mark A. Noll, David W. Bebbington, and George A. Rawlyk (New York: Oxford University Press, 1994), 24–28, 33; B. Daly Metcalf, *Islamic Revival in British India: Deoband, 1860–1900* (Princeton: Princeton University Press, 1982).

29. Nathan O. Hatch, *The Democratization of American Christianity* (New Haven: Yale University Pres, 1989).

30. Derek R. Peterson, *Ethnic Patriotism and the East African Revival: A History of Dissent, c. 1935–1972* (Cambridge: Cambridge University Press, 2012).

31. Henry Mitchell, "Malawian Intellectuals, Christianity and African Internationalism in 1920s Johannesburg," *Southern African Historical Journal* (forthcoming).

32. Cited in Terence Ranger, "Religious Movements and Politics in Sub-Saharan Africa," *African Studies Review* 29, no. 2 (1986): 20.

33. Alec Ryrie, *Protestants: The Faith that Made the Modern World* (New York: Viking, 2017), 2.

34. Bengt Sundkler, *Zulu Zion and Some Swazi Zionists* (Oxford: Oxford University Press, 1976); Philip Bonner, "South African Society and Culture, 1910–1948," in *The Cambridge History of South Africa,* Vol. 2, *1885–1994,* ed. Robert Ross, Anne Kelk Mager, and Bill Nasson (Cambridge: Cambridge University Press, 2014), 309–310.

35. Cabrita, *Text and Authority,* 175–177.

36. Ryrie, *Protestants,* 1.

37. *Leaves of Healing* 3, no. 21, 5 March 1897, 333.

38. Elders and Mrs Eugene Brooks, *Conflicts in the Narrow Way* (Zion, IL: n.p., 1944), 14.

39. *Leaves of Healing* 6, no. 25, 14 April 1900.

40. Cook, *Zion City,* 111.

41. Sidney E. Mead, *The Lively Experiment: The Shaping of Christianity in America* (Eugene, OR: Wipf & Stock, 1963), 108–109.

42. Archives of the School of Oriental and African Studies, University of London (hereafter SOAS), MS 380256, File 1 African Native Baptist Church of South Africa.

43. SOAS, MS 380256, File 38, Gazaland Zimbabwe Ethiopian Church.

44. S. M. Mokitimi, "African Religion," in *Handbook on Race Relations in South Africa,* ed. Ellen Hellman (Charlottesville, VA: Octagon Book, 1949), 565.

45. Bengt Sundkler, *Bantu Prophets in South Africa* (London: Lutterworth Press, 1961), 303.

46. David B. Barrett, *Schism and Renewal in Africa* (Nairobi: Oxford University Press, 1968).

47. Derek R. Peterson, "Nonconformity in Africa's Cultural History," *Journal of African History* 58, no. 1 (2017): 35–50.

48. Cook, *Zion City,* 94.

49. *Leaves of Healing* 12, no. 2, 22 November 1902.

50. Cook, *Zion City,* 93.

51. *Leaves of Healing* 17, no. 26, 14 October 1905, 855.

52. *Leaves of Healing* 9, no. 3, 10 May 1902.

53. James Campbell, *Songs of Zion: The African Methodist Episcopal Church in the United States and South Africa* (Oxford: Oxford University Press, 1995).

54. Fitzgerald, *The Evangelicals*, 3.

55. An important exception is Richard Elphick, *The Equality of Believers* (Charlottesville: University of Virginia Press, 2012).

56. E.g., Jean Comaroff and John Comaroff, *Of Revelation and Revolution: Christianity, Colonialism and Consciousness in South Africa* (Chicago: University of Chicago Press, 1997); Campbell, *Songs of Zion*.

57. Pnina Werbner, *Anthropology and the New Cosmopolitanism: Rooted, Feminist and Vernacular Perspectives* (Oxford: Berghahn Books, 2008).

58. Kwame Anthony Appiah, *Cosmopolitanism: Ethics in a World of Strangers* (New York: W. W. Norton, 2006).

1. TEMPERANCE, DIVINE HEALING AND URBAN REFORM IN NINETEENTH-CENTURY AUSTRALIA

1. A contemporary phrase referring to the high society of New York, and by extension social elites of other major world cities. John Russell Bartlett, *Dictionary of Americanisms* (Boston: Little, Brown, 1859), 494.

2. *Melbourne Punch*, 20 November 1884. All Australian periodicals referenced in this chapter are available at http://trove.nla.gov.au/newspaper/.

3. Heather D. Curtis, "Houses of Healing: Sacred Space, Spiritual Practice and the Transformation of Female Suffering in the Faith Cure Movement, 1870–1890," *Church History: Studies in Christianity and Culture* 75, no. 3 (2006): 598–611; James Opp, The *Lord for the Body: Religion, Medicine and Protestant Faith Healing in Canada, 1880–1930* (Montreal: McGill-Queen's University Press, 2005), 9.

4. Heather D. Curtis, *Faith in the Great Physician: Suffering and Divine Healing in American Culture, 1860–1900* (Baltimore: Johns Hopkins University Press, 2007), 167–191.

5. James Robinson, *Divine Healing* (London: Pickwick, 2011), 1:130.

6. An exception is Barry Chant's "The Australian Career of John Alexander Dowie" (paper presented to the Centre for the Study of Australian Christianity, 10 August 1992). There is also a brief entry on Dowie in H. J. Gibney, *Australian Dictionary of Biography*, Vol. 4 (Melbourne: Melbourne University Press, 1972), http://adb.anu.edu.au/biography/dowie-john-alexander-3434.

7. James Belich, *Replenishing the Earth: The Settler Revolution and the Rise of the Anglo World, 1783–1939* (Oxford: Oxford University Press, 2009), 356.

8. Stuart MacIntyre and Sean Scalmer, "Colonial States and Civil Society, 1860–1890," in *Cambridge History of Australia*, ed. Alison Bashford and Stuart MacIntyre (Cambridge: Cambridge University Press, 2013), 4:193.

9. Lionel Frost, "The Urban History Literature of Australia and New Zealand," *Journal of Urban History* 22, no. 1 (1995): 142.

10. Stephen Alomes, "Australian Nationalism in the Eras of Imperialism and Internationalism," *Australian Journal of Politics & History* 34, no. 3 (1988): 321.

11. David Hamer, *New Towns in the New World: Images and Perceptions of the Nineteenth-Century Urban Frontier* (New York: Columbia University Press, 1990), 226.

12. Penelope Edmonds, *Urbanizing Frontiers: Indigenous Peoples and Settlers in Nineteenth-Century Pacific Rim Cities* (Vancouver: University of British Columbia Press, 2010), 57, 157.

13. Shirley Fitzgerald, *Rising Damp: Sydney, 1870–1890* (Oxford: Oxford University Press, 1987), 200.

14. Graeme Davison, "Festivals of Nationhood: The International Exhibitions," in *Australian Cultural History*, ed. S. L. Goldberg and F. S. Smith (Cambridge: Cambridge University Press, 1988), 165.

15. Fitzgerald, *Rising Damp,* 147; Melissa Bellanta, "Leary Kin: Australian Larrikins and the Blackface Minstrel Dandy," *Journal of Social History* 42, no. 3 (2009): 685.

16. Fitzgerald, *Rising Damp,* 105; Alan J. Mayne, *Fever, Squalor and Vice: Sanitation and Social Policy in Victorian Sydney* (St Lucia: University of Queensland Press, 1982), 12.

17. Hamer, *New Towns in the New World,* 68.

18. Mayne, *Fever, Squalor and Vice,* 91–98.

19. Mayne, *Fever, Squalor and Vice,* 74, 167, 196, 220.

20. Bruce Haley, *The Healthy Body and Victorian Culture* (Cambridge, MA: Harvard University Press, 1978), 12; Robert Fuller, *Alternative Medicine and American Religious Life* (Oxford: Oxford University Press, 1989), 63–66.

21. Deana Heath, *Purifying Empire: Obscenity and the Politics of Moral Regulation in Britain, India and Australia* (Cambridge: Cambridge University Press, 2010), 109.

22. Laksiri Jayasuriya, David Walker and Jan Gothard, eds., *Legacies of White Australia: Race, Culture and Nation* (Crawley: University of Western Australian Press, 2003), 42–45.

23. Janet MacCalman and Rebecca Kippen, "Population and Health," in *Cambridge History of Australia*, 299.

24. Neville Hicks, *This Sin and Scandal: Australia's Population Debate, 1891–1911* (Canberra: Australia National University Press, 1978), 32, 85; Jayasuriya et al., *Legacies of White Australia,* 22; Alison Bashford, *Imperial Hygiene: A Critical History of Colonialism, Nationalism and Public Health* (London: Palgrave Macmillan, 2004), 2.

25. Stuart Piggin, *Evangelical Christianity in Australia: Spirit, Word and World* (Oxford: Oxford University Press, 1996), 51.

26. Walter Phillips, *Defending a "Christian Country": Churchmen and Society in New South Wales in the 1880s and After* (St Lucia: University of Queensland Press, 1981), 12; Piggin, *Evangelical Christianity in Australia,* 43, 57–59.

27. Diana Winston, *Red Hot and Righteous: The Urban Religion of the Salvation Army* (Cambridge, MA: Harvard University Press, 1999), 30; Clifford Putney, *Muscular Christianity: Manhood and Sports in Protestant America, 1880–1920* (Cambridge, MA: Harvard University Press, 2001), 40.

28. Phillips, *Defending a Christian Country,* 148.

29. Graeme Davison and David Dunstan, "This Moral Pandemonium: Images of Low Life," in *The Outcasts of Melbourne: Essays in Social History,* ed. Graeme Davison and David Dunstan, Kindle edition (Sydney: Allen and Unwin, 2005).

30. Kerreen Reiger, *The Disenchantment of the Home: Modernizing the Australian Family, 1880–1940* (Oxford: Oxford University Press, 1985), 33.

31. Graeme Davison, *The Rise and Fall of Marvelous Melbourne* (Melbourne: Melbourne University Press, 1978), 254.

32. Edward Sidney Kiek, *An Apostle in Australia: the Life and Reminiscences of Joseph Coles Kirby, Christian Pioneer and Social Reformer* (London: Independent Press, 1927), 94–95.

33. Ian Tyrrell, *Women's World, Women's Empire: The Women's Christian Temperance Union in International Perspective, 1880–1930* (Chapel Hill: University of North Carolina Press, 1991), 18.

34. Davison and Dunstan, "Moral Pandemonium."

35. Phillips, *Defending a Christian Country,* 64.

36. Phillips, *Defending a Christian Country,* 142.

37. Bernard Barrett, *The Inner Suburbs: The Evolution of an Industrial Area* (Melbourne: Melbourne University Press, 1971), 68–69.

38. Davison and Dunstan, "Moral Pandemonium."

39. Mayne, *Fever, Squalor and Vice,* 116–117.

40. Anne O'Brien, "Religion," in *Cambridge History of Australia,* 428.

41. Michelle Allen, *Cleansing the City: Sanitary Geographies in Victorian London* (Athens: Ohio University Press, 2008), 125; Gareth Stedman Jones, *Outcast London: A Study in the Relationship between Classes in Victorian Society* (Oxford: Clarendon Press, 1971), 289.

42. Robert Nye, "The Bio-Medical Origins of Urban Sociology," *Journal of Contemporary History* 20, no. 4 (1985): 664.

43. Graeme Davison, "Introduction," in *Outcast Melbourne.*

44. Melissa Bellanta, "Leary Kin," 686–687.

45. Melissa Bellanta and Simon Sleight, "The Leary Larrikin: Street Style in Colonial Australia," *Cultural and Social History* 11, no. 2 (2014): 263–283.

46. Bellanta, "Leary Kin," 685.

47. Bellanta, "Leary Kin," 685.

48. Bellanta and Sleight, "Leary Larrikin," 273.

49. William Booth, *In Darkest England and the Way Out* (London: Salvation Army, 1890), cited in Pamela Walker, *Pulling the Devil's Kingdom Down: The Salvation Army in Victorian Britain* (Berkeley: University of California Press, 2001), 236.

50. Walker, *Salvation Army,* 236.

51. Blair Ussher, "The Salvation War," in *Outcast Melbourne.*

52. Phillips, *Defending a Christian Country,* 5.

53. Winston, *Red Hot and Righteous,* 2.

54. *Mercury Weekly and Courier* (Collingwood and Fitzroy), 31 May 1884.

55. *Mercury Weekly and Courier* (Collingwood and Fitzroy), 5 January 1884.

56. Ussher, "Salvation War," in *Outcasts of Melbourne.*

57. Damon S. Adams, "Divine Healing in Australian Protestantism, 1870–1940," *Journal of Religious History* 40, no. 4 (2016): 1.

58. *Mercury Weekly and Courier* (Collingwood and Fitzroy), 27 September 1884.

59. *Mercury Weekly and Courier* (Collingwood and Fitzroy), 6 June 1885.

60. *Mercury Weekly and Courier* (Collingwood and Fitzroy), 21 June 1884.

61. *Mercury Weekly and Courier* (Collingwood and Fitzroy), 2 April 1886.

62. Ussher, "Salvation War."

63. *Mercury Weekly and Courier* (Collingwood and Fitzroy), 1 March 1884.

64. *Mercury Weekly and Courier* (Collingwood and Fitzroy), 13 October 1883.

65. David Bebbington, "Evangelicalism in Modern Scotland," *Scottish Bulletin of Evangelical Theology* 9 (1991): 6–7.

66. Edna Sheldrake, ed., *The Personal Letters of John Alexander Dowie* (Zion City: Wilbur Glenn Voliva, 1912), 13.

67. John Gordon Lindsay, *John Alexander Dowie: A Life Story of Trials, Tragedies and Triumphs* (Dallas: Christ for the Nations, 1980), 6.

68. *The Evangelical Magazine and Missionary Chronicle*, 21, 1843, 36

69. Sheldrake, *John Alexander Dowie*, 13.

70. Malcolm Prentis, *The Scots in Australia: A Study of New South Wales, Victoria and Queensland, 1788–1900* (Sydney: Sydney University Press, 1983), 27.

71. Eric Richards, "Immigrant Lives," *The Flinders History of South Australia*, ed. Eric Richards (Netley, SA: Wakefield Press, 1986), 160.

72. The *South Australian Register,* 24 January 1873 advertised "a large stock of best quality colonial boots and shoes manufactured at the South Australian Boot Factory, Alex. Dowie, proprietor."

73. Eric Richards, "The Peopling of South Australia, 1836–1986," in *Flinders History,* 118.

74. Chant, "John Alexander Dowie," 1–2.

75. Tony Denholm, "Adelaide: A Victorian Bastide," *The Origins of Australia's Capital Cities*, ed. Pamela Statham (Cambridge: Cambridge University Press, 1989), 179.

76. David Bebbington, *Victorian Religious Revivals: Culture and Piety in Local and Global Context* (Oxford: Oxford University Press, 2012), 197.

77. Bebbington, *Victorian Religious Revivals,* 193.

78. Kiek, *Apostle in Australia,* 297.

79. Phillips, *Defending a Christian Country,* 11.

80. Sheldrake, *John Alexander Dowie,* 14.

81. Chant, "John Alexander Dowie," 3.

82. Anna Blainey, "Australia," in *Alcohol and Temperance in Modern History: An International Encyclopedia,* ed. Jack S. Blocker, David M. Fahey, Ian Tyrell) (Oxford: ABC-CLIO, 2003), 75.

83. Blocker et al., *Alcohol and Temperance,* 75.

84. Diane Kirby, *Barmaids: A History of Women's Work in Pubs* (Cambridge: Cambridge University Press, 1997), 39.

85. Barrett, *The Inner Suburbs,* 68.

86. Phillips, *Defending a Christian Country,* 167.
87. Kiek, *Apostle in Australia,* 155, 193–194.
88. Sheldrake, *John Alexander Dowie,* 17, 20.
89. *South Australian Register,* 12 June 1873.
90. *South Australian Register,* 6 February 1873; *Sydney Mail and New South Wales Advertiser,* 26 December 1874.
91. Sheldrake, *John Alexander Dowie,* 18 September 1876, 101.
92. Sheldrake, *John Alexander Dowie,* 1 November 1873, 32.
93. Sheldrake, *John Alexander Dowie,* 18 September 1876, 101.
94. Sheldrake, *John Alexander Dowie,* 23.
95. *Adelaide Observer,* 18 May 1872.
96. *Sydney Mail and New South Wales Advertiser,* 30 October 1875.
97. *Sydney Evening News,* 28 November 1876.
98. *Sydney Morning Herald,* 12 May 1877.
99. *Sydney Morning Herald,* 12 May 1877.
100. *Australian Town and Country Journal,* 22 May 1880.
101. *Australian Town and Country Journal,* 22 May 1880.
102. Sheldrake, *John Alexander Dowie,* 29 October 1877, 138.
103. Sheldrake, *John Alexander Dowie,* 22 October 1877, 120.
104. Sheldrake, *John Alexander Dowie,* 18 September 1876, 101.
105. *Maitland Mercury and Hunter River General Advertiser,* 3 March 1877.
106. Kiek, *Apostle in Australia,* 297.
107. John Alexander Dowie, *Sin in the Camp: Being an Account of Nine Months Work in the Tabernacle, Sackville Street, Collingwood and a Vindication of Character by the Rev. John Alexander Dowie* (Melbourne: Henry Cooke, 1883), 7.
108. Sheldrake, *John Alexander Dowie,* 26 September 1879, 224.
109. Dowie, *Sin in the Camp,* 7.
110. John Alexander Dowie, *The Drama, The Press and the Pulpit, by the Rev. John Alexander Dowie, Being a Phonographic Report (Revised) of Two Lectures delivered by the Victoria Theatre, Sydney* (Sydney: Jarrett & Co., 1879), 49.
111. *Freeman's Journal,* 13 March 1880.
112. *Freeman's Journal,* 13 March 1880.
113. *Freeman's Journal,* 13 March 1880.
114. *South Australian Register,* 12 August 1876.
115. Sheldrake, *John Alexander Dowie,* 26 September 1879, 225.
116. *Sydney Evening News,* 16 October 1879.
117. *Sydney Morning Herald,* 17 December 1879.
118. Dowie, *Sin in the Camp,* 58.
119. Sheldrake, *John Alexander Dowie,* 12 February 1880, 266.
120. *Brisbane Telegraph,* 21 January 1886.
121. *South Australian Advertiser,* 15 June 1881.
122. *South Australian Advertiser,* 15 June 1881.
123. *South Australian Register,* 26 July 1881.

124. Jennifer Hein, "A Crisis of Leadership: John Alexander Dowie and the Salvation Army in South Australia," *Journal of the Historical Society of South Australia* 39 (2011): 65–77.

125. *Border Watch,* 6 August 1881.

126. Hein, "Dowie and the Salvation Army," 72.

127. Dowie, *Sin in the Camp,* 9.

128. Dowie, *Sin in the Camp,* 9.

129. Dowie, *Sin in the Camp,* 9.

130. Dowie, Sin in the Camp, 12.

131. The *Melbourne Argus,* 3 March and 7 March 1883.

132. Dowie, *Sin in the Camp,* 99.

133. Dowie, *Sin in the Camp,* 100.

134. *Mercury and Weekly Courier,* 9 August 1884; *Melbourne Argus,* 8 August 1885.

135. *Melbourne Argus,* 23 June 1883.

136. Dowie, *Sin in the Camp,* 103.

137. Dowie, *Sin in the Camp,* 103.

138. Curtis, *Faith in the Great Physician,* 175.

139. Curtis, *Faith in the Great Physician,* 176.

140. Curtis, *Faith in the Great Physician,* 178.

141. Curtis, *Faith in the Great Physician,* 168.

142. Lindsay, *John Alexander Dowie,* 14.

143. Chant, "John Alexander Dowie," 8. Sheldrake says 1884. Sheldrake, *John Alexander Dowie,* 314.

144. My argument here is contrary to Chant's, who claims it was "improbable" that Dowie was influenced by the international divine healing movement. Chant, "John Alexander Dowie," 9.

145. *South Australian Weekly Chronicle,* 10 May 1884.

146. Adams, "Australian Protestantism," 3–4.

147. William E. Boardman, *Record of the International Conference on Divine Healing and True Holiness, Held at the Agricultural Hall (St Mary's Agricultural Hall, Islington)* (London: J. Snow & Co., 1885), vi, 171–175.

148. Adams, "Australian Protestantism," 9.

149. Curtis, *Faith in the Great Physician,* 183.

150. John Alexander Dowie, *Record of the Fifth Annual Commemoration of the Rev. John Alexander Dowie and Mrs Dowie's Ministry of Healing Through Faith in Jesus, Held in the Free Christian Tabernacle, Fitzroy, Melbourne, Lord's Day December 4th and Monday December 5th, 1887. Containing Testimonies from Those Healed, and Ebenezer Address* (Melbourne: M. L. Hutchinson, 1888), 10.

151. Boardman, *International Conference on Divine Healing,* 69.

152. *Fitzroy City Press,* 20 August 1887.

153. *Leaves of Healing* 1, no. 1, July 1888, 52; F. B. Smith, "Spiritualism in Victoria in the Late Nineteenth Century," *Journal of Religious History* 3 (1965): 248.

154. Dowie, *Fifth Annual Commemoration,* 45.
155. Dowie, *Ministry of Healing Through Faith,* 18; Boardman, International Conference, 69.
156. Dowie, *Ministry of Healing Through Faith,* 25.
157. *Leaves of Healing* 1, no. 2, July 1888, 49–52.
158. *Mercury and Weekly Courier,* 15 September 1883.
159. *Fitzroy City Press,* 20 August 1887.
160. *Mercury and Weekly Courier* (Collingwood), 15 September 1883; *Geelong Advertiser,* 17 October 1884.
161. *Mercury and Weekly Courier* (Collingwood), 15 September 1883.
162. Boardman, *International Conference,* 69.
163. *Leaves of Healing* 1, no. 1, July 1888, 8.
164. *Freeman's Journal,* 18 March 1880.
165. *Leaves of Healing* 1, no. 1, July 1888, 24.
166. Dowie, *Fifth Annual Commemoration,* 7.
167. *Geelong Advertiser,* 29 April 1884.
168. *Clarence and Richmond Examiner and New England Enquirer,* 31 May 1887.
169. *Fitzroy City Press,* 20 August 1887.
170. John Alexander Dowie, *Rome's Polluted Springs, Being an Examination of and a Reply to Archbishop Vaughan's Address on Hidden Springs* (Sydney: William Maddock Publisher, 1877), 11.
171. *Bendigo Advertiser,* 21 September 1883. Dowie's polemical public debate with Thomas Walker, a Melbourne Spiritualist and member of the Victorian Association of Spiritualists was printed and published in tract form in 1882, John Alexander Dowie, *Spiritualism Unmasked, Being a Correspondence between the Rev. John Alex. Dowie and Mr. Thomas Walker, Lecturer for the Victorian Association of Spiritualists, Introduction by Mr Dowie* (Melbourne: George Robertson Publisher, 1882).
172. Sheldrake, *John Alexander Dowie,* 6 September 1888.
173. *Mercury and Weekly Courier,* 15 September 1883.
174. Boardman, *International Conference on Divine Healing,* 69.
175. Dowie, *Fifth Annual Commemoration,* 58.
176. Dowie, *Fifth Annual Commemoration,* 22.
177. Davison, "Introduction," in *Outcasts of Melbourne.*
178. Davison, "Introduction,"' in *Outcasts of Melbourne;* Davison, *Rise and Fall of Marvellous Melbourne,* 120.
179. Janet McCalman, *Sex and Suffering: Women's Health and a Women's Hospital: The Royal Women's Hospital, Melbourne, 1856–1996* (Melbourne: Melbourne University Press, 1999), 3.
180. McCalman, *Sex and Suffering,* 59–64.
181. Reiger, *Disenchantment of the Home,* 106.
182. Harold Love, *James Edward Neild: Victorian Virtuoso* (Melbourne: University of Melbourne Press, 1989), 148.
183. T. S. Pensabene, *The Rise of the Medical Practitioner in Melbourne* (Victoria, Canberra: Australian National University, 1981), 126.

184. *Clarence and Richmond Examiner and New England Enquirer,* 31 May 1887.

185. For a discussion of medical heterodoxies in colonial India, see Shinjini Das, "Biography and Homeopathy in Bengal: Colonial Lives of a European Heterodoxy," *Modern Asian Studies* 49, no. 6 (2015): 1732–1771.

186. *Mercury and Weekly Courier,* 15 September 1883.

187. Boardman, *International Conference,* 19.

188. Dowie, *Fifth Annual Commemoration,* 45.

189. Dowie, *Fifth Annual Commemoration,* 60.

190. Dowie, *Fifth Annual Commemoration,* 31.

191. *Clarence and Richmond Examiner and New England Advertiser,* 3 May 1887.

192. *The Colac Herald,* 3 October 1884; *The Mafra Spectator,* 4 January 1886.

193. *Bendigo Advertiser,* 21 September 1883. Dowie's polemical public debate with Thomas Walker, a Melbourne Spiritualist and member of the Victorian Association of Spiritualists was published in tract form in 1882, Dowie, *Spiritualism Unmasked.*

194. Sheldrake, *John Alexander Dowie,* 6 September 1888, 336.

195. *South Australian Advertiser,* 17 November 1881.

196. *Fitzroy City Press,* 27 June 1885.

197. *Mercury and Weekly Courier* (Collingwood), 5 October 1886.

198. Adams, "Australian Protestantism," 14; Raymond J. Cunningham, "From Holiness to Healing: The Faith Cure in America, 1872–1892," *Church History* 43 (1974): 506–512.

199. *Border Watch,* 17 May 1884.

200. *Border Watch,* 17 May 1884.

201. *Leaves of Healing* 1, no. 1, June 1888, 29.

202. *Melbourne Argus,* 3 March 1883.

203. *Australian Town and Country Journal,* 9 May 1885.

204. *South Australian Weekly Chronicle,* 6 June 1885.

205. *Fitzroy City Press,* 30 May 1885.

206. *Melbourne Advocate,* 6 June 1885.

207. *Fitzroy City Press,* 31 July 1886.

208. *South Australian Advertiser,* 5 July 1886.

209. *Fitzroy City Press,* 3 July 1886.

210. *Fitzroy City Press,* 3 July 1886.

211. Dowie, *Sin in the Camp,* 12.

212. Boardman, *International Conference on Divine Healing,* 51–52, 64.

213. Curtis, *Faith in the Great Physician,* 184.

214. *Leaves of Healing* 1, no. 1, 1 June 1888, 10.

215. Dowie, *Fifth Annual Commemoration,* 60.

216. *Leaves of Healing* 1, no. 1, 1 June 1888, 3.

217. *Leaves of Healing* 1, no. 1, 1 June 1888, 3.

2. CHRISTIAN COSMOPOLITANISM AND ZION CITY IN THE AMERICAN MIDWEST

1. Jean Miller Schmidt, *Souls or the Social Order: The Two-Party System in American Protestantism* (Brooklyn, NY: Carlson, 1991), xxxii; Martin Marty, *Righteous Empire: The Protestant Experience in America* (New York: Dial Press, 1970), 179, 183. For an overview of these debates, see J. Michael Utzinger, *Yet Saints Their Watch are Keeping: Fundamentalists, Modernists and the Development of Evangelical Ecclesiology, 1887–1937* (Macon, GA: Mercer University Press, 2006), 145–148.

2. Thekla Ellen Joiner, *Sin in the City: Chicago and Revivalism, 1880–1920* (Columbia: University of Missouri Press, 2007), 14, 36; Heath W. Carter, *Union Made: Working People and the Rise of Social Christianity in Chicago* (Oxford: Oxford University Press, 2015).

3. Philip L. Cook, *Zion City, Illinois, Twentieth-Century Utopia* (Syracuse: Syracuse University Press, 1996), ix.

4. *American First Fruits: Being a Brief Record of Eight Months Divine Healing Missions in the State of California, Conducted by the Rev. John Alexander Dowie and Mrs Dowie* (San Francisco: Leaves of Healing Office, 1889), 82; Robert C. Reinders, "Training for a Prophet: The West Coast Ministry of John Alexander Dowie, 1888–1890," *Pacific Historian* 30, no. 1 (Spring 1986): 20.

5. *Our Second Year's Harvest: Being a Brief Record of a Year of Divine Healing Missions on the Pacific Coast of America in California, Oregon, Washington and British Columbia, conducted by the Rev. John Alexander Dowie and Mrs Dowie* (Chicago: Headquarters of the International Divine Healing Association, 1891), 4, 20, 35.

6. Reinders, "West Coast Ministry," 10.

7. *Our Second Year's Harvest*, 172.

8. Reinders, "West Coast Ministry," 7.

9. Reinders, "West Coast Ministry," 7.

10. Curtis, *Faith in the Great Physician*, 193–201.

11. Heather D. Curtis, *Faith in Great Physician: Suffering and Divine Healing in American Culture, 1860–1900* (Baltimore: Johns Hopkins University Press, 2007), 198–200.

12. *Los Angeles Daily Herald*, 7 June 1889.

13. *American First Fruits*, 67.

14. *Leaves of Healing* 1, no. 35, 7 June 1895.

15. *Pittsburg Times*, 10 October 1891; A. B. Simpson, ed., *The Christian Alliance Yearbook, 1888* (New York: Word, World and Work Publishing Company, 1888), 60.

16. Carrie F. Judd, "Bethany Home in Pittsburg, PA," *Triumphs of Faith* 8 (March 1883): 98.

17. Simpson, *Christian Alliance Yearbook*, 65; *Pittsburgh Dispatch*, n.d., 1891.

18. *Pittsburg Dispatch*, 2 November 1891.

19. *Pittsburgh Times*, 10 November 1891.

20. Joiner, *Sin in the City*, 21.

21. Dominic A. Pacyga, *Polish Immigrants and Industrial Chicago: Workers on the South Side, 1880–1920* (Columbus: Ohio State University Press, 1991), 24; William Cronon, *Nature's Metropolis: Chicago and the Great West* (New York: Norton, 1991).

22. Bessie Louise Pierce, *A History of Chicago* (Chicago: University of Chicago Press, 1937), 20.

23. Pierce, *A History of Chicago*, 22.

24. John Bodnar, *The Transplanted: A History of Immigrants in Urban America* (Bloomington: Indiana University Press, 1985), 14.

25. Hartmut Keil and John B. Jentz, eds., *German Workers in Chicago: A Documentary History of Working-Class Culture from 1850 to World War I* (DeKalb: Northern Illinois University Press, 1988), 1.

26. Ulf Beijbom, *Swedes in Chicago: A Demographic and Social Study of the 1846–1880 Immigration* (Copenhagen: Vaxjo Press, 1971), 114.

27. Beijbom, *Swedes in Chicago*, 112.

28. H. Arnold Barton, "Swedish Travelers' Accounts of Chicago," in *Swedish-American Life in Chicago: Cultural and Urban Aspects of an Immigrant People*, ed. Philip J. Anderson and Dag Blanck (Uppsala: University of Uppsala Press, 1991), 105.

29. Beijbom, *Swedes in Chicago*, 349; Joy K. Lintelman, "America is the Woman's Promised Land: Swedish Immigrant Women and American Domestic Service," *Journal of American Ethnic History* 8, no. 2 (1989): 9–23.

30. James R. Barrett, *Work and Community in the Jungle: Chicago's Packinghouse Workers, 1894–1922* (Urbana: University of Illinois Press, 1987), 45–46; Pierce, *History of Chicago*, 33; Hartmut Keil, "Chicago's German Working Class in 1900," in *German Workers in Industrial Chicago, 1850–1910: A Comparative Perspective*, ed. Hartmut Keil and John B. Jentz (DeKalb: Northern Illinois University Press, 1983), 24.

31. Robert W. Rydell, *All the World's a Fair: Visions of Empire at American International Expositions, 1876–1916* (Chicago: University of Chicago Press, 1984), 38–71.

32. Richard Schneirov, Shelton Stromquist, and Nick Salvatore, eds., *The Pullman Strike and the Crisis of the 1890s: Essays on Labor and Politics* (Urbana: University of Illinois Press, 1999), 2.

33. Pierce, *History of Chicago*, 55; Stanley Buder, *Pullman: An Experiment in Industrial Order and Community Planning, 1880–1930* (Oxford: Oxford University Press, 1967), 34.

34. Buder, *Pullman*, 34.

35. Stephen G. Cobb, *Reverend William Carwardine and the Pullman Strike of 1894: The Christian Gospel and Social Justice* (Lewiston: Edwin Mellen Press, 1992), 36.

36. Richard Schneirov, Shelton Stromquist, and Nick Salvatore, "Introduction" in Schneirov et al., *Pullman Strike*, 7.

37. Carter, *Rise of Social Christianity in Chicago*, 7.

38. Richard Schneirov, "New Perspectives on Socialism: The Socialist Party Revisited," *Journal of the Gilded Age and Progressive Era* 2, no. 3 (2003): 245.

39. Edward Bellamy, *Looking Backward: 2000–1887* (Boston: Ticknor & Co., 1888).

40. Carl Smith, *Urban Disorder and the Shape of Belief: The Great Chicago Fire, the Haymarket Bomb and the Model Town of Pullman* (Chicago: University of Chicago Press, 1995), 111.

41. Heath W. Carter, "Scab Ministers, Striking Saints: Christianity and Class Conflict in 1894 Chicago," *American Nineteenth Century History* 11, no. 3 (2010): 323.

42. Smith, *Urban Disorder,* 4.

43. Barrett, *Work and Community in the Jungle,* 141.

44. Pacyga, *Polish Immigrants and Industrial Chicago,* 7.

45. Eric L. Hirsch, *Ethnic Revolt: Urban Politics in the Nineteenth-Century Chicago Labor Movement* (Berkeley: University of California Press, 1990), 144–145.

46. Carter, "Christianity and Class Conflict," 321–326.

47. Ken Fones-Wolf, "Religion and Trade Union Politics in the United States, 1880–1920," *International Labor and Working-Class History* 34 (Fall 1988): 45; William A. Mirola, "Asking for Bread, Receiving a Stone: The Rise and Fall of Religious Ideologies in Chicago's Eight-Hour Movement," *Social Problems* 50, no. 2 (2003): 288.

48. Amy Kittelstrom, "The International Social Turn: Unity and Brotherhood at the World's Parliament of Religions, Chicago, 1893," *Religion and American Culture: A Journal of Interpretation* 19 (2009): 249.

49. Carter, "Christianity and Class Conflict," 332.

50. Cobb, *Pullman Strike,* 42–43.

51. Cobb, *Pullman Strike,* 43.

52. Cobb, *Pullman Strike,* 44.

53. Carter, "Christianity and Class Conflict," 333.

54. Gutman, "Protestantism and the American Labor Movement: The Christian Spirit in the Gilded Age," *American Historical Review* 72, no. 1 (1966): 82.

55. Gutman, "American Labor Movement," 91.

56. Carter, "Christianity and Class Conflict," 334.

57. Joiner, *Sin in the City,* 66.

58. Joiner, *Sin in the City,* 85–108.

59. *Pittsburg Gazette,* 6 October 1891.

60. *Chicago Tribune,* 28 July 1890.

61. Kittelstrom, "World's Parliament of Religions," 243–274.

62. *Chicago Tribune,* 24 April 1894.

63. Rydell, *All the World's a Fair,* 62–64.

64. *Leaves of Healing* 1, no. 4, 21 September 1894.

65. *Leaves of Healing* 1, no. 9, 9 November 1894.

66. *Leaves of Healing* 4, no. 38, 15 July 1898.

67. *Leaves of Healing* 1, no. 39, 5 July 1895.

68. Reinders, *West Coast Ministry,* 11.

69. *Pittsburg Post,* 14 October 1891.

70. *Leaves of Healing* 2, no. 45, 4 September 1896.

71. *Zion Historical Society Magazine*, Series 4, 1971, "Who's Who in Zion."
72. *Zion Historical Society Magazine*, Series 4, 1971, "Who's Who in Zion."
73. *Leaves of Healing* 14, no. 19, 27 February 1904.
74. Interview with Luann and Tim Kuehl, Johannesburg, South Africa, 23 November 2015.
75. Monica Kusch, "Zion, Illinois: An Attempt at a Theocratic City" (PhD diss., University of California, 1954), 108.
76. Pierce, *History of Chicago*, 511; "Quondam," in *The Adventures of Uncle Jeremiah and Family at the Great Fair* (Chicago: Laird & Lee, 1893).
77. *Leaves of Healing* 6, no. 14, 27 January 1900.
78. *Leaves of Healing* 1, no. 13, 7 December 1894.
79. Bodnar, *The Transplanted*, 144–168.
80. Karl A. Olsson, "Dwight L. Moody and some Chicago Swedes," in *Swedish-American Life in Chicago*, 323.
81. Olsson, "Dwight L. Moody," 307–323; Lillian Taiz, "Applying the Devil's Works in a Holy Cause: Working Class Popular Culture and the Salvation Army in the United States, 1879–1900," *Religion and American Culture*, 7, 2 (1997), 199.
82. *Leaves of Healing* 10, no. 24, 5 April 1902.
83. *Leaves of Healing* 2, no. 37, 3 July 1896.
84. *Leaves of Healing* 3, no. 34, 19 June 1897.
85. *Leaves of Healing* 3, no. 43, 21 August 1897.
86. *Leaves of Healing* 17, no. 4, 13 May 1905.
87. *Leaves of Healing* 11, no. 16, 9 August 1902.
88. *Leaves of Healing* 1, no. 8, 19 October 1894.
89. *Chicago Tribune*, 27 February 1895.
90. Christ Community Church Archives, Zion, Illinois (hereafter CCC), Hand-written register book, 1 May 1896 to 1 May 1898.
91. *Leaves of Healing* 1, no. 39, 5 July 1895.
92. *Leaves of Healing* 10, no. 12, 11 January 1902.
93. *Leaves of Healing* 14, no. 9, 19 December 1903.
94. *Leaves of Healing* 8, no. 20, 9 March 1901.
95. *Leaves of Healing* 11, no. 22, 20 September 1092.
96. Warren Jay Beaman, "From Sect to Cult to Sect: The Christian Catholic Church in Zion" (PhD diss., Iowa State University, 1990), 130.
97. *Philadelphia Times*, 3 December 1899.
98. *Daily News*, Omaha Nebraska, 17 October 1903.
99. *Chicago Inter-ocean*, 16 April 1894.
100. *Leaves of Healing* 1, no. 1, 31 August 1894.
101. *Chicago Tribune*, 30 April 1894.
102. *Leaves of Healing* 1, no. 1, 31 August 1894.
103. *Leaves of Healing* 1, no. 1, 31 August 1894.
104. *Leaves of Healing* 1, no. 1, 7 September 1894.
105. *Leaves of Healing* 1, no. 1, 31 August 1894.
106. *Leaves of Healing* 1, no. 30, 26 April 1895.

107. *Leaves of Healing* 1, no. 30, 26 April 1895. For a discussion of Dowie's Apostolic "restorationism," see Grant Wacker, "Marching to Zion: Religion in a Modern Utopian Community," *Church History* 54, no. 4 (1985): 502–505.

108. E.g., "Sunday Observations" (*Fackel,* 14 September 1884), cited in Keil and Jentz, *German Workers in Chicago,* 357.

109. *Leaves of Healing* 2, no. 17, 31 January 1896.

110. *Leaves of Healing* 3, no. 3, 13 November 1896.

111. *Leaves of Healing* 4, no. 27, 30 April 1898.

112. *Leaves of Healing* 2, no. 4, 1 November 1895.

113. *Leaves of Healing* 2, no. 37, 3 July 1896; no. 3, 4, 20 November 1896; 4, no. 26, 21 April 1900.

114. James R. Grossman, *Land of Hope: Chicago, Black Southerners and the Great Migration* (Chicago: University of Chicago Press, 1989), 32.

115. Reed, *Black Chicago's First Century,* 242.

116. William Cohen, *At Freedom's Edge: Black Mobility and the Southern White Quest for Racial Control, 1861–1915* (Baton Rouge: Louisiana State University Press, 1991), 105–108; Christopher Robert Reed, *Black Chicago's First Century, Volume One, 1833–1900* (Columbus: University of Missouri Press, 2005), 339.

117. Reed, *Black Chicago's First Century,* 243.

118. Barrett, *Work and Community in the Jungle,* 47.

119. Pierce, *History of Chicago,* 48; Horace Cayton and St Clair Drake, *Black Metropolis: A Study in Negro Life in a Northern City* (New York: Harper & Row, 1962), 47.

120. Cohen, *Black Mobility,* 101.

121. Reed, *Black Chicago's First Century,* 340–342.

122. *Leaves of Healing* 4, no. 49, 1 October 1898.

123. Dowie, *Our Second Year's Harvest,* 40.

124. *Leaves of Healing* 2, no. 34, 12 June 1896.

125. *Leaves of Healing* 2, no. 34, 12 June 1896; CCC, Registration of Guests in Zion Home, John G. Speicher's handwritten log book, 1st May 1896–1st May 1898.

126. *Leaves of Healing* 15, no. 8, 11 June 1904.

127. *Leaves of Healing* 2, no. 27, 1 May 1896.

128. *Leaves of Healing* 4, no. 49, 1 October 1898.

129. *Leaves of Healing* 3, no. 39, 24 July 1897.

130. *Leaves of Healing* 3, no. 2, 6 November 1896.

131. *Zion Banner,* 2 August 1904.

132. *Leaves of Healing* 3, no. 41, 7 August 1897.

133. Reed, *Black Chicago's First Century,* 268.

134. *Leaves of Healing* 7, no. 19, 1 September 1900.

135. *Leaves of Healing* 3, no. 5, 27 November 1896.

136. *Leaves of Healing* 4, no. 11, 8 January 1898.

137. *Leaves of Healing* 5, no. 15, 4 February 1899.

138. *Leaves of Healing* 3, no. 5, 27 November 1896.

139. *Pittsburgh Gazette,* 6 November 1891.

140. Amy Kaplan and Donald E. Pease, eds., *Cultures of United States Imperialism* (Durham: Duke University Press, 1993).

141. *Leaves of Healing* 1, no. 9, 9 November 1894.

142. Reginald Horsman, *Race and Manifest Destiny: The Origins of American Racial Anglo-Saxonism* (Cambridge, MA: Harvard University Press, 1981), 116–138; Colin Kidd, *The Forging of Races: Race and Scripture in the Protestant Atlantic World, 1600–2000* (Cambridge: Cambridge University Press, 2006), 129.

143. Douglas Lorimer, "Theoretical Racism in Late-Victorian Anthropology, 1870–1900," *Victorian Studies* 31, no. 3 (1988): 405.

144. *Leaves of Healing* 15, no. 8, 11 June 1904.

145. *Leaves of Healing* 13, no. 22, 19 September 1903.

146. *Leaves of Healing* 13, no. 22, 19 September 1903.

147. Grant Wacker, "Playing for Keeps: The Primitivist Impulse in Early Pentecostalism," in *American Quest for the Primitive Church,* ed. Richard Hughes (Urbana: University of Illinois Press, 1988).

148. *Zion Banner,* 1 September 1905.

149. *Leaves of Healing,* 30 December 1905.

150. *Leaves of Healing* 17, no. 21, 9 September 1905.

151. Cayton and Drake, *Black Metropolis,* 22.

152. William T. Stead, *If Christ Came to Chicago: A Plea for the union of all who love in the service of all who suffer* (London: Published at the Office of the "Review of Reviews," 1894).

153. Stanley Buder, *Visionaries and Planners: The Garden City Movement and the Modern Community* (Oxford: Oxford University Press, 1990).

154. Daphne Spain, *How Women Saved the City* (Minneapolis: University of Minnesota Press, 2001), 16–17.

155. Richard Schneirov, Shelton Stromquist, and Nick Salvatore, "Introduction," in *The Pullman Strike and the Crisis of the 1890s: Essays on Labor and Politics* (Urbana: University of Illinois Press, 1999), 7.

156. *Chicago Tribune,* 28 February 1898.

157. *Chicago Inter-Ocean,* 2 July 1895. See also *Chicago Tribune,* 8 June 1895 for similar complaints.

158. Timothy Gloege, "Faith Healing, Medical Regulation and Public Religion in Progressive-Era Chicago," *Religion and American Culture: A Journal of Interpretation* 23, no. 2 (2013): 196.

159. *Leaves of Healing* 1, no. 36, 14 June 1895.

160. *Chicago Inter-Ocean,* 20 June 1895.

161. Hilary Marland and Anne Marie Rafferty, eds., *Midwives, Society and Childbirth: Debates and Controversies in the Modern Period* (London: Routledge, 1997), especially chapters 7 and 9.

162. *Chicago Tribune,* 29 July 1899.

163. *Chicago Tribune,* 29 July 1899, 17 August 1899.

164. *Chicago Tribune,* 10 December 1895.

165. *Leaves of Healing* 1, no. 22, 15 February 1895.

166. *Leaves of Healing* 2, no. 47, 18 September 1896.

167. *Leaves of Healing* 4, no. 11, 8 January 1898.

168. *Leaves of Healing* 6, no. 21, 17 March 1900.

169. *Leaves of Healing* 13, no. 7, 6 June 1903.

170. *Albany Journal* (New York), 6 January 1900.

171. *Zion Banner,* 3 May 1904; Kusch, "Zion, Illinois," 2.

172. Kusch, "Zion, Illinois," 98.

173. Kusch, "Zion, Illinois," 95.

174. Kusch, "Zion, Illinois," 102.

175. Rolvix Harlan, "John Alexander Dowie: The Christian Catholic Apostolic Church in Zion" (PhD diss., University of Chicago, 1906), 169.

176. Interview with Lee Deming, Zion, Illinois, 23 July 2013.

177. CCC, Lucille Bidille, "Zion Facts According to Lucille Bidille," 24.

178. *Outlook,* 13 September 1902.

179. *Leaves of Healing* 16, no. 26, 15 April 1905.

180. *Washington D.C. Times,* 25 November 1901.

181. *Marshfield News Wisconsin,* 19 February 1902.

182. *Boston Herald,* 11 November 1903.

183. *Leaves of Healing* 12, no. 5, 22 November 1902.

184. *Leaves of Healing* 17, no. 5, 24 May 1905.

185. *Leaves of Healing* 12, no. 21, 14 March 1903.

186. *Daily Express,* 10 January 1903, cited in *Leaves of Healing* 14, no. 14, 23 January 1904.

187. *Philadelphia Dispatch,* 9 June 1901.

188. *Sydney Daily Telegraph,* 16 May 1904.

189. *Zion Historical Society,* Series 4, 1971, "Who's Who in Zion."

190. *Zion Historical Society,* Series 4, 1971, "Who's Who in Zion."

191. *Leaves of Healing* 7, no. 8, 16 June 1900.

192. Cook, *Zion City,* 97.

193. John Halsey, *A History of Lake County, Illinois* (Chicago: Roy S. Bates, 1912), 36.

194. Bidille, "Zion Facts According to Lucille Biddle," 36.

195. *Leaves of Healing* 3, no. 42, 14 August 1897.

196. For an exception, see *Chicago Daily News,* 20 May 1901.

197. *Zion Banner,* 8 May 1903.

198. *Leaves of Healing* 12, no. 22, 21 March 1903.

199. *Chicago Journal,* 3 November 1905.

200. *Leaves of Healing* 16, no. 1, 22 October 1904; *Chicago Inter-Ocean,* 17 October 1904.

201. *Southern & Alabama Baptist,* Birmingham Alabama, 21 October 1903.

202. *World-Sun* (New York City), 18 October 1903.

203. *New York World,* 6 September 1904.

204. Cook, *Zion City, Illinois,* 47.

205. *Zion-Benton News,* "Zion City's Golden Anniversary," 24 April 1953.

206. Cook, *Zion City,* 47.

207. *Zion-Benton News,* "Zion City's Golden Anniversary."

208. Judge V. V. Barnes, "Civic Life in Zion, Illinois," in Halsey, *History of Lake County,* 747.

209. *Leaves of Healing* 14, no. 16, 6 February 1904.

210. *The Coming City,* 19 September 1900. See also *Municipal Journal and Enquirer,* "The Utopian City of Zion," October 1901.

211. *Leaves of Healing* 13, no. 9, 20 June 1903.

212. Jason D. Martinek, "The Working Man's Bible: Robert Blatchford's *Merrie England,* Radical Literacy and the Making of Debsian Socialism, 1895–1900," *Journal of the Gilded Age and the Progressive Era* 2, no. 3 (2003): 333.

213. Per Nordahl, "Swedish-American Labor in Chicago," in *Swedish-American Life in Chicago,* ed. Anderson and Blanck 216.

214. William A. Mirola, "Shorter Hours and the Protestant Sabbath: Religious Framing and Movement Alliances in late 19th Century Chicago," *Social Science History* 23, no. 3 (1999): 398.

215. *Municipal Journal and Enquirer,* October 1901.

216. *Zion Banner,* 6 November 1901.

217. Bidille, "Zion Facts According to Lucille Biddle," 17.

218. *Zion-Benton News,* "Zion City's Golden Anniversary."

219. *Leaves of Healing* 1, no. 22, 15 February 1895.

220. Interview with R. Mintern, Zion, Illinois, 18 July 2013.

221. *Leaves of Healing* 1, no. 16, 11 January 1895.

222. *London Leader,* 30 October 1900. See also *Nottingham Express,* 5 September 1900; *Nottingham Times,* 8 September 1900. The latter warned lace factory worker readers against "the voice of the charmer in the person of Dr. Dowie."

223. Evelyn Johnson Lampe, "The Founding of Zion City, Illinois" (PhD diss., University of Miami, 1966), 35.

224. Jan Jansen, *Battle for the Garden City* (Green Bay, WI: My Sister Publishing Company, 2011), 63.

225. Newberry Library, Chicago, Midwest MS Zion, Box 35, Folder 7, "The Lace Factory by Katherine Mair."

226. *Waukegan Gazette,* 4 April 1902.

227. *Scranton Times* (Pennsylvania), 18 January 1901.

228. Jansen, *Battle for the Garden City,* 63.

229. *Waukegan Daily Gazette,* 8 January 1900.

230. *Zion Banner,* "Editorial Greeting," 22 May 1901.

231. *Leaves of Healing* 11, no. 22, 20 September 1902.

232. *Leaves of Healing* 13, no. 18, 22 August 1903.

233. *Portland Journal, Oregon,* 6 November 1903.

234. *Waukegan Sun,* 5 April 1902.

235. *Pantagraph* (Bloomington, Illinois), 31 May 1902.

236. Bidille, "Zion Facts According to Lucille Biddle," 24.

237. Cook, *Zion City,* 123.

238. *Leaves of Healing* 11, no. 1, 26 April 1902.

239. Cook, *Zion City,* 122.

240. Cook, *Zion City,* 124.
241. *Philadelphia Post,* 29 July 1899.
242. *Chicago Record,* 5 February 1900.
243. *Leaves of Healing* 10, no. 23, 29 March 1902.
244. *Chicago Chronicle,* 16 April 1900.
245. *Chicago Chronicle,* 5 April 1902.
246. *Waukegan Sun,* 5 April 1902.
247. *Chicago Record,* 31 January 1901; *Hammond Indiana Tribune,* 31 January 1901.
248. *Portland Journal* (Oregon), 6 November 1903.
249. *Leaves of Healing* 10, no. 25, 12 April 1902.
250. *Leaves of Healing* 9, no. 7, 8 June 1901.
251. *Leaves of Healing* 15, no. 23, 24 September 1904.
252. *Leaves of Healing* 15, no. 16, 6 August 1904.
253. *Chicago Daily News,* 7 September 1899.
254. *Leaves of Healing* 14, no. 21, 12 March 1904.
255. Jansen, *Battle for Garden* City, 96.
256. *Zion City News,* 4 September 1908.
257. 13th Census of the United States, Zion, Illinois, 1910, 88.
258. Rolvix Harlan, "John Alexander Dowie and the Christian Catholic Apostolic Church" (PhD diss., University of Chicago, 1906), 17.

3. UNITY AND DIVISION IN EARLY TWENTIETH-CENTURY JOHANNESBURG AND IN TRANSATLANTIC ZION

1. During the period under discussion, this community was still referred to as "Dutch" and "Dutch-speaking." It was only later in the century that a distinct Boer, or Afrikaner, identity and language arose. For clarity's sake, this chapter uses the later term "Boer" to refer to Dutch-speaking migrants from the Cape settled in the interior of South Africa.
2. Charles van Onselen, *Studies in the Social and Economic History of the Witwatersrand, 1886–1914* (Harlow: Longman Group, 1982), 1:1.
3. CCC, Daniel Bryant, "Under the Southern Cross," unpublished manuscript, n.d., 11–12.
4. Shula Marks and Stanley Trapido, "Lord Milner and the South African State," *History Workshop Journal* 8, 1 (1979): 50–81; Saul Dubow, "Colonial Nationalism, The Milner Kindergarten and the Rise of South Africanism, 1902–1910," *History Workshop Journal* 43 (1997): 55.
5. Although see Liz Lang, *White, Poor and Angry: White Working Class Families in Johannesburg* (Aldershot: Ashgate, 2003) for a discussion on Anglicanism amongst working-class whites on the Witwatersrand.
6. *Zion City News,* 28 May 1907; Edith Blumhofer, *Restoring the Faith: The Assemblies of God, Pentecostalism and American Culture* (Champaign: University of Illinois Press, 1993), 31–34.
7. *Leaves of Healing* 5, no. 11, 7 January 1899.

8. *Leaves of Healing* 4, no. 27, 30 April 1898.

9. *Leaves of Healing* 5, no. 4, 8 April 1899; *Leaves of Healing* 5, no. 25, 15 April 1899; 6, no. 23, 31 March 1900; 6, no. 26, 21 April 1900.

10. *Leaves of Healing* 6, no. 3, 11 November 1899.

11. *Leaves of Healing* 5, no. 11, 7 January 1899.

12. *Leaves of Healing* 4, no. 11, 8 January 1898.

13. "Who's Who in Zion, 1901–1907," *Zion Historical Society,* Series 4, 1971, 18.

14. *Leaves of Healing* 6, no. 22, 24 March 1900.

15. *Leaves of Healing* 5, no. 32, 3 June 1899.

16. R. G. Tiedemann, *Reference Guide to Christian Missionary Societies in China: From the Sixteenth to the Twentieth Century* (Armonk, NY: M.E. Sharpe, 2009), 141.

17. *Leaves of Healing* 6, no. 22, 24 March 1900.

18. *Leaves of Healing* 6, no. 8, 16 December 1899.

19. *Leaves of Healing* 8, no. 20, 9 March 1901.

20. Hermann Giliomee, *The Afrikaners: Biography of a People* (London: C. Hurst, 2011), chap. 6.

21. Bill Nasson, *The Boer War: The Struggle for South Africa* (Stroud: History Press, 2010), 21–32.

22. *Leaves of Healing* 5, no. 23, 1 April 1899.

23. Bengt Sundkler, *Zulu Zion and Some Swazi Zionists* (Oxford: Oxford University Press, 1976), 28.

24. Andrew M. Eason, "Desperate Fighting at the Cape: The Salvation Army's Arrival and Earliest Work in Late-Victorian Cape Town," *Journal of Religious History* 33, no. 3 (2009): 273–282.

25. Interview with Edgar Mahon III, Durban, South Africa, 8 January 2016.

26. *The War Cry: Official Gazette of the Salvation Army in South Africa,* 17 October 1891, 6; Apostolic Faith Mission Archives, Johannesburg (hereafter AFM), Le Roux Collection, A. Murray to P. Le Roux, n.d.

27. van Onselen, *Social and Economic History of the Witwatersrand,* 5–7.

28. *Leaves of Healing* 3, no. 37, 10 July 1897.

29. *Leaves of Healing* 4, no. 7, 11 December 1897.

30. Sarah Duff, *Changing Childhoods in the Cape Colony: Dutch Reformed Church Evangelicalism and Colonial Childhood, 1860–1895* (London: Palgrave Macmillan, 2015), 26.

31. T. Dunbar Moodie, *The Rise of Afrikanerdom: Power, Apartheid and the Afrikaner Civil Religion* (Berkeley: University of California Press, 1975), 57ff.; Johann Du Plessis, *The Life of Andrew Murray in South Africa* (London: Marshall Bros, 1920), 230–231.

32. Duff, *Changing Childhoods,* 24–25.

33. Andrew Murray, *Divine Healing: a Series of Addresse*s (New York: Christian Alliance Pub. Co., 1900), preface.

34. Du Plessis, *Andrew Murray,* 337–338.

35. Andrew Le Roux, "My Parents," unpublished manuscript, n.d., property of Lynette Le Roux; Le Roux kept a diary between August to November 1890

describing his ox-cart journey from the Cape to Wakkerstroom; AFM, Diary of P. L. Le Roux, August–November 1890.

36. Le Roux, "My Parents."

37. AFM, Miscellaneous notes by P. L. Le Roux, 2 March 1902.

38. AFM, Le Roux to Revs. Kriel, Marais, Rossouw, Meiring, Bosman, 12 November 1898.

39. Le Roux, "My Parents."

40. AFM, Le Roux to Murray, 12 November 1898.

41. *Leaves of Healing* 5, no. 29, 13 May 1899.

42. *Leaves of Healing* 5, no. 23, 1 April 1899. ZAR stood for "Zuid-Afrikaansche Republiek" (South African Republic), also known as the Transvaal.

43. *Leaves of Healing* 4, no. 21, 19 March 1898.

44. van Onselen, *Social and Economic History of the Witwatersrand*, 111ff.

45. *Leaves of Healing* 5, no. 23, 1 April 1899.

46. Elaine Katz, *The White Death: Silicosis on the Rand Gold Mines, 1886–1910* (Johannesburg: Wits University Press, 1994), 2–3, 135.

47. *Leaves of Healing* 6, no. 25, 14 April 1900.

48. Donal Lowry, "The World's No Bigger Than a Kraal: The South African War and International Opinion," in *The Impact of the South African War*, ed. David Omissi and Andrew Thompson (London: Palgrave, 2002), 269ff.

49. Preben Kaarsholm, "Pro-Boers," in *Patriotism: The Making and Unmaking of British National Identity*, ed. Raphael Samuel (London: Routledge, 1999), 113.

50. Saul Dubow, *Racial Segregation and the Origins of Apartheid, 1919–1936* (London: Macmillan, 1989), 4.

51. *Leaves of Healing* 4, no. 16, 12 February 1898.

52. *Leaves of Healing* 12, no. 12, 10 January 1903.

53. Peter Warwick, *Black People and the South African War, 1899–1902* (Cambridge: Cambridge University Press, 1983), 19ff.

54. John Eddy and Deryck Schreuder, eds., *The Rise of Colonial Nationalism* (Sydney: Allen & Unwin, 1988), 20.

55. Reginald Horsman, *Race and Manifest Destiny: The Origins of American Racial Anglo-Saxonism* (Cambridge, MA: Harvard University Press, 1981), 4–5.

56. Saul Dubow, *Scientific Racism in Modern South Africa* (Cambridge: Cambridge University Press, 1995), 167.

57. Clifford Putney, *Muscular Christianity: Manhood and Sports in Protestant America, 1880–1920* (Cambridge, MA: Harvard University Press, 2001), 4.

58. Marilyn Lake and Henry Reynolds, *Drawing the Global Colour Line: White Men's Countries and the International Challenge of Racial Equality* (Cambridge: Cambridge University Press, 2008), 99–100.

59. Louis Creswicke, ed., *South Africa and its Future* (London: T. C. & E. C. Jack, 1903), 159; Morag Bell, "A Woman's Place in a White Man's Country: Rights, Duties and Citizenship in the New South Africa," *Ecumene* 2, no. 2 (1991): 138.

60. Morag Bell, "The Pestilence that Walketh in Darkness: Imperial Health, Gender and Images of South Africa, 1880–1910," *Transactions of the Institute of British Geographers* 18, no. 3 (1993): 331.

61. Dubow, "Rise of South Africanism," 57.

62. *Rand Daily Mail,* 30 October 1902.

63. *Rand Daily Mail,* 14 August 1903.

64. Katz, *The White Death,* 66, 78; Lis Lange, *White, Poor and Angry: White Working Class Families in Johannesburg* (Ashgate: Aldershot, 2003), 11–15.

65. van Onselen, *Social and Economic History of the Witwatersrand,* 31.

66. Dubow, "Colonial Nationalism," 69.

67. Dubow, "Colonial Nationalism," 70.

68. Shula Marks, "War and Union, 1899–1910," in *The Cambridge History of South Africa,* ed. Robert Ross et al (Cambridge: Cambridge University Press, 2012), 2:173.

69. W. K. Hancock, *Smuts: The Fields of Force* (Cambridge: Cambridge University Press, 1968), 199.

70. Dubow, "Colonial Nationalism," 69.

71. *Rand Daily Mail,* "Editorial," 30 May 1903.

72. Marks, "War and Union," 175.

73. Van Helten and Keith Williams, "The Crying Need of South Africa: The Emigration of Single British Women to the Transvaal, 1901–1910," *Journal of Southern African Studies* 10, no. 1 (1983): 17–18; Onselen, *Social and Economic History of the Witwatersrand,* 26–28.

74. *Rand Daily Mail,* 1 June 1910; *The Imperial Colonist: The Official Organ of the British Women's Emigration Association and the South African Colonization Society,* August 1903, 89–92.

75. *Transvaal Leader,* 2 February 1907.

76. *Transvaal Leader,* 2 February 1907.

77. *Star,* 10 May 1905.

78. *Rand Daily Mail,* 14 November 1903.

79. Sarah Stage, *Female Complaints: Lydia Pinkham and the Business of Women's Medicine* (New York: Norton, 1979), 63. In the years before the South African War, the Transvaal was dubbed a "quack's paradise . . . medico-legal work was performed by any practitioner at a tariff." Percy Ward Laidler and Michael Gelfand, *South Africa, Its Medical History, 1652–1898* (Cape Town: C. Struik, 1971), 406, 475.

80. *Star,* 19 April 1905; *Rand Daily Mail,* 22 September 1903.

81. *Rand Daily Mail,* 30 January 1904.

82. *Rand Daily Mail,* 25 October 1902.

83. *Rand Daily Mail,* 5 September 1903.

84. *The War Cry: Official Gazette of the Salvation Army in South Africa,* 20 April 1901.

85. *Rand Daily Mail,* 2 July 1904.

86. *Rand Daily Mail,* 1 July 1904.

87. Gipsy Smith, *A Mission of Peace: Evangelistic Triumphs in South Africa, 1904* (London: National Council of Evangelical Free Churches, 1905), 79.

88. Holt, *Gold Chains,* 11; *The Transvaal Leader,* 21 July 1906.

89. *Rand Daily Mail,* 27 January 1903.

90. *Rand Daily Mail,* 2 May 1904; *Star,* 27 August 1910.

91. *Rand Young Men's Journal* 2, no. 1 (October 1904).

92. *Rand Daily Mail,* 21 June 1904.

93. *Rand Daily Mail,* 14 February 1903.

94. *The Transvaal Leader,* 10 November 1906.

95. *Rand Young Men's Journal,* 3, no. 1 (October 1905).

96. *Rand Daily Mail,* 20 June 1904.

97. *Rand Daily Mail,* 22 November 1902, 30 December 1904, 21 July 1909.

98. *Leaves of Healing* 12, no. 7, 2 December 1902.

99. *Leaves of Healing* 9, no. 17, 17 August 1901; Isabel Hofmeyr, "South Africa's Indian Ocean: Boer Prisoners of War in India," *Social Dynamics: A Journal of African Studies* 38, no. 3 (2012): 366. See also E. H. Van Der Wall, "The Boers at Diyatalawa," *Journal of the Dutch Burger Union of Ceylon* 18, no. 3 (1929).

100. *Leaves of Healing* 9, no. 17, 17 August 1901.

101. *Leaves of Healing* 19, no. 4, 6 October 1906.

102. CCC, Missionary Correspondence Folder, E. Cox to W. Voliva, 16 October 1947.

103. *Leaves of Healing* 8, no. 14, 26 January 1901.

104. *Leaves of Healing* 6, no. 23, 31 March 1900.

105. *Leaves of Healing* 9, no. 17, 17 August 1901.

106. *Leaves of Healing* 6, no. 25, 14 April 1900.

107. Philip Cook, *Zion City, Illinois: Twentieth-Century Utopia* (Syracuse, NY: Syracuse University Press, 1996), 98–102.

108. Cook, *Zion City,* 98.

109. Olive Schreiner, *An English-South African's View of the Situation: Words in Season* (London, Hodder &Stoughton: 1899), 29, 76.

110. *Leaves of Healing* 10, no. 24, 5 April 1902.

111. *Leaves of Healing* 6, no. 23, 31 March 1900.

112. *Leaves of Healing* 11, no. 20, 6 September 1902.

113. *Leaves of Healing* 17, no. 14, 26 July 1905; 6, no. 20, 10 March 1900.

114. *Leaves of Healing* 6, no. 23, 31 March 1900.

115. William Nasson, "Tommy Atkins in South Africa," in *The South African War: The Anglo-Boer War, 1899–1902,* ed. Peter Warwick (London: Longmans, 1980), 127–137.

116. *Leaves of Healing* 9, no. 17, 17 August 1901.

117. *Kirkwell Arcadian,* June 27 1903.

118. *Kirkwell Arcadian,* June 27 1903.

119. *Kirkwell Arcadian,* June 27 1903.

120. *Leaves of Healing* 11, no. 20, 6 September 1902.

121. *Leaves of Healing* 11, no. 20, 6 September 1902.

122. *Leaves of Healing* 18, no. 8, 18 November 1905.

123. *Zion Banner,* 2 December 1901.

124. *Leaves of Healing* 14, no. 8, 12 December 1903; CCC, J. A. D. Dowie to D. Bryant and E. Bryant, 5 November 1903, 6.

125. CCC, Dowie to Bryants, 1.

126. CCC, Dowie to Bryants, 5.

127. CCC, Dowie to Bryants, 5.

128. CCC, Daniel P. Bryant to Bengt Sundkler, 4 January 1974; *Leaves of Healing* 9, no. 3, 11 May 1901.

129. *Leaves of Healing* 14, no. 10, 26 December 1903, 291.

130. *Leaves of Healing* 18, no. 8, 18 November 1905; CCC, Dowie to Bryants, 7.

131. *Leaves of Healing* 14, no. 10, 26 December 1903, 291; National Archives of South Africa (hereafter NASA), SAB (National Archives Repository, Public Records of Central Government since 1910), NTS 1430, 23/214, Clipping from *The Star,* 11 December 1922.

132. CCC, Dowie to Bryants, 12.

133. CCC, Dowie to Bryants, 9.

134. CCC, Daniel Bryant, "Beneath the Southern Cross," 11–12.

135. *Leaves of Healing* 18, no. 18, 17 February 1906.

136. NASA, SAB, Secretary for Native Affairs (hereafter SNA) 361, Sub-Native Commissioner (hereafter SNC) Witwatersrand to SNA, 13 May 1907.

137. *Leaves of Healing* 17, no. 14, 29 July 1905.

138. *Zion City News,* 17 April 1908.

139. *Zion City News,* 17 April 1908. See also CCC, Bryant, "Beneath the Southern Cross," 11.

140. *Leaves of Healing* 17, no. 13, 29 July 1905; 14, no. 10, 26 December 1903.

141. CCC, Bryant, "Beneath the Southern Cross," 11.

142. Saul Dubow, "South Africa: Paradoxes in the Place of Race," in *The Oxford Handbook of the History of Eugenics,* ed. Alison Bashford (Oxford: Oxford University Press, 2010), 276.

143. *Leaves of Healing* 17, no. 13, 29 July 1905.

144. *Leaves of Healing* 17, no. 13, 29 July 1905.

145. *Leaves of Healing* 17, no. 13, 29 July 1905.

146. *Leaves of Healing* 17, no. 13, 29 July 1905.

147. CCC, Bryant, "Beneath the Southern Cross," 17.

148. CCC, Dowie to Bryant, 10.

149. *Leaves of Healing* 13, no. 2, 2 May 1903, 60.

150. *Leaves of Healing* 5, no. 12, 14 January 1899.

151. *Leaves of Healing* 10, no. 17, 15 February 1902.

152. *Leaves of Healing* 10, no. 11, 4 January 1902.

153. *Leaves of Healing* 18, no. 8, 18 November 1905.

154. *Leaves of Healing* 6, no. 25, 14 April 1900.

155. CCC, Dowie to Bryant, 18–19.

156. Saul Dubow, "A Commonwealth of Science: The British Association in South Africa, 1905–1929," in *Science and Society in Southern Africa,* ed. Saul Dubow (Manchester: Manchester University Press, 2000), 77.

157. *Leaves of Healing* 8, no. 6, 1 December 1900.

158. *Leaves of Healing* 17, no. 19, 29 July 1905.

159. *Leaves of Healing* 18, no. 8, 18 November 1905.

160. *Transvaal Critic,* 24 April 1903.

161. *Rand Daily Mail,* 11 October 1904.

162. *Rand Daily Mail,* 18 October 1904.

163. *Rand Daily Mail,* 18 October 1904.

164. *The Transvaal Critic,* 24 April 1903.

165. *Free Press, Detroit Michigan,* 8 June 1901.

166. *Times* (Port Huron Michigan), 17 July 1901.

167. *Chicago Chronicle,* 26 February 1905.

168. *Portland Journal, Oregon,* 6 November 1903.

169. *Waukegan Gazette,* 4 October 1905.

170. Wacker, "Marching to Zion," 507.

171. *Chicago Chronicle,* 2 December 1906.

172. *Chicago Tribune,* 11 November 1906.

173. *Star,* "Editorial on Death of Dr Dowie." 11 March 1907; *Rand Daily Mail,* 11 March 1907, 14 March 1907; Cook, *Zion City,* 204ff.

174. *Waukegan Daily Sun,* 21 July 1906; *Chicago Inter-Ocean,* 11 April 1906.

175. *The Chicago Chronicle,* 15 March 1907.

176. Newberry Library, *Chicago Tribune,* 10 December 1906. See also *Chicago American,* 21 November 1906.

177. Newberry Library, *Chicago Tribune,* 11 December 1906; *Chicago Inter-Ocean,* 11 December 1906.

178. Newberry Library, *New York Mail and Express,* 12 February 1907. New York, Boston and California were also in revolt. *Chicago Tribune,* 23 February 1907.

179. Newberry Library, *Cincinnati Enquirer,* 1 February 1907.

180. Zion Historical Society, Zion, Illinois, *Zion City News,* 2 August 1907.

181. Zion Historical Society, Zion, Illinois, *Zion City News,* 2 August 1907.

182. Zion Historical Society, Zion, Illinois, *Zion City Independent,* 4 November 1910.

183. Zion Historical Society, Zion, Illinois, *Zion City Independent,* 9 September 1910; *Zion City News,* 1 January 1909.

184. Zion Historical Society, Zion, Illinois, *Zion City Independent,* 4 November 1910.

185. Zion Historical Society, Zion, Illinois, *Zion City Independent,* 4 November 1910.

186. Similar acts of insurrection followed amongst Zionists in Britain and Germany. *Zion City Independent,* 15 August 1910.

187. NASA, SAB, CS 709, copy of *Leaves of Healing.*

188. *Chicago Inter-Ocean,* 21 February 1907. See also *Chicago Tribune,* 23 February 1907.

189. NASA, SAB, SNA 361, SNC, Witwatersrand to SNA, 13 May 1907.

190. Edith Blumhofer, *Restoring the Faith: The Assemblies of God, Pentecostalism and American Culture* (Champaign: University of Illinois Press, 1993), 71–87.

191. Gordon P. Gardiner, *Out of Zion into All the World* (Shippensburg, PA: Companion Press, 1990).

192. *Zion Herald,* 2 August 1907.

193. *Leaves of Healing,* 25 July 1908.

194. *Zion City News,* 21 June 1907.

195. *Zion City News,* 4 September 1908; 4 October 1908.

196. Isak Burger and Marius Nel, *The Fire Falls in Africa: A History of the Apostolic Faith Mission of South Africa* (Vereeniging: Christian Art Publishers, 2008), 31.

197. Burger, *Fire Falls in Africa,* 34–35.

198. *Zion City News,* 4 October 1908.

199. AFM, *Trooster,* 9 May 1933; Christiaan de Wet, "The Apostolic Faith Mission in Africa: 1908–1980" (PhD diss., University of Cape Town, 1989), 38.

200. For example, the Van der Byl, Stuart, Ulyate, Shepherd, and Armstrong families from Johannesburg joined Lake's AFM, all prominent members of old Zion under Dowie. W. F. P. Burton, *When God Makes a Pastor* (London, Victory Press, 1934), 35; *Zion City News,* 4 October 1908.

201. *Zion City News,* 4 October 1908.

202. *Zion City News,* 4 October 1908.

203. *Rand Daily Mail,* 7 July 1909, 13 July 1909.

204. Giliomee, *Afrikaners,* 358; *Rand Daily Mail,* 19 October 1910, an editorial on how "racial feelings" were stirred up by anti-Boer articles printed in the *Star.*

205. Giliomee, *Afrikaners,* 362.

206. Giliomee, *Afrikaners,* 369.

207. Literally "bitter-ender," referring to those Dutch men and women who had long resisted surrender during the Boer War of 1899–1902.

208. Moodie, *Rise of Afrikanerdom,* 81–82.

209. Giliomee, *Afrikaners,* 330. See also van Onselen's "The Main Reef Road into the Working Class," in *Social and Economic History,* 309–367.

210. Berg, *Fire Falls Upon Africa,* 62.

211. AFM, *God's Latter Rain,* 18 November 1908.

212. AFM, *God's Latter Rain,* 18 November 1908.

213. *Zion City Independent,* 9 September 1910.

214. De Wet, *Apostolic Faith Mission,* 43.

215. John G. Lake (compiled by Curry R. Blake), *Writings from Africa* (Maitland, FL: Xulon Press, 2005), 26. In 1909 Lake noted that the AFM "has endeavored to be especially helpful to the Poor Dutch." University of Uppsala Archives, Uppsala, Sweden, Bengt Sundkler Collection, Box 111, J. G. Lake to L. Botha, 27 September 1909.

216. David Maxwell, "Historicizing Christian Independency: The Southern African Pentecostal Movement, 1908–1960," *Journal of African History* 40, no. 2 (1999): 248.

217. Lake, *Writings from Africa,* 44. One of the most widely reported of these was the healings of a van der Wall child, *Rand Daily Mail,* 7 July 1909.

218. *Rand Daily Mail,* 13 July 1909.

219. NASA, SAB, NTS 1427, Judicial Inspector Johannesburg to Director of Native Labor (hereafter DNL), 8 November 1916.

220. Burger, *Fire Falls in Africa,* 103.

221. De Wet, "Apostolic Faith Mission," 55.

222. Stuart Anderson, "Racial Anglo-Saxonism and the American Response to the Boer War," *Diplomatic History* 2, no. 3 (1978): 225.

223. *Leaves of Healing* 8, no. 8, 15 December 1900.

224. CCC, Dowie to Bryants, 12.

225. *Leaves of Healing* 8, no. 8, 15 December 1900.

226. *Leaves of Healing* 7, no. 8, 16 June 1900.

227. *Leaves of Healing* 8, no. 8, 15 December 1900.

228. CCC, Dowie to Bryants, 11.

229. William Tilchin, "The United States and the Boer War," in *The International Impact of the Boer War,* ed. Keith Wilson (Chesham: Acumen, 2001), 107ff.

230. *Leaves of Healing* 17, no. 15, 26 July 1905.

231. *Leaves of Healing* 8, no. 14, 22 January 1901.

232. *Leaves of Healing* 3, no. 37, 10 July 1897.

233. *Leaves of Healing* 8, no. 8, 15 December 1900.

234. *Leaves of Healing* 7, no. 8, 16 June 1900.

235. Burger, *Fire Falls in Africa,* 120.

236. AFM, Minute Book of the Executive Council, 1914, 161.

237. David du Plessis, *A Man Called Mr. Pentecost* (South Plainfield, NJ: Bridge, 1977), 45–54.

238. Lake, *Writings from Africa,* 88.

239. Lake, *Writings from Africa,* 88.

240. Lake, *Writings from Africa,* 113.

241. *Latter Rain Evangel,* November 1908.

242. "The Segregation Idea" was proposed as the only barrier against "the future nation [being] a coloured one." *Rand Daily Mail,* 23 May 1910. See also 15 September 1910 and 15 March 1911.

243. *Rand Daily Mail,* 7 July 1909.

244. Lindsay, *John G. Lake,* 36.

245. Lake, *Writings from Africa,* 19.

246. AFM, Minute Book, 6 November 1908.

247. AFM, Minute Book, 30 July 1909.

248. AFM, Minutes of the Executive Council, 4 July 1917.

249. Burger, *Fire Falls in Africa,* 200.

4. ZION'S EGALITARIAN PROMISES IN THE TRANSVAAL AND ORANGE RIVER COLONIES, SOUTH AFRICA

1. *Leaves of Healing* 17, no. 26, 14 October 1905, 855.

2. Paul Landau, *Popular Politics in the History of South Africa, 1400–1948* (Cambridge: Cambridge University Press, 2010), xii–xiii; 2–4.

3. Colin Bundy, *The Rise and Fall of the South African Peasantry* (Cape Town: David Philip, 1979), 205.

4. Timothy Keegan, *Rural Transformations in Industrializing South Africa: The Southern Highveld to 1914* (London: Macmillan, 1987), 18.

5. James Campbell, *Songs of Zion: The African Methodist Episcopal Church in the United States and South Africa* (Oxford: Oxford University Press, 1995), 161; Tim Keegan, *Facing the Storm: Portraits of Black Lives in Rural South Africa* (London: Zed Books, 1988), 133.

6. Peter Warwick, *Black People and the South African War, 1899–1902* (Cambridge: Cambridge University Press, 1983), 68.

7. James Campbell, *Songs of Zion,* 161; Keegan, *Facing the Storm,* 133; Tim Couzens, *The New African: A Study of the Life and Work of H. I. E. Dhlomo* (Johannesburg: Ravan Press, 1985), 82–124.

8. Richard Elphick, *The Equality of Believers: Protestant Missionaries and the Racial Politics of South Africa* (Charlottesville: University of Virginia Press, 2012).

9. Keegan, *Rural Transformations,* 74; Keegan, *Facing the Storm,* 75.

10. Keegan, *Facing the Storm,* 74, 77, 110.

11. Keegan, *Facing the Storm,* 76; Keegan, *Rural Transformations,* 195; Norman Etherington, *Preachers, Peasants and Politics in Southeast Africa, 1835–1880: African Christian Communities in Natal, Pondoland and Zululand* (London: Royal Historical Society, 1978), 115–134.

12. Timothy Keegan, "White Settlement and Black Subjugation on the South African Highveld: The Tlokoa Heartland in the North Eastern Orange Free State, 1850–1914," in William Beinart, Peter Delius and Stanley Trapido (eds.), *Putting a Plough to the Ground: Accumulation and Dispossession in Rural South Africa* (Johannesburg: Ravan Press, 1986), 227–229.

13. Keegan, "White Settlement and Black Subjugation," 227, 235.

14. Bundy, *Rise and Fall of the South African Peasantry,* 212.

15. Keegan, *Rural Transformations,* 72.

16. Keegan, *Rural Transformations,* 194.

17. Saul Dubow, "Colonial Nationalism, the Milner Kindergarten and the rise of South Africanism, 1902–1910," *History Workshop Journal* 43 (1997), 53–85.

18. Hoffie Hofmeyr, "Business and Farming," in Hoffie Hoymeyr and Krystyna Smith with Chris Smit, *Wakkerstroom: Jewel of Mpumalanga* (Centurion: Mediakor, 2009), 110.

19. NASA, SAB, LWM 25, Report for Wakkerstroom District, December 1903.

20. NASA, SAB, LWM 74, SNC Piet Retief to Native Commissioner (hereafter NC) South East Division, 10 February 1904.

21. *Leaves of Healing* 18, no. 11, 30 December 1905.

22. Harvey M. Feinburg, "The 1913 Natives Land Act in South Africa: Politics, Race and Segregation in the Early Twentieth Century," *International Journal of African Historical Studies* 26, no. 1 (1993): 68.

23. Keegan, *Facing the Story,* 89–90.

24. NASA, SAB, LWM 30, Native Affairs Department (hereafter NAD) to NC Wakkerstroom, 29 August 1903.

25. NASA, SAB, LWM 136, Clerk of the Peace to Magistrate Wakkerstroom, 5 September 1905.

26. *Leaves of Healing* 18, no. 11, 30 December 1905.

27. NASA, SAB, LWM 61, NC South East Division to SNA, 3 May 1904.

28. NASA, SAB, LWM 132, Maasdorp Attorney to SNC, Wakkerstroom, 20 August 1907.

29. *South African Native Affairs Commission, 1903–1905,* Vol. 4: *Minutes of Evidence* (Cape Town: Cape Times, 1904–1905), Testimony of the Hon. JG Fraser.

30. *Harrismith Chronicle,* "Farm Labour," 16 September 1905.
31. NASA, VAB (Free State Archives Repository, Bloemfontein), CO 414 Office of the Resident Magistrate, Vrede to Colonial Secretary, Bloemfontein, 28 December 1907; *Harrismith Chronicle,* "Editorial: Farm Labour," 1 July 1905.
32. *Native Affairs Commission,* Testimony of Mr Alec Wilson; VAC, NAB Office of the Resident Magistrate, Philippolis to Advisor Native Affairs, Bloemfontein, 22 July 1905. In the town of Harrismith alone, the second largest town in the Colony with a population of 8,300, 1,871 Africans were awarded a total of £12,600 in wartime compensation, with an average award of £78. *Harrismith Chronicle,* "Native Compensation Claims," 10 June 1905.
33. NASA, VAB, NAB 3, "Coloured Males: Passes to Enter Orange River Colony," 26 March 1906; *Harrismith Chronicle,* 3 February 1906.
34. NASA, VAB, MHT 2/1/8 Native Vigilance Committee to the Town Council of Harrismith Corporation, 16 March 1903; *Harrismith Chronicle,* "Census Returns," 21 May 1904.
35. NASA, VAB, NAB 4, B. Kumalo and H. R. Ngcaycya to His Excellency the High Commissioner, Lord Selbourne, 18 May 1906.
36. See Elphick, *Equality of Believers,* especially part 3, "'The Parting of the Ways,'" for the demise of the ideal of racial egalitarianism in missionary thought of the time.
37. Bengt Sundkler, *Bantu Prophets in South Africa* (London: Lutterworth Press, 1948), 29.
38. Elphick, *Equality of Believers,* 86.
39. Campbell, *Songs of Zion,* 110.
40. NASA, VAB, NAB 1 Rev. J. F. Goring to Commissioner for Native Affairs, Bloemfontein (1 September 1905).
41. *Native Affairs Commission,* Testimony of Rev. Heinrich Grutzner.
42. C. C. Saunders, "Tile and the Thembu Church: Politics and Independency on the Cape Eastern Frontier in the Late Nineteenth Century," *Journal of African History* 11, no. 4 (1970): 567.
43. Campbell, *Songs of Zion,* 119.
44. Sundkler, *Bantu Prophets,* 42–43.
45. NASA, VAB, NAB 3, "The History of the Ethiopian Movement in the Orange River Colony," 25 May 1906; Campbell, *Songs of Zion,* 180ff.
46. NASA, SAB, LWM 139, Lea to NC Wakkerstroom, 5 January 1907.
47. *Harrismith Chronicle,* 21 October 1911.
48. NASA, SAB, LWM 62, NC South East Division to SNA, 5 March 1904.
49. *Harrismith Chronicle,* 10 March 1906.
50. "Voice of Missions," cited in the *Bloemfontein Post,* 15 December 1904.
51. *Bloemfontein Post,* 15 December 1904.
52. NASA, SAB, LWM 25, NC Volksrust to NC South East Division, 8 February 1904.
53. NASA, VAB, NAB 3, Rev. Mareka, AME Church, Trumpsburg, ORC to Native Commission, Bloemfontein, 2 February 1904.
54. NASA, VAB, NAB 3, Rev. Mareka, AME Church, Trumpsburg, ORC to Native Commission, Bloemfontein.

55. *Native Affairs Commission,* Testimony of Rev. Joel Goronyane.

56. *Native Affairs Commission,* Testimony of Rev. Samuel Jacobs Brander (including telling the Commissioners that "he would like the white man to marry the native woman.").

57. AFM, Le Roux to Revs. Kriel, Marais, Rossouw, Meiring, Bosman, 12 November 1898.

58. AFM, Rev. Andrew Murray to Pieter Le Roux, 29 November 1898.

59. AFM, Pieter Le Roux to Rev. Andrew Murray, 12 November 1898.

60. E.g. A. J. Gordon's *The Ministry of Healing.* AFM, Le Roux to Local Mission Committee, 10 October 1901; *Leaves of Healing* 8, no. 8, 15 December 1900.

61. AFM, Local Mission Committee to P. Le Roux, 15 October 1901; Dutch Reformed Church Archives, Stellenbosch, "Notulen van de Zevende Algemeene Vergadering van de Ned. Herv. Of Geref. Kerk in Zuid-Afrika" (Kaapstad: Townshend, Taylor en Snashall, 1903).

62. Interview with Lynette Le Roux, Swaziland, 12 November 2015; interview with Marie Weidelmann, Harold Le Roux, Lynette Le Roux, Wakkerstroom, South Africa, 19 December 2015.

63. Interview with Edgar Mahon III, Durban, South Africa, 8 January 2016; interview with Netta Mahon, Pretoria, 23 November 2015.

64. *All the World: A Monthly Record of the Operation of the Salvation Army in all Lands,* 4, no. 10 (October 1888), 343; W. F. P. Burton, *When God Makes a Missionary* (London: Victory Press, 1936), 25–26.

65. Charles van Onselen, *Studies in the Social and Economic History of the Witwatersrand, 1886–1914* (Harlow: Longman Group, 1982), 1:20.

66. Interview with Edgar Mahon III, Durban, South Africa, 8 January 2016.

67. *Leaves of Healing* 5, no. 36, 1 July 1899.

68. James Opp, *The Lord for the Body: Religion, Medicine and Protestant Faith Healing in Canada, 1880–1930* (London: McGill-Queen's University Press, 2005), 89.

69. E. B. Hawkins, *The Story of Harrismith, 1849–1920* (Harrismith: Harrismith Rotary Club, 1982), 99.

70. Burton, *When God Makes a Missionary,* 25–26.

71. *Leaves of Healing* 5, no. 36, 1 July 1899, 690.

72. *Leaves of Healing* 4, no. 11, 8 January 1898.

73. CCC, J. A. D. Dowie to D. Bryant and E. Bryant, 5 November 1903, 14.

74. *Leaves of Healing* 5, no. 36, 1 July 1899, 690; 25, no. 25, 8 October 1904.

75. *Leaves of Healing* 25, no. 25, 8 October 1904.

76. *Leaves of Healing* 25, no. 25, 8 October 1904.

77. James Campbell, *Middle Passages: African American Journeys to Africa 1787–2005* (London: Penguin, 2006), 103ff.

78. *Zion City News,* 4 September 1908.

79. *Leaves of Healing* 25, no. 25, 8 October 1904; AFM, P. Le Roux to A. Murray, 12 November 1898.

80. NASA, SAB, LWM 111, Annual Report for Wakkerstroom, 1905.

81. *Leaves of Healing* 25, no. 25, 8 October 1904.

82. Dlamini, "Christian Catholic Apostolic Holy Spirit Church in Zion," 4.

83. *Leaves of Healing* 18, no. 11, 30 December 1905.

84. *Leaves of Healing* 18, no. 11, 30 December 1905; Grace Missionary Church Archives, Zion, Illinois (hereafter GMC), *The Zululand and Basutoland Missionary* 1, nos. 5–7, March–June 1914.

85. *Leaves of Healing* 15, no. 25, 8 October 1904.

86. *Leaves of Healing* 15, no. 25, 8 October 1904.

87. *Leaves of Healing* 15, no. 25, 8 October 1904.

88. *The Zululand and Basutoland Missionary* 2, no. 5, April 1915; 1, nos. 5–7, March–June 1914.

89. Timothy L. L. Dlamini, "The Christian Catholic Apostolic Holy Spirit Church in Zion as it Exists in Swaziland" (PhD diss., University of Botswana and Swaziland, 1976), 4.

90. *Leaves of Healing* 18, no. 11, 30 December 1905.

91. *Leaves of Healing* 25, no. 25, 8 October 1904.

92. *Leaves of Healing* 25, no. 25, 8 October 1904.

93. *Leaves of Healing* 15, no. 17, 13 August 1904.

94. NASA, VAB, MHT 2/1/27, Richard Mthembu to Harrismith Mayor, 14 April 1907. See also VAB, NAB 6, Assistant Native Adviser to Rev. Father Cretirion, Basutoland, 11 August 1908, with a list of churches in the ORC in 1908, in which the "Catholic Church in Zion" is number 8.

95. Burton, *When God Makes a Missionary,* 63–64, 36.

96. *Zion City News,* 3 June 1910.

97. *Leaves of Healing* 17, no. 7, 3 June 1905.

98. Karen Flint, *Healing Traditions: African Medicine, Cultural Exchange and Competition in South Africa, 1820–1948* (Athens: Ohio University Press, 2008), 65.

99. Flint, *Healing Traditions,* 37–66.

100. *Leaves of Healing* 17, no. 26, 14 October 1905.

101. *Leaves of Healing* 5, no. 36, 1 July 1899.

102. Alan Booth, "European Courts Protect Women and Witches," *Journal of Southern African Studies* 18, no. 2 (1992): 254.

103. NASA, VAB, NAB 3, Secretary to the Law Department to the Native Affairs Adviser, Bloemfontein, 16 March 1906.

104. *Harrismith Chronicle,* 26 September 1908.

105. *Leaves of Healing* 25, no. 25, 8 October 1904.

106. *Zion City News,* 3 June 1910.

107. *Zion City News,* 19 November 1909.

108. *Zion City News,* 22 October 1909.

109. *Leaves of Healing* 18, no. 11, 30 December 1905.

110. *Leaves of Healing* 5, no. 36, 1 July 1899.

111. *Zion City News,* 3 March 1910.

112. *Zion City News,* 19 November 1909.

113. *Leaves of Healing* 18, no. 11, 30 December 1905.

114. *Zion City News,* 19 November 1909.

115. NASA, SAB, LWM 123, Report for Wakkerstroom, November 1907.

116. *Harrismith Chronicle,* 1 April 1911.

117. *Zion City News,* 22 October 1909.

118. *Zion City News,* 22 October 1909.

119. *Leaves of Healing* 25, no. 25, 8 October 1904, 862–863.

120. Bengt Sundkler, *Zulu Zion and Some Swazi Zionists* (Oxford: Oxford University Press, 1976), 44.

121. NASA, SAB, LWM 25, NC Volksrust to NC SE Division, 8 February 1904.

122. NASA, SAB, LWM 91, Magistrate Wakkerstroom to SNC Wakkerstroom, 30 October 1905.

123. *Leaves of Healing* 28, no. 11, 30 December 1905.

124. NASA, VAB, CO 385, Commandant Witzieshoek to Native Affairs Bloemfontein, 13 November 1907.

125. Burton, *When God Makes a Missionary,* 48.

126. *Rand Daily Mail,* 16 December 1908. NASA, VAB, ORC 332, South African Native Affairs Commission, 1903–1905, vol. 4, Evidence of Mr Hugh Gunn (Director of Education in Orange River Colony).

127. CCC, Dowie to Bryant, 18.

128. *Leaves of Healing* 28, no. 11, 30 December 1905.

129. NASA, VAB, NAB 1, Lieutenant Commander Orange River Colony to Adviser for Native Affairs, Bloemfontein, 10 June 1905.

130. NASA, VAB, NAB 1, Lieutenant Commander Orange River Colony to Adviser for Native Affairs, Bloemfontein.

131. *Harrismith Chronicle,* 26 September 1908; Robert Vinson, *The Americans are Coming! Dreams of African American Liberation in Segregationist South Africa* (Athens: Ohio University Press, 2012), 16–17.

132. *Harrismith Chronicle,* 30 April 1910.

133. *Leaves of Healing* 27, no. 26, 14 October 1905.

134. Sundkler, *Zulu Zion,* 40.

135. *Zion City News,* 22 October 1909.

136. *Zion City Independent,* "Report of Native Workers' Conference," 15 July 1910.

137. *Zion City News,* 11 February 1910.

138. *Leaves of Healing* 27, no. 26, 14 October 1905.

139. *Leaves of Healing* 25, no. 25, 8 October 1904.

140. *Harrismith Chronicle,* 21 May 1904.

141. *Leaves of Healing* 25, no. 14, 23 July 1904.

142. *Leaves of Healing* 28, no. 11, 30 December 1905.

143. NASA, SAB, SNA 144, Le Roux to SNC, Wakkerstroom, 29 June 1903.

144. NASA, SAB, SNA 144, NC South Eastern Division to SNA, 23 July 1903.

145. NASA, VAB, CO 93, Department of Education to the Colonial Secretary Bloemfontein, 23 August 1902.

146. *Leaves of Healing* 28, no. 11, 30 December 1905.

147. *Leaves of Healing* 28, no. 11, 30 December 1905.

148. Burton, *When God Makes a Missionary*, 15.
149. NASA, VAB, NAB 2, List Showing Number of Heads of Native Families on Various Farms in the Harrrismith District, 1906; *Leaves of Healing* 25, no. 25, 8 October 1904, 857.
150. *Leaves of Healing* 25, no. 14, 23 July 1904.
151. *Zion City News*, 22 October 1909.
152. *Leaves of Healing* 28, no. 11, 30 December 1905.
153. *Leaves of Healing* 28, no. 11, 30 December 1905.
154. *Leaves of Healing* 28, no. 11, 30 December 1905.
155. *Zion City News*, 22 October 1909.
156. NASA, SAB, LWM 35, Sgd. Oriel J. Moilea to NC Volksrust, 9 June 1904.
157. NASA, SAB, LWM 36, Magistrate Wakkerstroom to NC Wakkerstroom, 17 May 1904.
158. *The Transvaal Critic*, 24 April 1903.
159. *Zion City News*, 11 February 1910.
160. NASA, VAB, CO 385 Application from Mr. E. H. Mahon to Commandant of Witzieshoek, 13 November 1907.
161. *Leaves of Healing* 5, no. 12, 14 January 1899.
162. *Leaves of Healing* 28, no. 11, 30 December 1905.
163. *Leaves of Healing* 28, no. 11, 30 December 1905.
164. NASA, SAB, LWM 132, Pieter Le Roux to SNC Wakkerstroom, 19 January 1907.
165. SOAS, MS 380256, File Number 1, African Christian Baptist Church of South Africa.
166. AFM, Minutes of Annual General Conference, 1 April 1915. Interview with Marie Weidelmann, Harold Le Roux, Lynette Le Roux, Wakkerstroom, Mpumalanga, South Africa, 19 December 2015.
167. AFM, *The Comforter*, 1913, 2.
168. C. De Wet, "The Apostolic Faith Mission in South Africa: 1908–1980" (PhD diss., University of Cape Town, 1989), 55.
169. AFM, Executive Committee Minutes, 1908–1914, 6 May 1910, 55.
170. AFM, Executive Committee Minutes, 1908–1914, 10 January 1909, 19.
171. *Zion City News*, 1 October 1909.
172. *Zion City News*, 4 June 1909.
173. GMC, *Grace Missionary Church, 100th anniversary publication, 1909–2009* (n.p., 2009).
174. De Wet, "Apostolic Faith Mission," 165. Paul's command is in 1 Corinthians 6:12 and 10:23.
175. AFM, Executive Committee Minutes, 7 March 1914; De Wet, "Apostolic Faith Mission," 164–165.
176. AFM, *The Comforter*, August 1921, 2.
177. De Wet, "Apostolic Faith Mission," 96; AFM, Executive Committee Minutes, 6 May 1910; 13 November 1913.
178. De Wet, "Apostolic Faith Mission," 126.

179. Le Roux's family continued to reside in Wakkerstroom and he commuted back and forth between there and Johannesburg for many years. Interview with Peter Le Roux, Elsa Le Roux and Louise Vonstaden, Pretoria, South Africa, 27 November 2015.
180. Sundkler, *Zulu Zion,* 48–49.
181. Sundkler, *Zulu Zion,* 40.
182. AFM, Executive Committee Minutes 1908–1914, 6 May 1910, 60.
183. De Wet, "Apostolic Faith Mission," 22.
184. *Leaves of Healing,* 9 May 1914.
185. *Leaves of Healing,* 9 May 1914.
186. *Leaves of Healing,* 9 May 1914.
187. Sundkler, *Zulu Zion,* 60–61.
188. GMC, Marian McElroy, *Church History Scrapbook* (n.p., n.d.).
189. *Zion City Independent,* 9 September 1910.
190. GMC, Church Record for the Christian Catholic Church, Minutes of Regular Meeting, 6 December 1911; see also McElroy, *Church History Scrapbook.*
191. GMC, Church Record for the Christian Catholic Church, Minutes of Council Meeting, 3 October 1917.
192. GMC, *Zulu and Basutoland Missionary* 12, no. 4, February 1925.
193. GMC, McElroy, *Church History.*
194. Burton, *When God Makes a Missionary,* 46; GMC, Church Record for the Christian Catholic Church, Minutes of Adjourned Business Meeting, 15 March 1916.
195. GMC, *Basutoland and Zululand Missionary* 1, no. 3, December 1913.
196. GMC, *Basutoland and Zululand Missionary* 3, no. 8, July–August 1913.
197. GMC, *Basutoland and Zululand Missionary* 1, no. 7, May 1914.
198. GMC, *Basutoland and Zululand Missionary* 3, no. 2, December 1915.
199. NASA, SAB, GG 178, Col. Garraway, Resident Commissioner to Resident Commissioner Maseru, 19 November 1921.
200. GMC, *Basutoland and Zululand Missionary* 3, no. 2, December 1915.
201. GMC, *Basutoland and Zululand Missionary* 1, no. 4, January and February 1914.
202. GMC, *Basutoland and Zululand Missionary* 5, no. 10, August 1918.
203. GMC, *Basutoland and Zululand Missionary* 6, no. 6, April 1919.
204. GMC, *Basutoland and Zululand Missionary* 16, no. 7, April 1929.
205. GMC, *Basutoland and Zululand Missionary,* February 1921.
206. GMC, *Basutoland and Zululand Missionary* 13, no. 6, April 1926.
207. NASA, VAB, SOO 1/1/178, Inspector of Native Locations, 24 October 1928, Report on Native School at Etembeni (Christian Catholic Church in Zion).
208. GMC, *Basutoland and Zululand Missionary* 1, no. 3, December 1913.
209. GMC, *Basutoland and Zululand Missionary* 1, no. 1, October 1913.
210. GMC, *Basutoland and Zululand Missionary* 22, no. 10, August 1935.
211. GMC, *Basutoland and Zululand Missionary,* November 1921.
212. GMC, *Basutoland and Zululand Missionary* 22, no. 10, August 1935.

5. SECTARIAN CREATIVITY AND POPULIST PROPHETS IN INTERWAR JOHANNESBURG

1. Ryrie, *Protestants*, 209.
2. Sundkler, *Bantu Prophets*, 168.
3. Phillip Bonner, "South African Society and Culture, 1910–1948," in *Cambridge History of South Africa*, ed. Robert Ross, Anne Mager, and Bill Nasson (Cambridge: Cambridge University Press, 2011), 2:296, 304.
4. Lucien van der Walt, "The Industrial Union is the Embryo of the Socialist Commonwealth: The International Socialist League and Revolutionary Syndicalism in South Africa, 1915–1920," *Comparative Studies of South Asia, Africa and the Middle East* 9, no. 1 (1999): 5–30.
5. Ellen Hellmann, *Rooiyard: A Sociological Survey of an Urban Native Slum* (Cape Town: Oxford University Press, 1948), 5.
6. Ray Phillips, *The Bantu in the City: A Study of Cultural Adjustment on the Witwatersrand* (Lovedale: Lovedale Press, 1938), xxii.
7. Philip Bonner, "African Urbanization on the Rand between the 1930s and the 1960s: Its Social Character and Political Consequences," *Journal of Southern African Studies* 21, no. 1 (1995): 116.
8. Bill Freund, "The Social Character of Secondary Industry in South Africa, 1915–1945," in *Organization and Economic Change, Southern African Studies*, ed. A. Mabin (Johannesburg: Ravan Press, 1989), 5:83.
9. Between 1911 and 1921, the number of black women in Johannesburg grew from 4,000 to 12,000. Paul La Hausse, *Brewers, Beer Halls and Boycotts: A History of Liquor in South Africa* (Johannesburg: Ravan Press, 1988), 40.
10. Cheryl Walker, "Gender and the Migrant Labour System," in *Women and Gender in Southern Africa to 1945*, ed. Cheryl Walker (London: James Currey, 1990), 177.
11. Bonner, "South African Society and Culture," 292.
12. Phillip Bonner, "The Transvaal Native Congress, 1917–1921: The Radicalization of the Black Petite Bourgeoisie on the Rand," in *Industrial and Social Change in South Africa, 1870–1930*, ed. Shula Marks and Richard Rathbone (London: Longman, 1982), 286–287.
13. T. D. Mweli Skota, *The African Yearly Register: Being an Illustrated National Biographical Dictionary of Black Folks in South Africa* (Johannesburg: R. L. Esson, ca. 1932), 71.
14. Skota, *African Yearly Register*, 142.
15. Deborah Gaitskell, "Housewives, Maids or Mothers: Some Contradictions of Domesticity for Christian Women in Johannesburg, 1903–1939," *Journal of African History* 24, no. 2 (1983): 241–256.
16. Phillips, *Bantu in the City*, xxvi.
17. Hellman, *Rooiyard*, 100; G. Ballenden, "Native Customs and Conditions," in *The Golden City: Johannesburg*, ed. Allister Macmillan (London: W. H. & L. Collingridge, 1933), 176.

18. David Goodhew, "Working Class Respectability: The Example of the Western Areas of Johannesburg, 1930–1955," *Journal of African History* 41, no. 2 (2000): 241.

19. Goodhew, "Working Class Respectability," 254.

20. Bengt Sundkler, *Bantu Prophets in South Africa* (London: Lutterworth Press, 1948), 81.

21. Sundkler, *Bantu Prophets*, 81.

22. NASA, Government Native Labour Bureau (hereafter GNLB), 206, DNL to SNA, 20 February 1923.

23. David Coplan, "The Emergence of African Working Class Culture," in *Industrial and Social Change in South Africa, 1870–1930*, ed. Shula Marks and Richard Rathbone (London: Longman, 1982), 367.

24. *Bantu World*, 10 June 1933.

25. *Bantu World*, 7 December 1940.

26. Phillips, *Bantu in the City*, 161.

27. Hellman, *Rooiyard*, 30, 67, 91.

28. Phillips, *Bantu in the City*, 162.

29. Les Switzer, "Bantu World and the Origins of a Captive African Commercial Press in South Africa," *Journal of Southern African Studies* 14, no. 2 (1998): 198.

30. *Bantu World*, 9 April 1932.

31. Lynn Thomas, "The Modern Girl and Racial Respectability in 1930s South Africa," *Journal of African History* 47, no. 3 (2006): 465.

32. Phillips, *Bantu in the City*, 293–302; *Umteteli wa Bantu*, 28 August 1920.

33. Hellman, *Rooiyard*, 114.

34. *Bantu World*, 11 April 1936.

35. Union of South Africa, *Union Statistics for Fifty Years, 1910–1960* (Pretoria: Bureau of Census and Statistics, 1960), table A-22.

36. Thomas, 'Modern Girl," 465.

37. *Bantu World*, 7 December 1940.

38. *Bantu World*, 14 May 1932.

39. *Umteteli wa Bantu*, 9 May 1925.

40. *Bantu World*, 7 December 1940.

41. *Bantu World*, 23 September 1933.

42. James Campbell, *Songs of Zion: The African Methodist Episcopal Church in the United States and South Africa* (New York: Oxford University Press, 1995), 272.

43. *Bantu World*, 15 December 1934.

44. Campbell, *Songs of Zion*, 272ff.

45. *Bantu World*, 20 February 1937.

46. Ellen Hellman, "Urban Areas," in *Handbook on Race Relations in South Africa*, ed. Ellen Hellman (Oxford: Oxford University Press, 1949), 233–234; "The Natives in the Towns," in *Report of the Native Affairs Commission, 1921* (Cape Town: Union Government, 1922), 25.

47. Phillips, *Bantu in the City*, 5.

48. An informal, offensive Afrikaans word for "get out of here," usually used with animals.

49. *Bantu World*, 26 June 1937.

50. The average monthly wage for an African family man was 4 pounds, 2 shillings, and 6 pence, and the minimum family budget for a month was £7, 10s. R. Phillips, *The Bantu Are Coming: Phases of South Africa's Race Problem* (London: Student Christian Movement Press, 1930), 62.

51. Bonner, "Radicalization of Black Petit Bourgeoisie," 272.

52. Shula Marks and Richard Rathbone, "Introduction," in *Industrial and Social Change in South Africa, 1870–1930* (London: Longman, 1982), 167.

53. Eddie Koch, "Doornfontein and Its African Working Class, 1914–1935: A Study of Popular Culture in Johannesburg" (PhD diss., University of Witwatersrand, 1983), 57–73; *Rand Daily Mail*, "No. 8 Marshall Street: House of Filth and Crime," 25 January 1923.

54. Bonner, "Radicalization of Black Petit Bourgeoisie," 272, 276.

55. Helen Bradford, *A Taste of Freedom: The ICU in Rural South Africa, 1924–1930* (New Haven: Yale University Press, 1987), 67–68.

56. *Bantu World*, 23 April and 30 July 1932.

57. *Bantu World*, 16 September 1933 (in isiZulu).

58. *Umteteli wa Bantu*, 27 February 1926.

59. *Bantu World*, 30 July 1932.

60. Switzer, "Bantu World," 196.

61. Walshe, *The Rise of African Nationalism in South Africa: The African National Congress 1912–1952* (Berkeley: University of California Press, 1970), 92.

62. Walshe, *Rise of African Nationalism*, 99.

63. Bradford, *A Taste of Freedom*, 64.

64. Bradford, *Taste of Freedom*, 67ff.

65. Richard Elphick, *The Equality of Believers: Protestant Missionaries and the Racial Politics of South Africa* (Charlottesville: University of Virginia Press, 2012).

66. *Umteteli wa Bantu*, 11 September 1920.

67. *Umteteli wa Bantu*, 26 May 1928.

68. Robert Vinson, *The Americans Are Coming! Dreams of African-American Liberation in Segregationist South Africa* (Athens: Ohio University Press, 2012).

69. *Umteteli wa Bantu*, 14 August 1920.

70. *Leaves of Healing*, 20 December 1913.

71. *Leaves of Healing*, 20 December 1913.

72. University of Uppsala Archives, Uppsala, Sweden (hereafter Uppsala), Bengt Sundkler Collection, Box 138, Membership Application Forms to Christian Catholic Apostolic Church in Zion.

73. SOAS, MS 380256, "Christian Apostolic Church in Zion of South Africa," Statement from Paulus Mabiletsa.

74. CCC, Membership Application Forms, Paulus Mabiletsa, 1912; Interview with Solomon Dube, Matshapa, 15 July 2016.

75. *Leaves of Healing*, 20 December 1913.

76. *Leaves of Healing,* 3 January 1914.

77. GMC, *Basutoland and Zululand Missionary* 12, no. 6, April 1925.

78. GMC, *Basutoland and Zululand Missionary* 12, no. 7, May 1925.

79. GMC, *Basutoland and Zululand Missionary* 14, no. 9, 1927.

80. GMC, *Basutoland and Zululand Missionary* 12, no. 12, October 1925.

81. GMC, *Basutoland and Zululand Missionary* 14, no. 3 January 1927.

82. NASA, SAB, GNLB 353, DNL to SNA, 14 October 1924.

83. SOAS, MS 380256, "Christian Apostolic Church in Zion of South Africa," Statement from Paulus Mabiletsa.

84. NASA, GNLB 205, File No. 1697/14/110, Mabiletsa to NC Johannesburg, 13 March 1917.

85. Father Hill, "Native Separatist Movements and their Relation to the Problem of Evangelisation," in *The Evangelisation of South Africa, being the Report of the Sixth General Missionary Conference of South Africa* (Cape Town: Nasionale Pers, 1925), 112; SOAS, MS 380256, "Christian Catholic Apostolic Church in Zion of South Africa," statement from Abraham Mabilikama.

86. NASA, GNLB 205 File No. 1697/14/110, File No. 26, Christian Catholic Apostolic Church in Zion of South Africa.

87. Uppsala, Bengt Sundkler Collection, Box 123, City of Johannesburg Non-European Affairs Department, Separatist Churches, Survey 1958.

88. *Bantu World,* 6 October 1934 (in isiZulu).

89. Bengt Sundkler, *Zulu Zion and Some Swazi Zionists* (Oxford: Oxford University Press, 1976), 60; SOAS, MS 380256, "Christian Apostolic Church in Zion of South Africa," statement from Jacob Ndlovu; *Bantu World,* 28 August 1937.

90. Uppsala, Bengt Sundkler Collection, Box 127, *Constitution of the Holy Catholic Apostolic Church in Zion* (Doornfontein, 1937), last chapter by Jane Phillips, "A Brief History of the Life of the Rev. John George Philips." My thanks to Henry Mitchell for providing further information on Phillips, in particular, and Nyasa migration to the Rand, in general.

91. Robert Boeder, *Malawians Abroad: The History of Labor Emigration from Malawi to its Neighbours 1890 to the Present* (University Microfilms, 1978), 114–115.

92. NASA, DGO 77, File No. 120/4/71, "A Brief History of the Holy Catholic Apostolic Church in Zion," by Archbishop S. Nkosi.

93. Phillips, "A Brief History of the Life of the Rev. John George Philips."

94. Phillips, "A Brief History of the Life of the Rev. John George Philips."

95. Phillips, "A Brief History of the Life of the Rev. John George Philips."

96. *Leaves of Healing,* 20 December 1913.

97. NASA, GNLB 363, Phillips to NAD, 28 August 1925.

98. NASA, GNLB 363, Phillips to NAD, 28 August 1925.

99. NASA, GNLB 363, Phillips to NAD, 28 August 1925.

100. NASA, GNLB 363, DNL to SNA, 9 June 1927.

101. NASA, GNLB 353, DNL to SNA, 14 October 1924; Interview with Philemon Mvubu, Manzini, Swaziland, 15 August 2016.

102. NASA, DGP 76, References for Phillip Mabiletsa from Wesley House, Fort Hare, South African Native College, 21 August 1937.

103. *Bantu World,* 30 May 1936 (in isiZulu); for information on E. P. Mart Zulu, see Philip Bonner and Noor Nieftagodien, *Alexandra: A History* (Johannesburg: Wits University Press, 2008), 35, 53. For Mdlalose, see Bengt Sundkler, "Chief and Prophet in Zululand and Swaziland," in *African Systems of Thought,* ed. Meyer Fortes and Germaine Dieterlen (Oxford: Oxford University Press, 1965), 277.

104. *Bantu World,* 28 July 1934 (in isiZulu).

105. SOAS, MS 380256, File No. 1, "Congregational Church of South Africa"; *Bantu World,* 19 August 1939 (in Setswana).

106. *Bantu World,* 24 August 1935.

107. *Bantu World,* 15 July 1933 ("Rev Mabiletsa and Mrs Mabiletsa left Durban on Tuesday night and will return to Johannesburg on July 18"); 28 August 1937.

108. *Bantu World,* 21 July 1934.

109. Skota, *African Yearly Register,* 319.

110. Grant Wacker, *Heaven Below: Early Pentecostals and American Culture* (Cambridge, MA.: Harvard University Press, 2001), 151–153.

111. NASA, SAB, NTS 1428, File No. 21/214, Snelling to Native Affairs Department, 10 September 1930.

112. Fiona Armitage, "Abakamoya: People of the Spirit: A Study of the Zionist Movement in Swaziland with Special Reference to the Swazi Christian Church in Zion of South Africa and the Nazarethe Branch" (PhD diss., University of Aberdeen, 1976), 66, 91.

113. *Bantu World,* 15 April 1939.

114. NASA, SAB, GNLB 205, File No. 23, Bethesda Zion Apostolic Church of Africa.

115. NASA, SAB, GNLB 216, T. Snider, SA Police to the Inspector, SA Police, Western Area, Johannesburg, 17 March 1920.

116. NASA, GNLB 216, T. Snider to South African Police, Western Area, Johannesburg, 16 and 17 March 1920.

117. SOAS, MS 380256, Folder 23, "Bethesda Zion Apostolic Church of Africa."

118. Uppsala, Bengt Sundkler Collection, Box 123, City of Johannesburg Non-European Affairs Department, Survey into Separatist Churches in Orlando, 1958.

119. SOAS, MS 380256, Folder 44, "Congregational Apostolic Evangelical Church."

120. *Bantu World,* 16 September 1933 (in isiZulu).

121. Uppsala, Bengt Sundkler Collection, Box 123, City of Johannesburg Non-European Affairs Department, Separatist Churches, Survey 1958.

122. Sundkler, *Zulu Zion,* 125–126.

123. NASA, GG 1569, File No. 50/1471.

124. NASA, DGO 55, File No. 120/3/111.

125. SOAS, MS 380256, Folder 62, "Zion Apostolic Faith Mission."

126. Sundkler, *Bantu Prophets,* 245.

127. Sundkler, *Zulu Zion,* 81–82.

128. Allen Lea, "The Separatist Church Movement of South Africa," *International Review of Missions* 26, no. 104, October 1937, 456.

129. Phillips, *Bantu in the City*, 255.

130. SOAS, MS 380256 "Constitution and Laws, Byelaws, Rules and Regulations of the CAC in Zion of SA."

131. Mia Brandel-Syrier, *Reeftown Elite: A Study of Social Mobility in a Modern African Community on the Reef* (London: Routledge and Kegan Paul, 1971), 68.

132. SOAS, MS 380256, Christian Apostolic Church in Zion of South Africa Constitution, Laws, Byelaws, Rules and Regulations, 1920.

133. *Bantu World*, 21 April 1934.

134. NASA, NTS 1428, Edgar Mahon to Chief Native Commissioner, 11 April 1933.

135. GMC, *Light is Springing Up: A Pictorial Story of the Mahon Mission* (Etembeni: Mahon Mission Press, 1955).

136. *Bantu World*, 16 September 1933 (in isiZulu).

137. *Bantu World*, 7 May 1932.

138. *Bantu World*, 13 July 1939. See also 'Preachers Need Training," 12 August 1939 and 'Intellectuals and Untrained Preachers," 23 September 1939.

139. *Bantu World*, 16 September 1933 (in isiZulu).

140. *Bantu World*, 14 December 1940.

141. *Bantu World*, 16 September 1933 (in isiZulu).

142. Seth Mokitimi, "African Religion," in *Handbook on Race Relations in South Africa*, ed. Ellen Hellmann (Oxford: Oxford University Press, 1949), 569. Mokitimi had trained for the Methodist ministry at Fort Hare, alongside none other than Phillip Mabiletsa, son of Paulus Mabiletsa, the most prominent representative of the older Zionist tradition in the city.

143. Phillips, *Bantu Are Coming*, 55.

144. Robert Edgar, "The Prophet Motive: Enoch Mgijima, the Israelites and the Background to the Bulhoek Massacre," *International Journal of African Historical Studies*, 15, 3 (1982), 401–422.

145. *Ilanga lase Natal*, 22 July 1921.

146. *Ilanga lase Natal*, 1 July 1921, 5.

147. *Ilanga lase Natal*, 15 July 1921.

148. *Umteteli wa Bantu*, 21 May 1921.

149. *Umteteli wa Bantu*, 10 October 1925.

150. *Report of the Native Churches Commission* (Pretoria: Union Government Printers, 1926), 7–17.

151. *Native Churches Commission*, 17.

152. *Native Churches Commission*, 18.

153. Sundkler, *Bantu Prophets*, 77–78.

154. Hill, "Native Separatist Movements," 110.

155. Charles Loram, "The Separatist Church Movement," *International Review of Missions* 15, no. 59 (July 1926): 477.

156. Mokitimi, "African Religion," 565.

157. Sundkler, *Bantu Prophets*, 81.

158. *Bantu World,* 19 August 1933; Sundkler, *Bantu Prophets,* 81–82.

159. Rosenthal, "Johannesburg, Home of Many Religions," 252.

160. *Bantu World,* 19 August 1933; 5 June 1937.

161. *Bantu World,* 19 August 1933.

162. Sundkler, *Bantu Prophets,* 47–48.

163. Koch, *Doorfontein,* 103; Phillips, *Bantu Are Coming,* 163; Hellman, *Rooiyard,* 8; Susan Parnell, "Race, Power and Urban Control: Johannesburg's Inner-City Slumyards, 1910–1923," *Journal of Southern African Studies* 29, no. 3 (2003), 631.

164. *Rand Daily Mail,* 16 January 1923; *Star,* 18 December 1924.

165. Dunbar Moodie, "Mine Culture and Miners' Identity of the South African Gold Mines," in *Town and Countryside in the Transvaal,* ed. Belinda Bozzoli (Johannesburg: Ravan Press, 1983), 180.

166. Alan H. Jeeves, *Migrant Labour in South Africa's Mining Economy* (Montreal: McGill-Queens University Press, 1985), 22.

167. Jonathan Crush, Alan H. Jeeves, and David Yudelman, *South Africa's Labour Empire: A History of Black Migrancy to the Gold Mines* (Oxford: Westview Press, 1991), 33–45.

168. Jeeves, *Migrant Labour,* 26.

169. *Bantu World,* 11 September 1937.

170. Karen Flint, *Healing Traditions: African Medicine, Cultural Exchange and Competition in South Africa, 1820–1948* (Athens: Ohio University Press, 2008), 132.

171. Hellman, *Rooiyard,* 107.

172. Phillips, *Bantu in the City,* 16.

173. Hellman, *Rooiyard,* 104.

174. *Bantu World,* 16 April 1932.

175. Bonner and Nieftagodien, *Alexandra,* 103.

176. Phillips, *Bantu in the City,* 16.

177. Phillips, *Bantu in the City,* 130; *Rand Daily Mail* 18 January 1923; 31 January 1923; 23 February 1923.

178. Phillips, *Bantu in the City,* 132; *Rand Daily Mail,* 21 May 1918; Wulf Sachs, *Black Hamlet* (Baltimore: Johns Hopkins University Press, 1996), 5–6.

179. Sachs, *Black Hamlet,* 178.

180. *Bantu World,* 9 April 1932.

181. *Bantu World,* 21 April 1934.

182. Anne Digby, "Early Black Doctors in South Africa," *Journal of African History* 46, no. 3 (2005): 426–454.

183. Digby, "Black Doctors," 442–443; Leo Kuper, *An African Bourgeoisie: Race, Class and Politics in South Africa* (New Haven: Yale University Press, 1965), 234.

184. *Bantu World,* 19 November 1932.

185. Skota, *African Yearly Register,* 152.

186. *Umteteli wa Bantu,* 13 March 1926.

187. *Bantu World,* 22 December 1934.

188. *Bantu World,* 14 March 1936.

189. *Umteteli wa Bantu,* 1 May 1920.

190. *Bantu World,* 7 January 1939.

191. *Leaves of Healing,* 4 October 1913.

192. *Rand Daily Mail,* 19 August 1913.

193. Les Switzer, ed., *South Africa's Alternative Press: Voices of Protest and Resistance, 1880–1960* (Cambridge: Cambridge University Press, 1997), 200.

194. *Bantu World,* 19 June 1937.

195. *Bantu World,* 23 September 1933.

196. *Bantu World,* 31 March 1934.

197. *Bantu World,* 16 September 1933 (in isiZulu).

198. Sundkler, *Bantu Prophets,* 86.

199. *Bantu World,* 31 March 1934.

200. *Bantu World,* 16 September 1933 (in isiZulu).

201. Interview with Emmanuel Tsotetse and Interview with Thami Hlatshwayo, both in Soweto, Johannesburg, 16 June 2016.

202. *Bantu World,* 16 September 1933 (in isiZulu).

203. *Bantu World,* 16 September 1933 (in isiZulu).

204. Sundkler, *Bantu Prophets,* 255–256.

205. *Bantu World,* 16 September 1933 (in isiZulu).

206. GMC, *Zululand & Basutoland Missionary* 15, no. 7, May 1928.

207. Sundkler, *Bantu Prophets,* 258.

208. Timothy L. L. Dlamini, "The Christian Catholic Apostolic Holy Spirit Church in Zion as it Exists in Swaziland" (PhD diss., University of Botswana and Swaziland, 1976), 4.

209. Sundkler, *Bantu Prophets,* 245.

210. Sundkler, *Bantu Prophets,* 247.

211. GMC, *Zululand and Basutoland Missionary* 20, no. 2, December 1932.

212. Sundkler, *Bantu Prophets,* 260–261.

213. Sundkler, *Bantu Prophets,* 241.

214. Uppsala, Bengt Sundkler Collection, Box 130, Constitution of Holy Catholic Apostolic Church in Zion.

215. NASA, GNLB 205 File No. 1697/14/110; Uppsala, Bengt Sundkler Collection, Box 123, City of Johannesburg Non-European Affairs Department, Separatist Churches, Survey 1958.

216. *Bantu World,* 16 September 1933 (in isiZulu).

217. *Bantu World,* 16 September 1933 (in isiZulu).

218. *Bantu World,* 16 September 1933 (in isiZulu).

219. Interview with Godfrey Maseko, Soweto, Johannesburg, South Africa, 24 November 2015.

220. Interview with Philemon Mvubu, Manzini, Swaziland, 15 August 2016.

221. *Bantu World,* 21 April 1934 (in isiZulu).

222. *Bantu World,* 31 March 1934.

223. Bonner and Nieftagodien, *Alexandra,* 103.

224. *Bantu World,* 20 November 1937; 13 November 1937.

225. *Bantu World,* 20 November 1937. See also editorial in *Umteteli wa Bantu,* 10 October 1925.

226. *Bantu World,* 10 June 1933; see also *Bantu World,* 16 September 1933 (in isiZulu).

227. Dikobe, *Marabi Dance.*

228. *Umteteli wa Bantu,* 18 June 1921.

229. *Bantu World,* 15 June 1940.

6. COSMOPOLITANISM, ETHNICITY, AND MIGRANT LABOR NETWORKS IN SOUTHERN AFRICAN ZION

1. *Bantu World,* 16 April 1932 (in isiZulu).

2. Philip Bonner, "South African Society and Culture, 1910–1948," in *The Cambridge History of South Africa,* ed. Robert Ross, Anne Kelk Mager, and Bill Nasson (Cambridge: Cambridge University Press, 2012), 2:305.

3. Leroy Vail, ed., *The Creation of Tribalism in Southern Africa* (Berkeley: University of California Press, 1986).

4. Nicholas Cope, *To Bind the Nation: Solomon kaDinuzulu and Zulu Nationalism* (Pietermaritzburg: University of Natal Press, 1993); Hugh Mac-Millan, "Swaziland, Decolonization and the Triumph of Tradition," *Journal of Modern African Studies* 23, no. 4 (1985): 643–666.

5. Sean Moroney, "Mine Married Quarters: The Differential Stabilization of the Witwatersrand Workforce, 1900–1920," in *Industrialization and Social Change in South Africa: African Class Formation, Culture and Consciousness,* ed. Shula Marks and Richard Rathbone (Harlow, Essex: Longman, 1982), 261.

6. Modikwe Dikobe, *The Marabi Dance* (London: Heinemann, 1973), 75.

7. P. Spurr, "Street Scenes and Impressions," in *The Golden City, Johannesburg,* ed. Allister Macmillan (London: W. H. & L. Collingridge, 1933), 205.

8. Keith Breckenridge, "Migrancy, Crime and Faction Fighting: The Role of the Isitshozi in the Development of Ethnic Organizations in Compounds," *Journal of Southern African Studies* 16, no. 1 (1990): 56; Jeff Guy and Motlatsi Thabane, "Technology, Ethnicity and Ideology: Basuto Miners and Shaft Sinking on the South African Gold Mines," *Journal of Southern African Studies* 14, no. 2 (1988): 259.

9. Peter Delius, "Sebatakgomo: Migrant Organizations, the ANC and the Sekhukhuneland Revolt," *Journal of Southern African Studies* 15, no. 4 (1989): 583; Sekibakiba Peter Lekgoathi, "Migrants from Zebediela and Shifting Identities on the Rand, 1930s to 1970s," in *A Long Way Home: Migrant Worker Worlds, 1880–2014,* ed. Peter Delius, Laura Phillips and Fiona Rankin-Smith (Johannesburg: Wits University Press, 2014), 158–161.

10. William Beinart, "A Century of Migrancy from Mpondoland," *African Studies* 73, no. 3 (2014): 394.

11. J. D. Taylor, "The Rand as Mission Field," *International Review of Missions* 15, no. 60 (October 1926): 650.

12. Ray Phillips, *Bantu in the City: A Study of Cultural Adjustment on the Witwatersrand* (Alice: Lovedale Press, 1938), 254.

13. Patrick Harries, *Work, Culture and Identity: Migrant Labourers in Mozambique and South Africa, 1860–1910* (Johannesburg: University of Witwatersrand Press, 1994), 217.

14. Harries, *Work, Culture and Identity,* 217.

15. University of Uppsala Archives, Uppsala, Sweden (hereafter Uppsala), Bengt Sundkler Papers, Box 92, "Separatist Churches in the Hostels."

16. Uppsala, Bengt Sundkler Papers, Box 112 'A Second Study of Life in the Townships," Market Research Africa, Johannesburg, 1967.

17. Philip Bonner and Noor Nieftagodien, *Alexandra: A History* (Johannesburg: University of Witwatersrand Press, 2008), 53.

18. Peter Walshe, *The Rise of African Nationalism in South Africa* (Berkeley: University of California Press, 1971), 213.

19. Walshe, *African Nationalism,* 242.

20. Uppsala, Bengt Sundkler Papers, Box 132, *Africa's Golden Harvest* 9, no. 13, August 1914.

21. Uppsala, Bengt Sundkler Papers, Box 132.

22. Uppsala, Bengt Sundkler Papers, Box 132.

23. *Leaves of Healing,* 20 December 1913.

24. *Leaves of Healing,* 21 March 1914.

25. NASA, GNLB 216, T. Snider to South African Police, Western Area, Johannesburg, 16 and 17 March 1920.

26. Uppsala, Bengt Sundkler Papers, Box 127, *Constitution of the Holy Catholic Apostolic Church in Zion* (Doornfontein, 1937), last chapter by Jane Phillips, "A Brief History of the Life of the Rev. John George Philips." City Deep Mine Compound, for example, allowed Zionist services in their rooms; NASA, NTS 1430 File No. 23/214, Missao Christao Catholica Apostolica em Zion to SNA, 18 September 1928.

27. Ray E. Phillips, *The Bantu Are Coming: Phases of South Africa's Race Problem* (London: Student Christian Movement, 1930), 55.

28. NASA, NTS 1427 File No. 16/214, South African Police Report, Boksburg, 12 August 1918.

29. Bengt Sundkler, *Bantu Prophets in South Africa* (London: Lutterworth Press, 1948), 366, 373.

30. Bonner and Nieftagodien, *Alexandra,* 103.

31. NASA, NTS 1430 23/214, Jack Taju, Lourenco Marques to Secretary for Native Affairs, 18 September 1928.

32. Bengt Sundkler, *Zulu Zion and some Swazi Zionists* (Oxford: Oxford University Press, 1976), 61–65.

33. NASA, GNLB 205 File No. 1697/14/110; Uppsala, Bengt Sundkler Papers, Box 123, City of Johannesburg Non-European Affairs Department, Separatist Churches, Survey 1958.

34. Interview with Asa Mmango, Soweto, Johannesburg, 16 July 2016.

35. Interview with Godfrey Maseko, Soweto, Johannesburg, South Africa, 24 November 2015.

36. Uppsala, Bengt Sundkler Papers, Box 123, City of Johannesburg Non-European Affairs Department, Separatist Churches, Survey 1958.
37. Interview with Thami Hlathshwayo, Soweto, Johannesburg, 14 July 2016.
38. Uppsala, Bengt Sundkler Papers, Box 96, P. Mkize's interview with P. Mahlangu, 18 December 1973.
39. SOAS, MS 380256, Christian Apostolic Church in Zion of South Africa Constitution, Laws, Byelaws, Rules and Regulations, 1920.
40. NASA, GG 1569, File No. 50/1471, Lion to GG, 7 February 1933.
41. NASA, GNLB 216, "Constitution of the Bethesda Zion Apostolic Church of Africa," 11 July 1921.
42. Sundkler, *Zulu Zion,* 64.
43. Uppsala, Bengt Sundkler Papers, Box 113, Constitution of Congregational Catholic Apostolic Church of Zion in South Africa.
44. Uppsala, Bengt Sundkler Papers, Box 130, Constitution of Christian Catholic Apostolic Holy Spirit Church in Zion, 1923.
45. Zacarias Muiambo, *Titus Ndhlovu: Sigwaba Inkani* (Maputo: Mozambique School of the Bible, 2013), 14.
46. Uppsala, Bengt Sundkler Papers, Box 132, *Africa's Golden Harvest,* January 1914.
47. NASA, GNLB 216, Native Inspector of Mines to DNL, 14 June 1916.
48. SOAS, MS 380256, File Number 1, Folder on "East African Gaza Church," Report of Rev AW Baker, 1921.
49. Interview with Thami Hlatshwayo, Soweto, Johannesburg, 14 July 2016.
50. Liz Gunner, "Soft Masculinities, *Isicathamiya* and Radio," *Journal of Southern African Studies,* 40, 2 (2014), 343–360; Deborah James, "*Basade ba baeng:* Visiting Women: Female Migrant Performance from the Northern Transvaal," in *Politics and Performance: Theatre, Poetry and Song in Southern Africa,* ed. Liz Gunner (Johannesburg: University of Witwatersrand Press, 1994), 85.
51. Interview with Emmanuel Tsotetse; Thami Hlatshwayo, Soweto, Johannesburg, 16 June 2016.
52. Muiambo, *Titus Ndhlovu,* 14.
53. Uppsala, Bengt Sundkler Papers, Box 132, *Africa's Golden Harvest,* January 1914.
54. Uppsala, Bengt Sundkler Papers, Box 96, P. Mkize interview with P. Mahlangu, 18 December 1973.
55. Interview with Thami Hlatshwayo, Soweto, 14 July 2016.
56. Henry Mitchell'Patience and Perseverance Overcome Mountains': The Prudent Struggles of Malawians Migrating to South Africa, 1913–1960," *Journal of South African Studies* (forthcoming).
57. *Leaves of Healing,* 3 January 1914.
58. *Native Churches Commission,* "Section 9: Anti-European Feeling."
59. NASA, NTS 1459, Rev. Mazibuko to SNA, 4 January 1929.
60. Uppsala, Bengt Sundkler Papers, Box 130, *Constitution of the Zion Apostolic Faith Mission of the World* (Ladybrand: n.p., 1922).

61. Uppsala, Bengt Sundkler Papers, Box 130 "Constitution of the Holy Catholic Apostolic Church in Zion."

62. Uppsala, Bengt Sundkler Papers, Box 130 "Constitution of the Holy Catholic Apostolic Church in Zion."

63. *Bantu World,* 16 April 1932 (in isiZulu).

64. NASA, NTS 1427, File No. 16/214 "The Native Work of the Apostolic Faith Mission," 15 December 1917.

65. Phillips, *Bantu Are Coming,* 31.

66. Uppsala, Bengt Sundkler Papers, *Africa's Golden Harvests,* January 1914, "The Story of the South African Compounds Mission."

67. *Bantu World,* 7 January 1939.

68. Botswana National Archives (hereafter BNA), Secretariat 291, S.291/18/1, Memorandum on Motsisi Ralefala, 17 December 1940, District Commissioner's Office, Mochudi; Secretariat Box No. 497, S.497/5/1, District Commissioner Mochudi to Government's Secretary, Mafeking, 9 December 1947.

69. NASA, GG 1550, Government House, Zomba, Nyasaland to Governor General, Pretoria, 22 December 1919.

70. NASA, NTS 1451, File No. 76/214, Native Sub-Commissioner Johannesburg to DNL, Johannesburg, 17 September 1923.

71. Interview with Philemon Mvubu, Manzini, Swaziland, 15 August 2016.

72. Muiambo, *Titus Ndhlovu,* 5–6.

73. Interview with Zacarias Muiambo, Maputo, Mozambique, 22 June 2016.

74. NASA, GNLB 353, Native Sub-Commissioner Johannesburg to DNL, Johannesburg, 9 August 1923.

75. BNA, Secretariat 291, S. 291/18/1, Memorandum on Motsisi Ralefala, 17 December 1940, District Commissioner's Office, Mochudi.

76. *Bantu World,* 7 January 1939.

77. *Bantu World,* 15 October 1938.

78. *Bantu World,* 10 June 1939.

79. *Bantu World,* 15 October 1938.

80. Muiambo, *Titus Ndhlovu,* 10.

81. Muiambo, *Titus Ndhlovu,* chap. 2.

82. Muiambo, *Titus Ndhlovu,* chap. 2.

83. John Lambert, "Chiefship in Early Colonial Natal, 1843–1879," *Journal of Southern African Studies* 21: 2 (1995): 269–285.

84. Helen Bradford, *A Taste of Freedom: The ICU in Rural South Africa, 1924–1930* (New Haven: Yale University Press, 1987), 88–104.

85. Aran MacKinnon, "Chiefly Authority, Leapfrogging Headmen and the Political Economy of Zululand, South Africa, ca. 1930–1950," *Journal of Southern African Studies* 27, no. 3 (2001): 567–590.

86. Aran MacKinnon, "The Persistence of the Cattle Economy in Zululand, 1900–1950," *Canadian Journal of African Studies* 33, no. 1 (1999): 113.

87. Muiambo, *Titus Ndhlovu,* chap. 2.

88. Sundkler, *Zulu Zion,* 156.

89. *Bantu World,* 15 October 1938.

90. BNA, DIV.COM.S/3/17, Notes of Discussion between Acting Resident Commissioner and Chiefs of the Bechuanaland Protectorate, Mafeking, 17 April 1957.

91. BNA, DIV.COM.S/3/17, Notes of Discussion between Acting Resident Commissioner and Chiefs of the Bechuanaland Protectorate, Mafeking, 17 April 1957.

92. Marks, "Patriotism, Patriarchy and Purity," 220–228.

93. BNA, Secretariat, 291, S. 291/18/1. Notes of Meeting Held in Bokaa Kgotla, 31 July 1940.

94. BNA, DIV.COM.S/3/17, Notes of Discussion between Acting Resident Commissioner and Chiefs of the Bechuanaland Protectorate, Mafeking, 17 April 1957.

95. BNA, DIV.COM.S.3/17, Chief Bathoen II to District Commissioner Lobatsi, 23 September 1957.

96. Sundkler, *Bantu Prophets*, 96.

97. BNA, DIV.COM.S.3/17, Notes of Discussions between Acting Resident Commissioner and the Chiefs of the Bechuanaland Protectorate, Mafeking, 17 April 1957.

98. NASA, NTS 1451 File No. 76/214, Native Sub-Commissioner Johannesburg to DNL, Johannesburg, 17 September 1923.

99. NASA, GNLB 353, J. G. Phillips to NAD, Johannesburg, 11 June 1924.

100. NASA, GNLB 353, J. G. Phillips to DNL, Johannesburg, 3 October 1924.

101. National Archives of Swaziland, Lobamba (hereafter NAS), RCS File No. 320/40.

102. NASA, KJB 100, File No. 198/33, Paulus Mabiletsa, "Application for Church Recognition," F. B. Wessels to Native Commissioner, Johannesburg, 23 June 1944.

103. NASA, URU 1270, Governor General Memorandum, 24 March 1932.

104. NASA, GNLB 369, Printed Constitution of "Zion Apostolic Faith Mission," ca. 1921.

105. NASA, GNLB 353, Native Sub-Commissioner Johannesburg to Director for Native Labour, Johannesburg, 9 August 1923.

106. NAS, RCS 155/37, W. Mkize to Resident Native Commissioner, Swaziland, 22 January 1937.

107. Uppsala, Bengt Sundker Papers, Box 123, City of Johannesburg Non-European Affairs Department, "Survey into Separatist Churches in Orlando," 1958.

108. Sundkler, *Bantu Prophets*, 85.

109. Uppsala, Bengt Sundkler Papers, Box 96, P. Mkize interview with P. Mahlangu, 18 December 1973.

110. NASA, GNLB 353, Philips to NAD Johannesburg, 11 June 1924.

111. NASA, NTS 1430 File No. 23/214, J. Maduna to SNA, 29 August 1936.

112. NASA, GNLB 353, Philips to NAD Johannesburg, 11 June 1924.

113. *Bantu World*, 15 October 1938.

114. Interview with Thami Hlatshwayo, Soweto, Johannesburg, South Africa, 14 June 2016.

115. NASA, GG 1550, Government House, Zomba, Nyasaland to Governor General, Pretoria, 22 December 1919.

116. Church documents in the possession of Soul Sibandze, Swazi Christian Church in Zion of South Africa, Lobamba loMdzala, Swaziland.

117. NASA, GG 1575 File No. 50/1783, Evangelist's Certificate from The Catholic Apostolic Church of Witness in Zion of South Africa.

118. NASA, GNLB 353, Preachers' Certificate of Holy Catholic Apostolic Church in Zion, n.d.

119. NASA, DGO 75 T. N. Ngubane to SNA, 29 August 1938.

120. NASA, GNLB 216 File No. 150/15/317, "Constitution of the Bethesda Zion Apostolic Church of Africa."

121. Interview with Asa Mmango, Soweto, Johannesburg, South Africa, 16 July 2016.

122. Interview with Soul Sibandze, Lobamba Lomdzala, Swaziland, 29 June 2016.

123. *Bantu World,* 22 April 1939 (in isiZulu); 6 April 1940 (in isiZulu).

124. NASA, GNLB 299, Ulyate to NAD, Johannesburg, 21 August 1915.

125. NASA, GNLB 299, Ulyate to NAD, Johannesburg, 21 August 1915; DGO 75 T. N. Ngubane to SNA, 29 August 1938.

126. *Bantu World,* 27 April 1935 (in isiZulu).

127. Allan Anderson, "The Lekganyanes and Prophecy in the Zion Christian Church," *Journal of Religion in Africa,* 29, 3 (1999), 287; AFM, Executive Committee Minutes, 1908–1914, 9 September 1914.

128. Uppsala, Bengt Sundkler Papers, Box 96, P. Mkize interview with P. Mahlangu, 18 December 1973.

129. Anderson, "Lekganyanes," 287–288.

130. NASA, GNLB 369, "Zion Apostolic Faith Mission of South Africa."

131. Anderson, "Lekganyanes," 289.

132. Samuel Mutendi was a migrant laborer to the Rand from Zimbabwe who became Lekganyane's influential overseer for that region, leading a community of eventually 250,000. Vengesayi Chimininge, "Zion Christian Church," in *Multiplying in the Spirit: African Initiated Churches in Zimbabwe,* ed. Ezra Chitando, Masiiwa Ragies Gunda and Joachim Kuegler (Bamberg: University of Bamberg Press, 2014), 33–48.

133. Anderson, "Lekganyanes," 289–291; Sundkler, *Zulu Zion,* 219; *Drum* July 1954.

134. BNA, Secretariat 435 Box 435, S.435/3/1, J. Lekganyane, Pietersburg to Acting Government Secretary, Bechuanaland Protectorate, Mafeking, 16 September 1953.

135. Anderson, "Lekganyanes," 289.

136. *Drum,* July 1954.

137. *Drum,* July 1954.

138. Anderson, "Lekganyanes," 296.

139. J. Cabrita, "Isaiah Shembe's Theological Nationalism, 1920s–1935," *Journal of Southern African Studies* 35, no. 3 (2009): 611.

140. N. Cope, *To Bind the Nation: Solomon kaDinuzulu and Zulu Nationalism, 1913–1933* (Pietermaritzburg: University of Natal Press, 1993), 171–200.

141. Cabrita, "Theological Nationalism," 611.
142. Sundkler, *Zulu Zion*, 63.
143. NASA, NTS 1451 File No. 76/214, NAD Johannesburg to SNA, 27 June 1927.
144. Uppsala, Bengt Sundkler Papers, Box 96, P. Mkize interview with P. Mahlangu, 18 December 1973; NASA, NTS 1451 File No. 76/214, E. Mahlangu to SNA, 28 July 1926.
145. Joel Cabrita, *Text and Authority in the South African Nazaretha Church* (Cambridge: Cambridge University Press, 2014), 143.
146. NASA, NTS 1451 File No. 76/214, E. Mahlangu to SNA, 28 July 1926.
147. NASA, NTS 1451 File No. 76/214, E. Mahlangu to SNA, 28 July 1926; General Manager South African Railways and Harbours to SNA, 29 March 1927.
148. NASA, NTS 1451 File No. 76/214, E. Mbonambi to S. Seheri 5 and 13 February 1926.
149. Uppsala, Bengt Sundkler Papers, Box 96, P. Mkize interview with P. Mahlangu, 18 December 1973.
150. NASA, NTS 1451 File No. 76/214, E. Mbonambi to SNA, 26 April 1928.
151. NASA, NTS 1451 File No. 76/214, clipping from *Ilanga lase Natal*, 26 October 1928, "The Remarks of Rev. E. J. Mbonambi to the Editor' (in isiZulu).
152. NASA, NTS 1451 File No. 76/214, Statement from Zion Apostolic Church, Etete Bridge, Groutville, Natal, n.d.
153. Sundkler, "Chief and Prophet," 277.
154. Uppsala, Bengt Sundkler Papers, Box 138, Daniel Nkonyane Membership Application Form to Christian Catholic Apostolic Church in Zion, Zion City, Illinois.
155. J. S. M. Matsebula, *A History of Swaziland* (Cape Town: Longman, 1988), 161ff., 184–185; MacMillan, "Triumph of Tradition," 645.
156. Timothy L. L. Dlamini, "The Christian Catholic Apostolic Holy Spirit Church in Zion as It Exists in Swaziland" (PhD diss., University of Botswana and Swaziland, 1976), 6–7.
157. Fiona Armitage, "Abakamoya: People of the Spirit: A Study of the Zionist Movement in Swaziland with Special Reference to the Swazi Christian Church in Zion of South Africa and the Nazarethe Branch" (PhD diss., University of Aberdeen, 1976), 77.
158. Sundkler, *Zulu Zion*, 209.
159. Interview with Soul Sibandze, Lobamba Lomdzala, Swaziland, 27 June 2016. Zwane had previously belonged to Snelling's church before affiliating to Nkonyane. Sundkler, *Zulu Zion*, 214.
160. Hugh Macmillan, "A Nation Divided? The Swazi in Swaziland and the Transvaal, 1865–1986," in *The Creation of Tribalism in Southern Africa*, ed. Leroy Vail (Berkeley: University of California Press, 1986), 292.
161. Interview with Simon/Dabete Mavimbela, Mbabane, 11 July 2016.
162. Interview with Herbert Mavimbela and Pastor Dlamini, Ludzeludze, Manzini, Swaziland, 23 June 2016.

163. Interview with Simon/Dabete Mavimbela, Mbabane, 11 July 2016.

164. Uppsala, Bengt Sundkler Papers, Box 115, Town Clerk Wakkerstroom to Resident Magistrate, Wakkerstroom, 14 December 1909.

165. Sundkler, *Zulu Zion*, 209–210.

166. Interview with Simon/Dabete Mavimbela, Mbabane, 11 July 2016.

167. Sundkler, *Zulu Zion*, 210.

168. Interview with Simon/Dabete Mavimbela, Mbabane, 11 July 2016.

169. McMillan, "A Nation Divided?," 300ff.

170. McMillan, "A Nation Divided?," 301.

171. Sundkler, *Zulu Zion*, 224.

172. NAS, RCS 791/36, Swaziland Police to Chief of Police, 6 January 1937.

173. Interview with Herbert Mavimbela and Pastor Dlamini, Ludzeludze, Manzini, Swaziland, 23 June 2016.

174. NAS, RCS 282/1941, District Commissioner Central District to Government Secretary Mbabane, 21 October 1941.

175. Interview with Soul Sibandze, Lobamba Lomdzala, Swaziland, 29 June 2016.

176. Interview with Simon/Dabete Mavimbela, Mbabane, 11 July 2016.

177. NAS, RCS 791/36, Assistant District Commissioner to Government Secretary, Mbabane, 9 November 1936.

178. Interview with Bishop Maziya, Manzini, Swaziland (interview conducted by Dr. Sonene Nyawo), 4 August 2016.

179. Interview with Bishop Maziya, Manzini, Swaziland (interview conducted by Dr. Sonene Nyawo), 4 August 2016.

180. Hebron Ndhlovu, Sonene Nyawo, David Nhlabatsi, Patrick Mkhonta, "The League of African Christian Churches in Swaziland: Challenges and Prospects' (Kwaluseni: University of Swaziland, 2011), 34.

181. Interview with Nhlanhla Magongo, Manzini, Swaziland, 8 June 2016.

182. NAS, RCS 282/1941, District Commissioner Central District to Government Secretary, Mbabane, 28 July 1941; Ekuphumleni Church Papers (kept by Soul Sibandze), Examination and Ordination Certificates of Swazi Christian Church in Zion, ca. 1940.

183. Ndhlovu et al, "African Christian Churches in Swaziland," 32.

184. NAS, RCS 791/36, District Commissioner to Government Secretary, 11 February 1937; Sundkler, *Zulu Zion*, 216.

185. Sundkler, *Zulu Zion*, 224.

186. Interview with Bishop Maziya, Manzini, Swaziland (interview conducted by Dr. Sonene Nyawo), 4 August 2016.

187. Sundkler, *Zulu Zion*, 207.

188. *Izwi lama Swazi*, 8 December 1956, cited in Sundkler, *Zulu Zion*, 233.

189. NAS, RCS 791/36 District Commissioner to Government Secretary, Mbabane, 2 February 1937.

190. Interview with Bishop Maziya, Manzini, Swaziland (interview conducted by Dr. Sonene Nyawo), 4 August 2016.

191. Hilda Kuper, "A Ritual of Kingship Among the Swazi," *Africa: Journal of the International African Institute* 14, no. 5 (1944): 232–233.

7. YOUTHFUL REFORMERS AND THE POLITICS OF BIBLE SCHOOLS IN THE KINGDOM OF SWAZILAND

1. Zion Bible College meeting, Manzini, Swaziland, 4 August 2016.
2. Paul Cummergen, "Zionism and Politics in South Africa," *Journal of Religion in Africa* 30, no. 3 (2000): 376; Peter Kasenene, "Swazi Civil Religion: An Emerging Ideology for Swaziland," *UNISWA Research Journal* 1 (1988) and "Church and State in Swaziland," *UNISWA Research Journal* 4 (1991); Hebron Ndhlovu, "Zionist Churches and the Promotion of Civil Society—the Case of the Kingdom of Swaziland," *Theologia Viatorum* 24 (1997).
3. Anders Fogelqvist, *The Red-Dressed Zionists: Symbols of Power in a Swazi Independent Church* (Uppsala: Uppsala Research Reports in Cultural Anthropology, 1986), 35–36; Timothy L. L. Dlamini, "The Christian Catholic Apostolic Holy Spirit Church in Zion in Swaziland" (PhD diss., University of Botswana and Swaziland, 1978), 25; Sandile Nyawo, "Religious Organizations in Swaziland: The Case of the Zionists" (PhD diss., University of Swaziland, 1998), 17.
4. Roger Cazziol, "The Swazi Zionists: An Indigenous Religious Movement in Southern Africa" (working paper, University of Swaziland, 1987), 82.
5. Dlamini, "Holy Spirit Church," 18.
6. Martin West, *Bishops & Prophets in a Black City: African Independent Churches in Soweto* (Johannesburg: David Philip, 1975), 55.
7. Dlamini, "Holy Spirit Church," 20; Fogelqvist, *Red-Dressed Zionists,* 36; Fiona Armitage, "Abakaymoya: People of the Spirit, A Study of the Zionist Movement in Swaziland" (PhD diss., University of Aberdeen, 1976), 253.
8. Fogelqvist, *Red-Dressed Zionists,* 349; Dlamini, "Holy Spirit Church," 354.
9. Interview with Meshack Dlamini, Matsapha, Swaziland, 19 August 2016.
10. *Fulfilling the Vision: Swaziland Evangelism Task Report* (n.p., 1995), 67.
11. Interview with Linda Hlatshwayo, Soweto, Johannesburg, South Africa, 14 June 2016. For a description of a *siguco* from the 1960s, see West, *Bishops and Prophets,* 92–93.
12. Interview with Nhlanhla Magongo, Manzini, Swaziland, 8 June 2016.
13. Interview with Sifiso Dlamini, Manzini, Swaziland, 29 June 2016.
14. Interview with Jerome Sangweni, Manzini, Swaziland, 8 June 2016.
15. Interview with Sifiso Dlamini, Manzini, Swaziland, 29 June 2016.
16. West, *Bishops and Prophets,* 181.
17. Interview with Zac Muiambo, Maputo, Mozambique, 22 June 2016.
18. Interview with Khanyakwezwe Vilakati, Makanyane, Swaziland, 30 July 2016; *Times of Swaziland,* 11 April 1998.
19. Fogelqvist, *Red-Dressed Zionists,* 76.
20. Fogelqvist, *Red-Dressed Zionists,* 114.
21. Armitage, "Abakamoya," 350.
22. Interview with Vusimuzi Mkhatshwa, Mbabane, Swaziland, 17 August 2016; G. C. Oosthuizen, *The Healer-Prophet in Afro-Christian Churches* (Leiden: E. J. Brill, 1992), 32.

23. Interview with Meshack Dlamini, Matsapha, Swaziland, 19 August 2016; J. P. Kiernan, "Prophet and Preacher: An Essential Partnership in the Work of Zion," *MAN* 11, no. 3 (1976): 356–366.
24. Fogelqvist, *Red-Dressed Zionists,* 63.
25. *Times of Swaziland,* 22 July 2001.
26. *Times of Swaziland,* 19 August 1994.
27. Interview with Solomon Dube, Matsapha, Swaziland, 15 July 2016.
28. Fogelqvist, *Red-Dressed Zionists,* 129.
29. Interview with Solomon Dube, Matsapha, Swaziland, 15 July 2016. A similar pattern is noted by J.P. Kiernan in "The Social Stuff of Revelation: Pattern and Purpose in Zionist Dreams and Visions," *AFRICA: Journal of the International African Institute* 55, no. 3 (1985): 312–314.
30. Hugh MacMillan, "A Nation Divided? The Swazi in Swaziland and the Transvaal, 1865–1985," in *The Creation of Tribalism in Southern Africa,* ed. Leroy Vail (Berkeley: University of California Press, 1986), 306.
31. Hugh MacMillan, "Swaziland, Decolonization and the Triumph of Tradition," *Journal of Modern African Studies* 23, no. 4 (1985): 661.
32. Macmillan, "Swaziland," 664.
33. Paul Cummergen, "Zionism and Politics in Swaziland," *Journal of Religion in Africa* 30, no. 3 (2000): 376.
34. Fogelqvist, *Red-Dressed Zionists,* 80.
35. Fogelqvist, *Red-Dressed Zionists,* 80.
36. *Times of Swaziland,* 23 January 1993.
37. *Times of Swaziland,* 6 December 1993, Letter to the Editor from Dumisani Hlophe.
38. *Fulfilling the Vision,* 48.
39. *Fulfilling the Vision,* 47.
40. *Times of Swaziland,* 2 December 1993 and 1 December 1994; Casey Colomski, "Risk, Mistake and Generational Context in Bodily Rituals of Swazi Jerikho Zionism," *Journal of Contemporary Religion* 31, no. 3 (2016): 353.
41. *Times of Swaziland,* 18 December 1993.
42. *Times of Swaziland,* 8 September 1996.
43. *Times Higher Education,* 24 March 1995; *Times of Swaziland,* 7 August 1994.
44. *Times of Swaziland,* 15 December 1993.
45. *Times of Swaziland,* 7 April 1996.
46. *Times of Swaziland,* 20 April 2003.
47. *Times of Swaziland,* 12 April 1998.
48. Armitage, "Abakaymoya," 256.
49. Fogelqvist, *Red-Dressed Zionists,* 81.
50. Nyawo, "Zionist Churches," 26.
51. Golomski, "Swazi Jerikho Zionism," 355; Dlamini, "Holy Spirit Church," 313.
52. Fogelqvist, *Red-Dressed Zionists,* 164.
53. Golomski, "Swazi Jerikho Zionism," 358.
54. Interview with Simon Nzima, Manzini, Swaziland, 1 October 2016.

55. Interview with Meshack Dlamini Matsapha, Swaziland, 19 August 2016.

56. Richard Quebedeaux, *The New Charismatics: The Origins, Development and Significance of Neo-Pentecostalism* (New York: Doubleday, 1976).

57. Ogbu Kalu, *African Pentecostalism: An Introduction* (Oxford: Oxford University Press, 2008), especially chap. 5; Paul Gifford, *The New Crusaders: Christianity and the New Right in Southern Africa* (London: Pluto Press, 1991).

58. Cazziol, "Swazi Zionists," 35–36.

59. Growth rate for Council churches was the lowest at 23 percent and the League stood at 71 percent. *Fulfilling the Vision,* 36.

60. Cazziol, "Swazi Zionists," 88; *Times of Swaziland,* 31 January 1993 and 4 June 1993; Armitage, "Abakamoya," 253; interview with Nhlanhla Magongo, Manzini, Swaziland, 8 June 2016.

61. *Fulfilling the Vision,* 82–83.

62. *Times of Swaziland,* 31 January 1993.

63. *Times of Swaziland,* Letter To Editor from Jabulani Nkambule, 15 March 1994.

64. *Times of Swaziland,* 19 June 1993.

65. *Times of Swaziland,* 14 June 1993.

66. *Fulfilling the Vision,* 82–83.

67. Cazziol, "Red-Dressed Zionists," 97.

68. Interview with Sifiso Dlamini, Manzini, Swaziland, 29 June 2016; Darrel Hostetter, "Isaac Dlamini: My Best Friend!" (n.p., n.d.).

69. Interview with Elizabeth Dlamini and Lungile Dlamini, Ludzeludze, Swaziland, 23 June 2016.

70. Interview with Jerome Sangweni, Manzini, Swaziland, 8 June 2016.

71. Meshack Mduduzi Dlamini, *My Story* (n.p., 2016), 4; interview with Meshack Dlamini, Matsapha, Swaziland, 19 August 2016.

72. Interview with Meshack Dlamini, Matsapha, Swaziland, 19 August 2016.

73. Interview with Xolile Tshuma, Jeppes Reef, South Africa, 4 June 2016.

74. Interview with Jerome Sangweni, Manzini, Swaziland, 8 June 2016.

75. Interview with Sifiso Dlamini, Manzini, Swaziland, 29 June 2016.

76. Interview with Elizabeth Dlamini and Lungile Dlamini, Ludzeludze, Swaziland, 23 June 2016.

77. Interview with Meshack Dlamini, Matsapha, Swaziland, 19 August 2016.

78. *Zion Banner,* "Testimony of Pastor Nkosinathi Mchunu," 2, no. 1 (2015).

79. Interview with Jerome Sangweni, Manzini, Swaziland, 8 June 2016.

80. Interview with Nhlanhla Magongo, Manzini, Swaziland, 8 June 2016.

81. Interview with Erickson Dlamini, Motjane, Swaziland, 10 August 2016.

82. Interview with Nhlanhla Magongo, Manzini, Swaziland, 8 June 2016.

83. Interview with Simon Nzima, Manzini, Swaziland, 1 October 2016.

84. Interview with Erickson Dlamini, Motjane, Swaziland, 10 August 2016.

85. *Times of Swaziland,* 25 March 2008.

86. Interview with Erickson Dlamini, Motjane, Swaziland, 10 August 2016.

87. Interview with Simon/Dabete Mavimbela, Mbabane, 11 July 2016.

88. Telephone Interview with Darrel Hostetter, Lancaster, Pennsylvania 19 October 2016.

89. Vusumuzi Mkhatshwa, Mbabane, Swaziland, 17 August 2016.

90. *Times of Swaziland,* 5 March 1998.

91. Interview with Philemon Mvubu, Manzini, Swaziland, 15 August 2016.

92. *Times of Swaziland,* 13 April 2004.

93. Interview with Erickson Dlamini, Motjane, Swaziland, 10 August 2016.

94. Interview with Simon Nzima, Manzini, Swaziland, 1 October 2016.

95. Interview with Jerome Sangweni, Manzini, Swaziland, 8 June 2016.

96. The city was renamed Zion from Zion City in the 1950s.

97. Voliva's branch of the church maintained a limited presence in South Africa by sending Van Buren Shumaker and his wife to Johannesburg as missionaries in the 1920s. *Leaves of Healing* 54, no. 6, 26 April 1924.

98. GMC, *Mahon Missionary Messenger,* March 1952, L. S. McCordic, "The White Robers."

99. McCordic, "The White Robers."

100. NASA, NTS 1429, File No. 21/214, Edgar Mahon to Chief Native Commissioner, Natal, 11 April 1933.

101. GMC, *Light Is Springing Up: A Pictorial History of the Mahon Mission* (Mahon Mission Press, Etembeni, ca. 1955).

102. GMC, *Mahon Missionary Messenger,* May 1950, Rev. and Mrs. H. Suttie, "Pray for the Latter Rains."

103. GMC, Lyle Mahon, "One Hundred Years of Zion, Success and Failure," lecture, 1996; interview with Cleburn McIlhany and family, Kenosha, Illinois, 26 March 2014.

104. David Barrett, *Schism and Renewal in Africa: An Analysis of Six Thousand Contemporary Religious Movements* (Nairobi: Oxford University Press, 1968).

105. University of Uppsala Archives, Uppsala, Sweden, Bengt Sundkler Papers, Box 96, Carl Lee to Evangeline Barrett, 1 December 1959.

106. GMC, *Zululand and Basutoland Missionary* 7, no. 3, March 1920.

107. Links between the Christian Catholic Church (now renamed Christ Community Church or CCC) and its branches (now fully autonomous) in the Philippines are still strong. Church leaders from the Philippines attended CCC's annual missions conference in October 2015.

108. Dana Robert, "Shifting Southward: Global Christianity since 1945," *International Bulletin of Missionary Research* 24, no. 2 (2000): 52.

109. Sathianathan Clarke, "World Christianity and Postcolonial Mission: A Path Forward for the Twenty-First Century," *Theology Today* 71, no. 2 (2014): 196.

110. Clarke, "World Christianity," 201.

111. Andrew Walls and Clark Ross, eds., *Mission in the Twenty-First Century* (Maryknoll, NY: Orbis Books, 2008), 196–197.

112. On TEAM, see https://team.org/about/our-mission/what-we-do, accessed 5 January 2018.

113. Adam Mohr, "Roaring Twenties: Faith Tabernacle Congregation and Early Pentecostalism in Colonial West Africa, 1918–1929" (unpublished manuscript, n.d.), 31–35.

114. E.g., G. C. Oosthuizen, *Post-Christianity in Africa: A Theological and Anthropological Study* (London: Hurst, 1968).

115. Joel Cabrita, *Text and Authority in the South African Nazaretha Church* (Cambridge: Cambridge University Press), 32–61.
116. Mrs. Ford Wilson and Mrs. Harold K. Light, "50th Anniversary, 1909–1959, Grace Missionary Church, Zion, Illinois" (unpublished booklet, 1959.
117. Interview with Grant and Barbara Sisson, Zion, Illinois, 18 July 2014.
118. Interview with Grant and Barbara Sisson, Zion, Illinois, 18 July 2014.
119. "Report of Missionary Trip Made by General Overseer and Mrs Ottersen to England, Egypt, Israel, South Africa and Venezuela," *Leaves of Healing,* January–February 1981.
120. *Leaves of Healing,* September–October 1985.
121. Interview with Tim and Luann Kuehl, Johannesburg, South Africa, 23 November 2015.
122. *Leaves of Healing,* September–October 1985; interview with Tim and Luann Kuehl, Johannesburg, South Africa, 23 November 2015.
123. Interview with Richard and Geraldine Akers, Nelspruit, South Africa, 18 November 2015.
124. Interview with Greg and Carlene Seghers, Sunbury, South Africa, 17 August 2015.
125. On ZEMA, see www.zema.org/about.html, accessed 5 January 2018.
126. Interview with Greg and Carlene Seghers, Sunbury, South Africa, 17 August 2015.
127. Interview with Andrew Sisson, Sunbury, South Africa, 8 January 2016.
128. See www.zema.org/about.html.
129. CCC, Harold Froise, "Zion Christian Church: A Study to Evaluate the Theology and Practice of South African Zionists with a View to Designing a Strategy to Win Them for Christ" (PhD diss., Columbia Biblical Seminary, 1989), 69.
130. Froise, "Zion Christian Church," 78; interview with Peter Kopp, Mbabane, Swaziland, 30 September 2016.
131. Froise, "Zion Christian Church," 74.
132. Interview with Greg and Carlene Seghers, Sunbury, South Africa, 18 August 2015.
133. Interview with Tim and Luann Kuehl, Johannesburg, South Africa, 23 November 2015.
134. Interview with Mike McDowell, Zion, Illinois, 19 July 2012.
135. Interview with Greg and Carlene Seghers, Sunbury, South Africa, 18 August 2015.
136. Interview with Richard and Geraldine Akers, Nelspruit, South Africa, 18 November 2015.
137. Interview with Greg and Carlene Seghers, Sunbury, South Africa, 18 August 2015.
138. Interview with Greg and Carlene Seghers, Sunbury, South Africa, 18 August 2015.
139. Sunbury Archives, Darnell, South Africa, Zion Evangelical Bible Schools (ZEBS) Pamphlet.

140. Sunbury Archives, Folder on Misc. Notes on ZEBS Curriculum Material, "Synopsis of Curriculum."
141. Interview with Brett and Evelyn Miller, Manzini, Swaziland, 9 August 2016.
142. Froise, "Zion Christian Church," 74.
143. Interview with Greg and Carlene Seghers, Sunbury, South Africa, 18 August 2015.
144. Visit to Sunbury for Annual ZEMA Missionaries Conference, 5 January 2015.
145. Interview with Tim and Luann Kuehl, Johannesburg, South Africa, 23 November 2015.
146. CCC, *Mahon Mission Messenger,* 1992.
147. Interview with Mike McDowell, Zion, Illinois, 19 July 2012; interview with Mike McDowell, Grant Sisson, Barbara Sisson, Greg Seghers, Carlene Seghers, Zion, Illinois, 20 July 2012.
148. CCC, *TEAM Horizons Magazine* 8, no. 2 (2008).
149. Elijah Maswanganyi and Bruce Britten, *Power of Jesus: Power for You to Be a Man of God, Woman of God* (Covington, LA: Insight Books, n.d.), 137.
150. Interview with Richard and Geraldine Akers, Nelspruit, South Africa, 18 November 2015.
151. Interview with Godfrey Maseko, Pimville, Johannesburg, South Africa, 24 November 2015.
152. *Times of Swaziland,* 17 January 1993.
153. Interview with Jerome Sangweni, Manzini, Swaziland, 8 June 2016.
154. Hostetter, "Isaac Dlamini," 1.
155. Interview with Zac Muiambo, Maputo, Mozambique, 22 June 2016; "Isaac Dlamini," in *Dictionary of African Christian Biography,* accessed 5 January 2018, http://www.dacb.org/stories/swaziland/dlamini-isaac.html.
156. Interview with Elizabeth Dlamini and Lungile Dlamini, Ludzeludze, Manzini, Swaziland, 23 June 2016; Froise, "Zion Christian Church," 75; Cazziol, "Swazi Zionists," 81.
157. Sundkler, *Zulu Zion,* 235.
158. Interview with Sifiso Dlamini, Manzini, Swaziland, 29 June 2016.
159. "Isaac Dlamini," in *Dictionary of African Christian Biography.*
160. Robert Bruce Yoder, "Mennonite Missionaries and African Independent Churches: The Development of an Anabaptist Missiology in West Africa, 1958–1967" (PhD diss., Boston University, 2016).
161. Interview with Darrel Hostetter, Lancaster, Pennsylvania, 17 October 2016.
162. Interview with Elizabeth Dlamini and Lungile Dlamini, Ludzeludze, Manzini, Swaziland, 23 June 2016.
163. Interview with Erickson Dlamini, Motjane, Swaziland, 10 August 2016.
164. Interview with Elizabeth Dlamini and Lungile Dlamini, Ludzeludze, Manzini, Swaziland, 23 June 2016.
165. Interview with Elizabeth Dlamini and Lungile Dlamini, Ludzeludze, Manzini, Swaziland, 23 June 2016.
166. Interview with Darrel Hostetter, Lancaster, Pennsylvania, 19 October 2016.

167. Interview with Bruce and Carol Britten, Ohio, 24 July 2016.

168. Interview with Philemon Mvubu, Manzini, Swaziland, 15 August 2016.

169. Zion Bible College information pamphlet (courtesy of Brett Miller).

170. Interview with Bruce and Carol Britten, Ohio, 24 July 2016.

171. Interview with Nhlanhla Magongo, Manzini, Swaziland, 8 June 2016.

172. Skype Interview with Bruce and Carol Britten, Ohio, 24 July 2016.

173. Interview with Vusumuzi Jonathan Mkhatshwa, Mbabane, Swaziland, 17 August 2016.

174. Interview with Meshack Mduduzi Dlamini, Matsapha, Swaziland, 19 August 2016.

175. Interview with Sipho Masilela, Jeppes Reef, South Africa, 26 June 2016.

176. Interview with Solomon Dube, Matsapha, Swaziland, 15 July 2016. A similar phenomenon was also described by Thami Hlatshwayo, Bishop of the Holy Catholic Apostolic Church in Zion in Johannesburg. Interview with Thami Hlatshwayo, Soweto, Johannesburg, South Africa, 16 June 2016.

177. Interview with Solomon Dube, Matsapha, Swaziland, 15 July 2016.

178. Fogelqvist, *Red-Dressed Zionists,* 161.

179. Maswanganyi and Britten, *Power of Jesus,* 78–80.

180. Interview with Vusumuzi Jonathan Mkhatshwa, Mbabane, Swaziland, 17 August 2016.

181. Interview with Vusumuzi Jonathan Mkhatshwa, Mbabane, Swaziland, 17 August 2016.

182. Meshack Dlamini, "Story of My Life," 4.

183. Meshack Dlamini, "Story of My Life," 6.

184. Interview with Anastase and Immaculee Nzabilinda, Zion, Illinois, 19 July 2012.

185. Maswanganyi and Britten, *Power of Jesus,* 116, 126; Skype interview with Bruce and Carol Britten, Ohio, 24 July 2016.

186. Interview with Meshack Mduduzi Dlamini, Matsapha, Swaziland, 19 August 2016.

187. Maswanganyi and Britten, *Power of Jesus,* 116.

188. Maswanganyi and Britten, *Power of Jesus,* 136.

189. Interview with Simon Nzima, Manzini, Swaziland, 1 October 2016. Matthew 7:15–23 refers to false prophets.

190. Interview with Erickson Dlamini, Motjane, Swaziland, 10 August 2016.

191. Interview with Meshack Dlamini, Matsapha, Swaziland, 19 August 2016.

192. Interview with Solomon Dube, Matsapha, Swaziland, 15 July 2016.

193. Maswanganyi and Britten, *Power of Jesus,* 123.

194. *Fulfilling the Vision,* 69.

195. *Times of Swaziland,* 25 September 1998.

196. Interview with Sipho Masilela, Jeppes Reef, South Africa, 15 May 2016.

197. CCC, *Team Horizons Magazine* 8, no. 2 (2008).

198. Interview with Philemon Mvubu, Manzini, Swaziland, 15 August 2016.

199. Interview with Jerome Sangweni, Manzini, Swaziland, 8 June 2016.

200. *Times of Swaziland,* 24 August 1998.

201. Interview with Jerome Sangweni, Manzini, Swaziland, 8 June 2016.

202. Interview with Brett and Evelyn Miller, Manzini, Swaziland, 9 August 2016.

203. E.g., *Times of Swaziland*, 15 August 2016.

204. Interview with Simon/Dabete Mavimbela, Mbabane, 11 July 2016.

205. *Fulfilling the Vision*, 68.

AFTERWORD

1. *Zion City News*, 25 June 1909.

2. Allan Anderson, *An Introduction to Pentecostalism* (Cambridge: Cambridge University Press, 2004), 144–165; Edith Blumhofer, *Restoring the Faith: The Assemblies of God, Pentecostalism and American Culture* (Urbana: University of Illinois Press, 1993), chaps. 9, 10.

3. Ogbu Kalu, *African Pentecostalism: An Introduction* (Oxford: Oxford University Press, 2008), chap. 5.

4. Sword and Spirit Ministries, accessed 1 November 2017, https://www.facebook.com/Sword.and.Spirit.Ministries.Intl/. See "About" and then "Story."

5. TB Joshua Fanclub, accessed 17 August 2017, Etbjoshuafanclub.wordpress.com.

6. *Times of Swaziland*, 1 April 2007.

7. Enjoli Liston, "Inside the Most Powerful Church in South Africa," *Independent,* 20 June 2010, http://www.independent.co.uk/news/world/africa/inside-the-most-powerful-church-in-south-africa-2006129.html.

8. *Times of Swaziland*, 9 April 2016.

9. Pew Research Center, "Historical Overview of Pentecostalism in South Africa," 5 October 2006, http://www.pewforum.org/2006/10/05/historical-overview-of-pentecostalism-in-south-africa/.

10. Pew Research Center, "Historical Overview of Pentecostalism in South Africa: Origins and Growth," http://www.pewforum.org/2006/10/05/historical-overview-of-pentecostalism-in-south-africa/#origins-and-growth.

11. Interview with Godfrey Maseko, Pimville, Johannesburg, South Africa, 24 November 2015.

12. Interview with Simon/Dabete Mavimbela, Mbabane, Swaziland, 11 July 2016.

Acknowledgments

The bulk of this research was generously supported by a two-year Early Career Fellowship from the Arts and Humanities Research Council of the UK. I am also grateful to the British Academy Small Research Grant Scheme for funding that allowed me to develop my ideas for this book at an early stage. I want to thank the University of Cambridge's Humanities Research Grant Scheme for extensive financial support; and the Faculty of Arts and Humanities at SOAS, University of London, for research funding.

A number of universities have supported me in various ways as I have conducted my research for this book and written it. The Faculty of Divinity at the University of Cambridge has offered me a collegial home for my teaching and research. I am grateful to Peter Harland for the administrative assistance he has provided. I have been hosted as a visiting scholar at three institutions over the past several years, to all of whom I am grateful: the Department of History at the Graduate Center, CUNY, in New York City; the Department of Theology and Religious Studies at University of Swaziland; and the Wits Institute for Social and Economic Research at the University of the Witwatersrand in Johannesburg, South Africa. I am grateful for the opportunities to present various chapters of this book at a number of research seminars, including at WISER, University of Cambridge, University of Oxford, University of Birmingham, University of Uppsala, the African Studies Association annual meeting, Yale Intellectual Histories Workshop, Oxford Global Histories of Africa Workshop, The Ecclesiastical History Society Annual Meeting, Ecumenism and Christianity conference at the University of Botswana, and the Cadbury Conference at the University of Birmingham.

My research for this book has been greatly assisted by the resources of several research libraries and archives. I am grateful to the archivists at the School of Oriental and African Studies, London; the Flower Pentecostal Heritage Center in Springfield, Missouri, for supplying many of the images illustrating this book; the Newberry Library in Chicago; the Carolina Reddiva Library and Manuscripts Collection at Uppsala University; the Historical Papers Research Collection at the William Cullen Library at the University of the Witwatersrand; the Africana Collection at the University of Swaziland; the Mbabane-based archives of *The Times of Swaziland*; the Zion-Benton Public Library. In particular, I thank Angela Westphal from the Zion-Benton Public Library, who helped me follow leads in Zion, Illinois, from afar. The Baptist Union Theological Seminary Archives in Johannesburg and the YMCA Archives at the University of Minnesota Libraries were also very helpful resources. Also within Zion, I am grateful to the expertise of Chuck Paxton, the archivist at the Christ Community Church archives, as well as to Timothy Morse of the Zion Historical Society, who offered me extensive assistance in locating documents and periodicals. Sadly, Tim passed away before the publication of this book. Miles Irving created the two maps that appear at the beginning of the book.

Many individuals have given me assistance in undertaking my research as well as with formulating my ideas for this book, and I gratefully acknowledge the research assistance provided by Jamie Boulding, Marco Derks, Jamie Klair, Nthlakgiso Molantoa, Zac Muiambo, and Thato Sukati. In the United States, I am grateful to Christ Community Church in Zion, as well as to Ken Langley and Mike McDowell, former director of ZEMA, at Christ Community Church in Zion, Illinois, as well as ZEMA's current director, Andrew Sisson. I am also grateful to Beverly Easterly, Dan Hess, Sherill Hostetter, David Kirkpatrick, Cleburn and Alyce McIlhany, Rose Simon, and Grant and Barbara Sisson. I am especially thankful to Rose and Beverly for frequently accommodating me within the Zion Faith Homes during my trips to Zion. Within Southern Africa, I am grateful to all the ZEMA missionaries, including Richard Akers, ZEMA field director, and to Greg and Carlene Seghers for hosting me at Sunbury and guiding me through the archives there. I thank Andy Sullivan, whose research into ZEMA's work in Southern Africa was very helpful for me. I am also grateful to Andrew Bank, Biebie de Vos, Derek du Bruyn, Erickson Dlamini, Sarah Duff, Natasha Erlank, Liz Gunner, Thami Hlatshwayo, Hoffie Hofmeyr, Isabel Hofmeyr, Edgar Mahon III, Brett Miller, the Le Roux family, Godfrey Maseko, Khuba Mpungose, Hebron Ndlovu, Noor Nieftagodien, Sonene Nyawo, Simon Nzima, Jeremo Sangweni, Soul Sibandze, Chris Smit, Charles van Onselen, and Martin West. In the UK, I am indebted to assistance I received from Fiona Armitage, David Beckingham, Timothy Jenkins, Frances Knight, David Maxwell, Henry Mitchell, Insa Nolte, Richard Werbner, and Emma Wild-Wood. In Sweden, my thanks are due to Johannes Zeiler and Kajsa Ahlstrand at the University of Uppsala. In Australia, I am grateful to Barry Chant and Stuart Piggin. I am most grateful to Sabelo Mlangeni for permission to reproduce his photograph as the cover image.

Finally, at Harvard University Press, my most grateful thanks are due to Ian Malcolm and Olivia Woods.

Index